SAMURAI GIRL

REAL BOUT HIGH SCHOOL

リアルバウトハイスクール

Volume 3

Art by Sora Inoue
Story by Reiji Saiga

TOKYOPOP®

Los Angeles • Tokyo

Translator – Lucan Duran
Graphic Designer – Justin Renard
English Adaptation – Dana Pupkin
Cover Designer – Rod Sampson

Senior Editor – Luis Reyes
Production Manager – Joaquin Reyes
Art Director – Matt Alford
Brand Manager – Kenneth Lee
VP of Production – Ron Klamert
Publisher – Stuart Levy

Email: editor@TOKYOPOP.com
Come visit us at www.TOKYOPOP.com

A  manga

TOKYOPOP® Presents
Real Bout High School Vol. 3 by Sora Inoue and Reiji Saiga
TOKYOPOP® is a registered trademark of Mixx Entertainment, Inc.

Real Bout High School Volume 3 © 2000 REIJI SAIGA/SORA INOUE. First pub-
lished in 2000 by KADOKAWA SHOTEN PUBLISHING CO., LTD., Tokyo. English
translation rights arranged with KADOKAWA SHOTEN PUBLISHING CO., LTD.,
Tokyo through TUTTLE-MORI AGENCY, INC., Tokyo. English text © 2002 by
Mixx Entertainment, Inc. TOKYOPOP® and the Robofish logo are trademarks of
Mixx Entertainment, Inc.

ISBN: 1-59182-020-0
First TOKYOPOP® Printing: August 2002

10 9 8 7 6 5 4 3 2 1

Printed in Canada

THE STORY THUS FAR . . .

More than anything else, Ryoko wants to be a great woman, and she has emarked on achieving this goal in life by taking up the code of the warrior and becoming one of the best Kendo combatants at Daimon High School. However, she buries her insecurities and emotions well beneath her gruff exterior, especially a romantic longing for her Kendo sparing partner, Tatsuya. Competition for Tatsuya is tough - bad-ass fighter Azumi and the Drama Club President Shiori both volley for the lithe Kendo Captain's affections. But to make things worse, Tatsuya, Ryoko's reason for even wanting to fight in the first place, is transferring to another school, leaving our little samurai girl to find her own emotional strength.

Of course, life at Daimon High Shool isn't exactly the easiest stretch in a student's academic career. Too many martial arts groups vie for too few training studios prompting sponatenous and large scale battles on campus. Luckily, Principal Todo - a man defined as much by his bloodlust as by his committment to education - has set up the K-Fight system in which students and teachers can settle disputes, differences of opinion and personal vendettas through sanctioned combat. When do students find time to study? When they're laid up in the hospital licking their tender wounds.

SAMURAI GIRL

REAL BOUT
HIGH SCHOOL

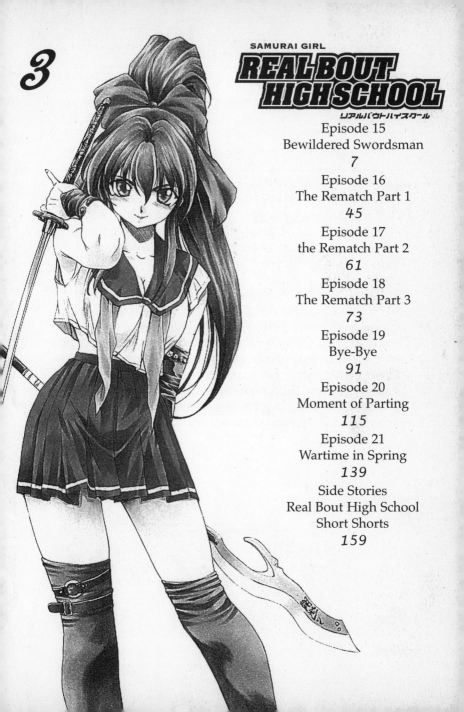

3

SAMURAI GIRL

REAL BOUT HIGH SCHOOL

リアルバウトハイスクール

Episode 15 Bewildered Swordsman

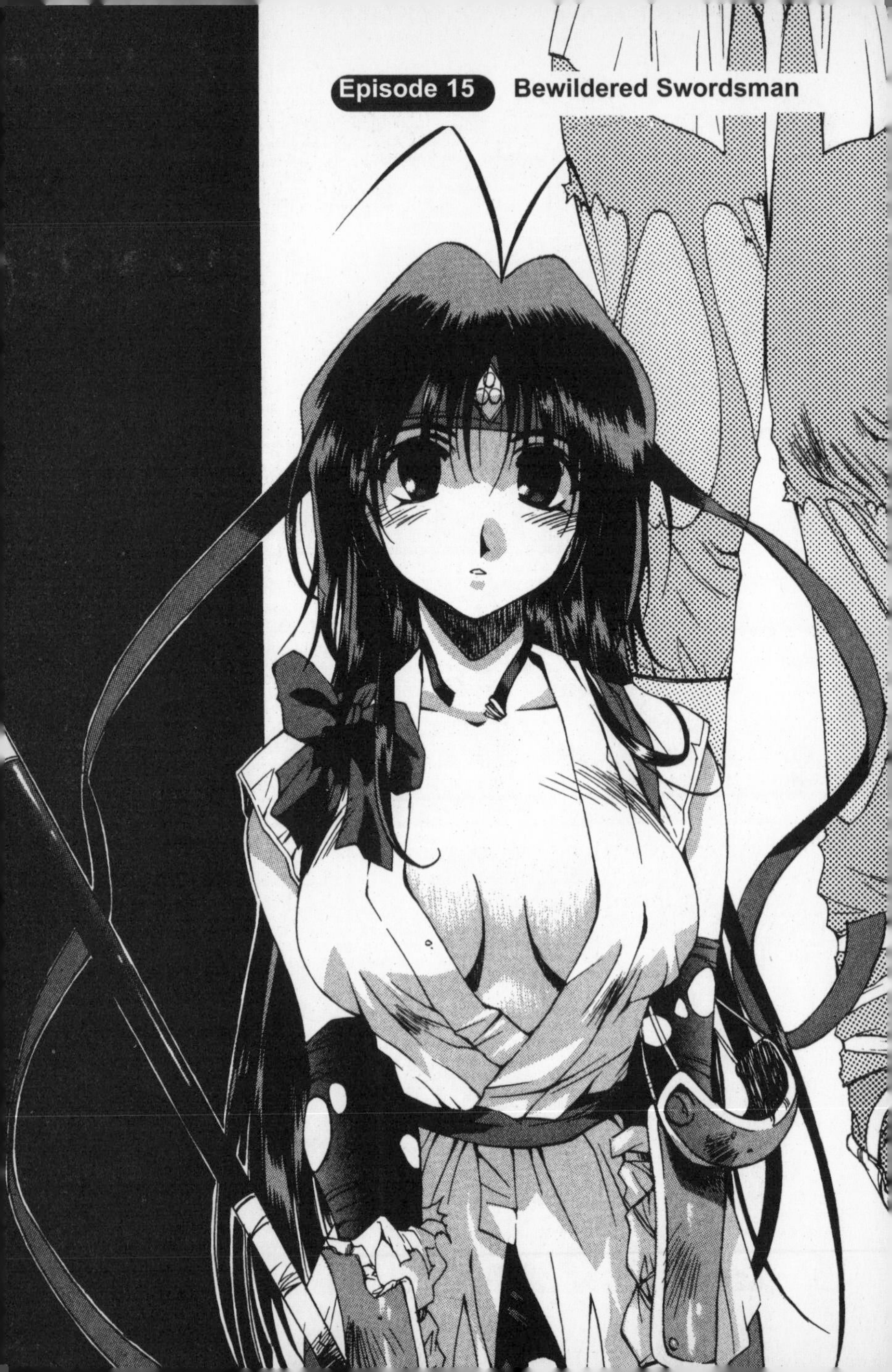

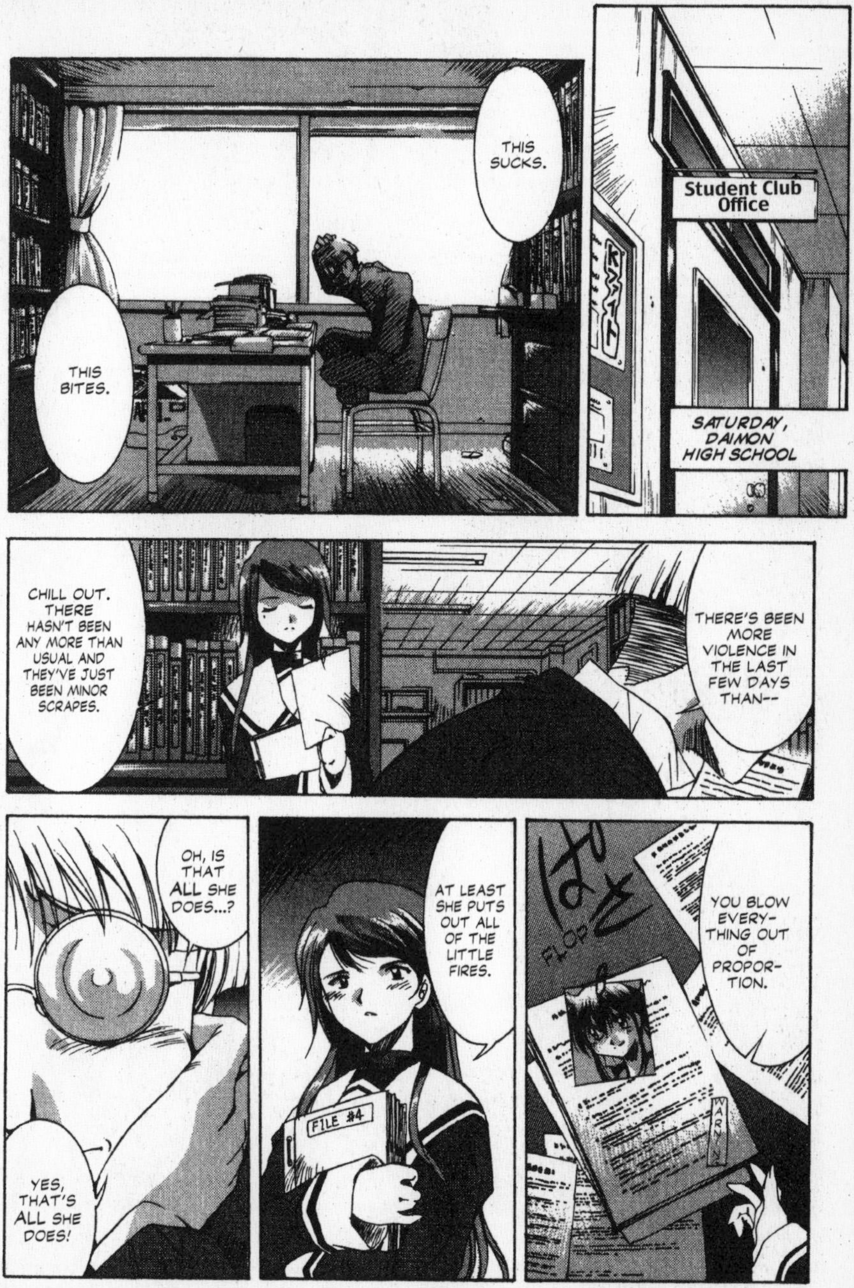

Student Club Office
SATURDAY, DAIMON HIGH SCHOOL
THIS SUCKS.
THIS BITES.
THERE'S BEEN MORE VIOLENCE IN THE LAST FEW DAYS THAN--
CHILL OUT. THERE HASN'T BEEN ANY MORE THAN USUAL AND THEY'VE JUST BEEN MINOR SCRAPES.
YOU BLOW EVERY-THING OUT OF PROPOR-TION.
FLOP
AT LEAST SHE PUTS OUT ALL OF THE LITTLE FIRES.
FILE #4
OH, IS THAT ALL SHE DOES...?
YES, THAT'S ALL SHE DOES!

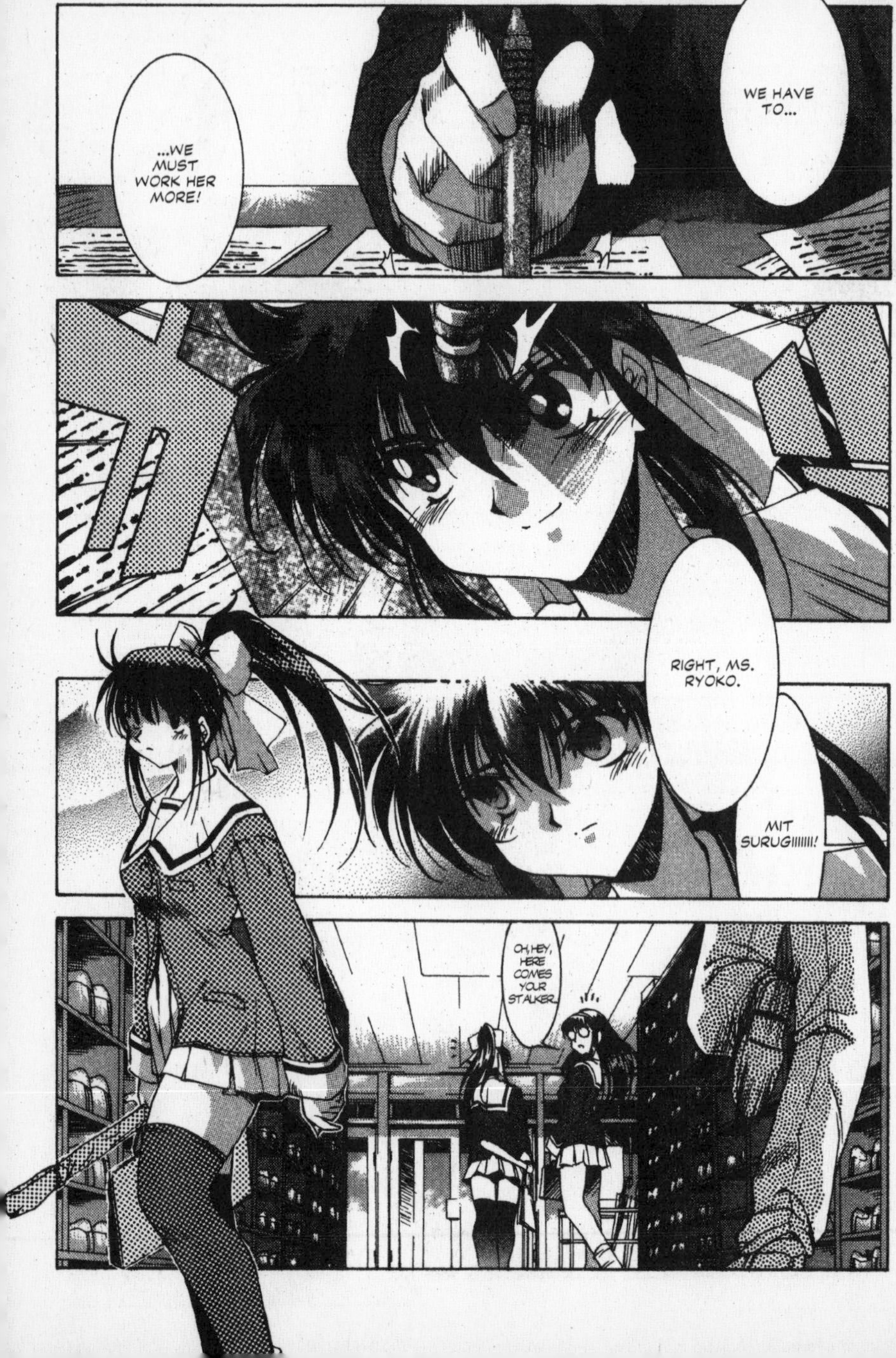
WE HAVE TO...
...WE MUST WORK HER MORE!
RIGHT, MS. RYOKO.
MIT SURUGIIIIIII!
OH, HEY, HERE COMES YOUR STALKER.

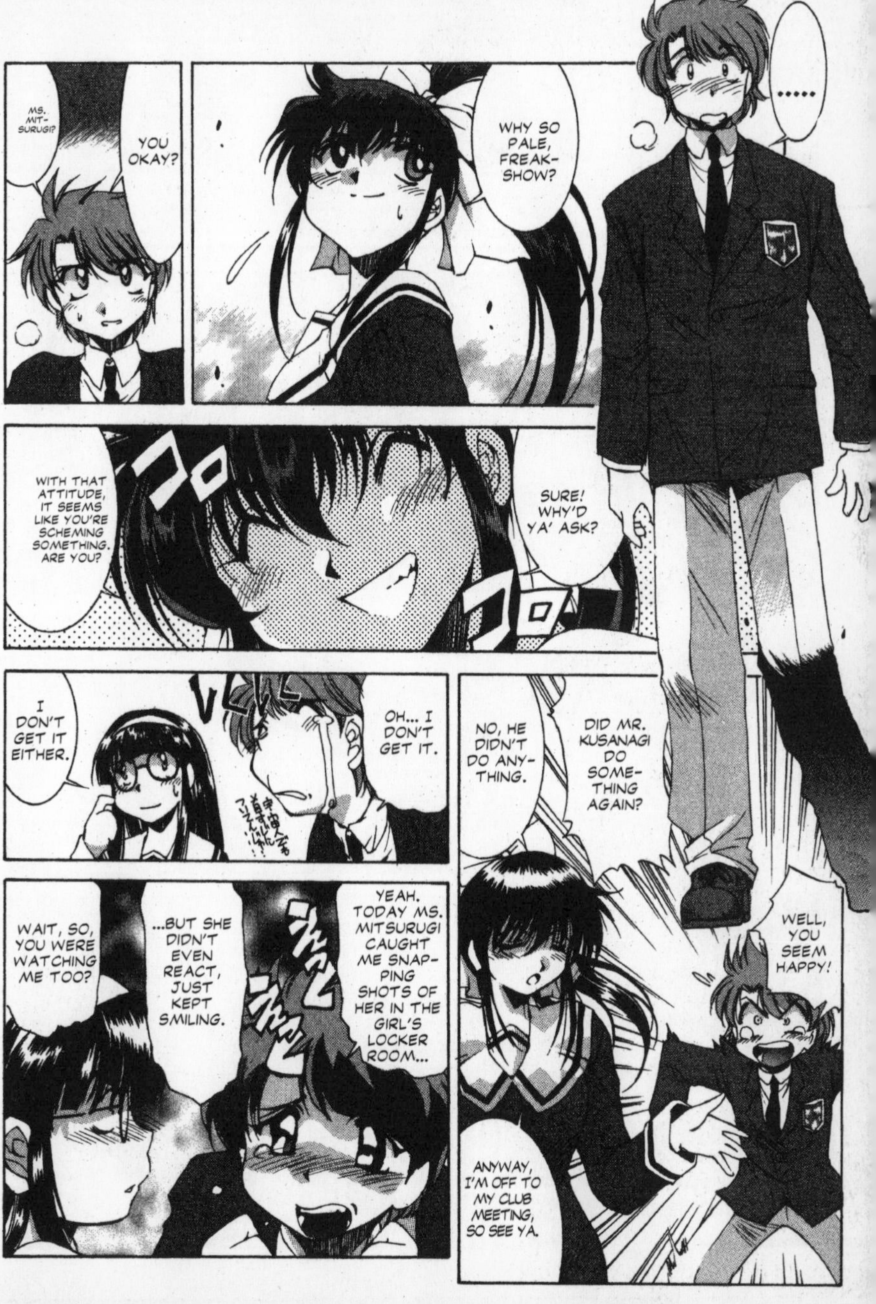
.....
WHY SO PALE, FREAK-SHOW?
YOU OKAY?
MS. MIT-SURUGI?
SURE! WHY'D YA' ASK?
WITH THAT ATTITUDE, IT SEEMS LIKE YOU'RE SCHEMING SOMETHING. ARE YOU?
DID MR. KUSANAGI DO SOMETHING AGAIN?
NO, HE DIDN'T DO ANYTHING.
WELL, YOU SEEM HAPPY!
ANYWAY, I'M OFF TO MY CLUB MEETING, SO SEE YA.
OH... I DON'T GET IT.
I DON'T GET IT EITHER.
YEAH. TODAY MS. MITSURUGI CAUGHT ME SNAPPING SHOTS OF HER IN THE GIRL'S LOCKER ROOM...
...BUT SHE DIDN'T EVEN REACT, JUST KEPT SMILING.
WAIT, SO, YOU WERE WATCHING ME TOO?

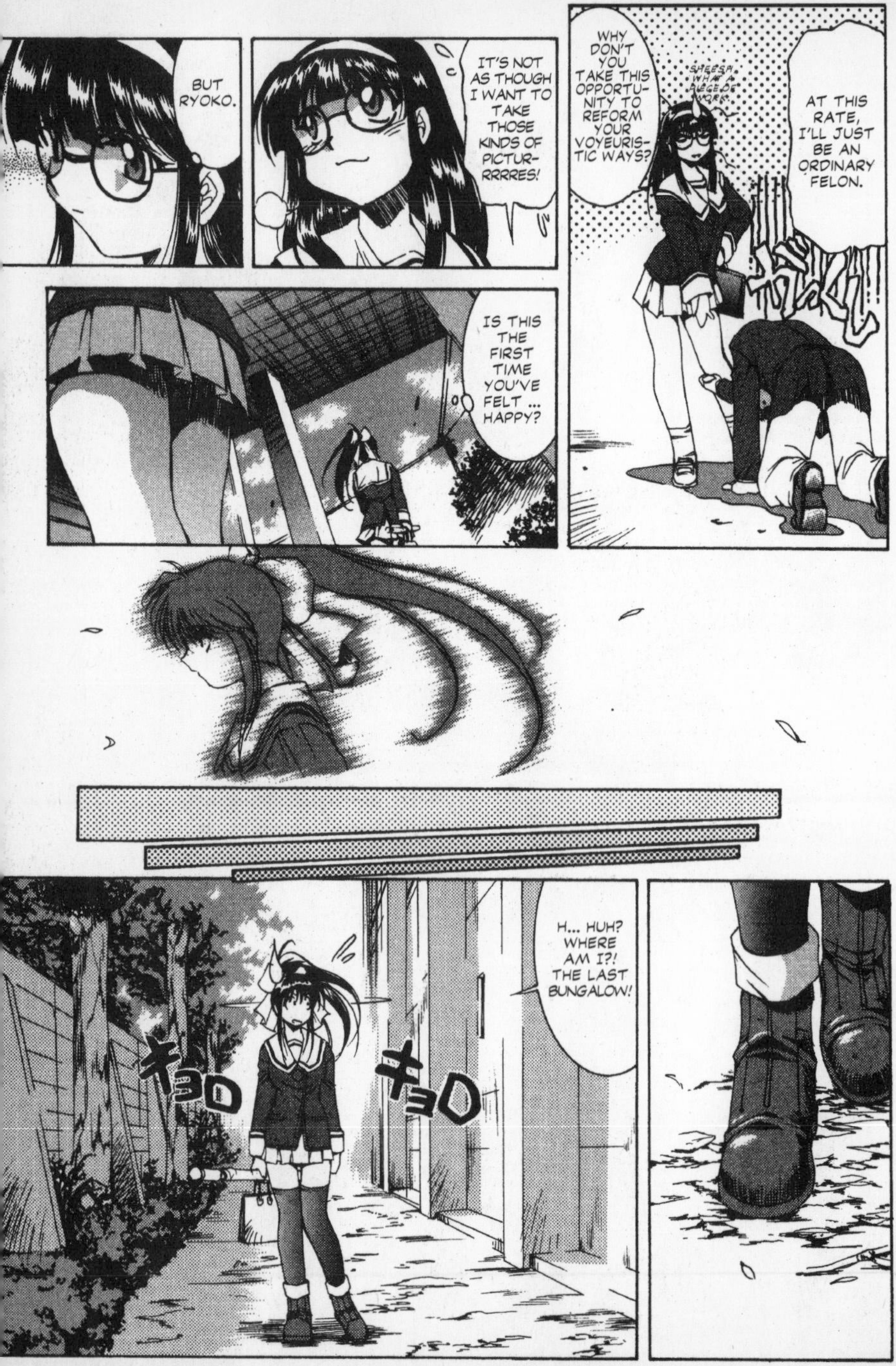
AT THIS RATE, I'LL JUST BE AN ORDINARY FELON.
WHY DON'T YOU TAKE THIS OPPORTUNITY TO REFORM YOUR VOYEURISTIC WAYS?
SHEESH! WHAT A PIECE OF WORK.
IT'S NOT AS THOUGH I WANT TO TAKE THOSE KINDS OF PICTURRRRRES!
BUT RYOKO.
IS THIS THE FIRST TIME YOU'VE FELT ... HAPPY?
H... HUH? WHERE AM I?! THE LAST BUNGALOW!
キョロ
キョロ

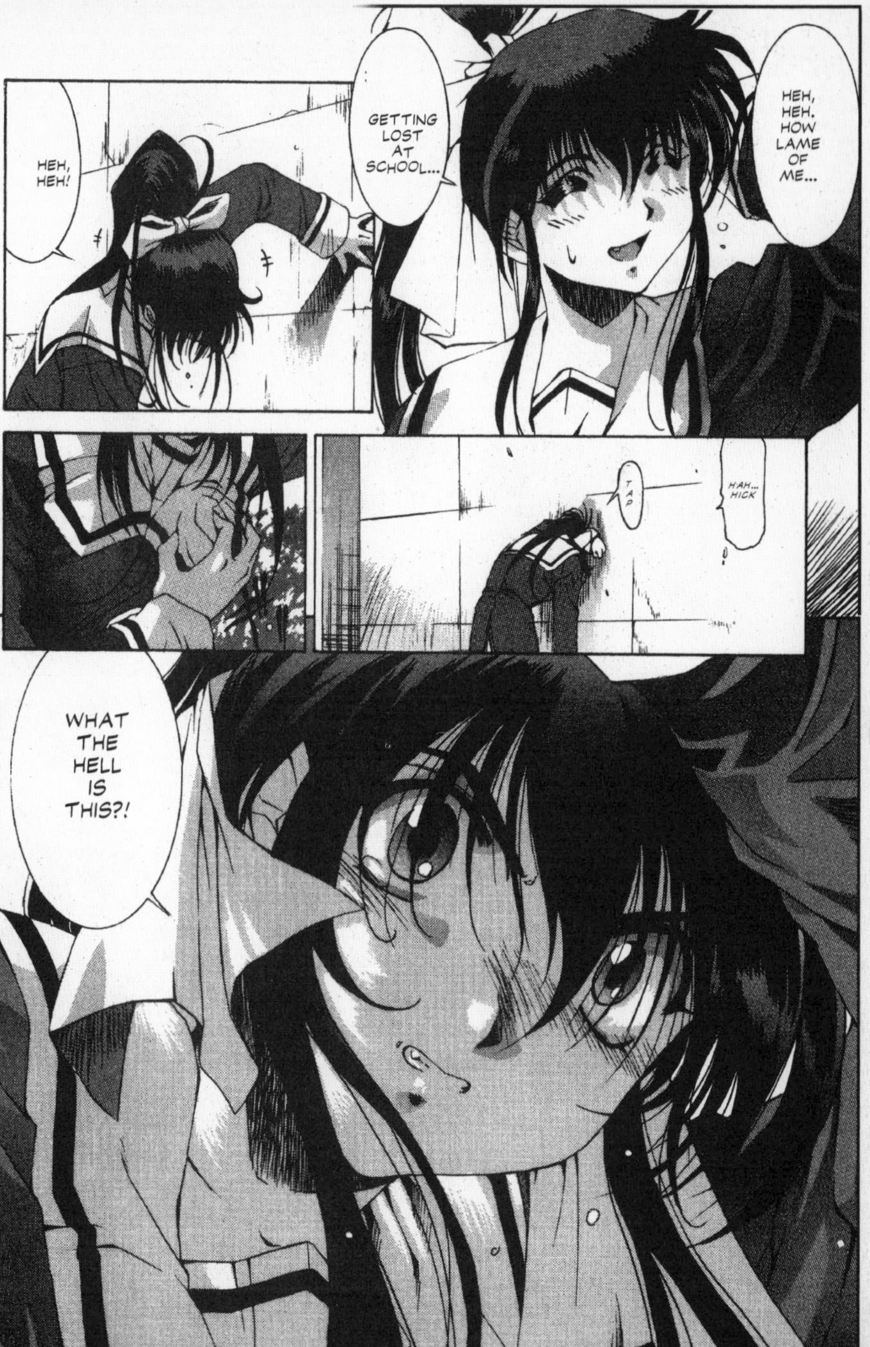
HEH, HEH. HOW LAME OF ME...
GETTING LOST AT SCHOOL...
HEH, HEH!
HAH... HICK
TAP
WHAT THE HELL IS THIS?!

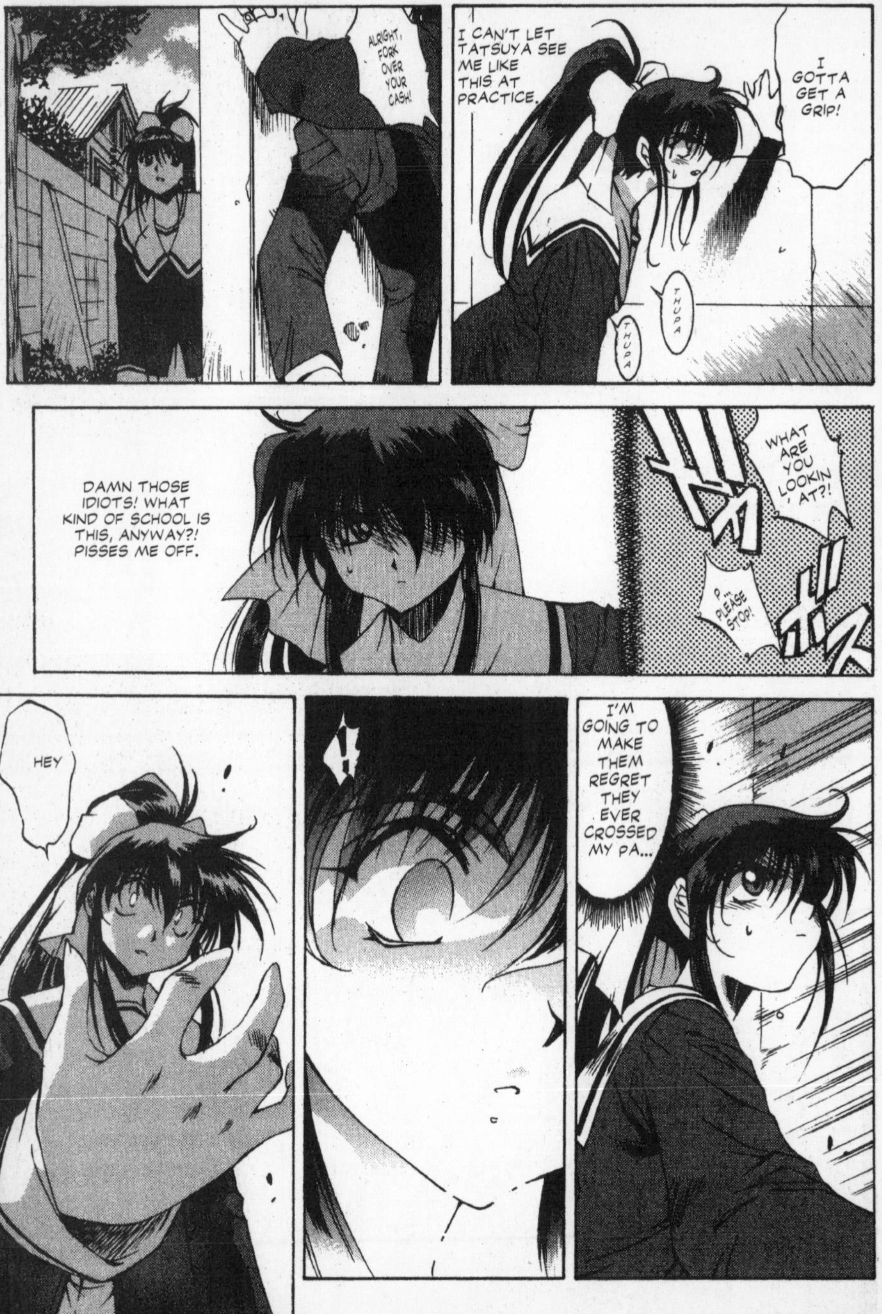
I GOTTA GET A GRIP!
I CAN'T LET TATSUYA SEE ME LIKE THIS AT PRACTICE.
THUPA
THUPA
ALRIGHT, FORK OVER YOUR CASH!
WHAT ARE YOU LOOKIN' AT?!
P... PLEASE STOP!
DAMN THOSE IDIOTS! WHAT KIND OF SCHOOL IS THIS, ANYWAY?! PISSES ME OFF.
I'M GOING TO MAKE THEM REGRET THEY EVER CROSSED MY PA...
!
HEY
!

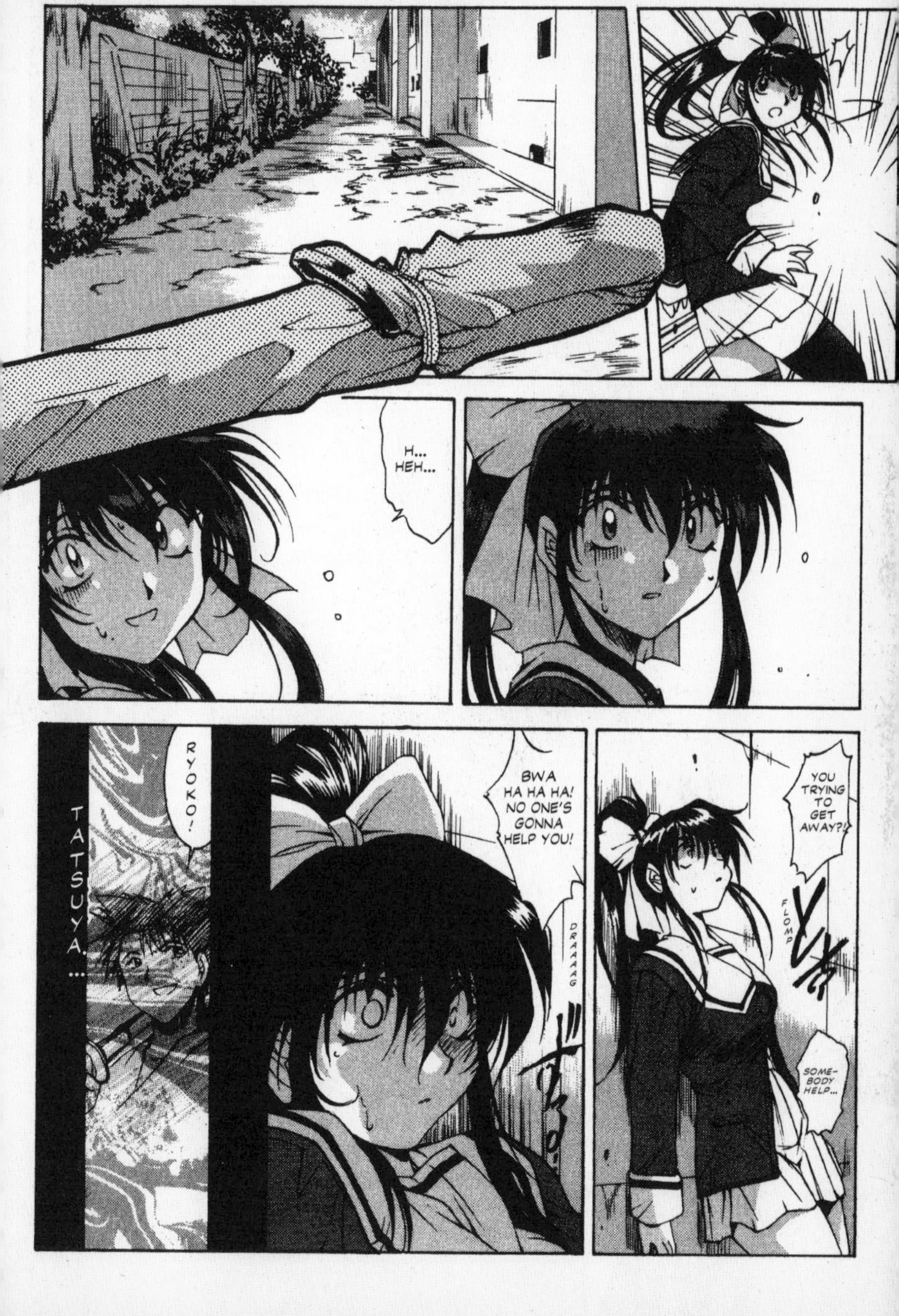
H... HEH...
YOU TRYING TO GET AWAY?!
FLOMP
SOMEBODY HELP...
BWA HA HA HA! NO ONE'S GONNA HELP YOU!
DRAAAAAG
RYOKO!
TATSUYA...

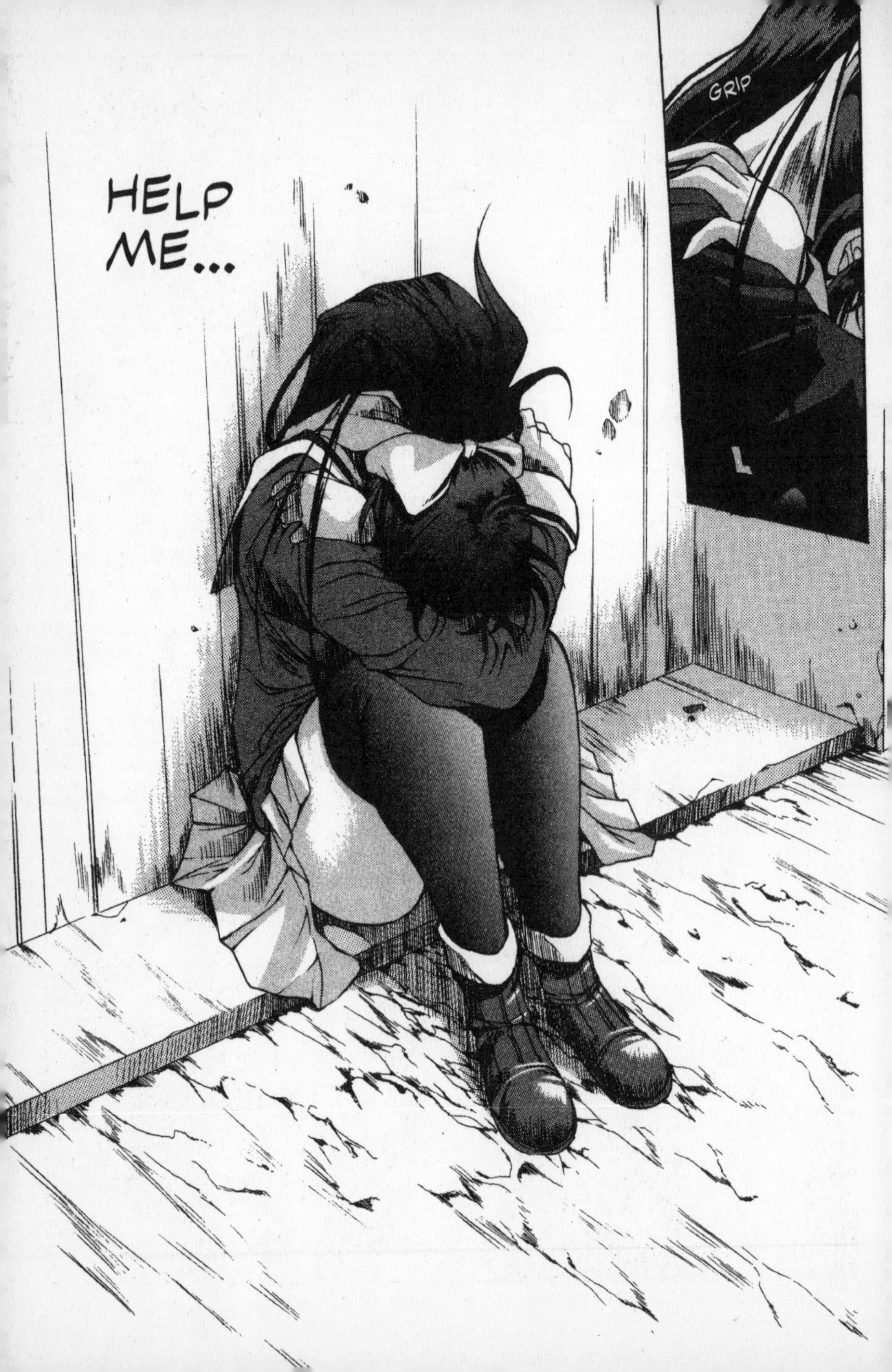
GRIP
HELP ME...

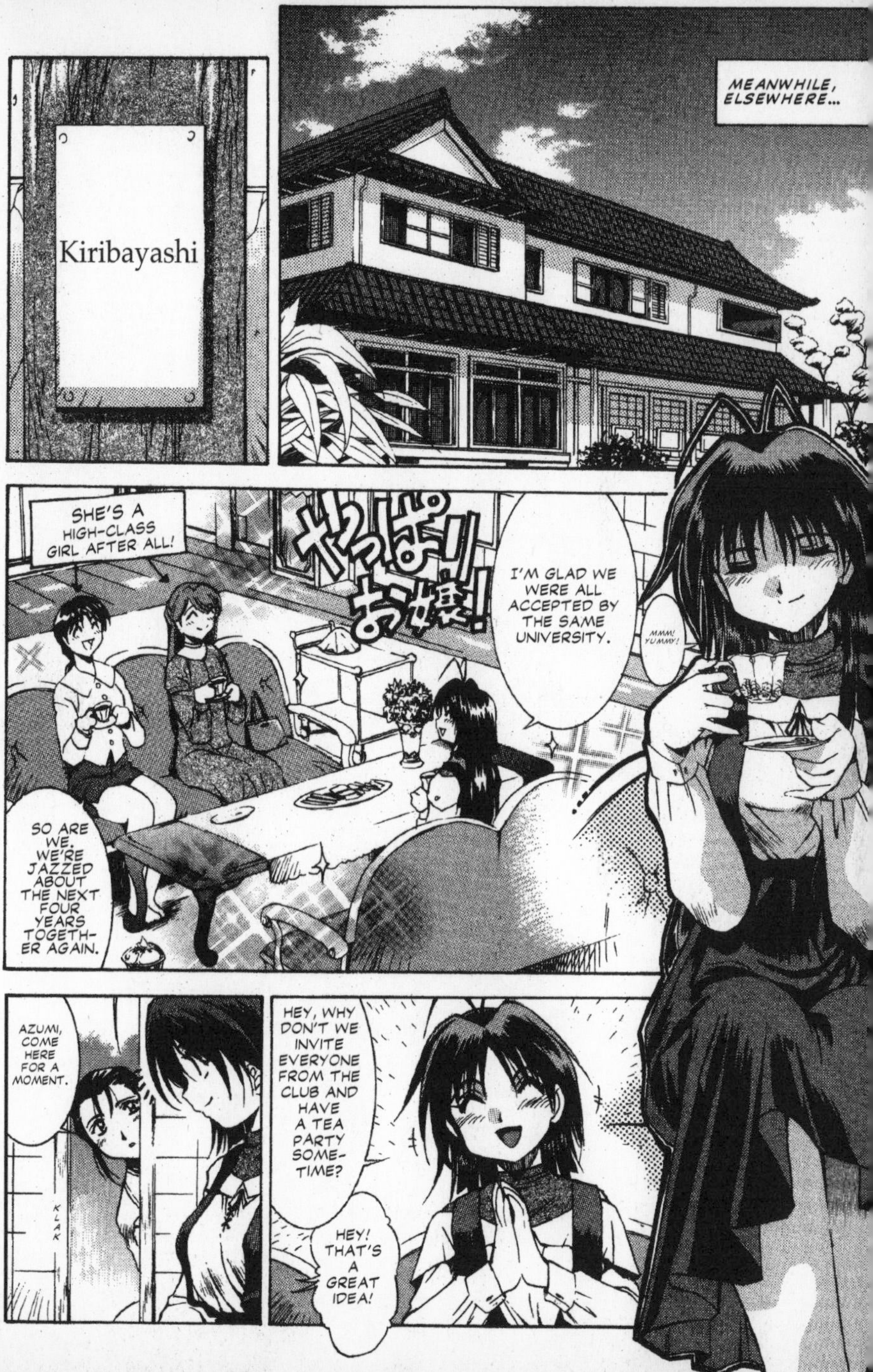
MEANWHILE, ELSEWHERE...
Kiribayashi
MMM! YUMMY!
やっぱり!! お嬢!
I'M GLAD WE WERE ALL ACCEPTED BY THE SAME UNIVERSITY.
SHE'S A HIGH-CLASS GIRL AFTER ALL!
SO ARE WE. WE'RE JAZZED ABOUT THE NEXT FOUR YEARS TOGETH-ER AGAIN.
HEY, WHY DON'T WE INVITE EVERYONE FROM THE CLUB AND HAVE A TEA PARTY SOME-TIME?
HEY! THAT'S A GREAT IDEA!
AZUMI, COME HERE FOR A MOMENT.
KLAK

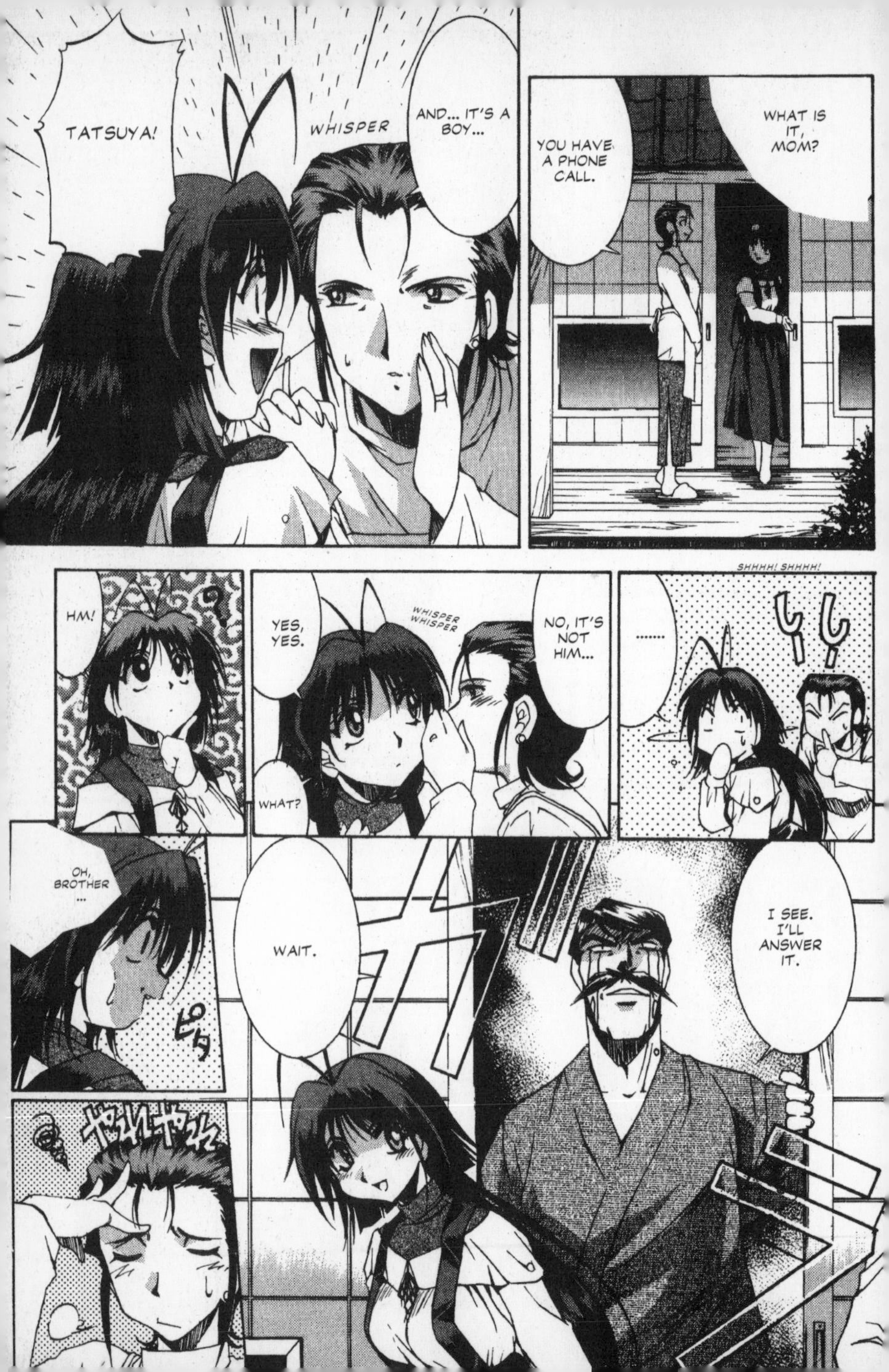
WHAT IS IT, MOM?
YOU HAVE A PHONE CALL.
AND... IT'S A BOY...
WHISPER
TATSUYA!
SHHHH! SHHHH!
....
NO, IT'S NOT HIM...
WHISPER WHISPER
YES, YES.
WHAT?
HM!
I SEE. I'LL ANSWER IT.
WAIT.
OH, BROTHER ...

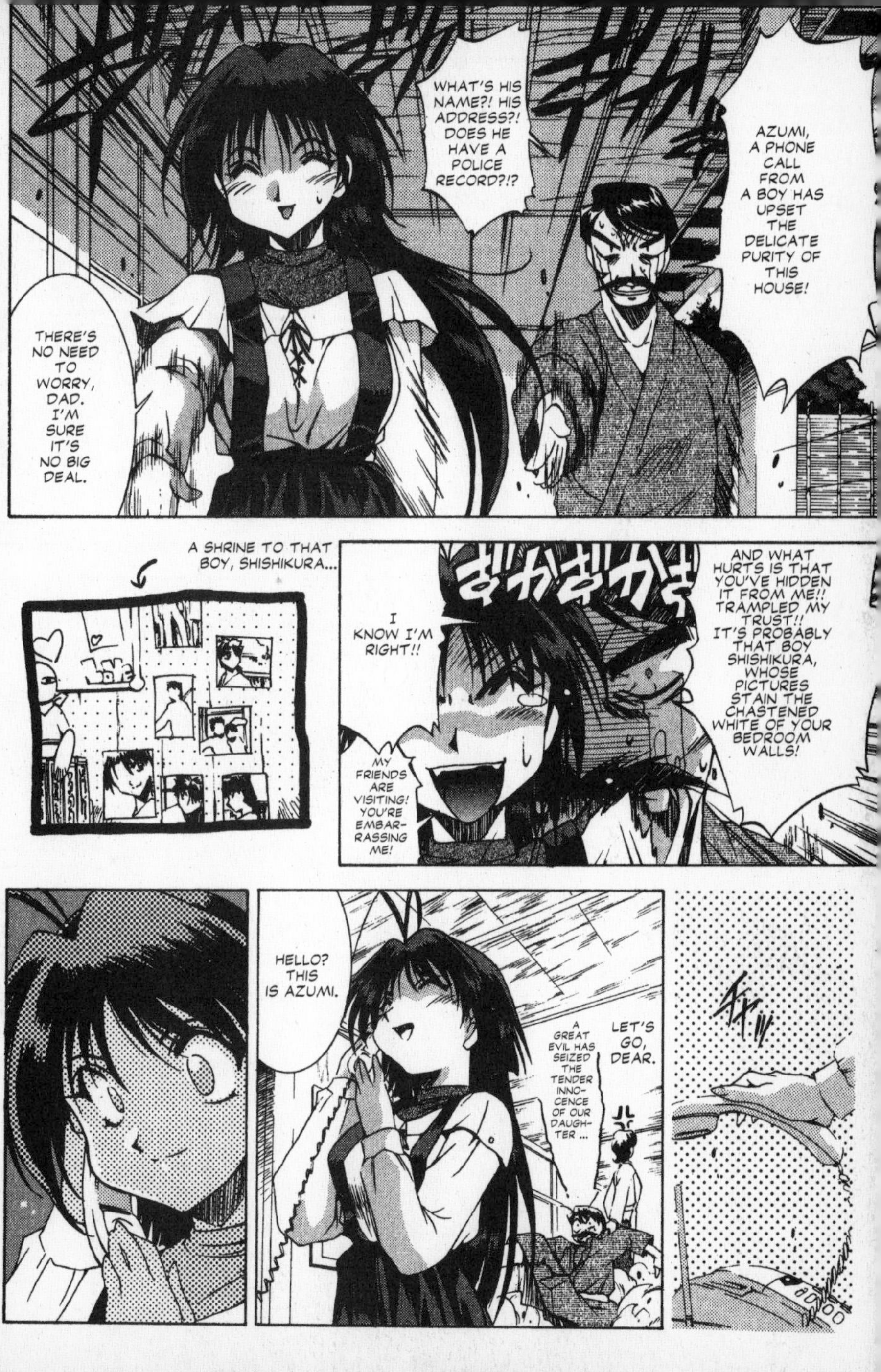
AZUMI, A PHONE CALL FROM A BOY HAS UPSET THE DELICATE PURITY OF THIS HOUSE!
WHAT'S HIS NAME?! HIS ADDRESS?! DOES HE HAVE A POLICE RECORD?!?
THERE'S NO NEED TO WORRY, DAD. I'M SURE IT'S NO BIG DEAL.
AND WHAT HURTS IS THAT YOU'VE HIDDEN IT FROM ME!! TRAMPLED MY TRUST!! IT'S PROBABLY THAT BOY SHISHIKURA, WHOSE PICTURES STAIN THE CHASTENED WHITE OF YOUR BEDROOM WALLS!
I KNOW I'M RIGHT!!
MY FRIENDS ARE VISITING! YOU'RE EMBARRASSING ME!
A SHRINE TO THAT BOY, SHISHIKURA...
LET'S GO, DEAR.
A GREAT EVIL HAS SEIZED THE TENDER INNOCENCE OF OUR DAUGHTER ...
HELLO? THIS IS AZUMI.

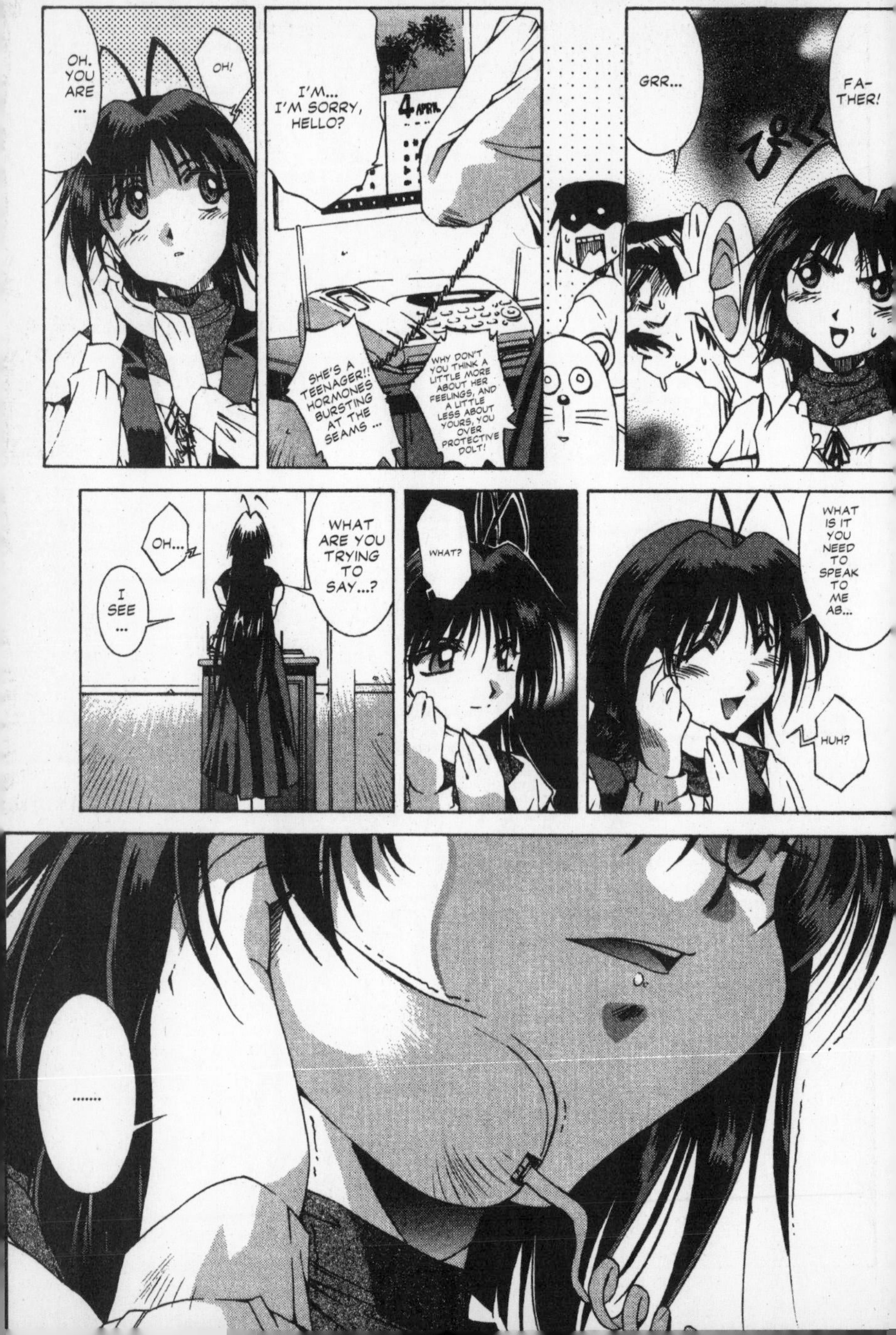
FA-
THER!
GRR...
I'M...
I'M SORRY,
HELLO?
WHY DON'T YOU THINK A LITTLE MORE ABOUT HER FEELINGS, AND A LITTLE LESS ABOUT YOURS, YOU OVER PROTECTIVE DOLT!
SHE'S A TEENAGER!! HORMONES BURSTING AT THE SEAMS ...
OH!
OH. YOU ARE ...
WHAT IS IT YOU NEED TO SPEAK TO ME AB...
HUH?
WHAT?
WHAT ARE YOU TRYING TO SAY...?
OH...
I SEE ...
....

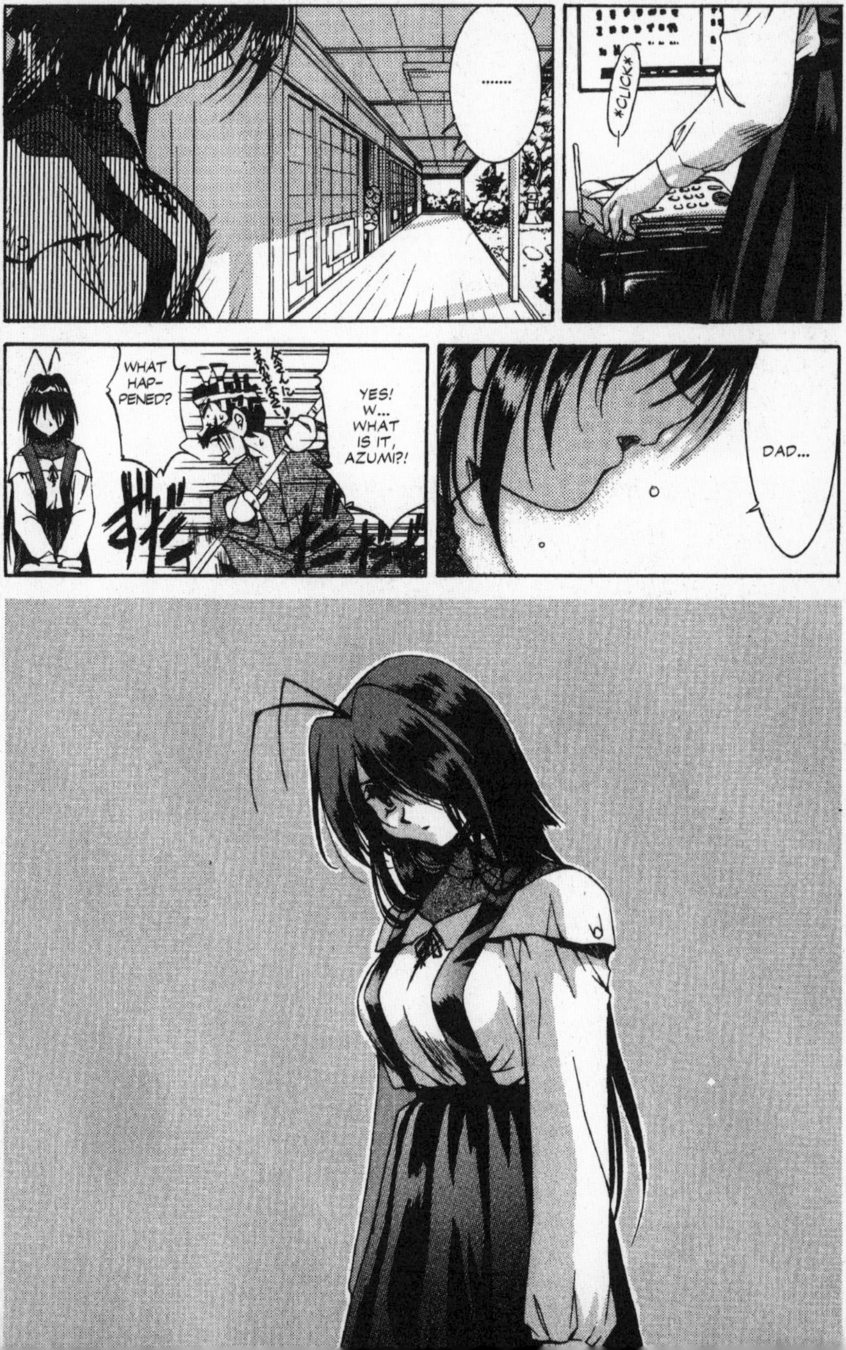
CLICK
......
DAD...
YES! W... WHAT IS IT, AZUMI?!
WHAT HAP-PENED?

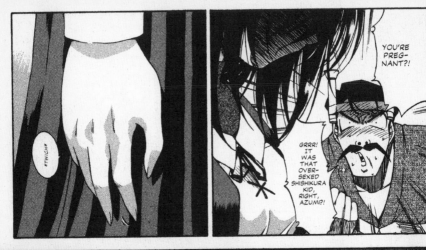

TWICH

YOU'RE PREG- NANT?!

GRRR! IT WAS THAT OVER- SEXED SHISHIKURA KID, RIGHT, AZUMI?!

COULD YOU... PULL THE CAR OUT?

HUH?

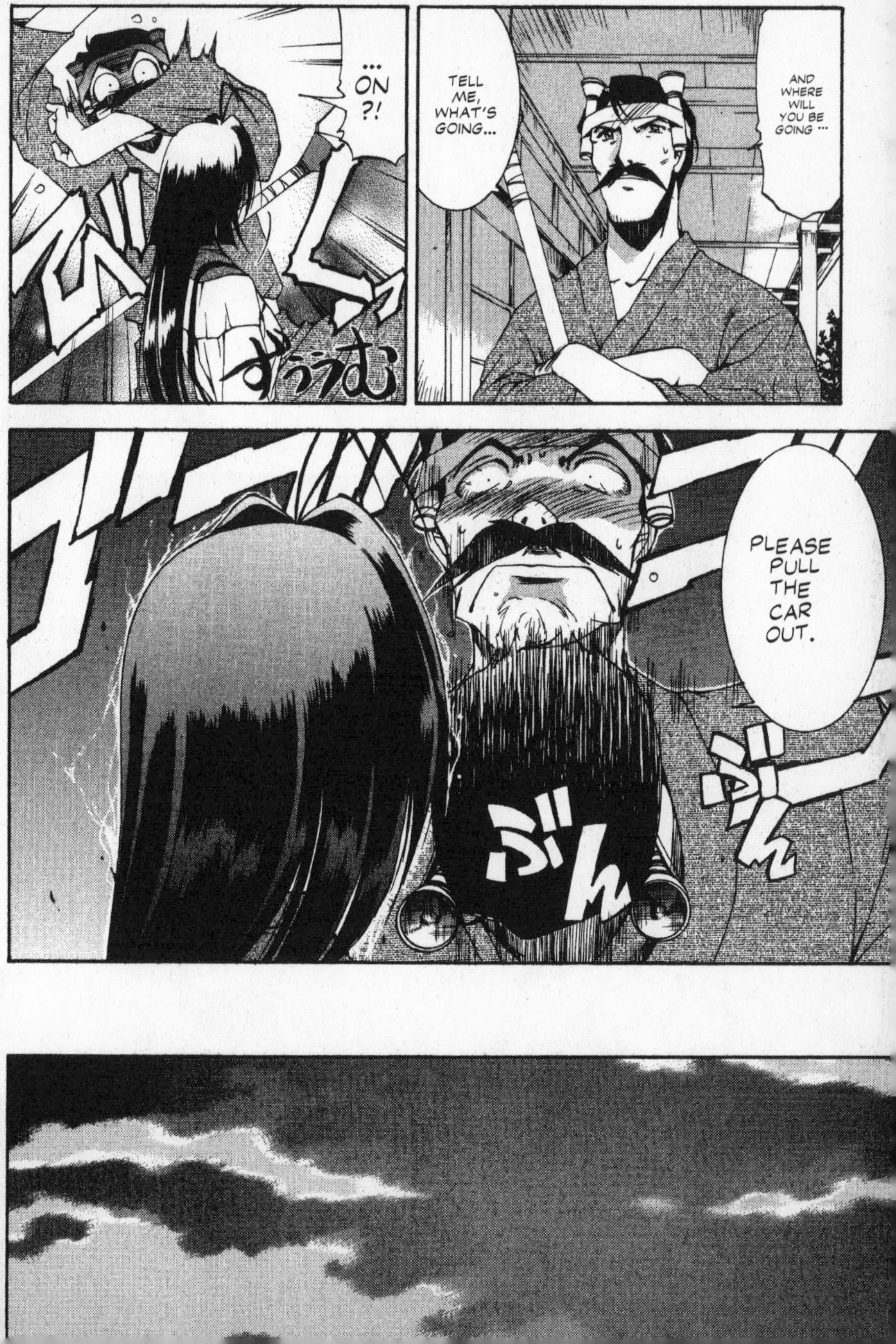
AND WHERE WILL YOU BE GOING ...
TELL ME, WHAT'S GOING...
... ON ?!
PLEASE PULL THE CAR OUT.

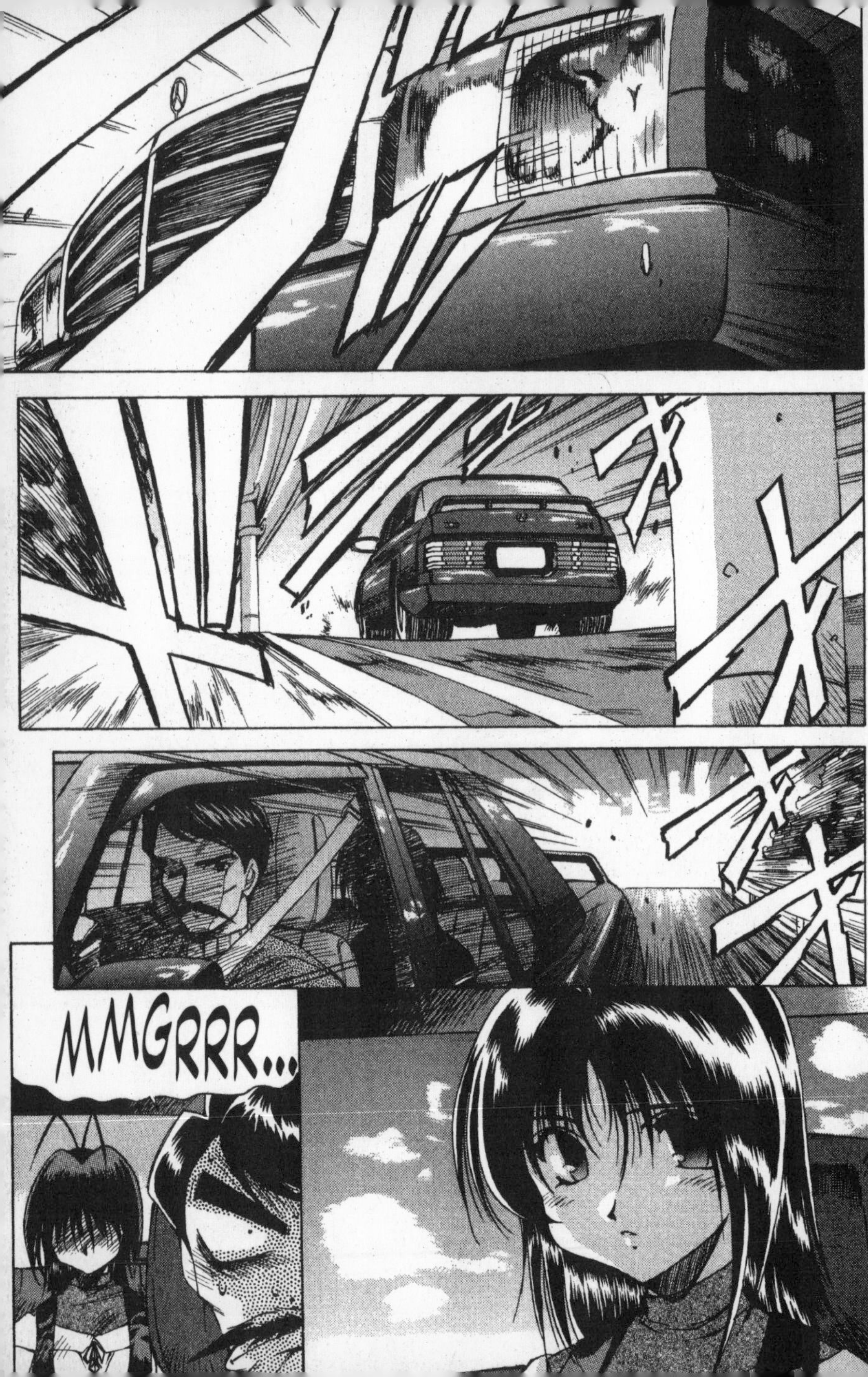
MMGRRR...

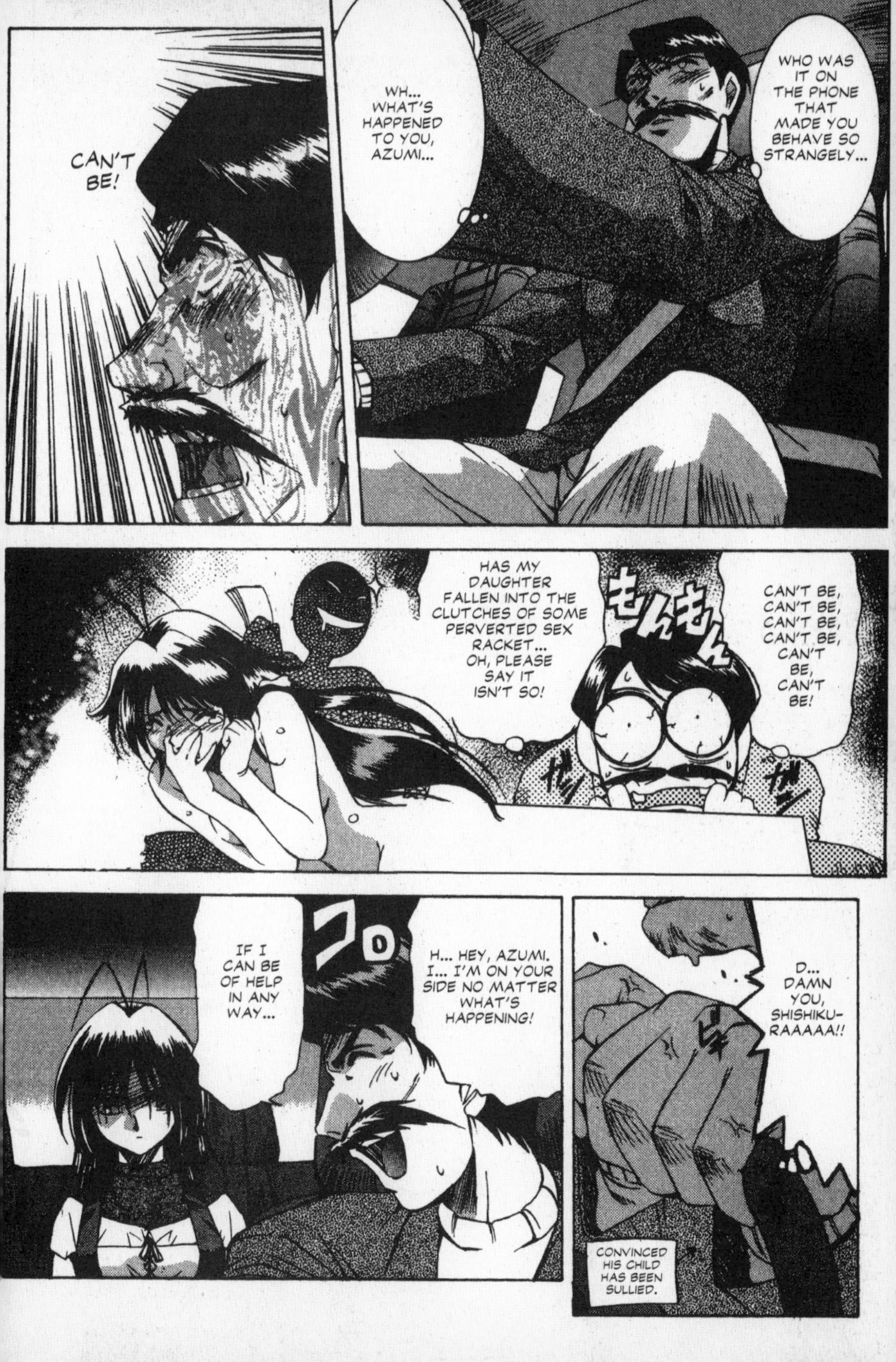
WHO WAS IT ON THE PHONE THAT MADE YOU BEHAVE SO STRANGELY...
WH... WHAT'S HAPPENED TO YOU, AZUMI...
CAN'T BE!
CAN'T BE, CAN'T BE, CAN'T BE, CAN'T BE, CAN'T BE, CAN'T BE!
もんもん
HAS MY DAUGHTER FALLEN INTO THE CLUTCHES OF SOME PERVERTED SEX RACKET... OH, PLEASE SAY IT ISN'T SO!
D... DAMN YOU, SHISHIKU-RAAAAA!!
CONVINCED HIS CHILD HAS BEEN SULLIED.
H... HEY, AZUMI. I... I'M ON YOUR SIDE NO MATTER WHAT'S HAPPENING!
IF I CAN BE OF HELP IN ANY WAY...

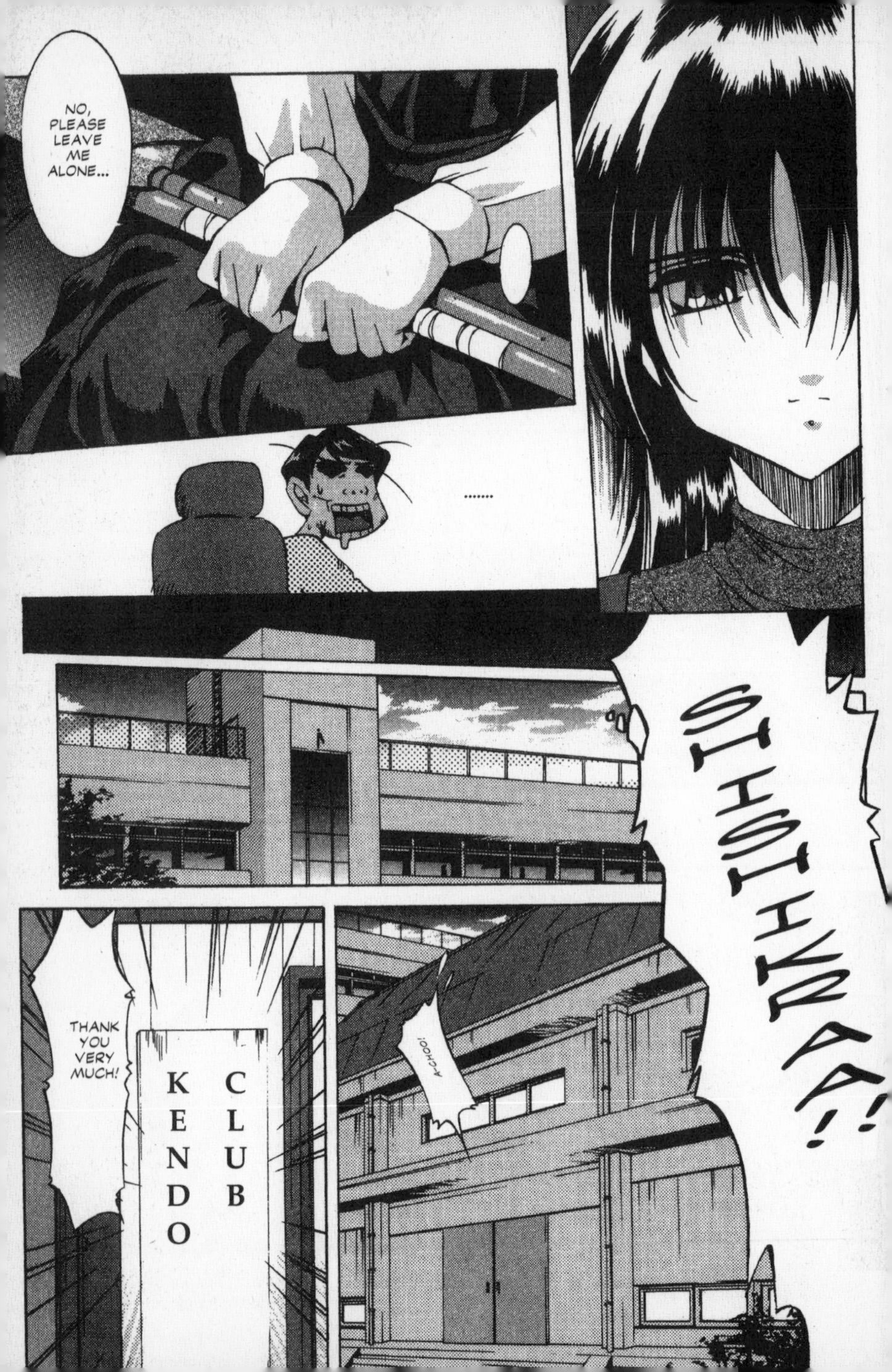
NO, PLEASE LEAVE ME ALONE...
......
A-CHOO!
KENDO CLUB
THANK YOU VERY MUCH!

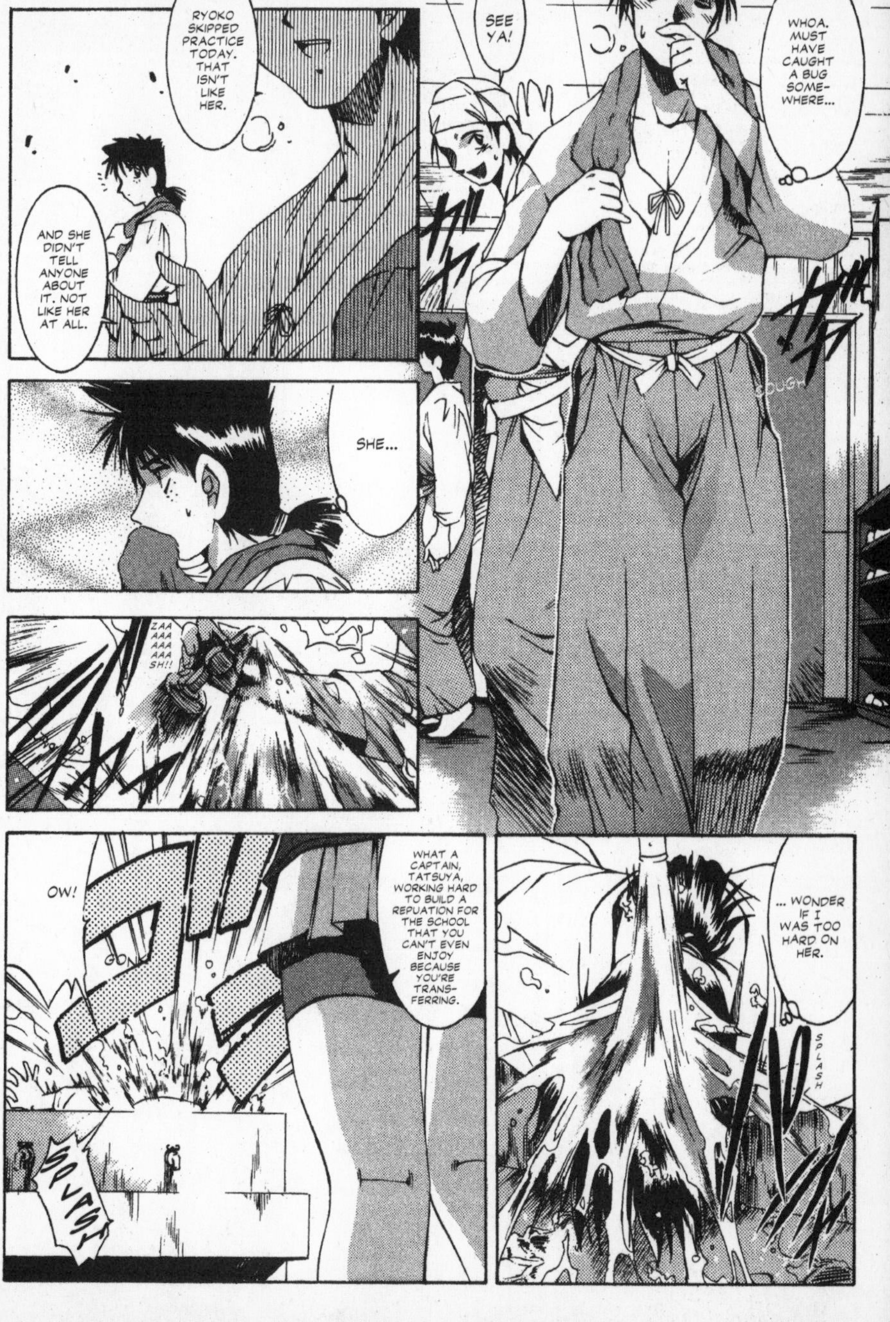

WHOA. MUST HAVE CAUGHT A BUG SOME-WHERE...
SEE YA!
COUGH
RYOKO SKIPPED PRACTICE TODAY. THAT ISN'T LIKE HER.
AND SHE DIDN'T TELL ANYONE ABOUT IT. NOT LIKE HER AT ALL.
SHE...
ZAAAAAAAAAASH!!
... WONDER IF I WAS TOO HARD ON HER.
SPLASH
WHAT A CAPTAIN, TATSUYA, WORKING HARD TO BUILD A REPUATION FOR THE SCHOOL THAT YOU CAN'T EVEN ENJOY BECAUSE YOU'RE TRANS-FERRING.
OW!
GONK
SPLASH

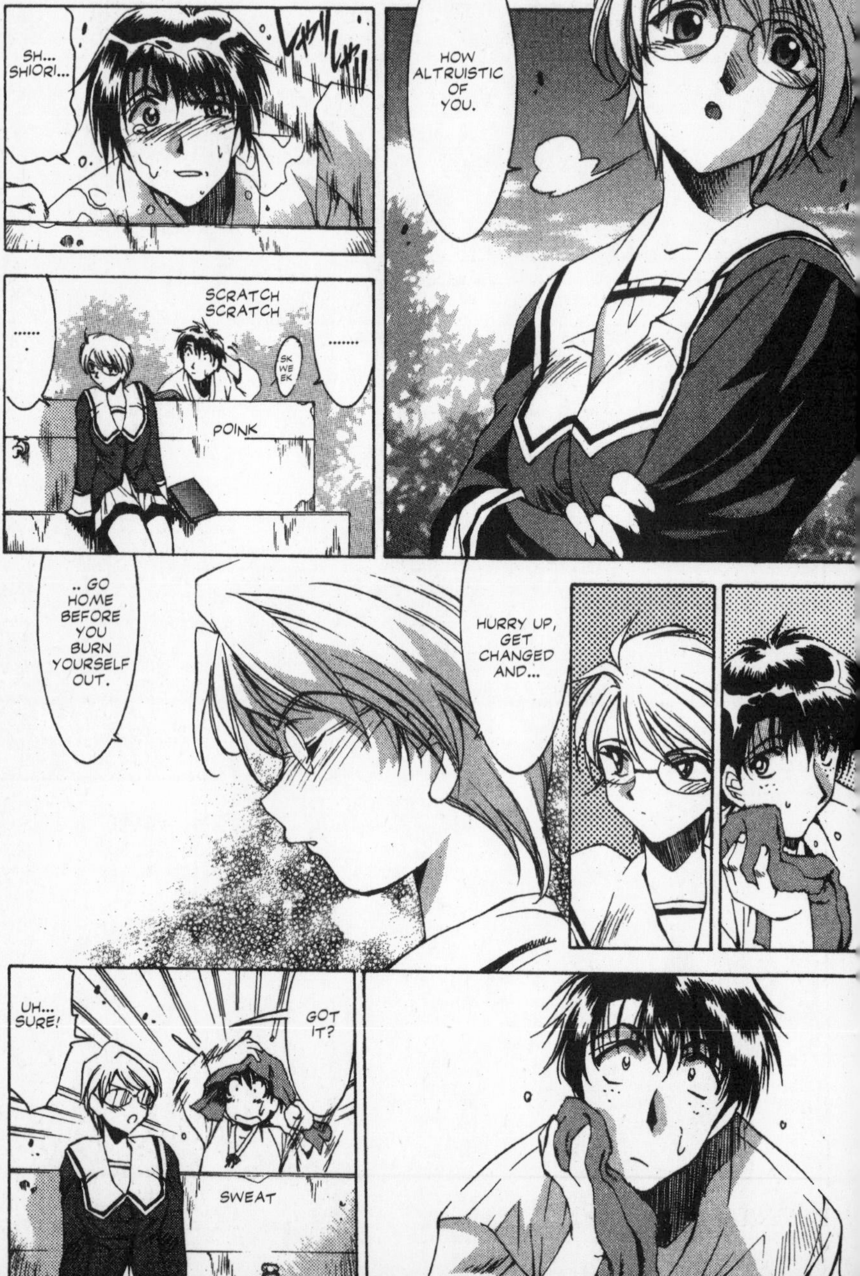
HOW ALTRUISTIC OF YOU.
SH... SHIORI...
....
SCRATCH SCRATCH
SK WE EK
....
POINK
HURRY UP, GET CHANGED AND...
.. GO HOME BEFORE YOU BURN YOURSELF OUT.
GOT IT?
UH... SURE!
SWEAT

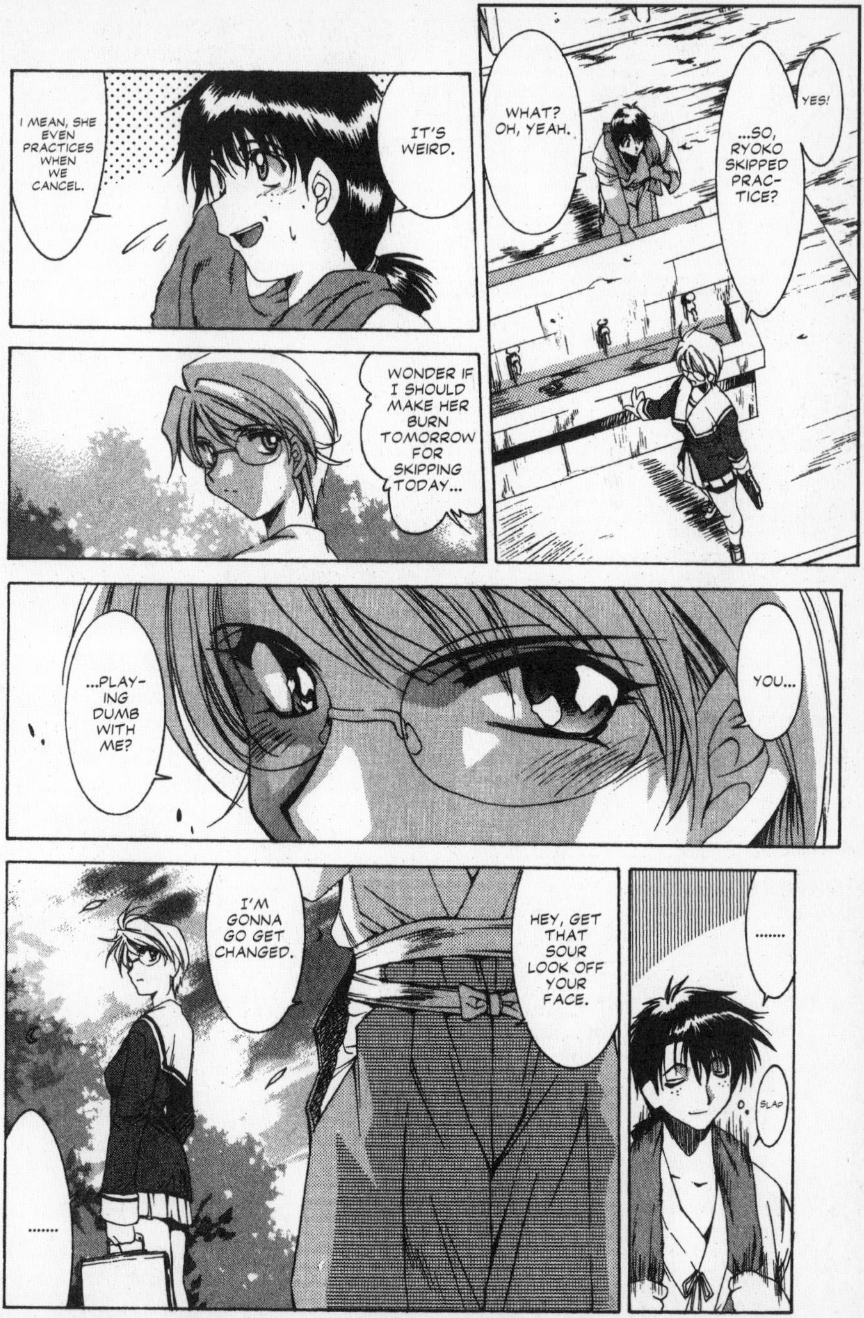
YES!
...SO, RYOKO SKIPPED PRAC-TICE?
WHAT? OH, YEAH.
IT'S WEIRD.
I MEAN, SHE EVEN PRACTICES WHEN WE CANCEL.
WONDER IF I SHOULD MAKE HER BURN TOMORROW FOR SKIPPING TODAY...
YOU...
...PLAYING-ING DUMB WITH ME?
....
SLAP
HEY, GET THAT SOUR LOOK OFF YOUR FACE.
I'M GONNA GO GET CHANGED.
....

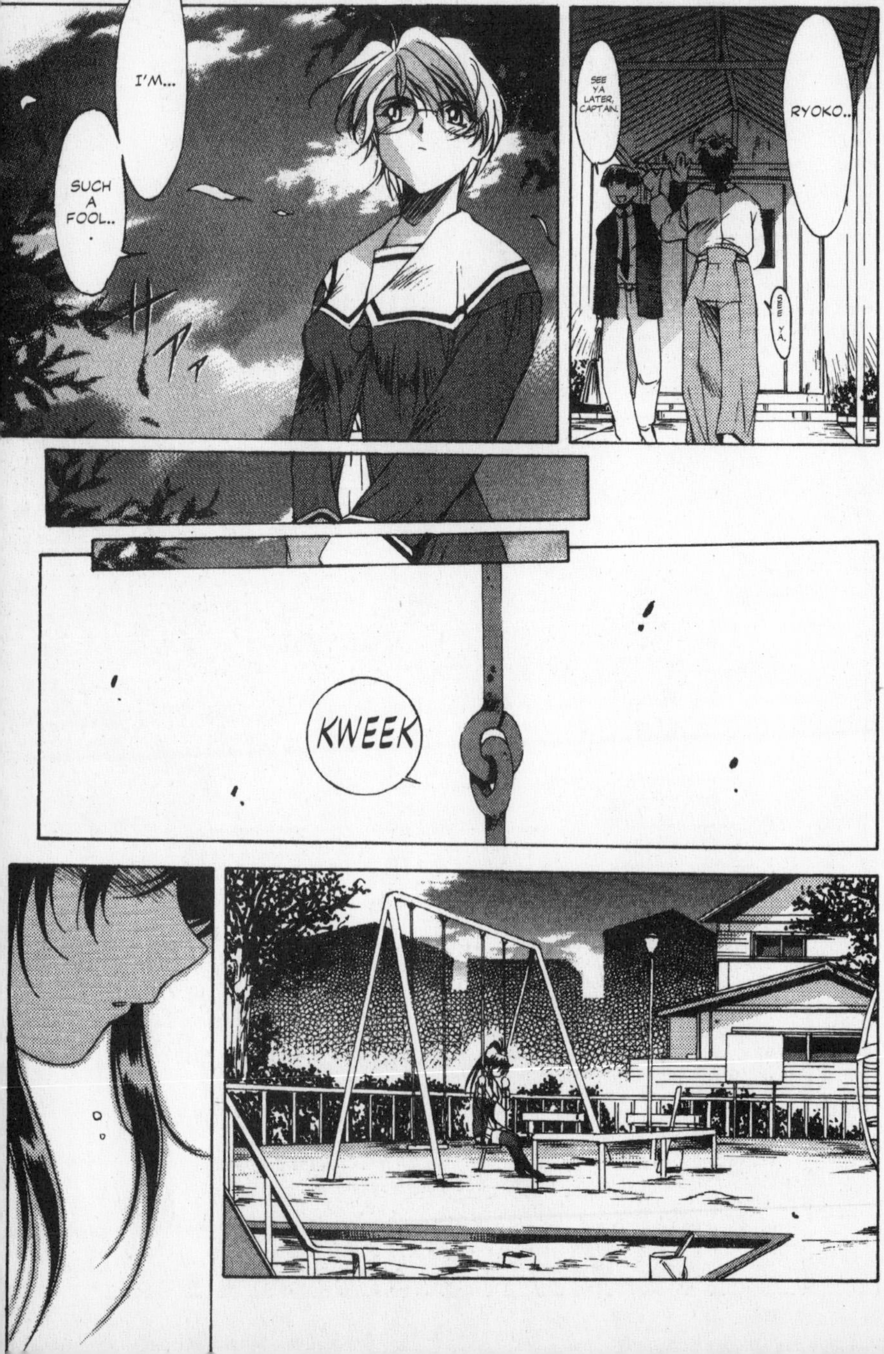
RYOKO..
SEE YA LATER, CAPTAIN.
SEE YA.
I'M...
SUCH A FOOL...
KWEEK

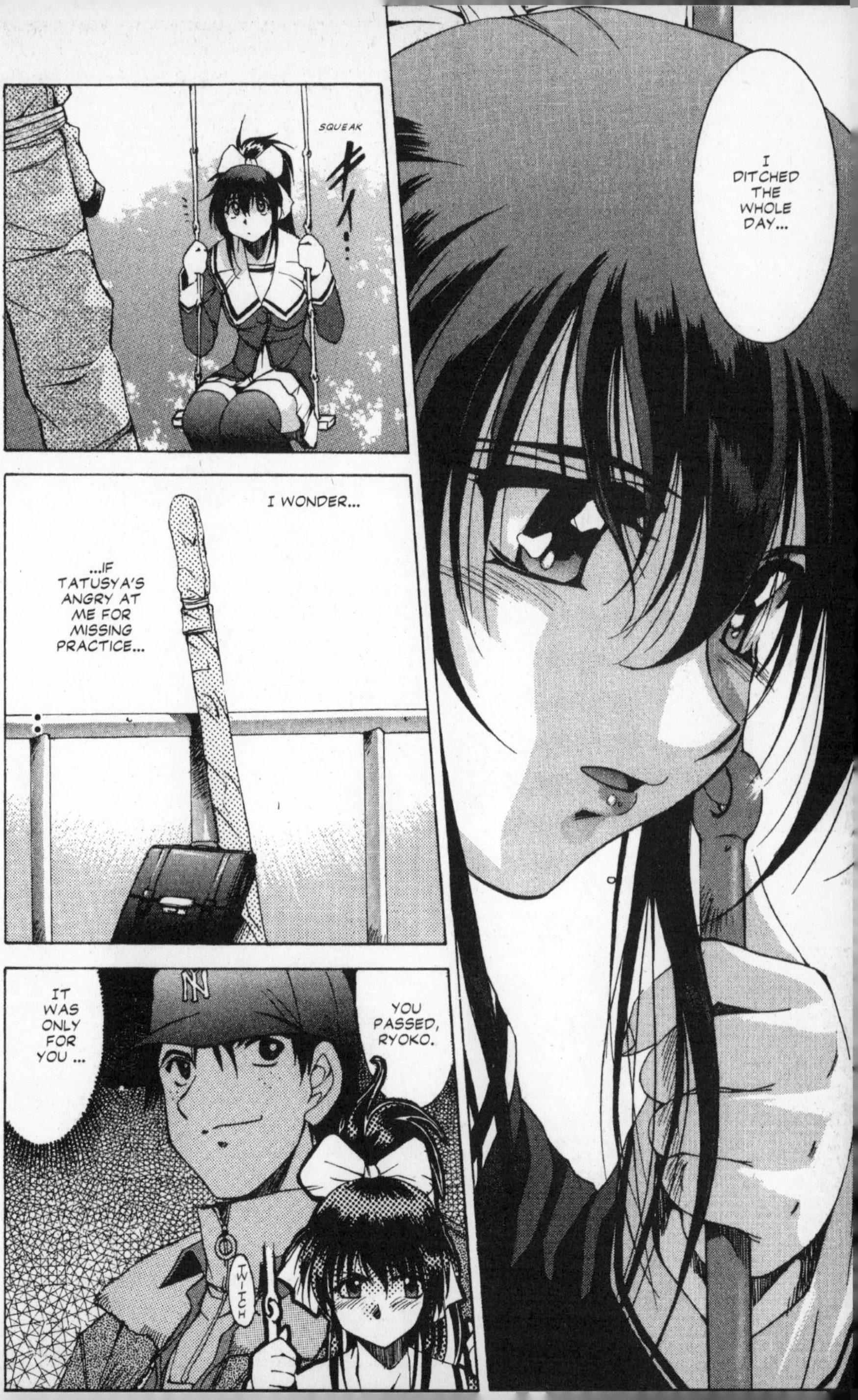
I DITCHED THE WHOLE DAY...
SQUEAK
I WONDER...
...IF TATUSYA'S ANGRY AT ME FOR MISSING PRACTICE...
YOU PASSED, RYOKO.
IT WAS ONLY FOR YOU ...
TWITCH

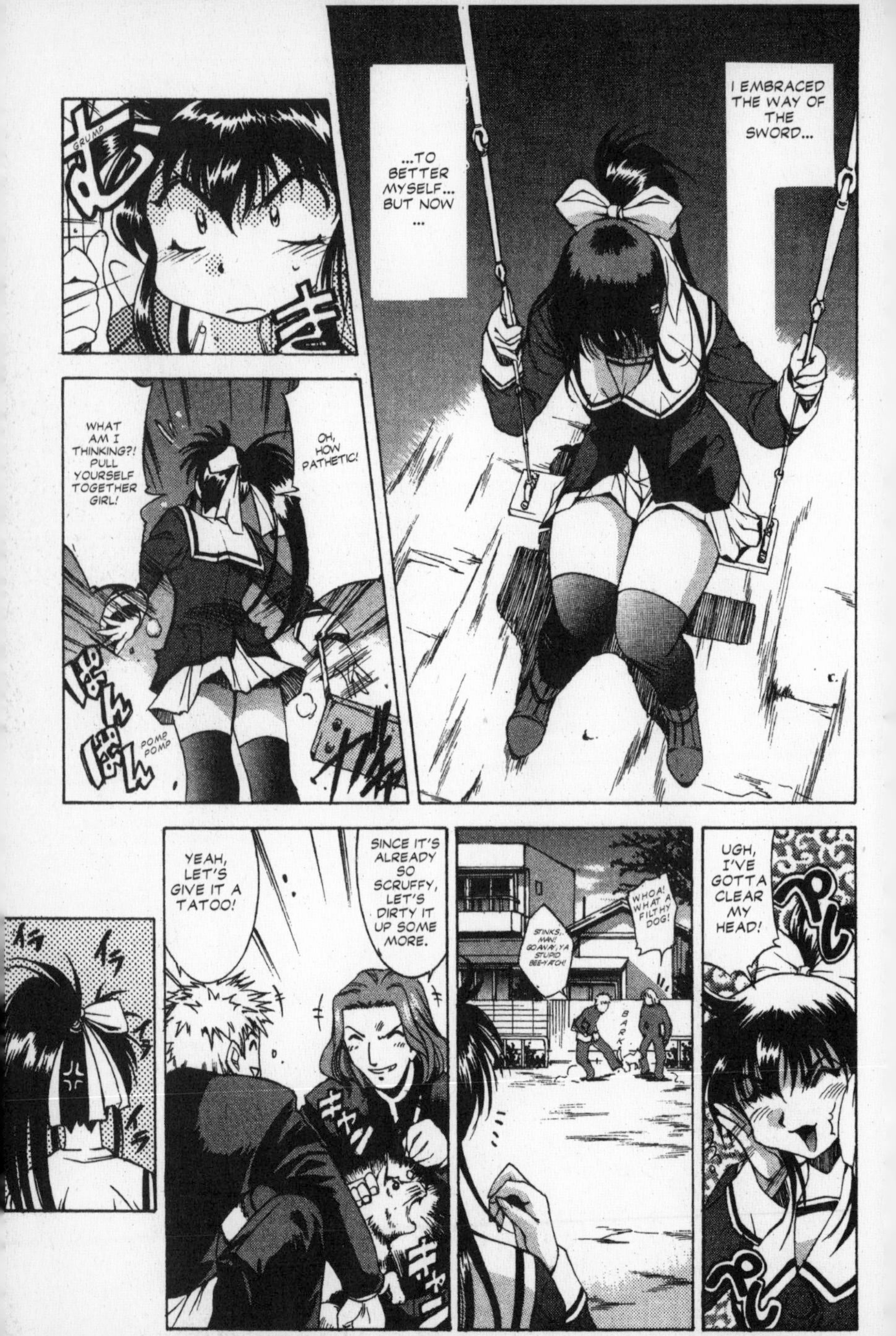
I EMBRACED THE WAY OF THE SWORD...
...TO BETTER MYSELF... BUT NOW ...
GRUMP
OH, HOW PATHETIC!
WHAT AM I THINKING?! PULL YOURSELF TOGETHER GIRL!
POMP POMP
UGH, I'VE GOTTA CLEAR MY HEAD!
WHOA! WHAT A FILTHY DOG!
STINKS, MAN! GO AWAY, YA STUPID BEE-YATCH!
BARK
SINCE IT'S ALREADY SO SCRUFFY, LET'S DIRTY IT UP SOME MORE.
YEAH, LET'S GIVE IT A TATOO!

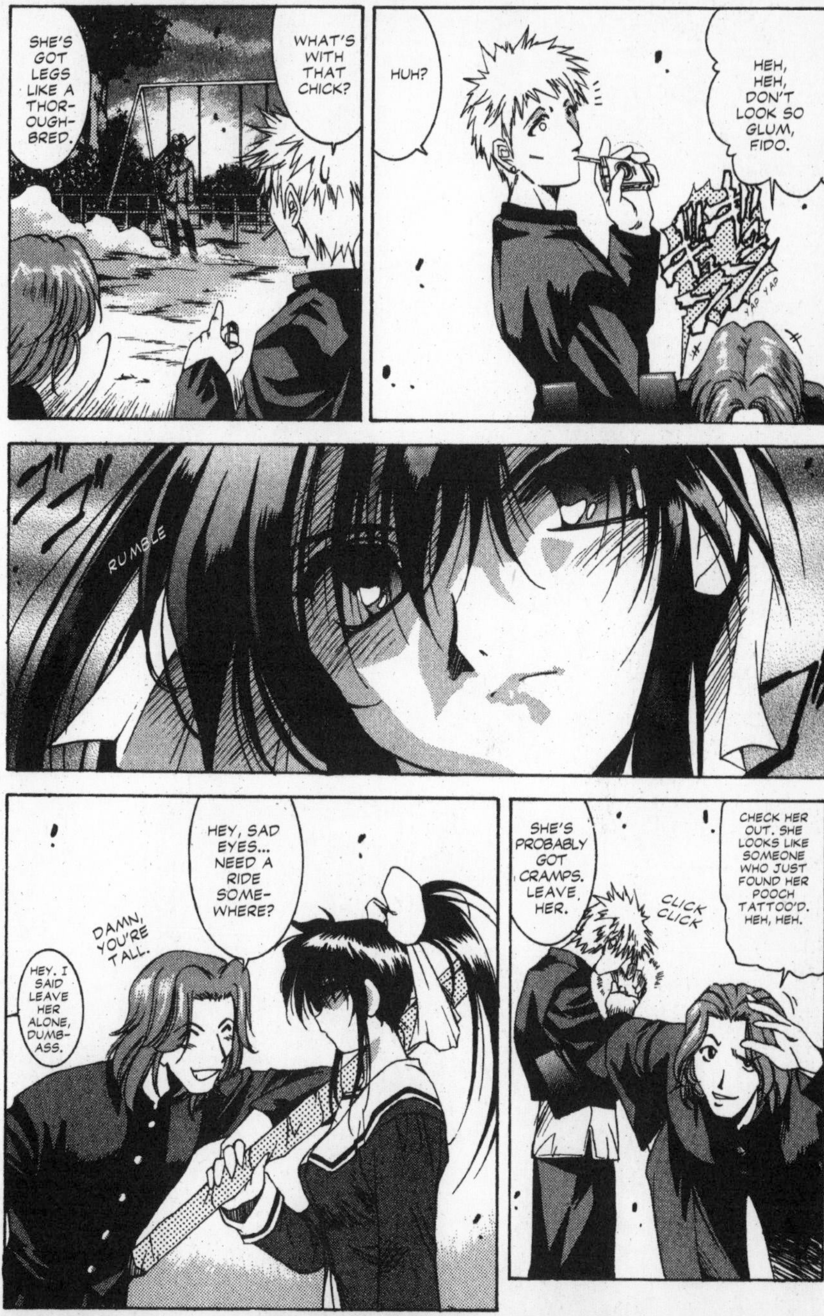
HEH, HEH, DON'T LOOK SO GLUM, FIDO.
YAP YAP
HUH?
WHAT'S WITH THAT CHICK?
SHE'S GOT LEGS LIKE A THOROUGHBRED.
RUMBLE
CHECK HER OUT. SHE LOOKS LIKE SOMEONE WHO JUST FOUND HER POOCH TATTOO'D. HEH, HEH.
CLICK CLICK
SHE'S PROBABLY GOT CRAMPS. LEAVE HER.
HEY, SAD EYES... NEED A RIDE SOMEWHERE?
DAMN, YOU'RE TALL.
HEY. I SAID LEAVE HER ALONE, DUMBASS.

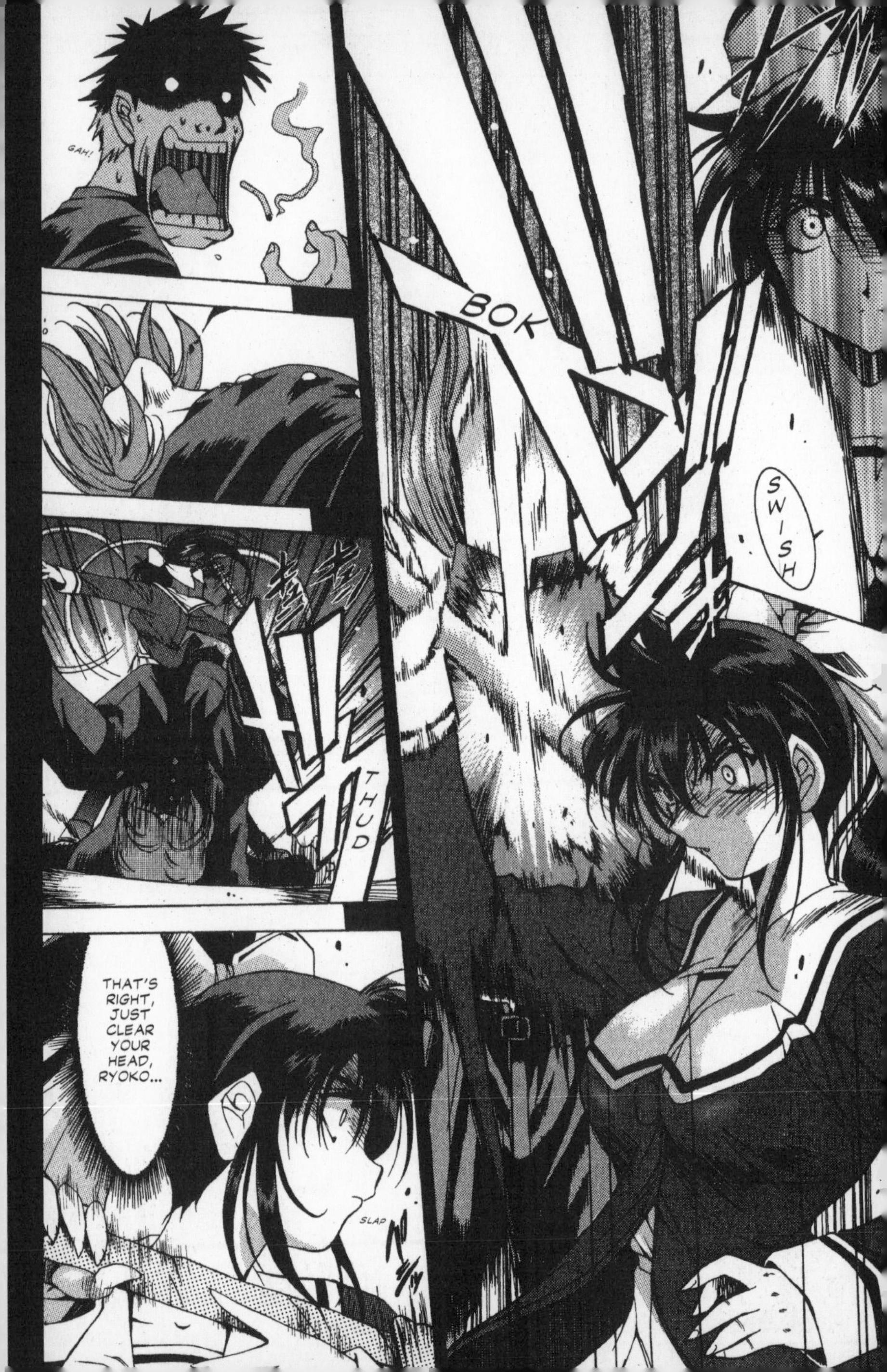
BOK
SWISH
GAH!
THUD
THAT'S RIGHT, JUST CLEAR YOUR HEAD, RYOKO...
SLAP

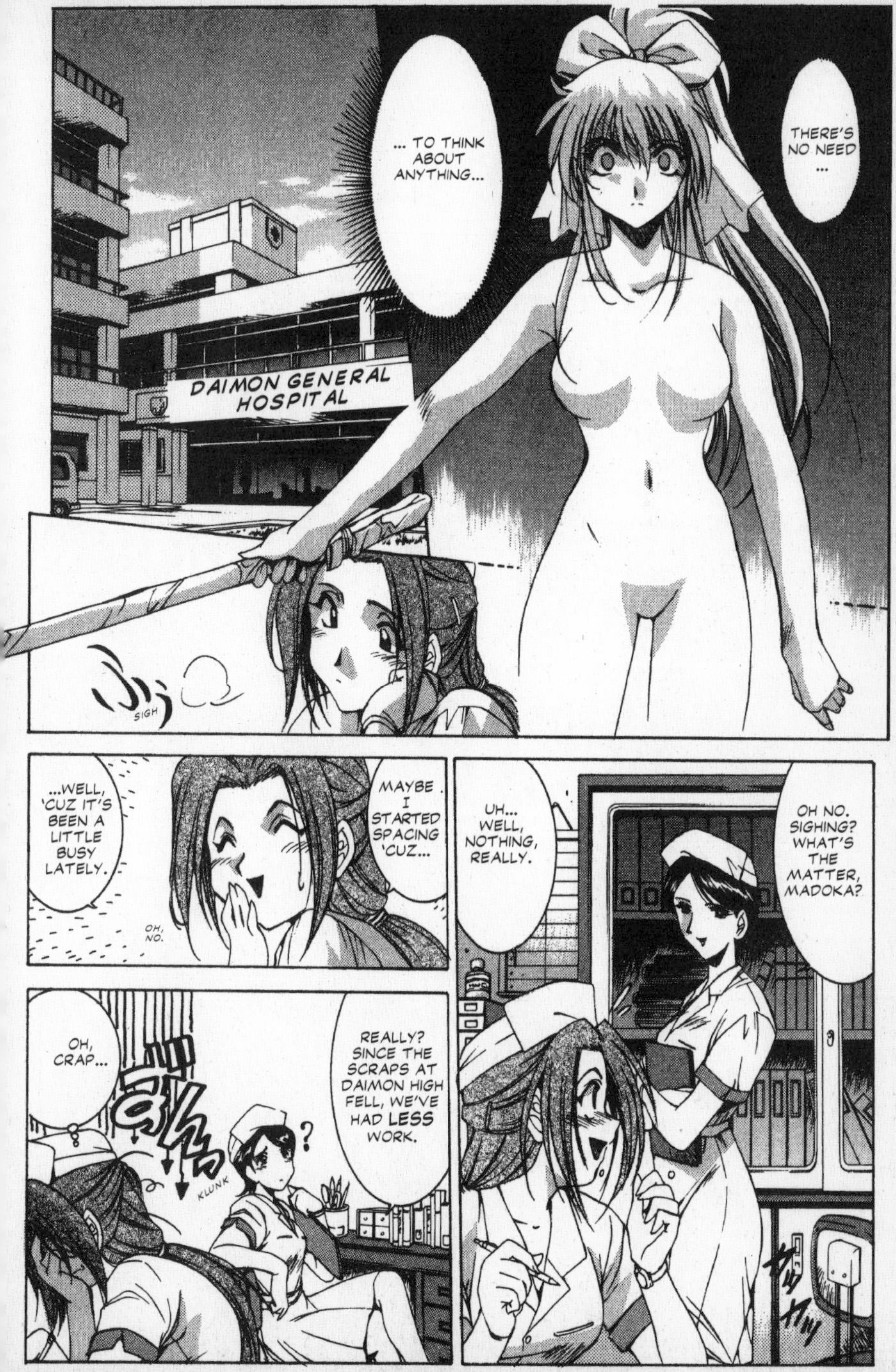

THERE'S NO NEED ...
... TO THINK ABOUT ANYTHING...
DAIMON GENERAL HOSPITAL
SIGH
OH NO. SIGHING? WHAT'S THE MATTER, MADOKA?
UH... WELL, NOTHING, REALLY.
MAYBE I STARTED SPACING 'CUZ...
...WELL, 'CUZ IT'S BEEN A LITTLE BUSY LATELY.
OH, NO.
REALLY? SINCE THE SCRAPS AT DAIMON HIGH FELL, WE'VE HAD LESS WORK.
?
KLUNK
OH, CRAP...

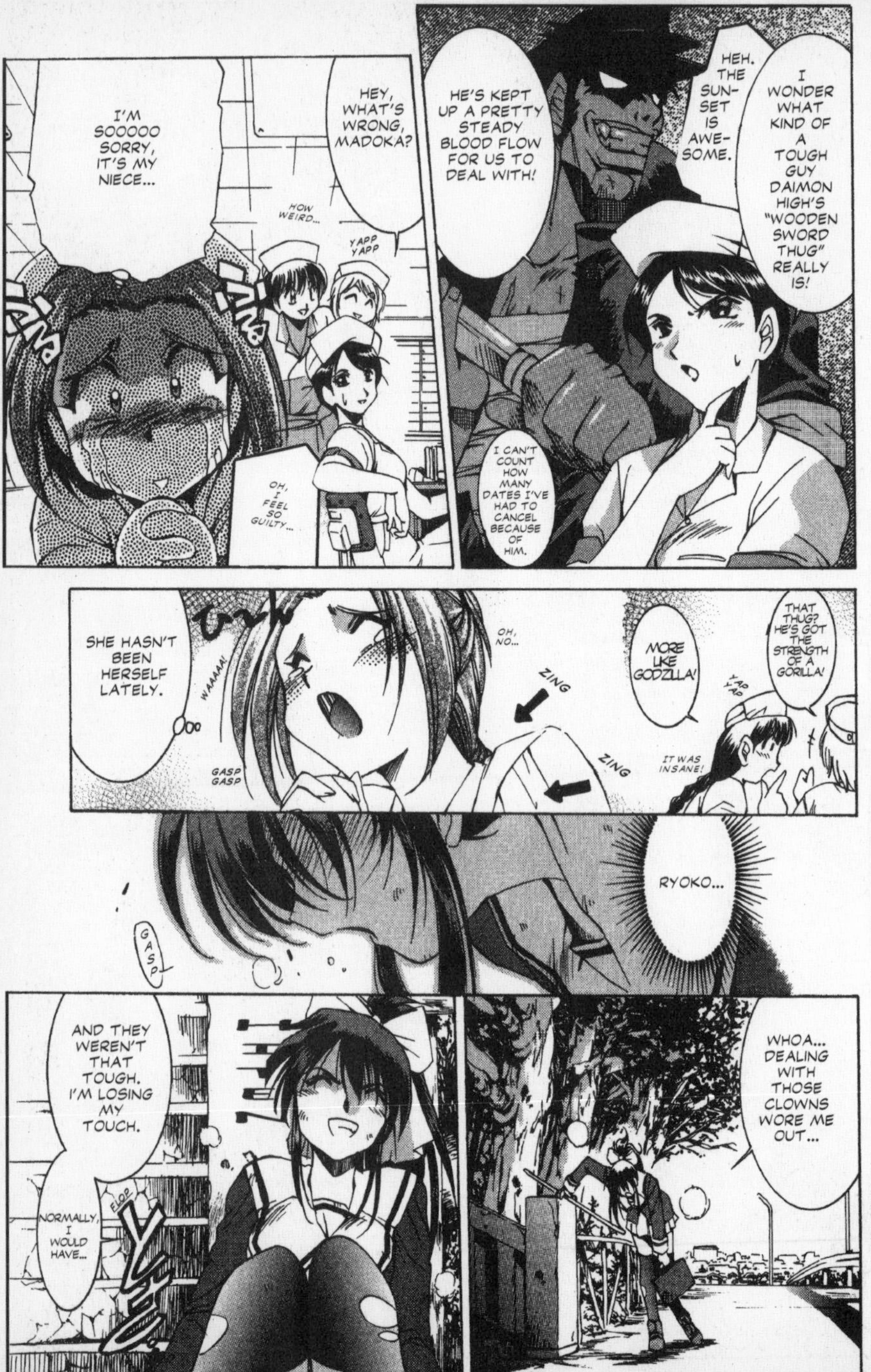
I WONDER WHAT KIND OF A TOUGH GUY DAIMON HIGH'S "WOODEN SWORD THUG" REALLY IS!
HEH. THE SUN-SET IS AWE-SOME.
HE'S KEPT UP A PRETTY STEADY BLOOD FLOW FOR US TO DEAL WITH!
I CAN'T COUNT HOW MANY DATES I'VE HAD TO CANCEL BECAUSE OF HIM.
HEY, WHAT'S WRONG, MADOKA?
HOW WEIRD...
YAPP YAPP
I'M SOOOOO SORRY, IT'S MY NIECE...
OH, I FEEL SO GUILTY...
THAT THUG? HE'S GOT THE STRENGTH OF A GORILLA!
YAP YAP
MORE LIKE GODZILLA!
IT WAS INSANE!
ZING
ZING
OH, NO...
SHE HASN'T BEEN HERSELF LATELY.
WAAAAA!
GASP GASP
RYOKO...
GASP
WHOA... DEALING WITH THOSE CLOWNS WORE ME OUT...
AND THEY WEREN'T THAT TOUGH. I'M LOSING MY TOUCH.
NORMALLY, I WOULD HAVE...
FLOP

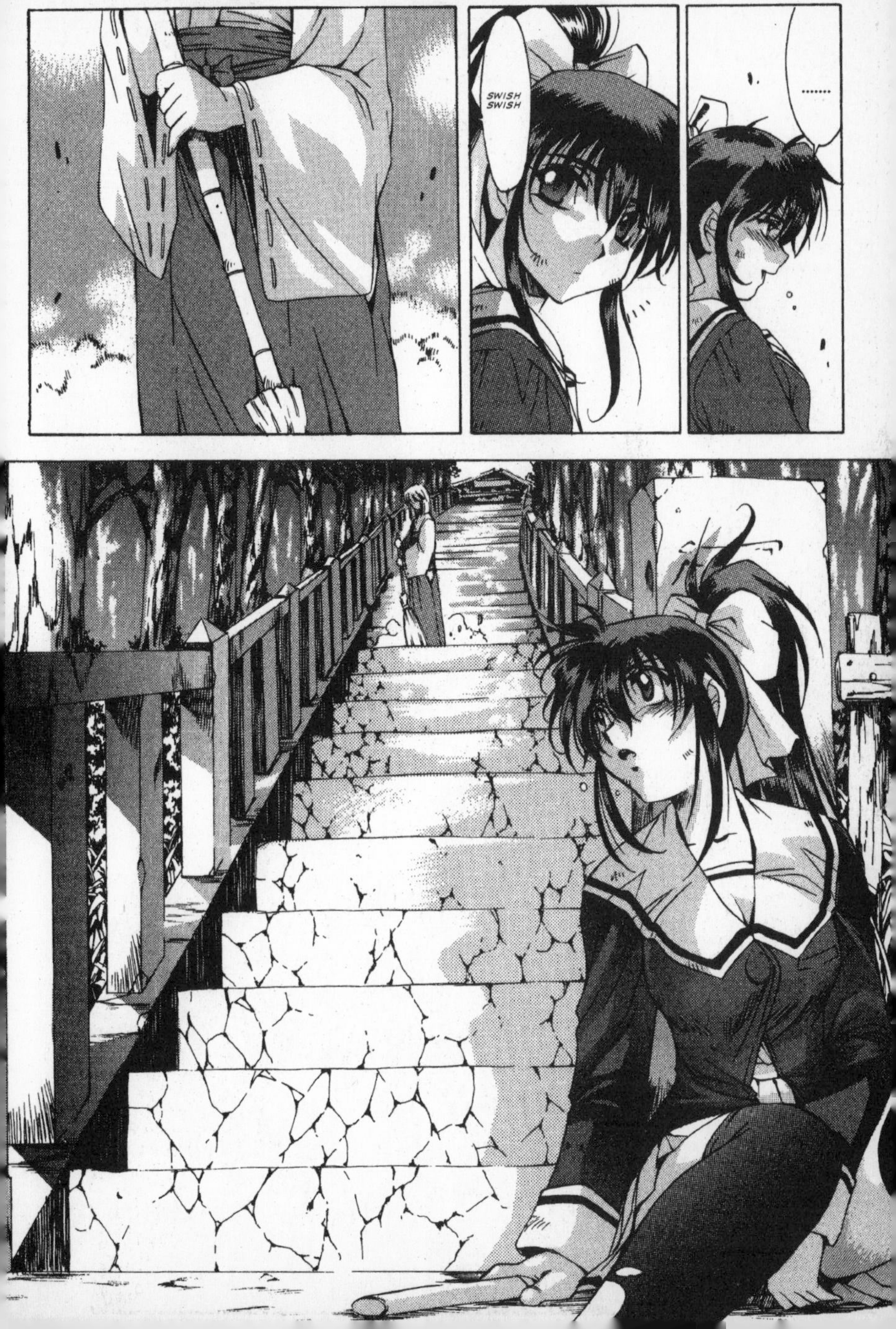

....
SWISH SWISH

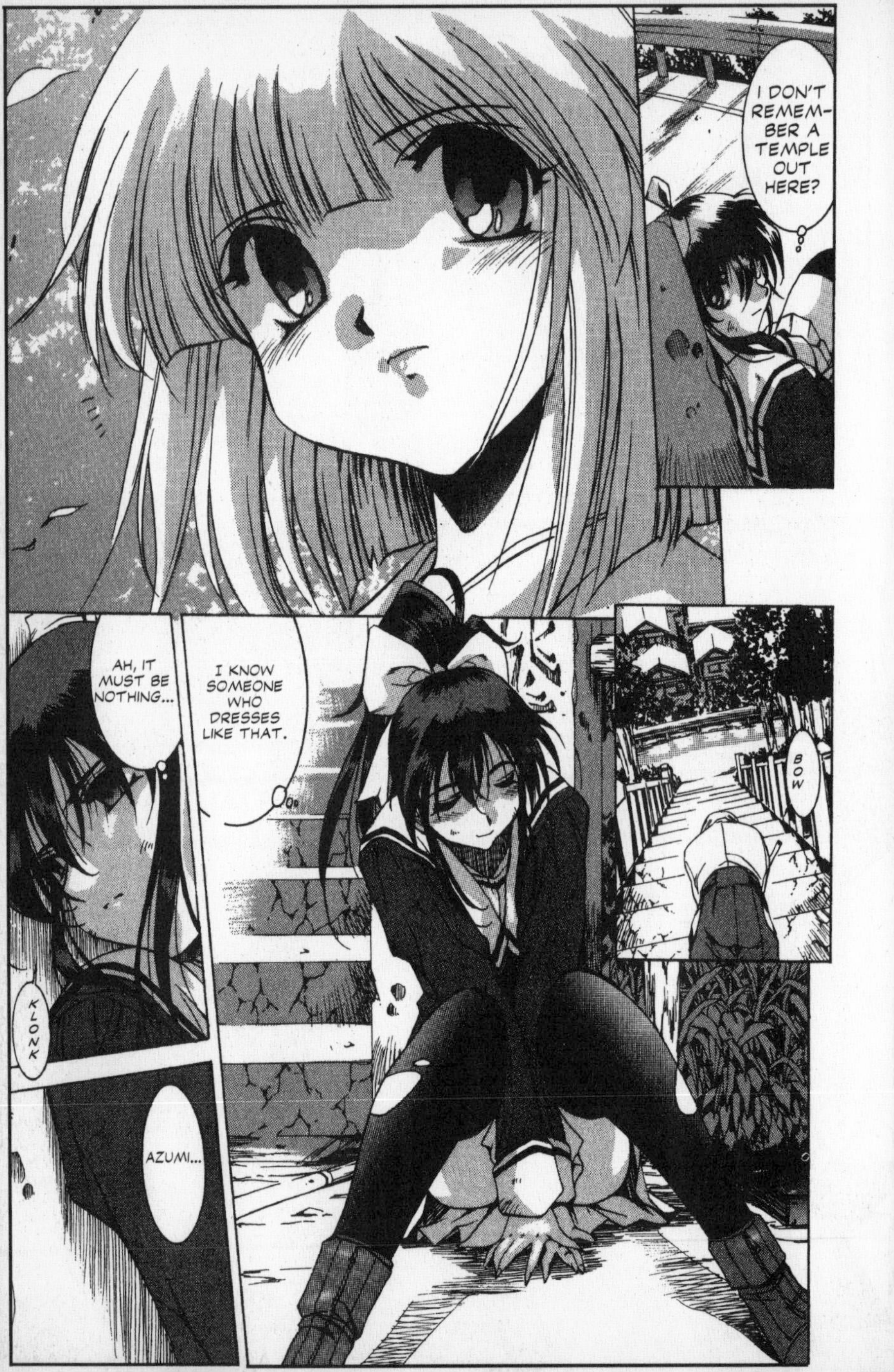
I DON'T REMEM-BER A TEMPLE OUT HERE?
BOW
I KNOW SOMEONE WHO DRESSES LIKE THAT.
AH, IT MUST BE NOTHING...
KLONK
AZUMI...

MIGHT AS WELL GO HOME...

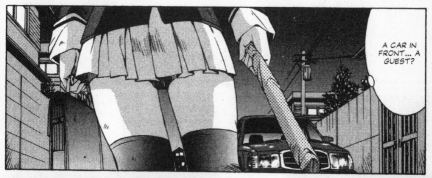

A CAR IN FRONT... A GUEST?

YOU'RE WIDE OPEN.

GASP

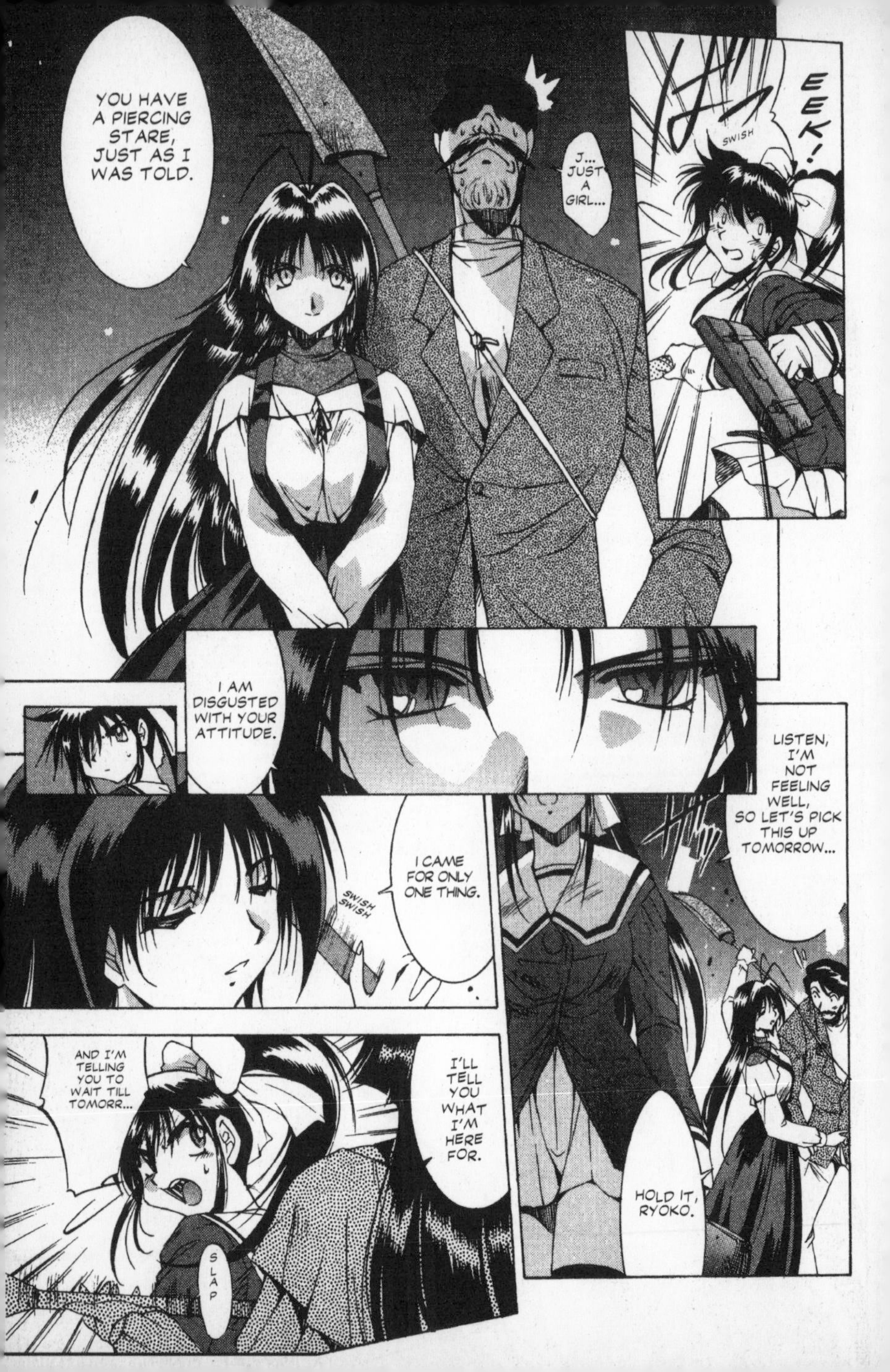
EEK!
SWISH
YOU HAVE A PIERCING STARE, JUST AS I WAS TOLD.
J... JUST A GIRL...
I AM DISGUSTED WITH YOUR ATTITUDE.
LISTEN, I'M NOT FEELING WELL, SO LET'S PICK THIS UP TOMORROW...
HOLD IT, RYOKO.
I CAME FOR ONLY ONE THING.
SWISH SWISH
I'LL TELL YOU WHAT I'M HERE FOR.
AND I'M TELLING YOU TO WAIT TILL TOMORR...
SLAP

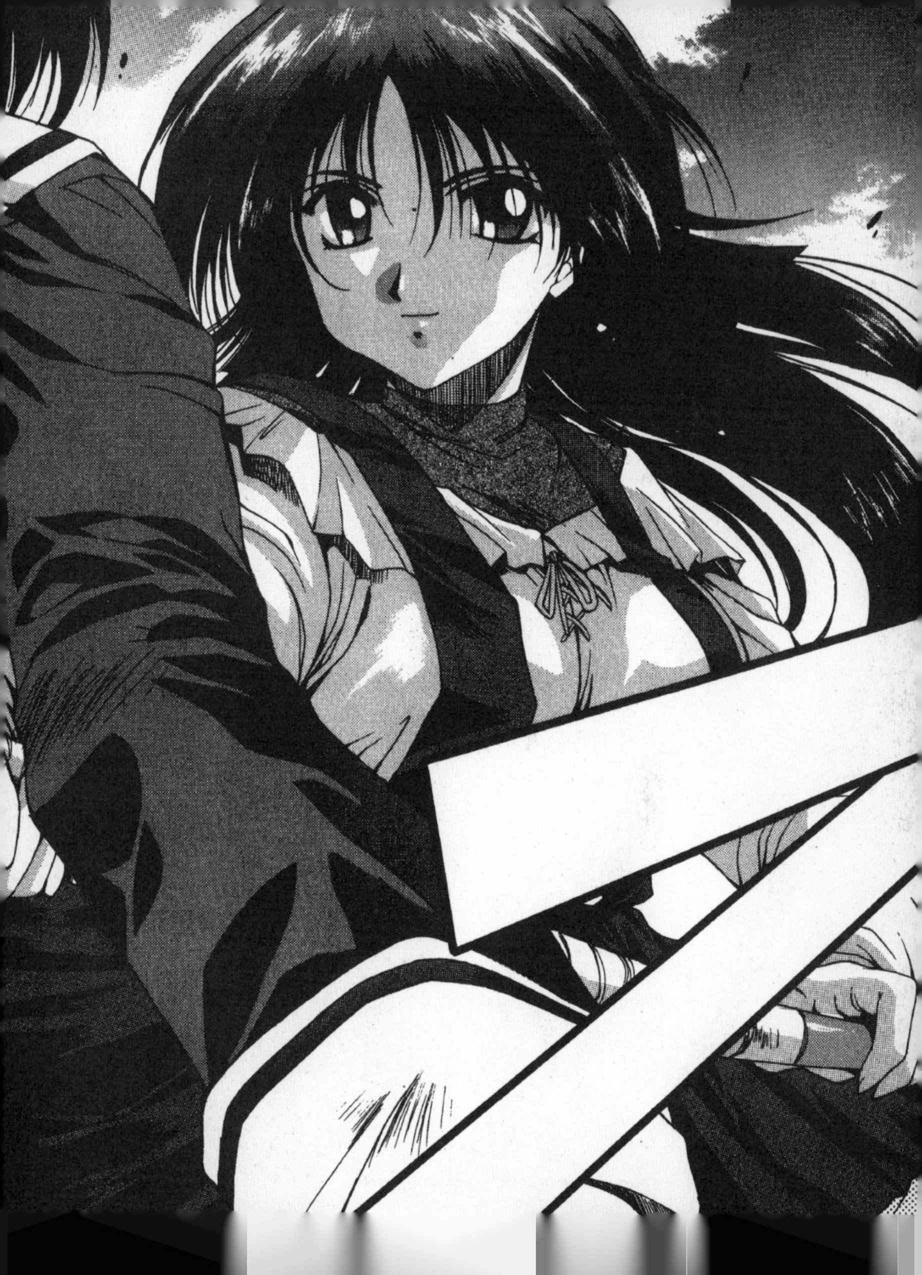

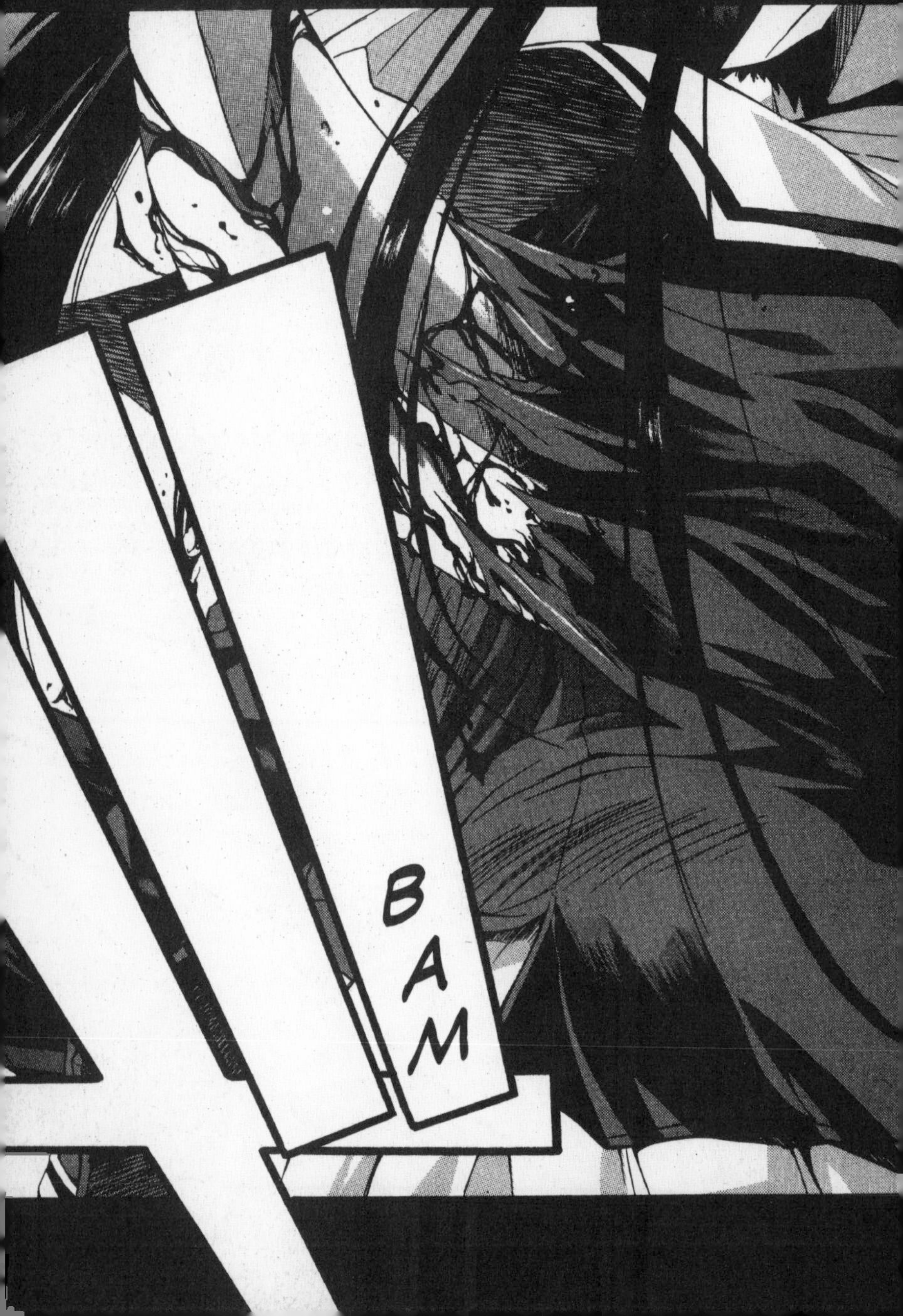
BAM

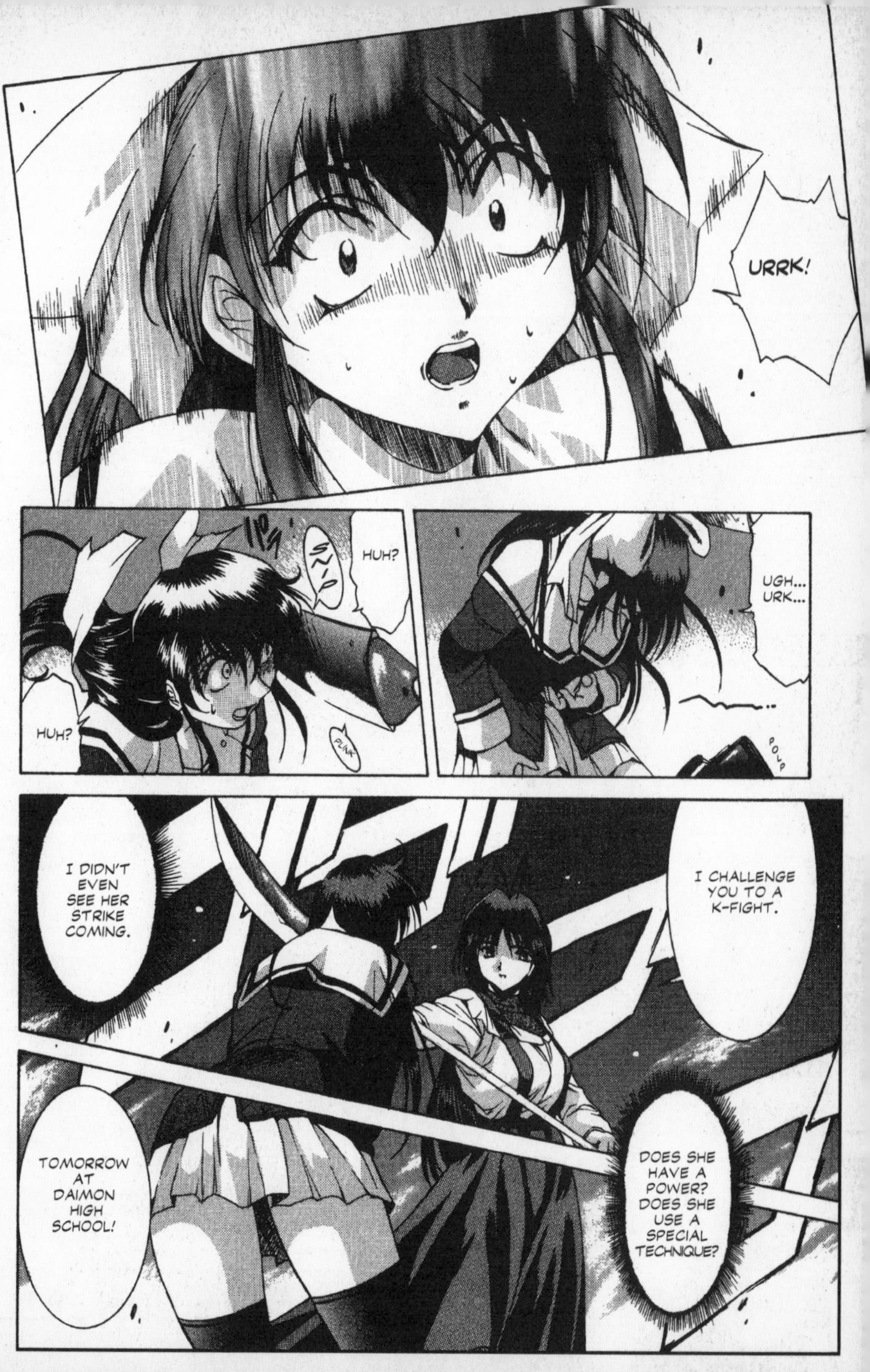
URRK!
UGH... URK...
...
POLP
HUH?
HUH?
PLINK
I CHALLENGE YOU TO A K-FIGHT.
I DIDN'T EVEN SEE HER STRIKE COMING.
DOES SHE HAVE A POWER? DOES SHE USE A SPECIAL TECHNIQUE?
TOMORROW AT DAIMON HIGH SCHOOL!

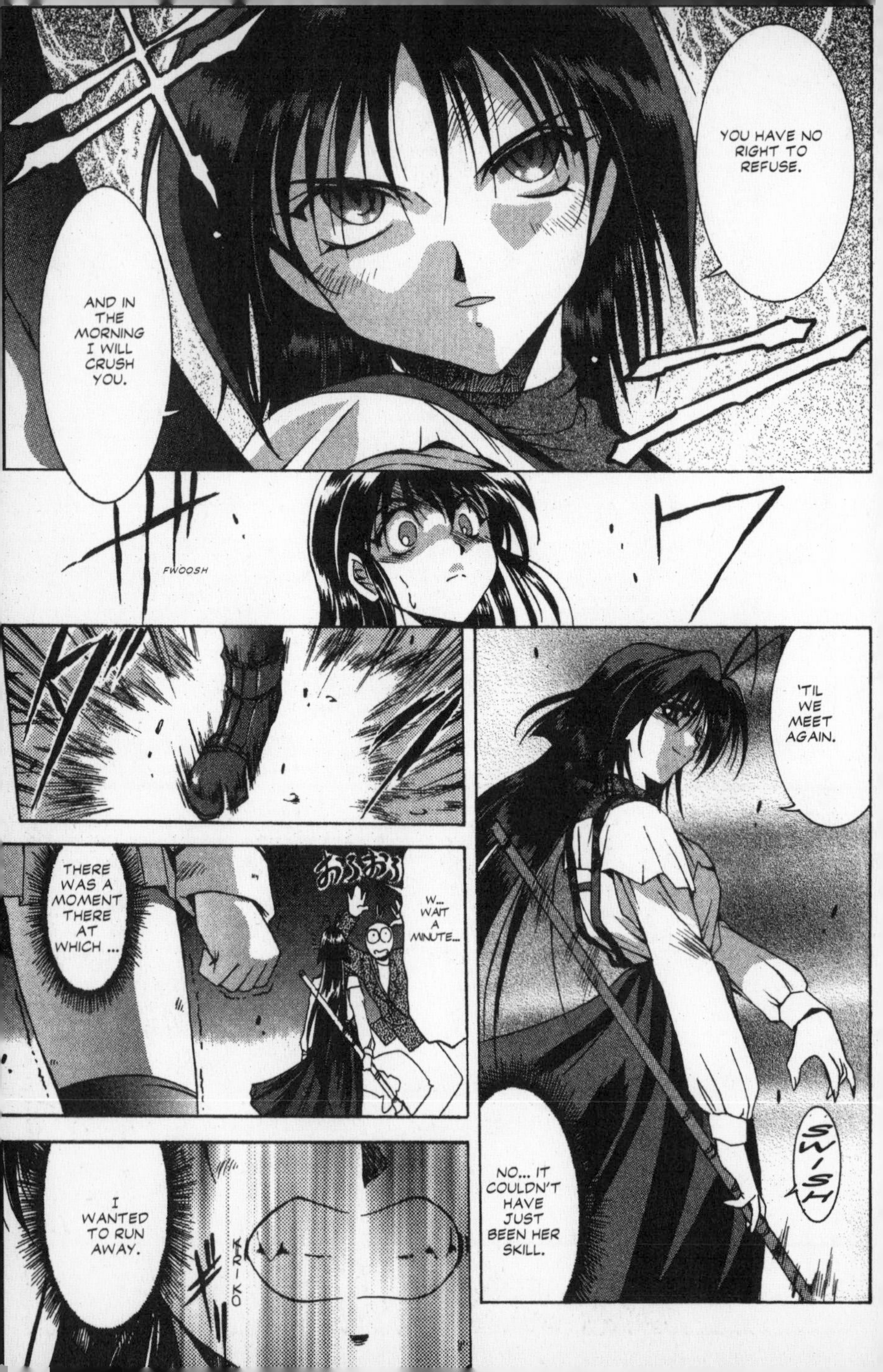

YOU HAVE NO RIGHT TO REFUSE.
AND IN THE MORNING I WILL CRUSH YOU.
FWOOSH
'TIL WE MEET AGAIN.
SWISH
NO... IT COULDN'T HAVE JUST BEEN HER SKILL.
W... WAIT A MINUTE...
おろおろ
THERE WAS A MOMENT THERE AT WHICH ...
KI-RI-KO
I WANTED TO RUN AWAY.

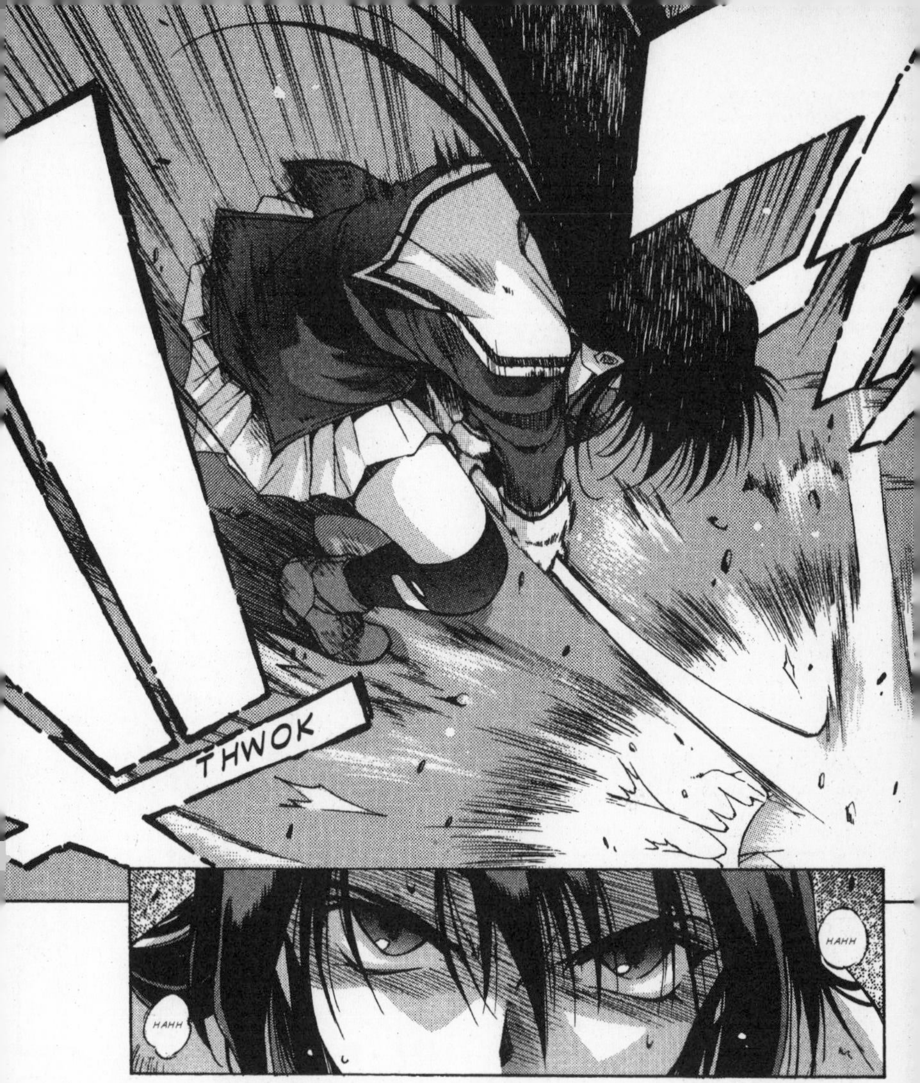
THWOK
HAHH
HAHH

NO NEED TO THINK ABOUT ANYTHING...

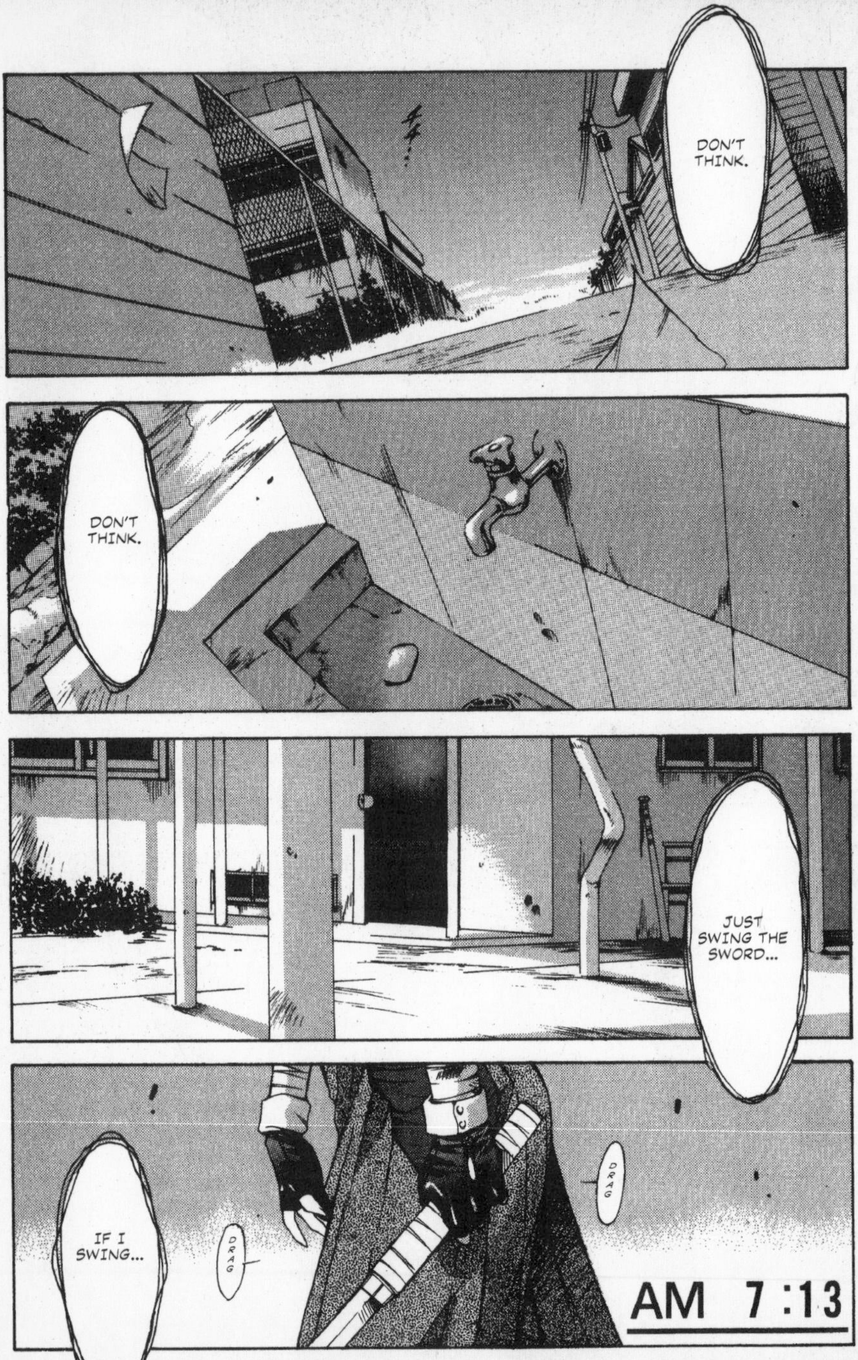

DON'T THINK.
DON'T THINK.
JUST SWING THE SWORD...
DRAG
DRAG
IF I SWING...
AM 7:13

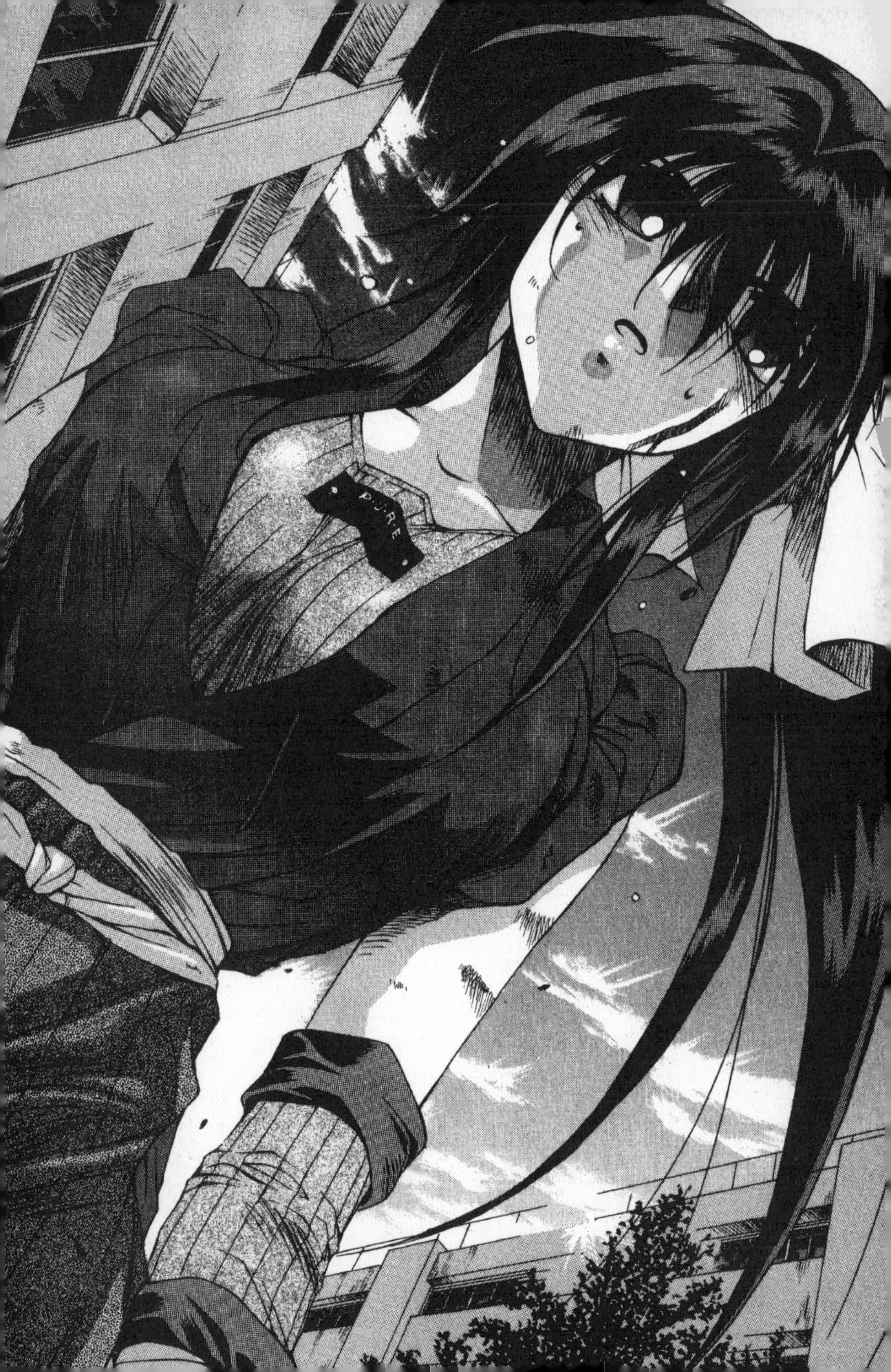
PURE

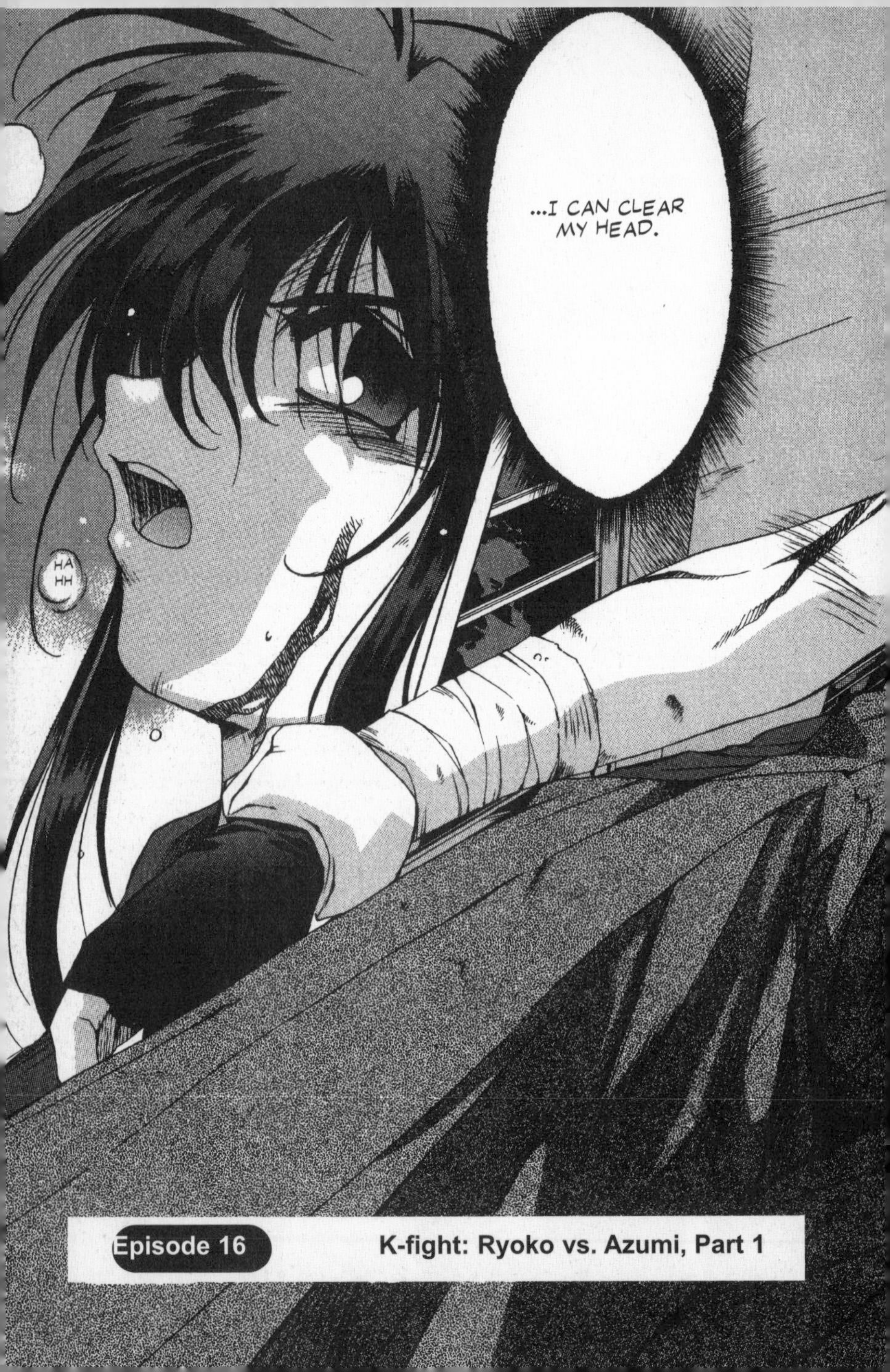
...I CAN CLEAR MY HEAD.
HA HH

Episode 16 K-fight: Ryoko vs. Azumi, Part 1

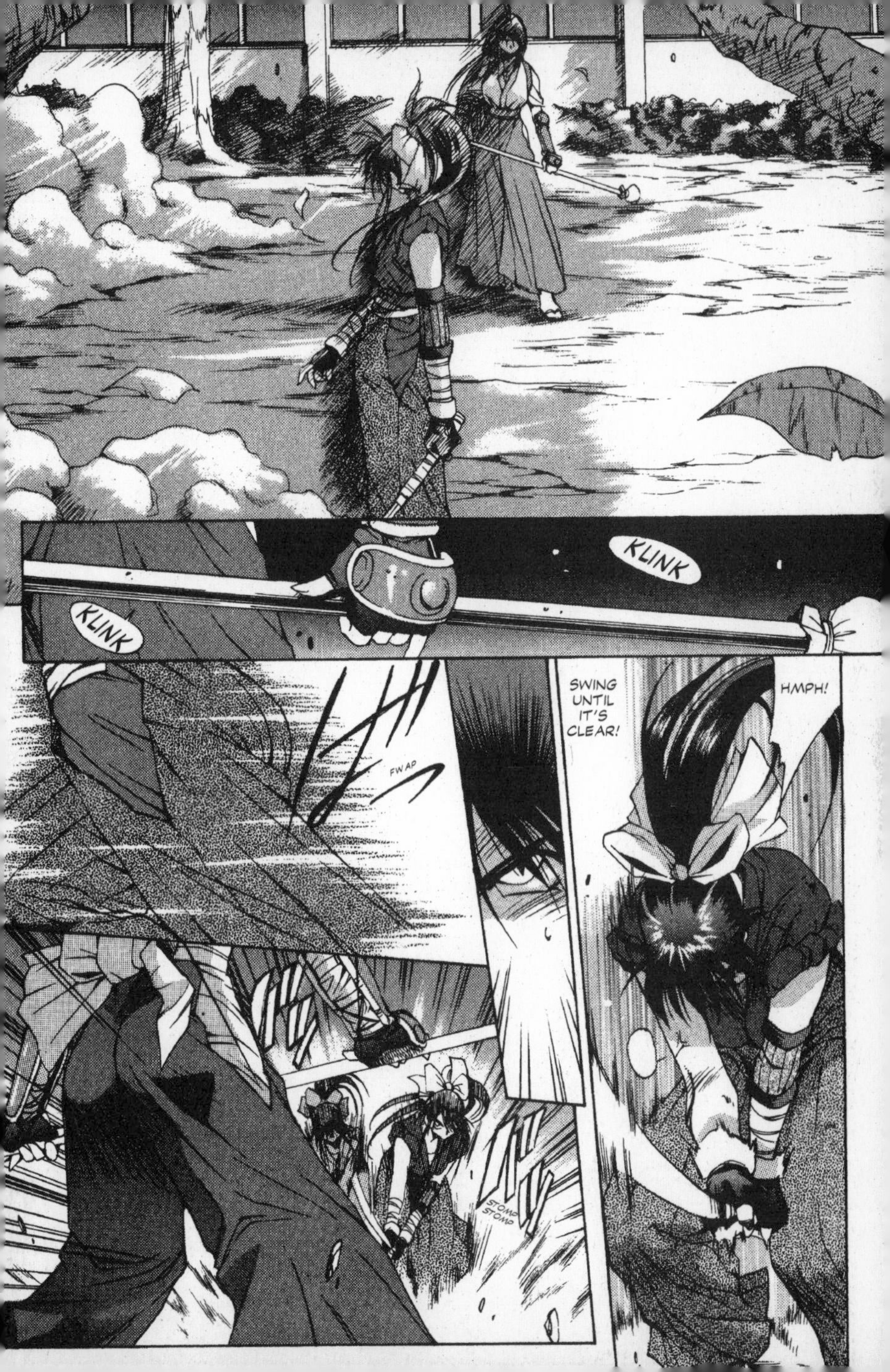
KLINK
KLINK
HMPH!
SWING UNTIL IT'S CLEAR!
FWAP
STOMP STOMP

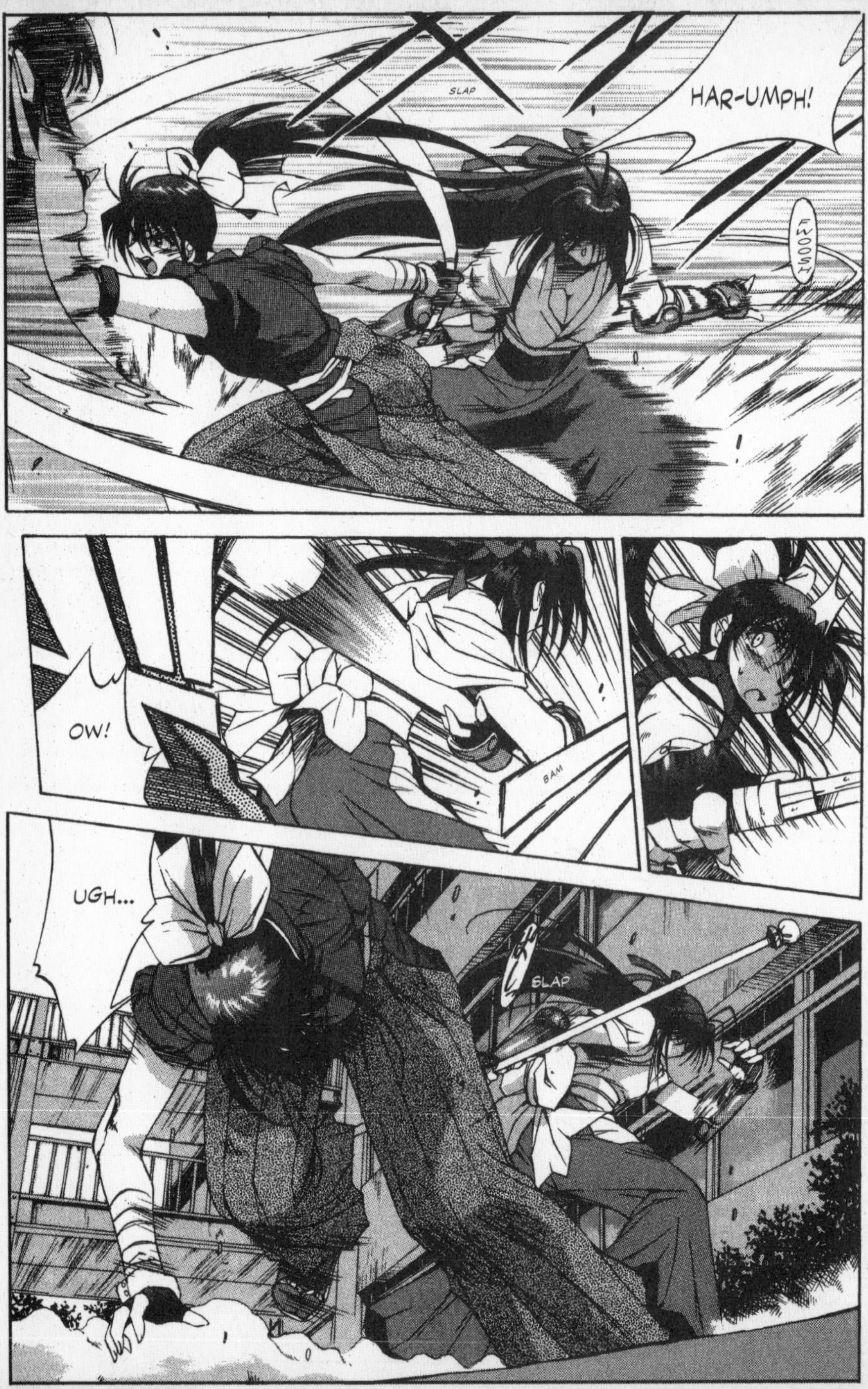
HAR-UMPH!
SLAP
FWOOSH
BAM
OW!
SLAP
UGH...

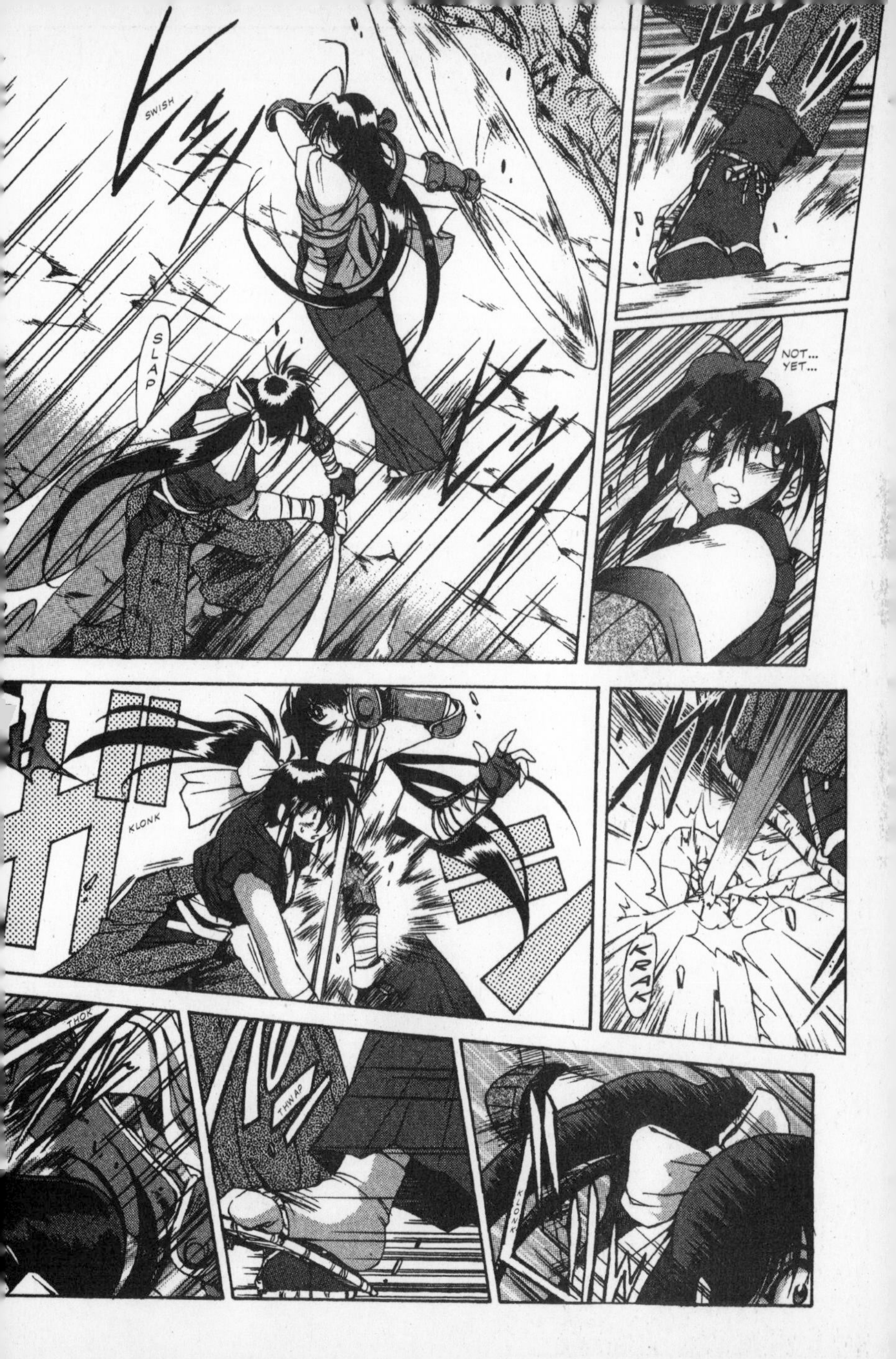
NOT... YET...
SWISH
SLAP
KRAK
KLONK
KLONK
THWAP
THOK

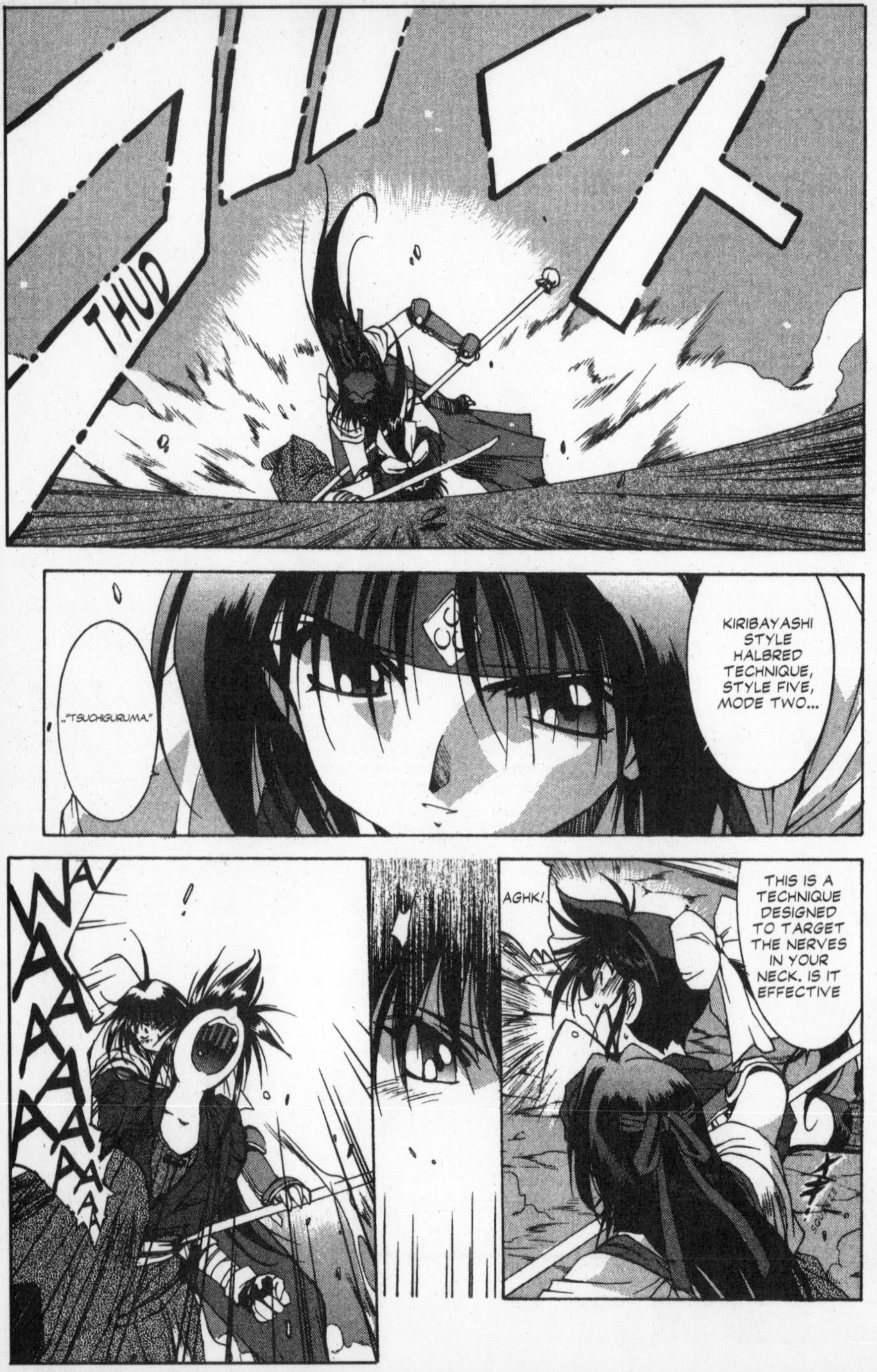
THUD
KIRIBAYASHI STYLE HALBRED TECHNIQUE, STYLE FIVE, MODE TWO...
..."TSUCHIGURUMA."
THIS IS A TECHNIQUE DESIGNED TO TARGET THE NERVES IN YOUR NECK. IS IT EFFECTIVE
AGHK!
WAAAAAAAAA

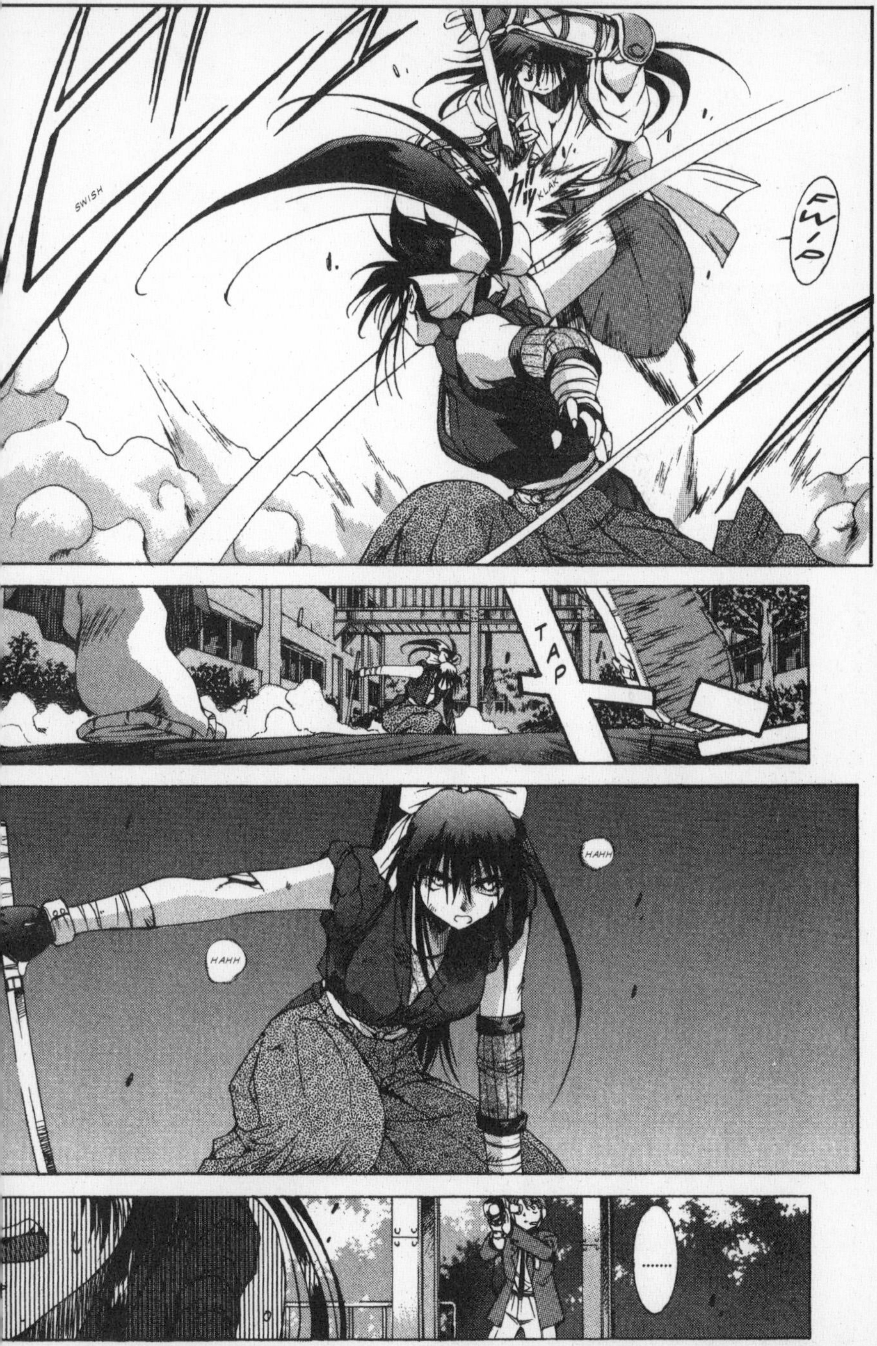
FWIP
KLAK
SWISH
TAP
HAHH
HAHH
....

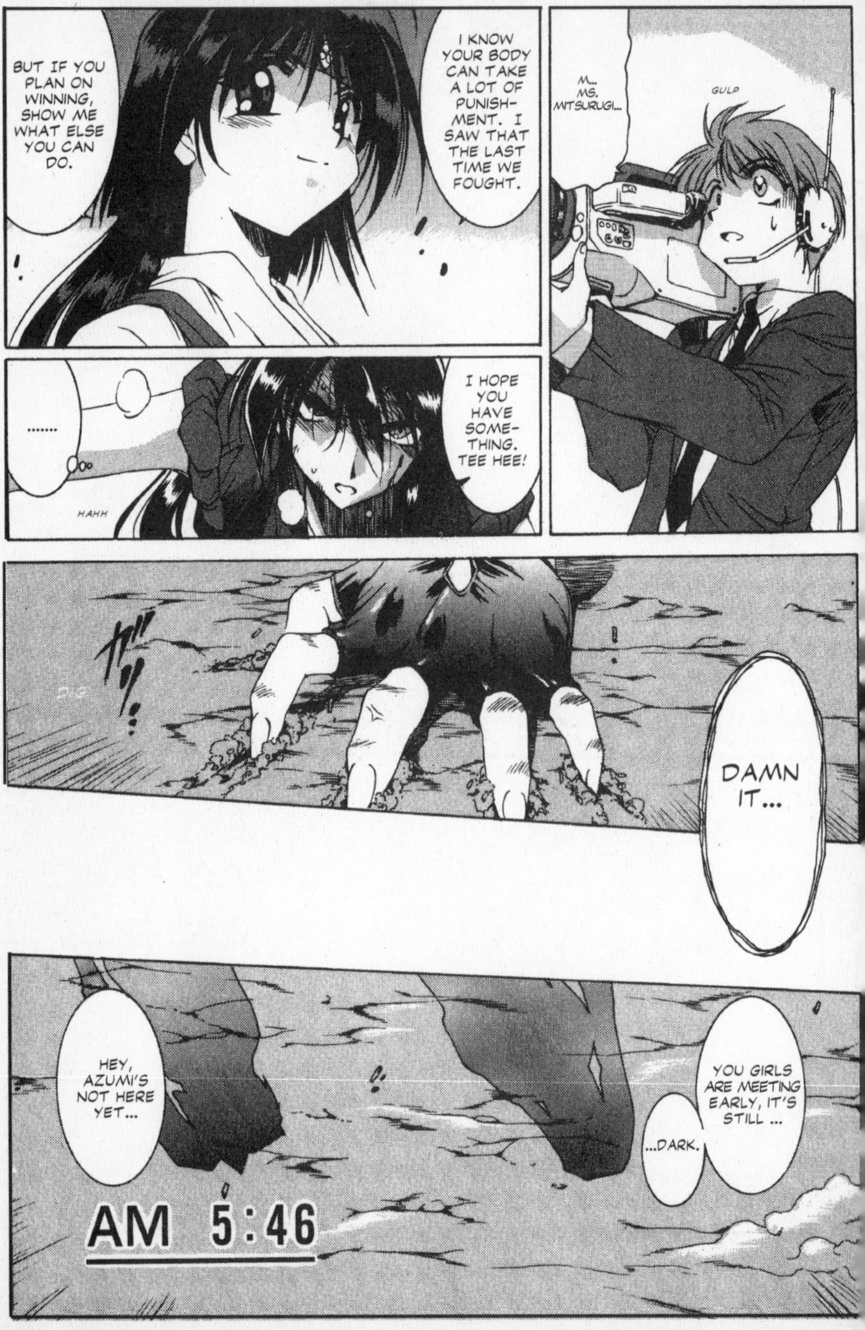
M... MS. MITSURUGI...
GULP
I KNOW YOUR BODY CAN TAKE A LOT OF PUNISH-MENT. I SAW THAT THE LAST TIME WE FOUGHT.
BUT IF YOU PLAN ON WINNING, SHOW ME WHAT ELSE YOU CAN DO.
I HOPE YOU HAVE SOME-THING. TEE HEE!
....
HAHH
DIG
DAMN IT...
YOU GIRLS ARE MEETING EARLY, IT'S STILL ...
...DARK.
HEY, AZUMI'S NOT HERE YET...
AM 5:46

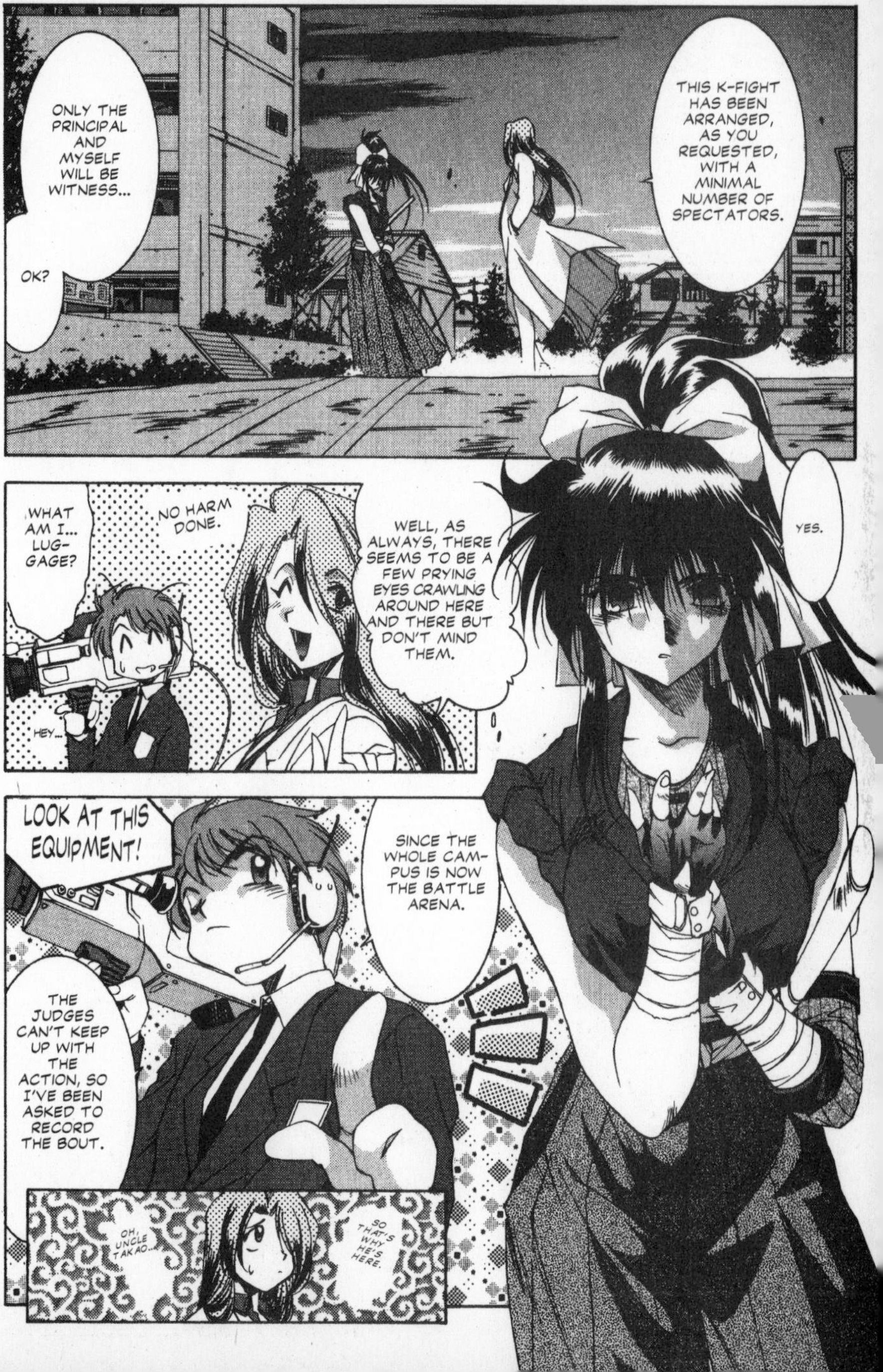
THIS K-FIGHT HAS BEEN ARRANGED, AS YOU REQUESTED, WITH A MINIMAL NUMBER OF SPECTATORS.
ONLY THE PRINCIPAL AND MYSELF WILL BE WITNESS...
OK?
YES.
WELL, AS ALWAYS, THERE SEEMS TO BE A FEW PRYING EYES CRAWLING AROUND HERE AND THERE BUT DON'T MIND THEM.
NO HARM DONE.
WHAT AM I... LUG-GAGE?
HEY...
SINCE THE WHOLE CAM-PUS IS NOW THE BATTLE ARENA.
LOOK AT THIS EQUIPMENT!
THE JUDGES CAN'T KEEP UP WITH THE ACTION, SO I'VE BEEN ASKED TO RECORD THE BOUT.
SO THAT'S WHY HE'S HERE.
OH, UNCLE TAKAO...

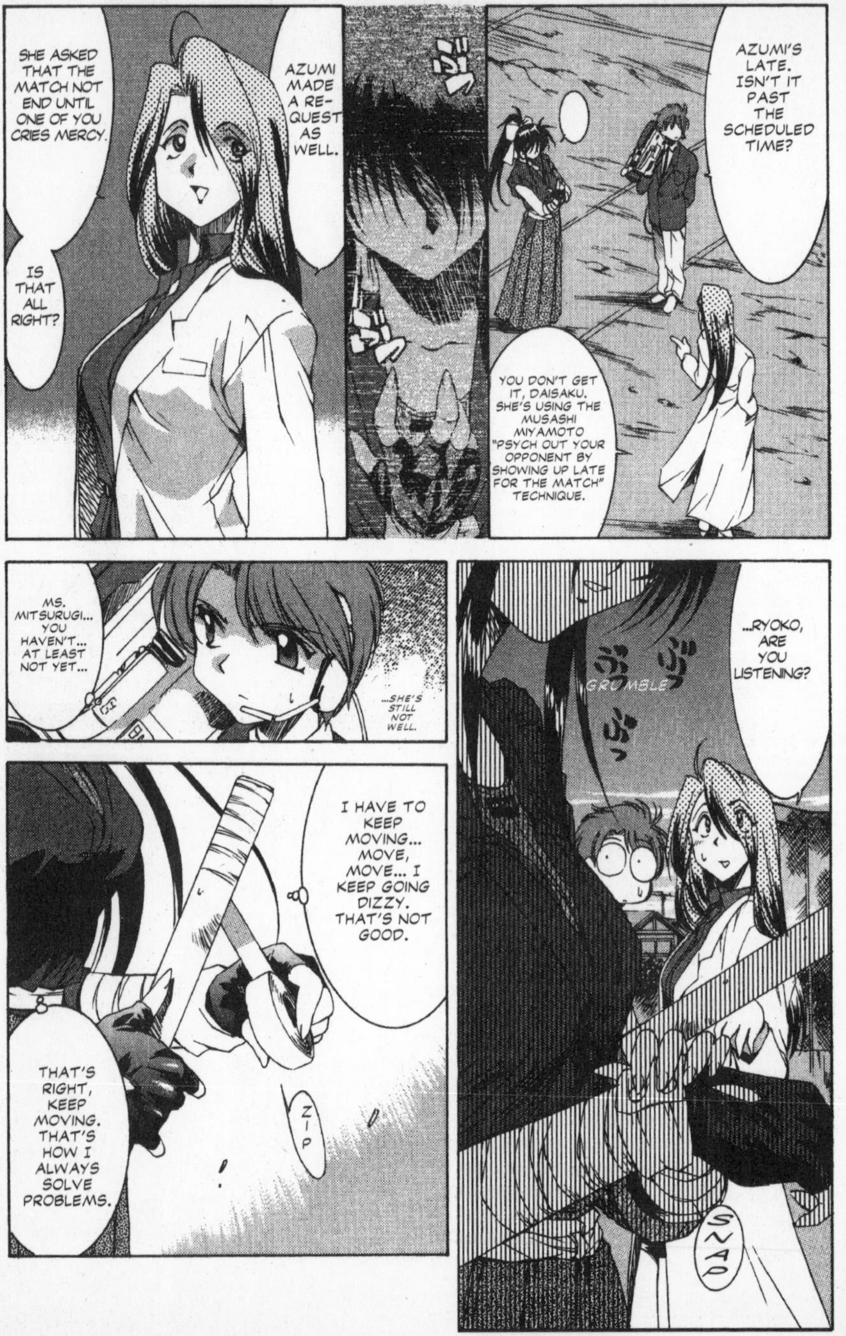
AZUMI'S LATE. ISN'T IT PAST THE SCHEDULED TIME?
...
YOU DON'T GET IT, DAISAKU. SHE'S USING THE MUSASHI MIYAMOTO "PSYCH OUT YOUR OPPONENT BY SHOWING UP LATE FOR THE MATCH" TECHNIQUE.
AZUMI MADE A RE-QUEST AS WELL.
SHE ASKED THAT THE MATCH NOT END UNTIL ONE OF YOU CRIES MERCY.
IS THAT ALL RIGHT?
...RYOKO, ARE YOU LISTENING?
ぶつぶつ
GRUMBLE
SNAP
MS. MITSURUGI... YOU HAVEN'T... AT LEAST NOT YET...
...SHE'S STILL NOT WELL.
I HAVE TO KEEP MOVING... MOVE, MOVE... I KEEP GOING DIZZY. THAT'S NOT GOOD.
ZIP
THAT'S RIGHT, KEEP MOVING. THAT'S HOW I ALWAYS SOLVE PROBLEMS.

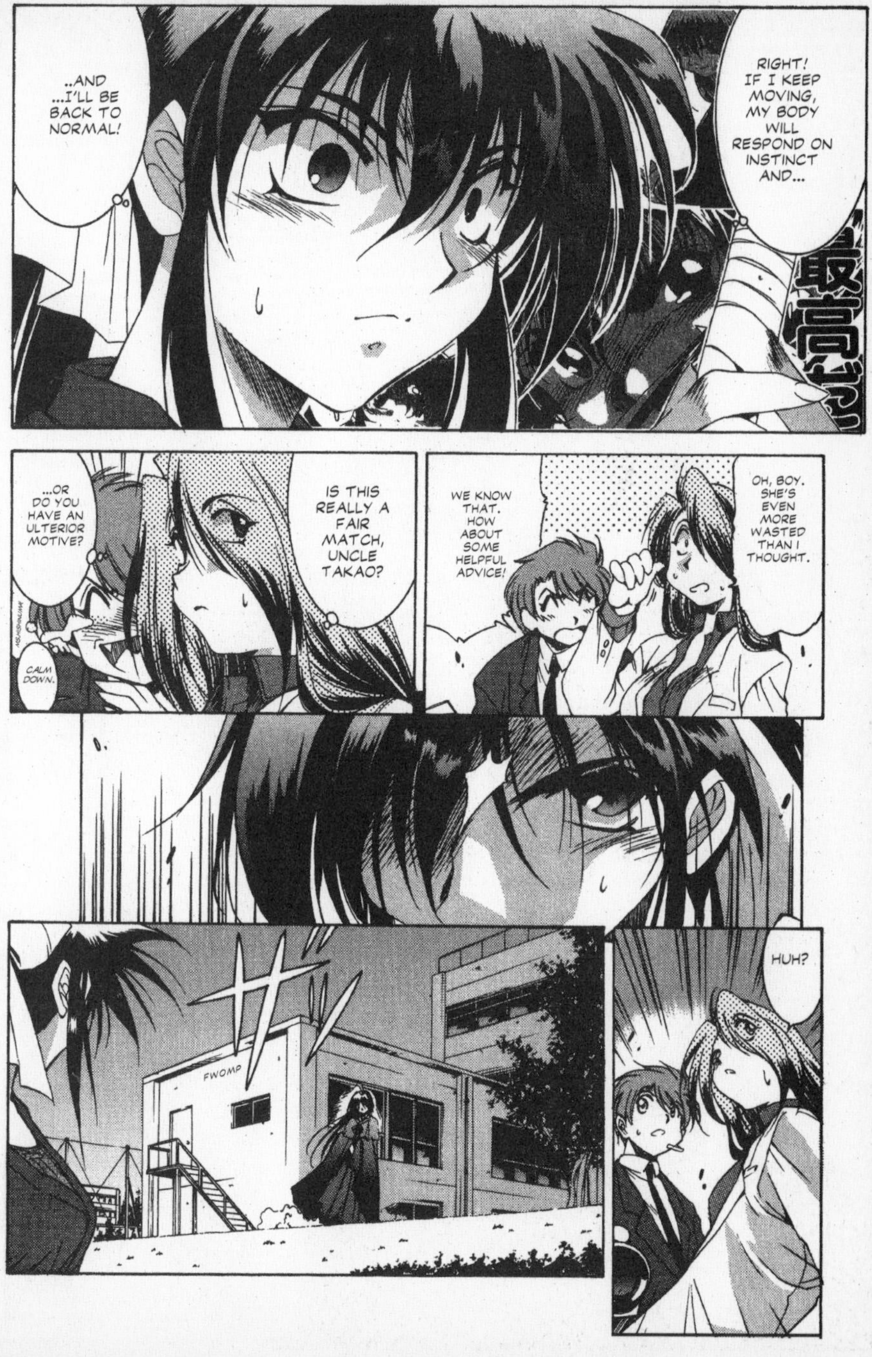
RIGHT! IF I KEEP MOVING, MY BODY WILL RESPOND ON INSTINCT AND...
..AND ...I'LL BE BACK TO NORMAL!
最高
OH, BOY. SHE'S EVEN MORE WASTED THAN I THOUGHT.
WE KNOW THAT. HOW ABOUT SOME HELPFUL ADVICE!
IS THIS REALLY A FAIR MATCH, UNCLE TAKAO?
...OR DO YOU HAVE AN ULTERIOR MOTIVE?
CALM DOWN.
HUH?
FWOMP

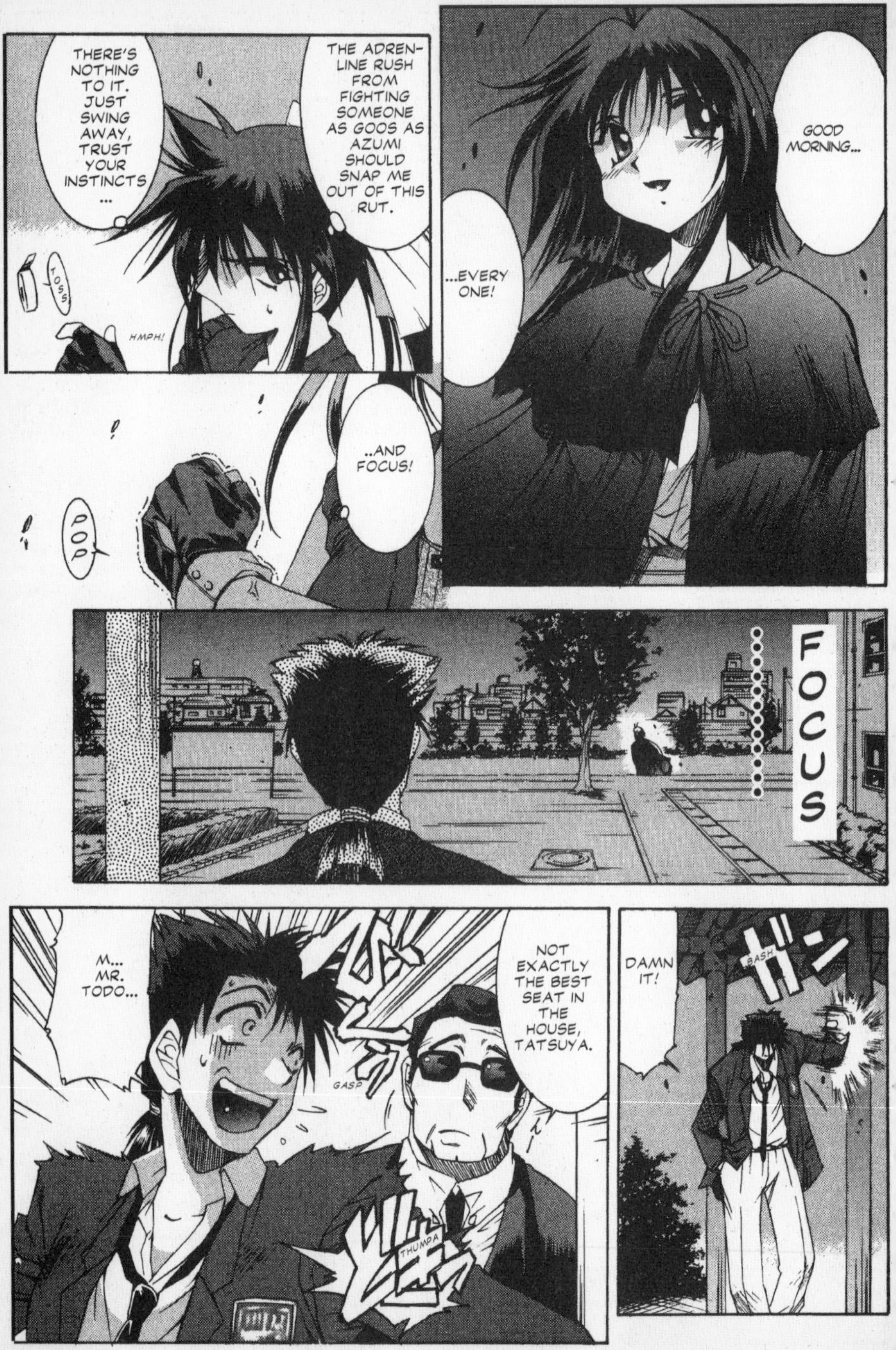
GOOD MORNING...
...EVERY ONE!
THE ADREN-LINE RUSH FROM FIGHTING SOMEONE AS GOOS AS AZUMI SHOULD SNAP ME OUT OF THIS RUT.
THERE'S NOTHING TO IT. JUST SWING AWAY, TRUST YOUR INSTINCTS ...
TOSS
HMPH!
..AND FOCUS!
POP
FOCUS
DAMN IT!
BASH
NOT EXACTLY THE BEST SEAT IN THE HOUSE, TATSUYA.
M... MR. TODO...
GASP
THUMPA

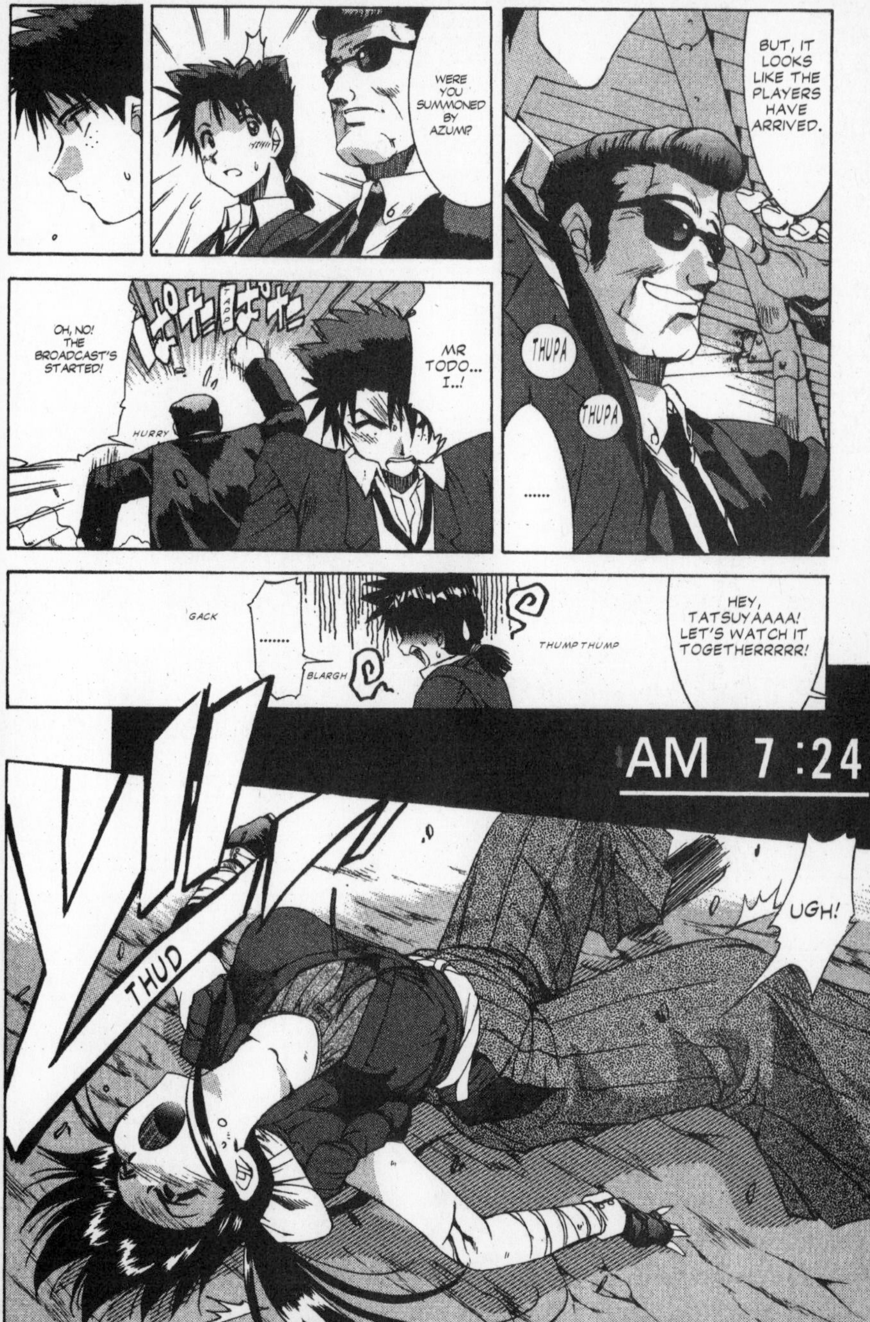
BUT, IT LOOKS LIKE THE PLAYERS HAVE ARRIVED.
THUPA
THUPA
......
WERE YOU SUMMONED BY AZUMI?
MR TODO... I..!
TADD
OH, NO! THE BROADCAST'S STARTED!
HURRY
HEY, TATSUYAAAA! LET'S WATCH IT TOGETHERRRRR!
THUMP THUMP
....
GACK
BLARGH
AM 7:24
UGH!
THUD

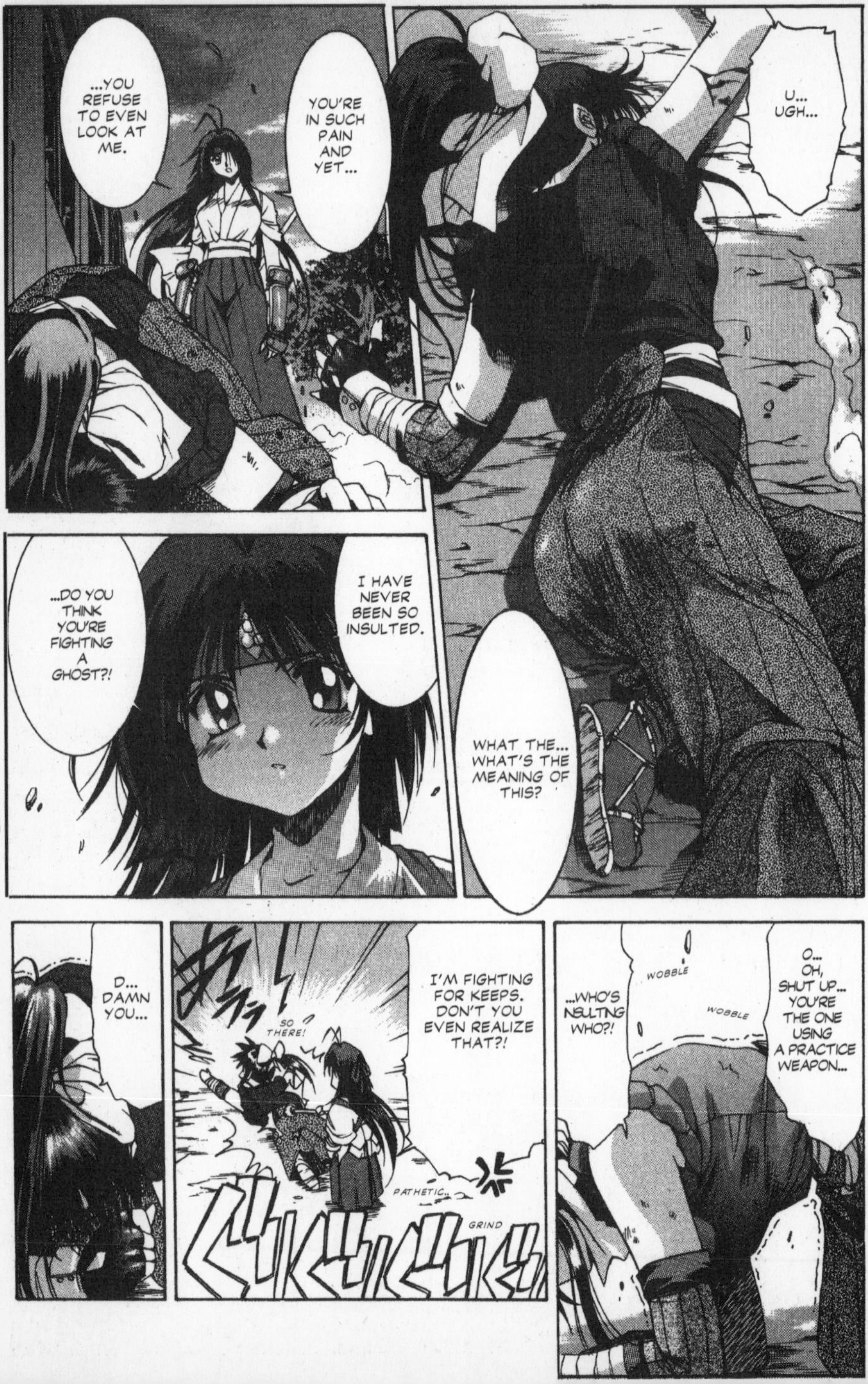
U... UGH...
WHAT THE... WHAT'S THE MEANING OF THIS?
YOU'RE IN SUCH PAIN AND YET...
...YOU REFUSE TO EVEN LOOK AT ME.
I HAVE NEVER BEEN SO INSULTED.
...DO YOU THINK YOU'RE FIGHTING A GHOST?!
O... OH, SHUT UP... YOU'RE THE ONE USING A PRACTICE WEAPON...
WOBBLE
WOBBLE
...WHO'S NSULTNG WHO?!
I'M FIGHTING FOR KEEPS. DON'T YOU EVEN REALIZE THAT?!
SO THERE!
PATHETIC..
GRIND
D... DAMN YOU...

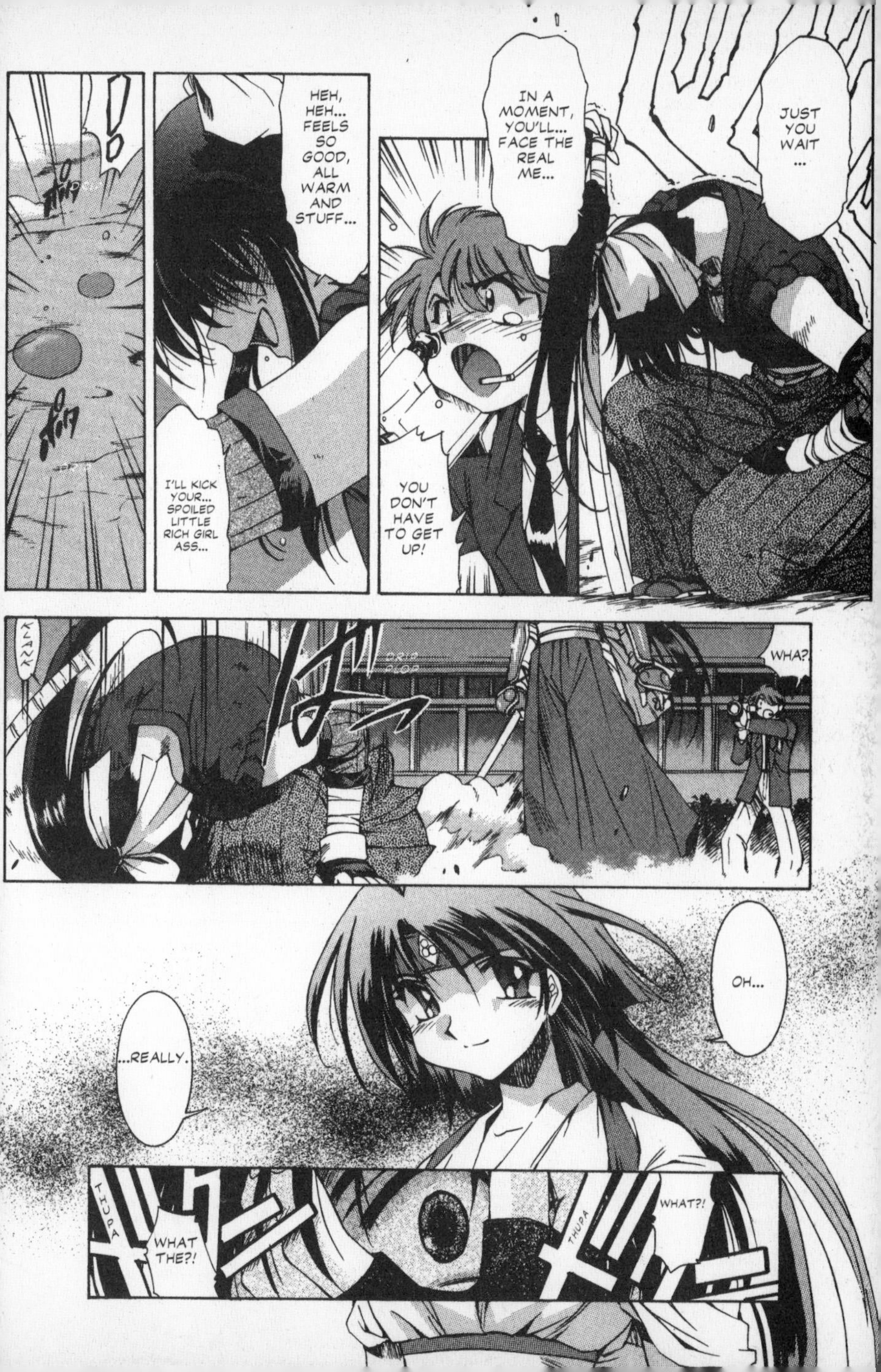
JUST YOU WAIT ...
IN A MOMENT, YOU'LL... FACE THE REAL ME...
YOU DON'T HAVE TO GET UP!
HEH, HEH... FEELS SO GOOD, ALL WARM AND STUFF...
I'LL KICK YOUR... SPOILED LITTLE RICH GIRL ASS...
WHA?
DRIP PLOP
KLANK
OH...
...REALLY.
WHAT?!
THUPA
THUPA
WHAT THE?!

Episode 17

K-fight: Ryoko vs. Azumi, Part 2

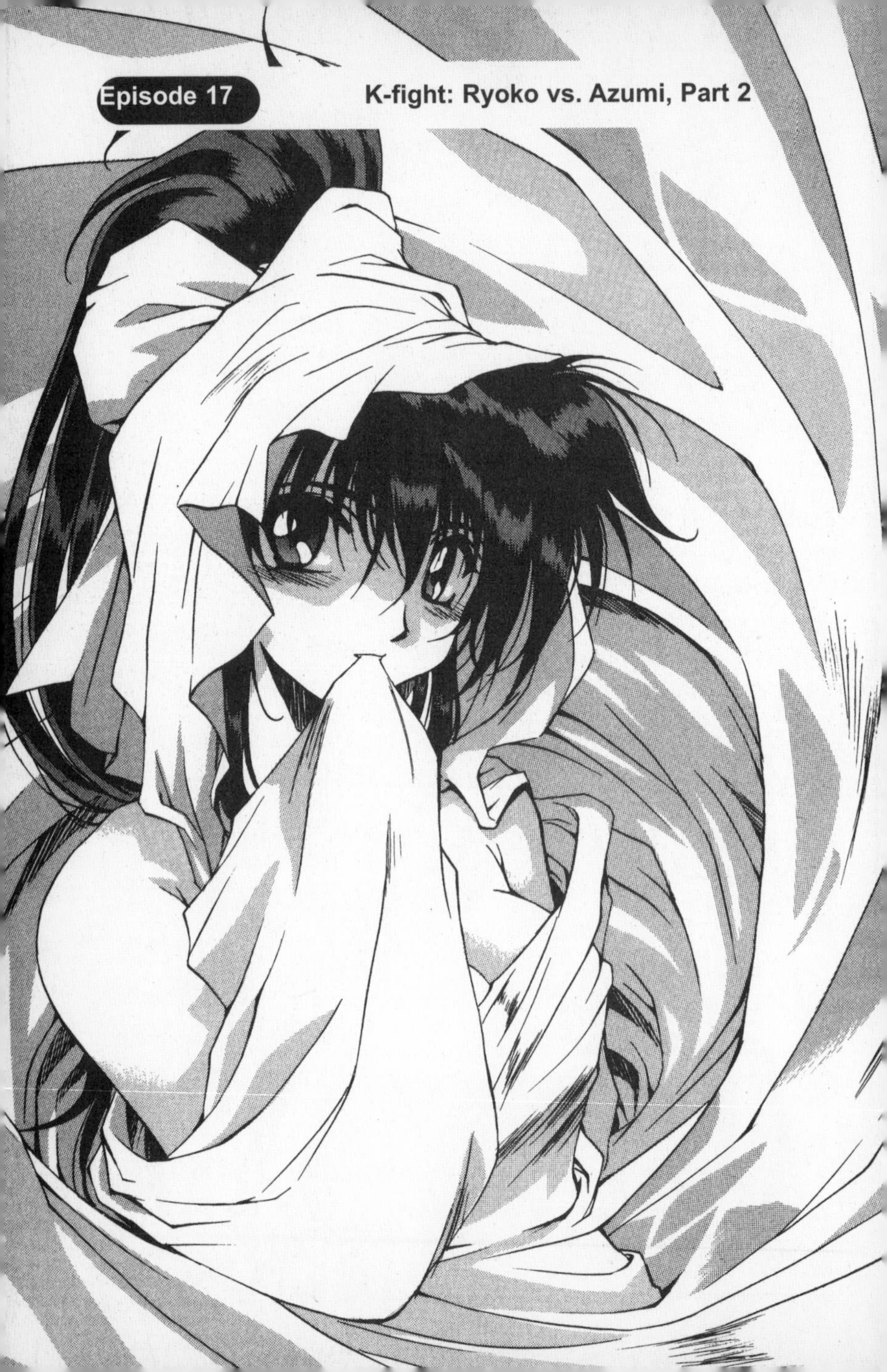

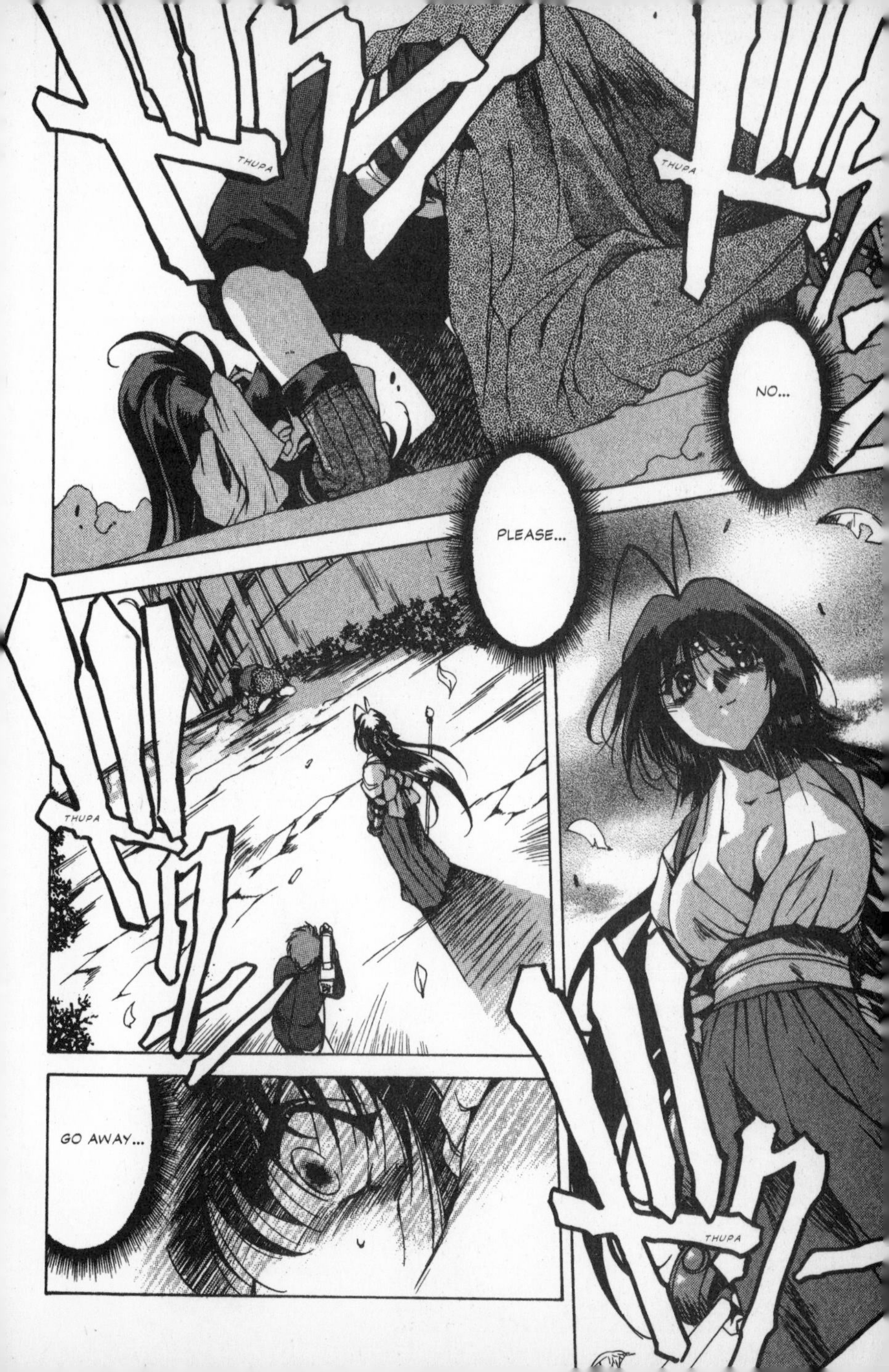
THUPA
THUPA
NO...
PLEASE...
THUPA
THUPA
GO AWAY...

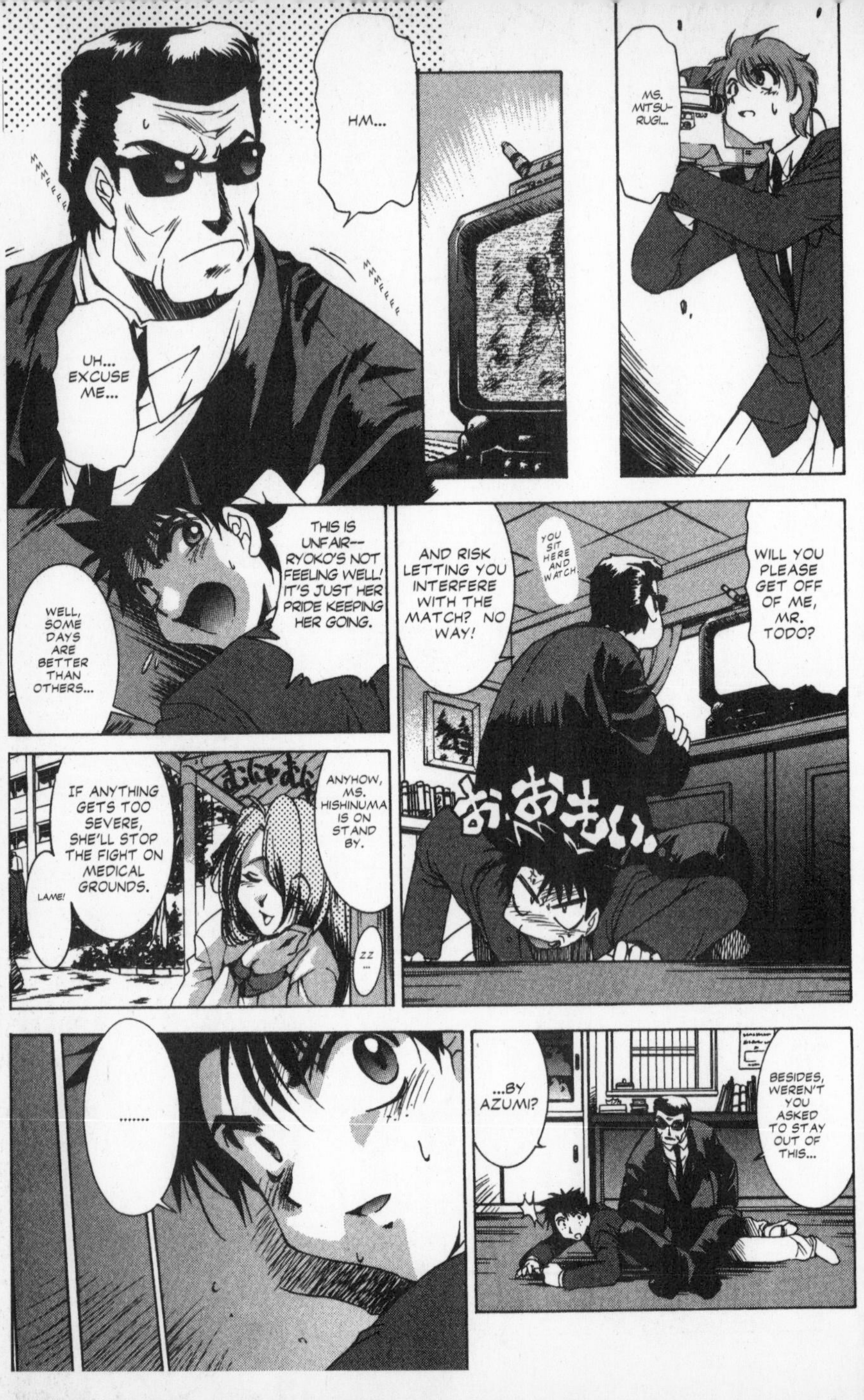
MS. MITSU-RUGI...
HM...
MMMEEEE
MMMEEEE
UH... EXCUSE ME...
WILL YOU PLEASE GET OFF OF ME, MR. TODO?
AND RISK LETTING YOU INTERFERE WITH THE MATCH? NO WAY!
YOU SIT HERE AND WATCH.
お、おもい
THIS IS UNFAIR--RYOKO'S NOT FEELING WELL! IT'S JUST HER PRIDE KEEPING HER GOING.
WELL, SOME DAYS ARE BETTER THAN OTHERS...
ANYHOW, MS. HISHINUMA IS ON STAND BY.
IF ANYTHING GETS TOO SEVERE, SHE'LL STOP THE FIGHT ON MEDICAL GROUNDS.
LAME!
ZZ ...
BESIDES, WEREN'T YOU ASKED TO STAY OUT OF THIS...
...BY AZUMI?
....

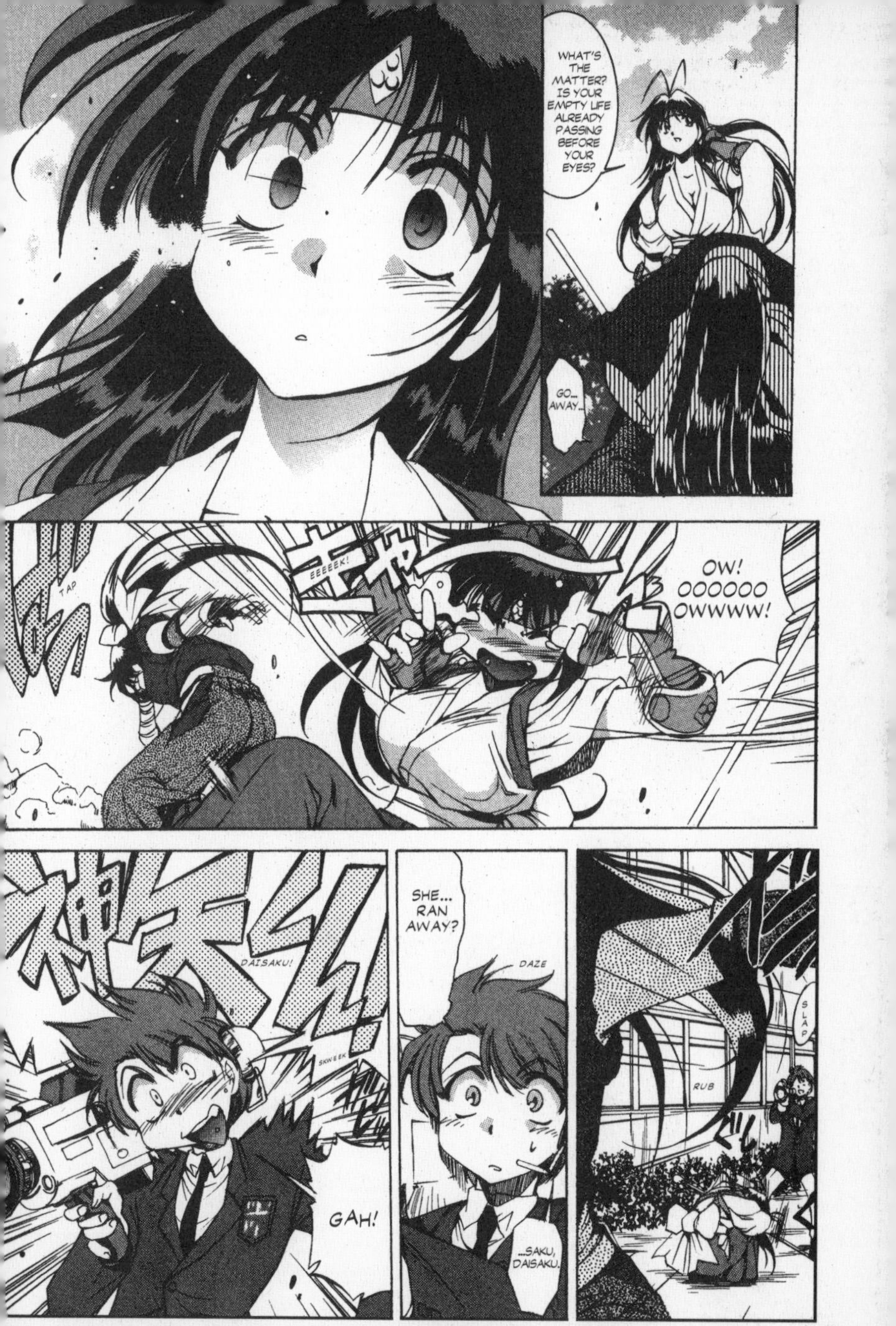
WHAT'S THE MATTER? IS YOUR EMPTY LIFE ALREADY PASSING BEFORE YOUR EYES?
GO... AWAY...
OW! OOOOOO OWWWW!
EEEEEK!
TAP
SLAP
RUB
SHE... RAN AWAY?
DAZE
...SAKU, DAISAKU.
DAISAKU!
SKWEEK
GAH!

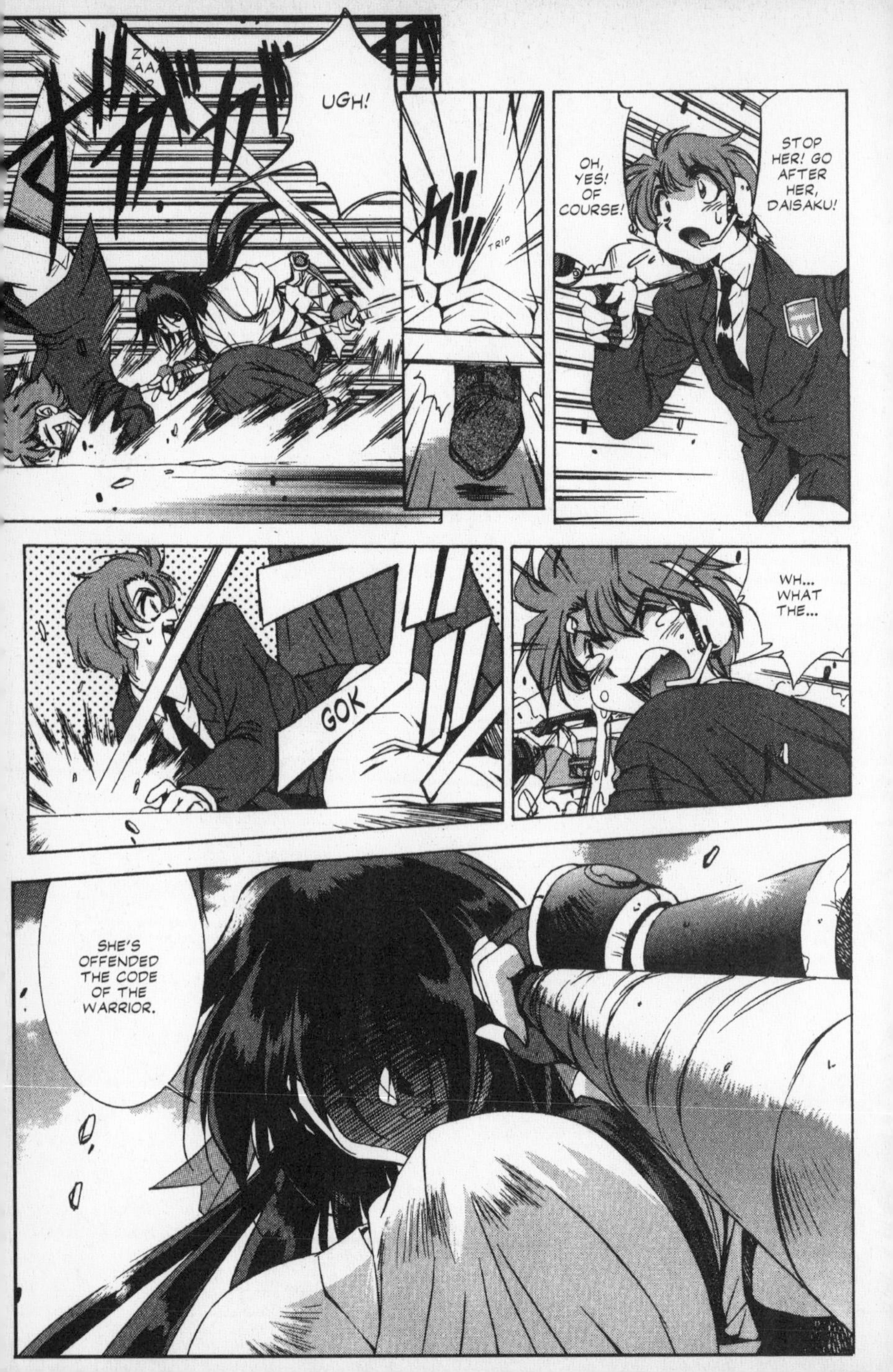
STOP HER! GO AFTER HER, DAISAKU!
OH, YES! OF COURSE!
TRIP
UGH!
WH... WHAT THE...
GOK
SHE'S OFFENDED THE CODE OF THE WARRIOR.

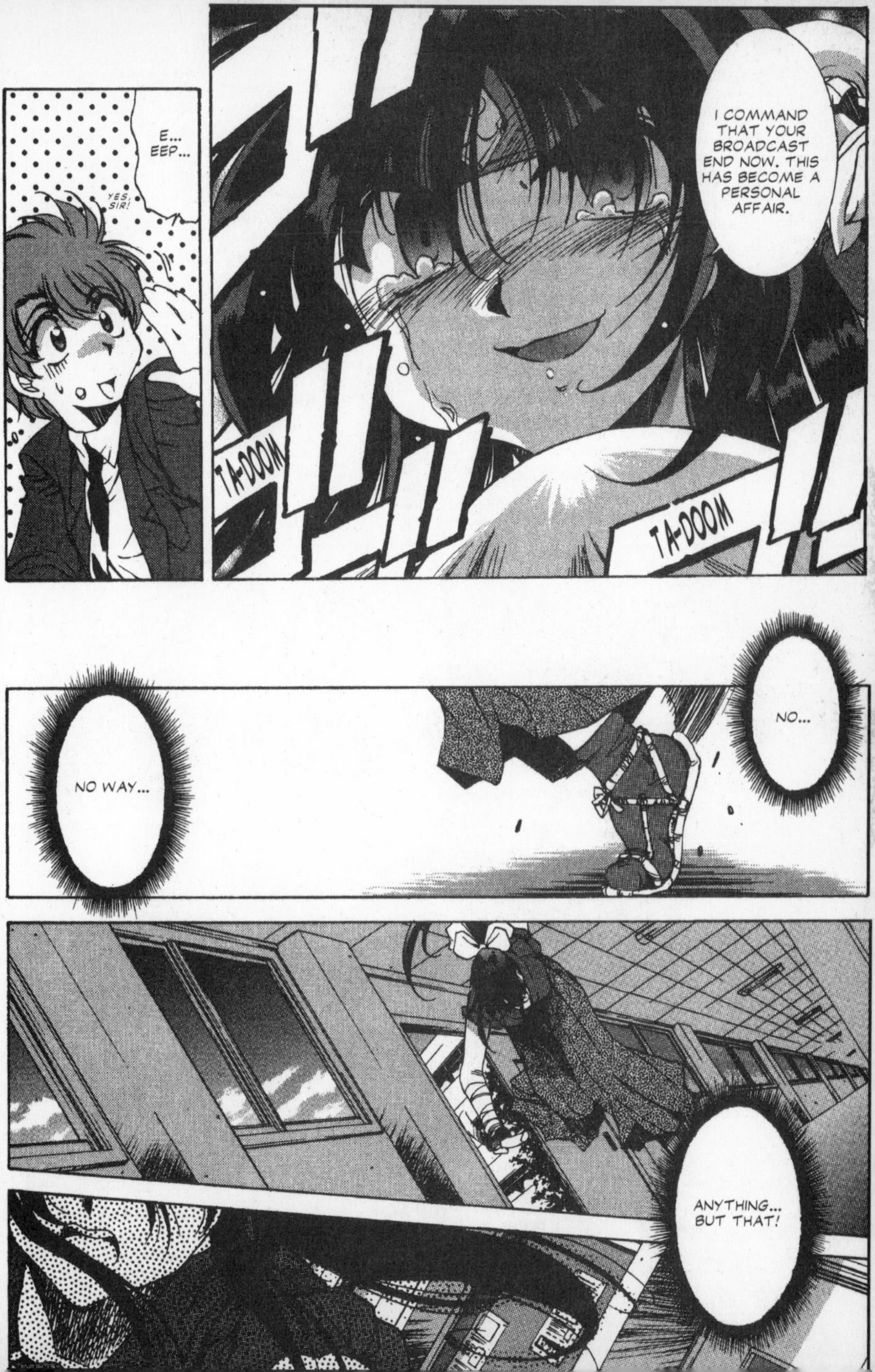
I COMMAND THAT YOUR BROADCAST END NOW. THIS HAS BECOME A PERSONAL AFFAIR.
TA-DOOM
TA-DOOM
E... EEP...
YES, SIR!
NO...
NO WAY...
ANYTHING... BUT THAT!

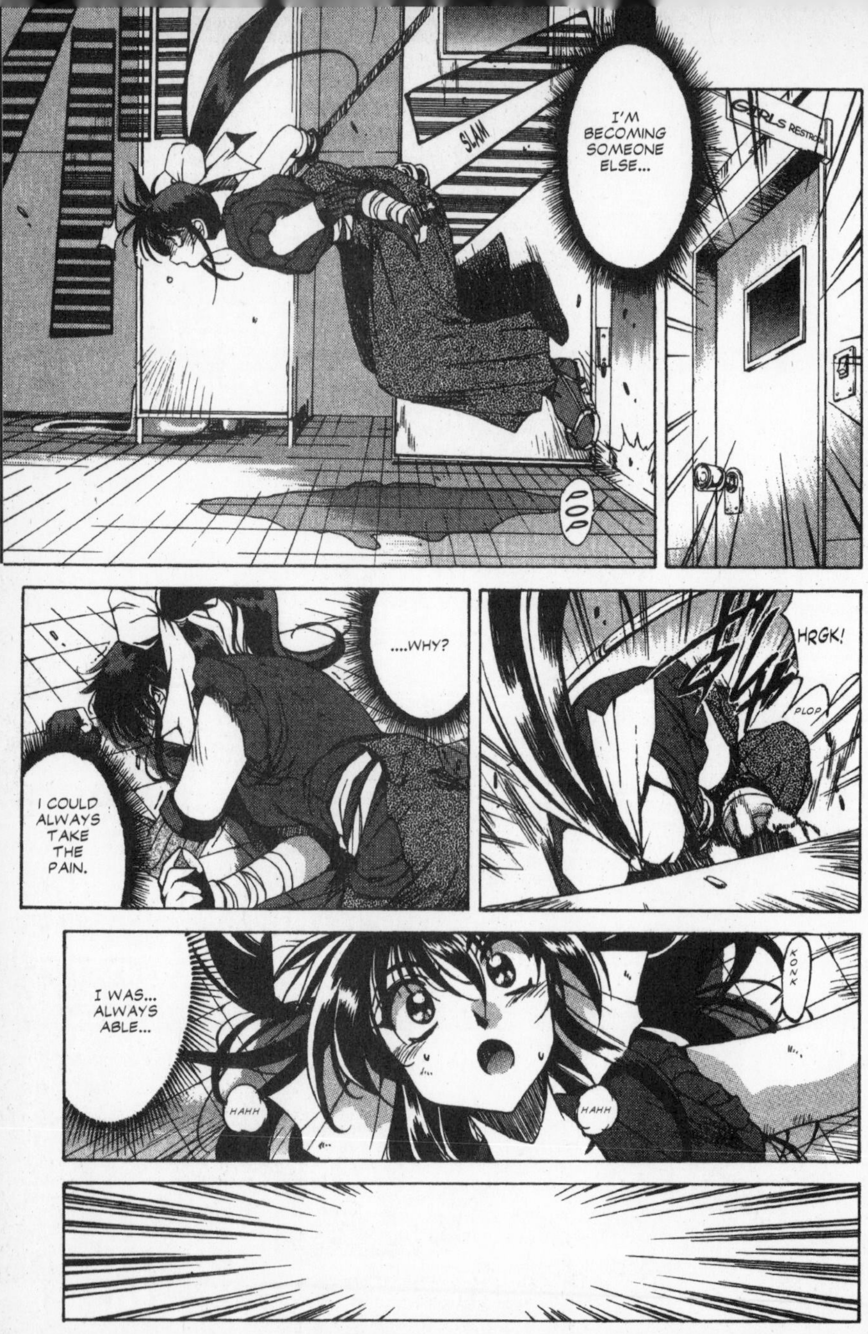
GIRLS RESTROOM
I'M BECOMING SOMEONE ELSE...
SLAM
POP
HRGK!
PLOP
...WHY?
I COULD ALWAYS TAKE THE PAIN.
KONK
I WAS... ALWAYS ABLE...
HAHH
HAHH

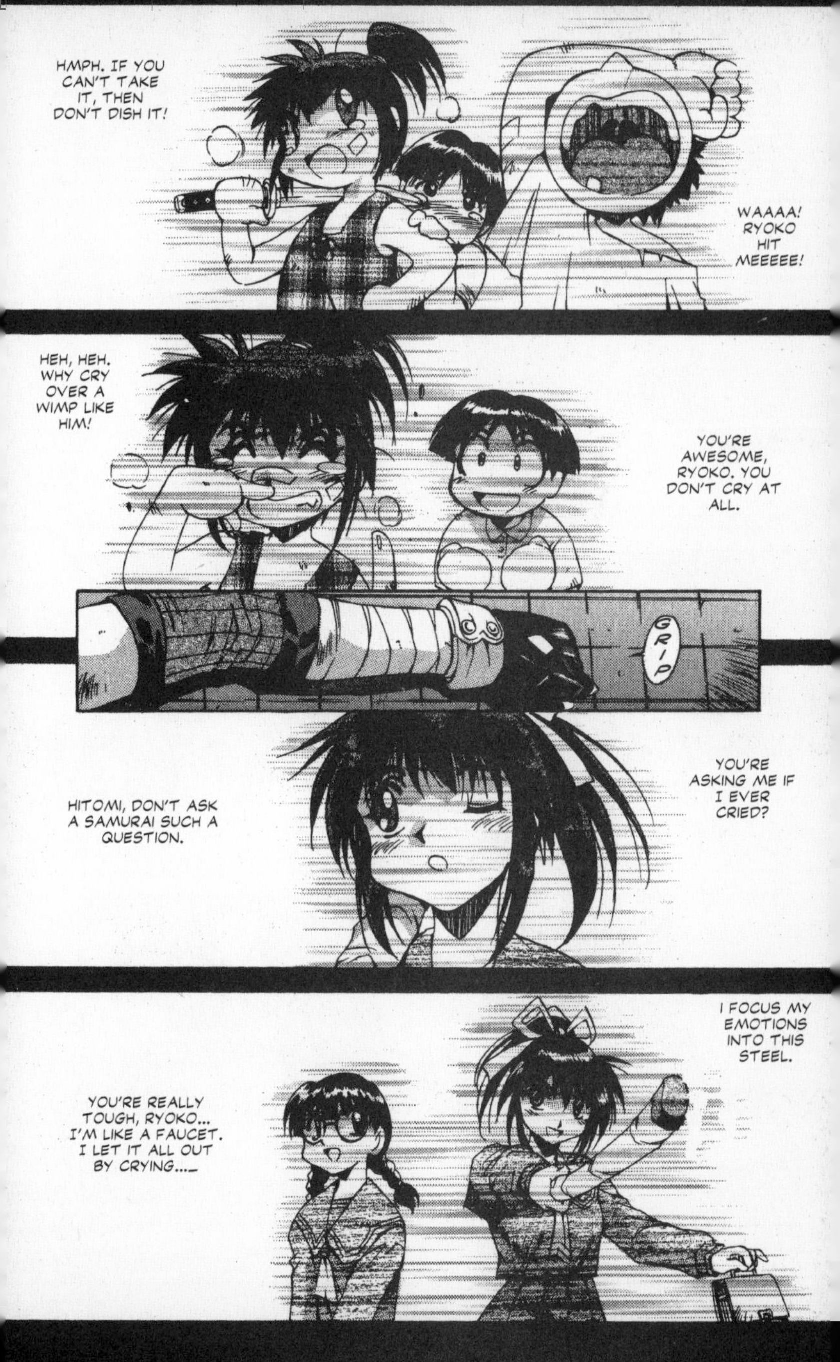
WAAAA! RYOKO HIT MEEEEE!
HMPH. IF YOU CAN'T TAKE IT, THEN DON'T DISH IT!
YOU'RE AWESOME, RYOKO. YOU DON'T CRY AT ALL.
HEH, HEH. WHY CRY OVER A WIMP LIKE HIM!
GRIP
YOU'RE ASKING ME IF I EVER CRIED?
HITOMI, DON'T ASK A SAMURAI SUCH A QUESTION.
I FOCUS MY EMOTIONS INTO THIS STEEL.
YOU'RE REALLY TOUGH, RYOKO... I'M LIKE A FAUCET. I LET IT ALL OUT BY CRYING...

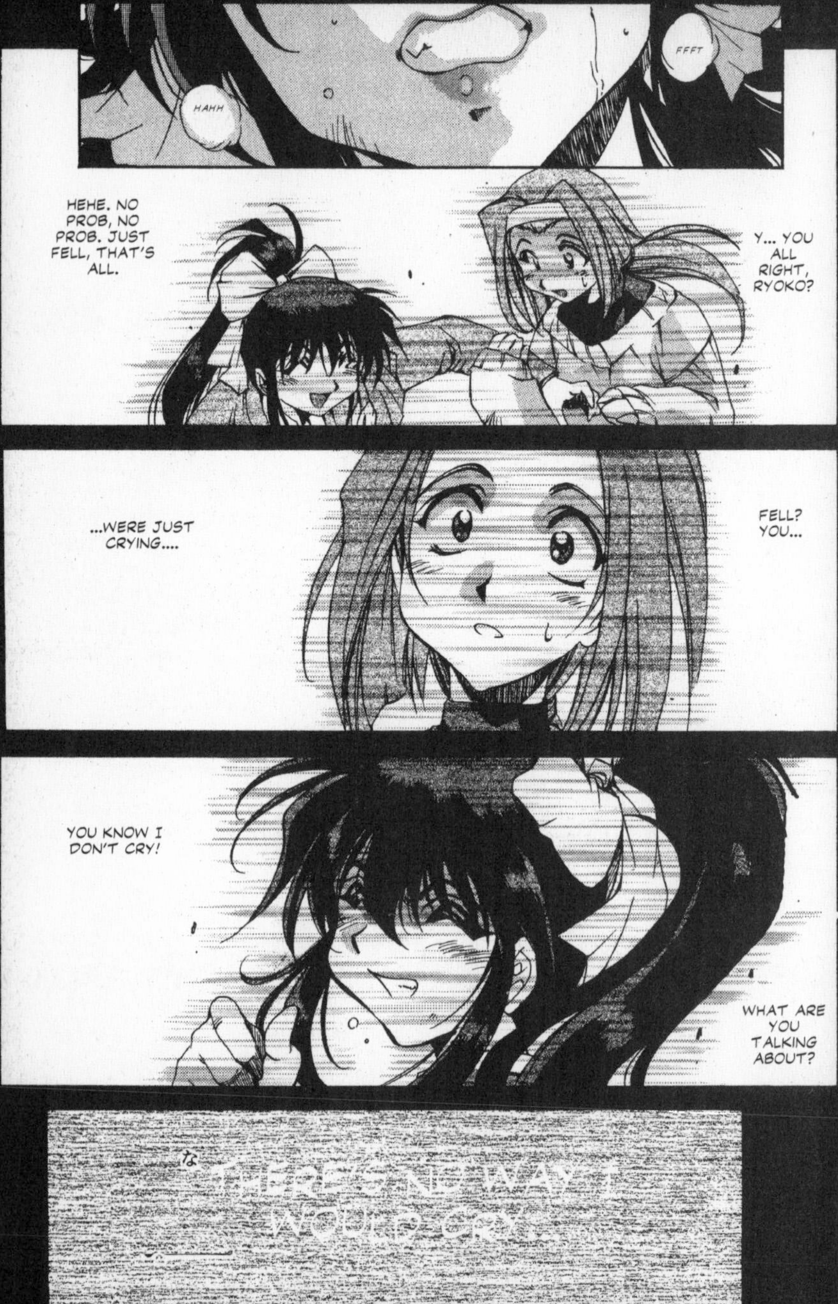
FFFT
HAHH
Y... YOU ALL RIGHT, RYOKO?
HEHE. NO PROB, NO PROB. JUST FELL, THAT'S ALL.
FELL? YOU...
...WERE JUST CRYING....
WHAT ARE YOU TALKING ABOUT?
YOU KNOW I DON'T CRY!
THERE'S NO WAY I WOULD CRY...

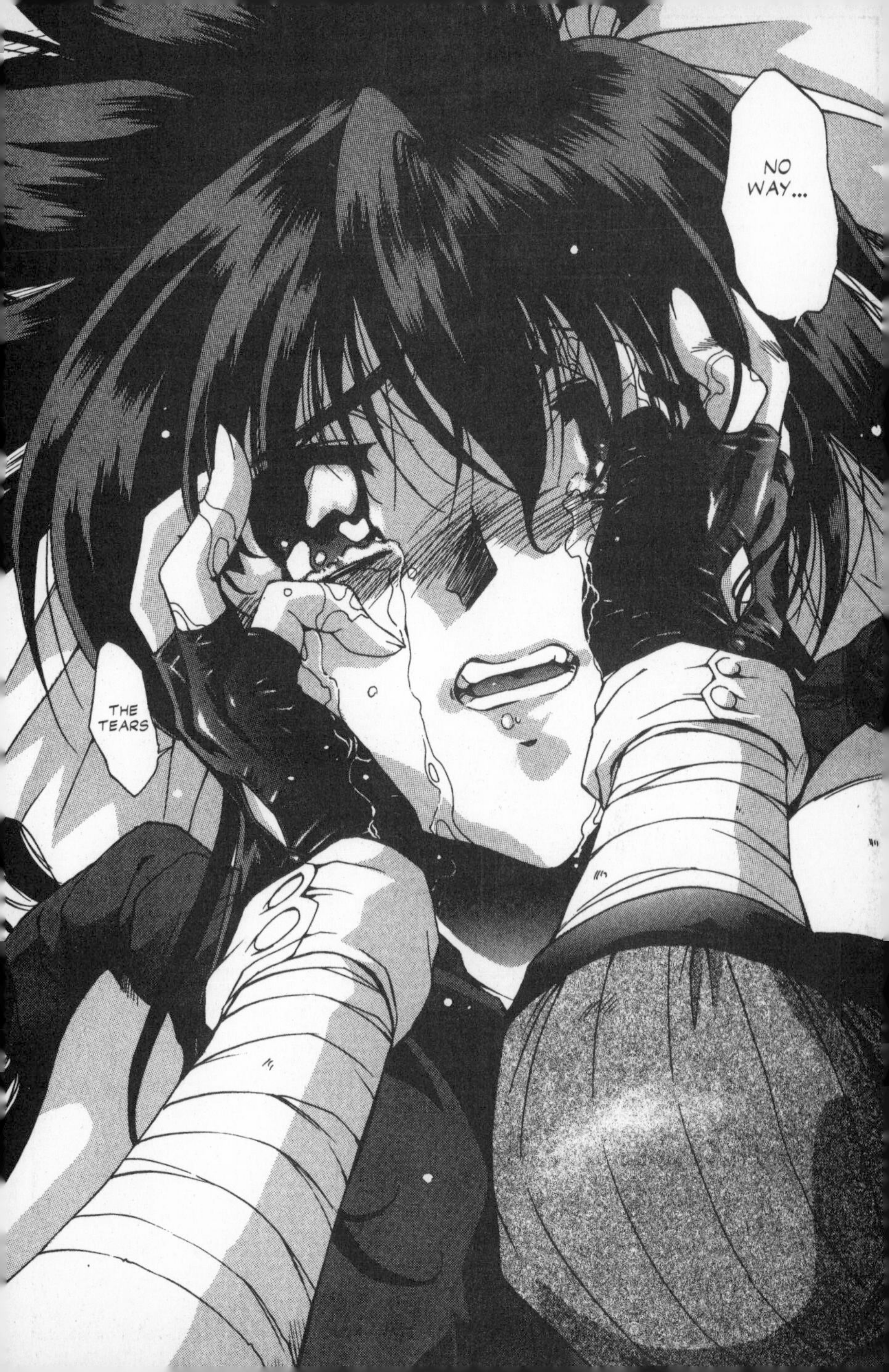
NO WAY...
THE TEARS

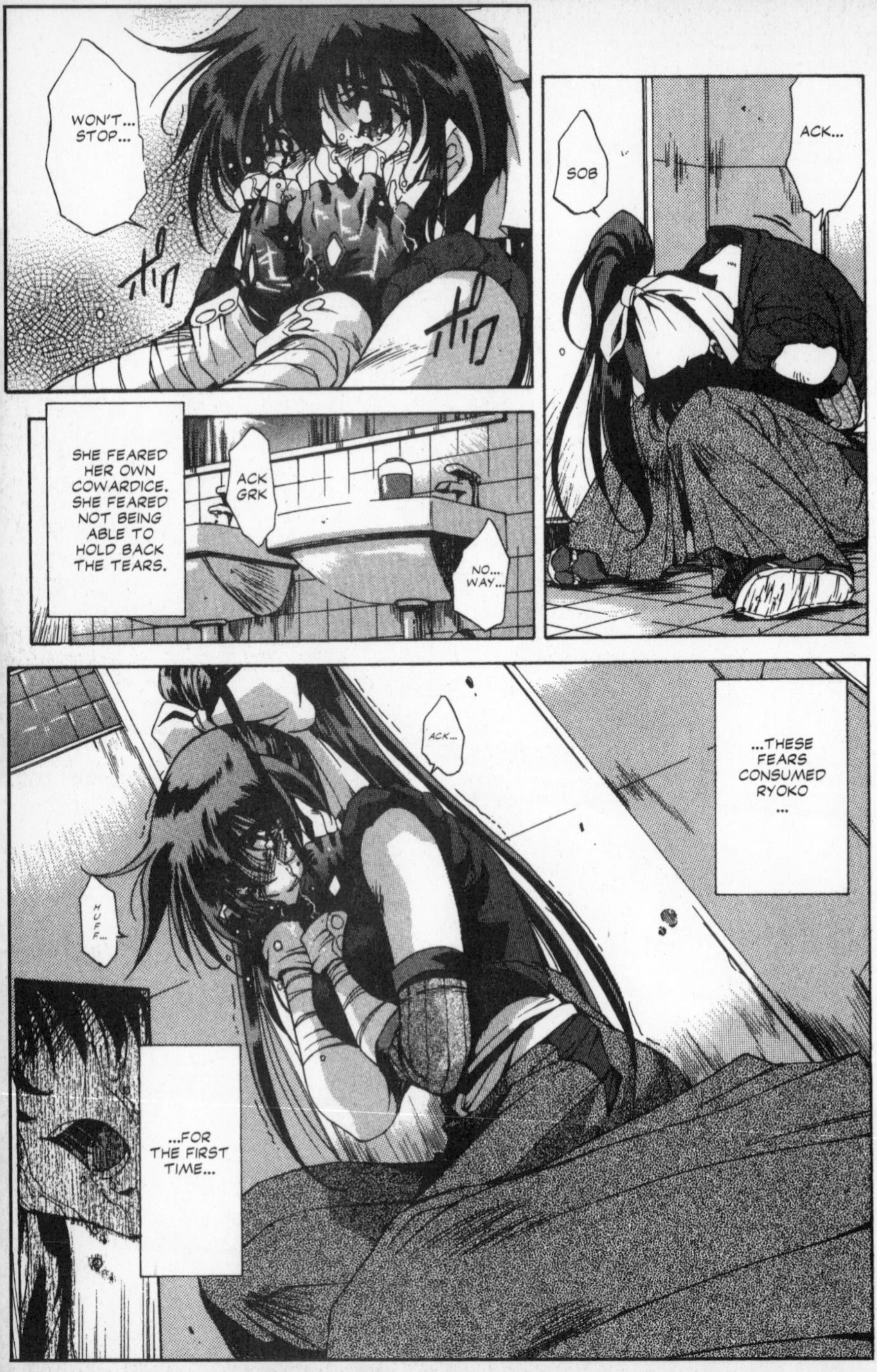
ACK...
SOB
WON'T... STOP...
ポロ
ポロ
ACK GRK
NO... WAY...
SHE FEARED HER OWN COWARDICE. SHE FEARED NOT BEING ABLE TO HOLD BACK THE TEARS.
...THESE FEARS CONSUMED RYOKO ...
ACK...
HUFF...
...FOR THE FIRST TIME...

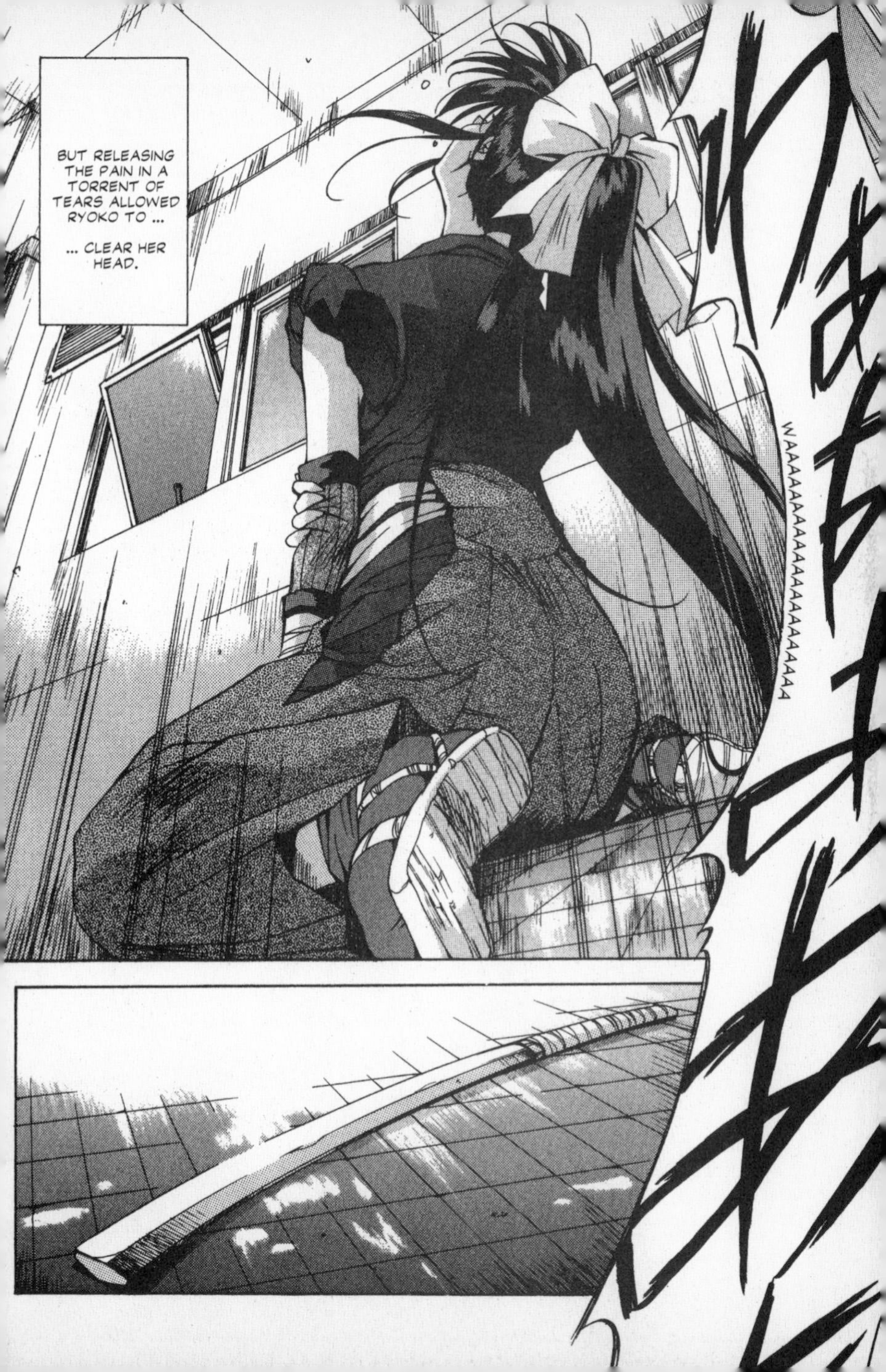
BUT RELEASING THE PAIN IN A TORRENT OF TEARS ALLOWED RYOKO TO ...
... CLEAR HER HEAD.
WAAAAAAAAAAAAAAAAAAAAA

Episode 18 K-fight Again, Ryoko vs. Azumi Part 3

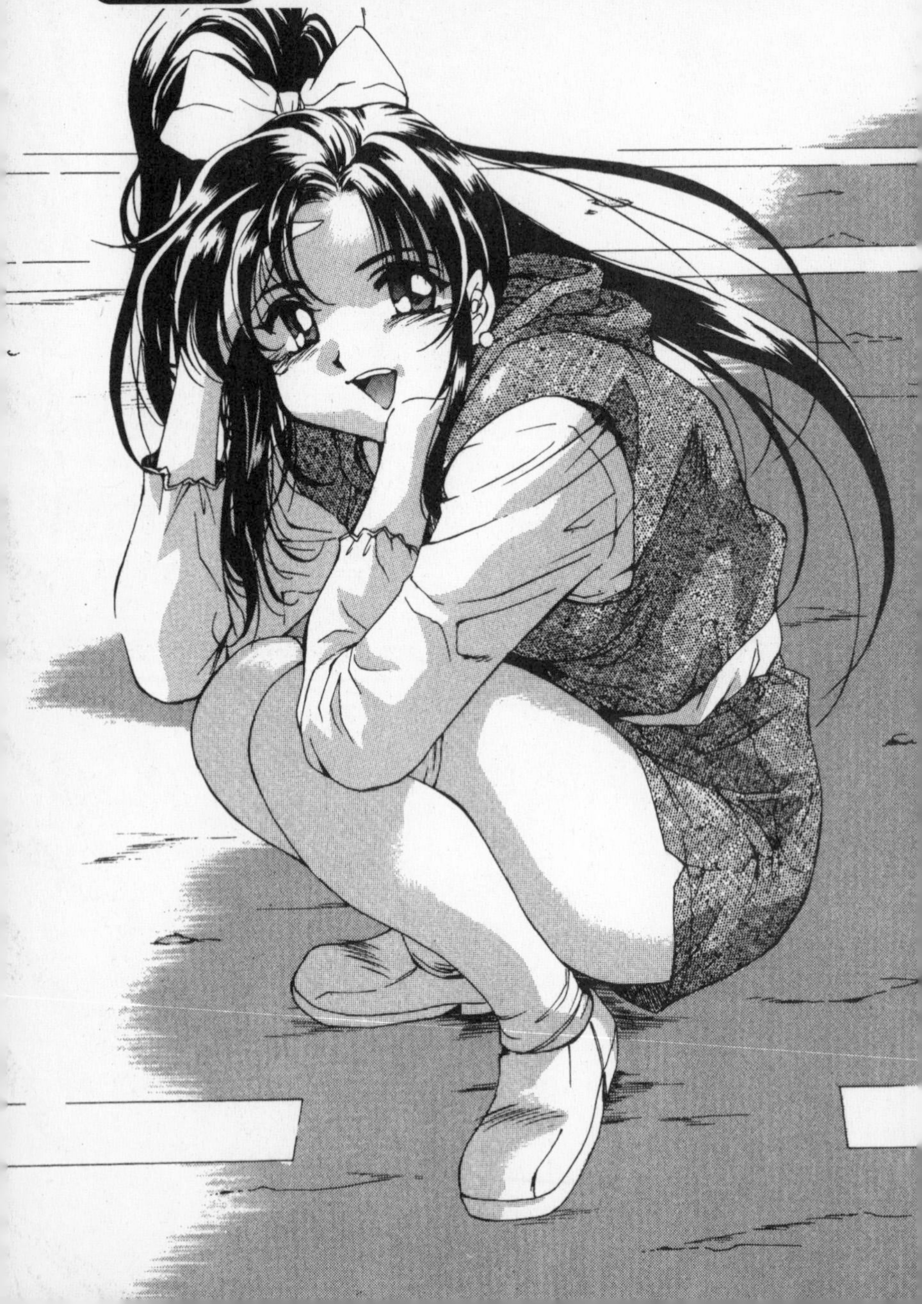

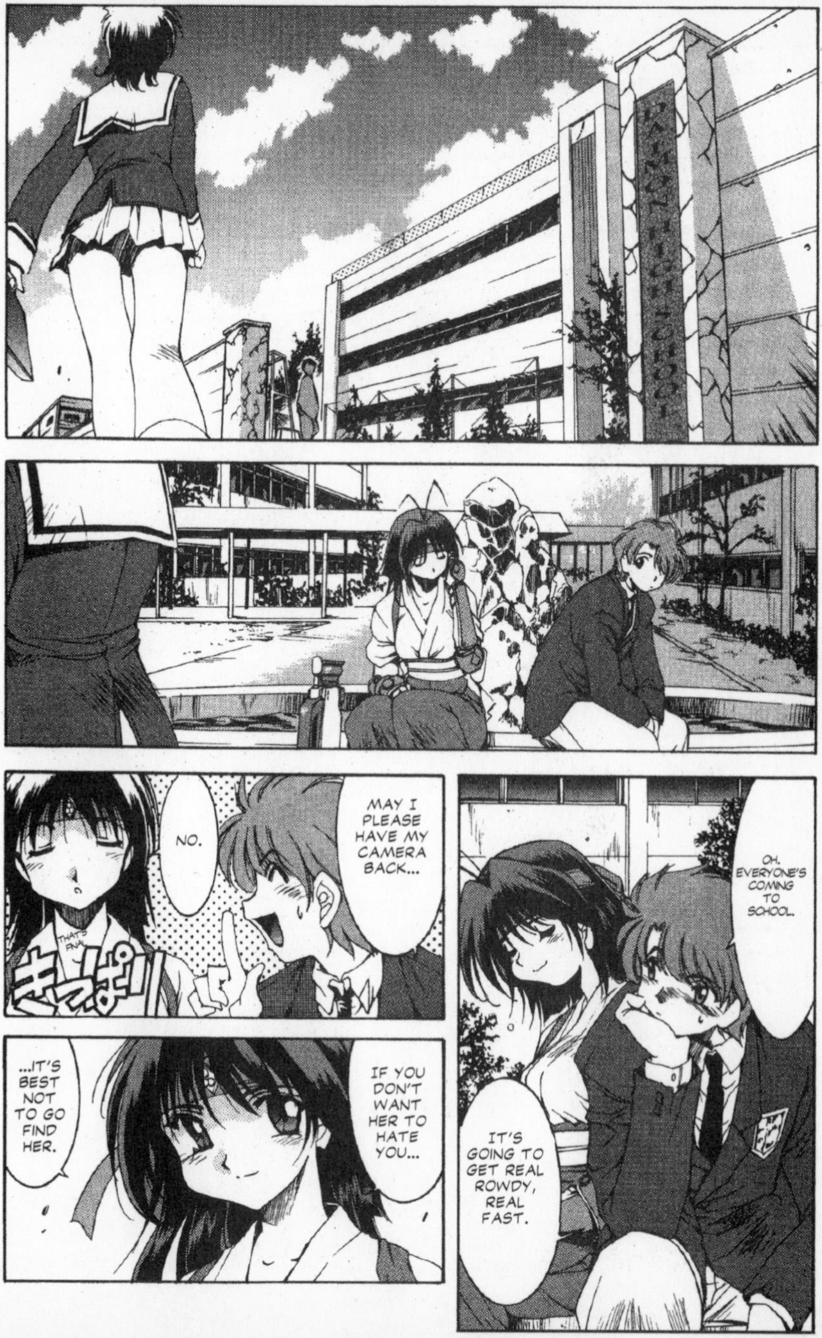
DAIMON HIGH SCHOOL
OH. EVERYONE'S COMING TO SCHOOL.
IT'S GOING TO GET REAL ROWDY, REAL FAST.
MAY I PLEASE HAVE MY CAMERA BACK...
NO.
THAT'S FINAL
IF YOU DON'T WANT HER TO HATE YOU...
...IT'S BEST NOT TO GO FIND HER.

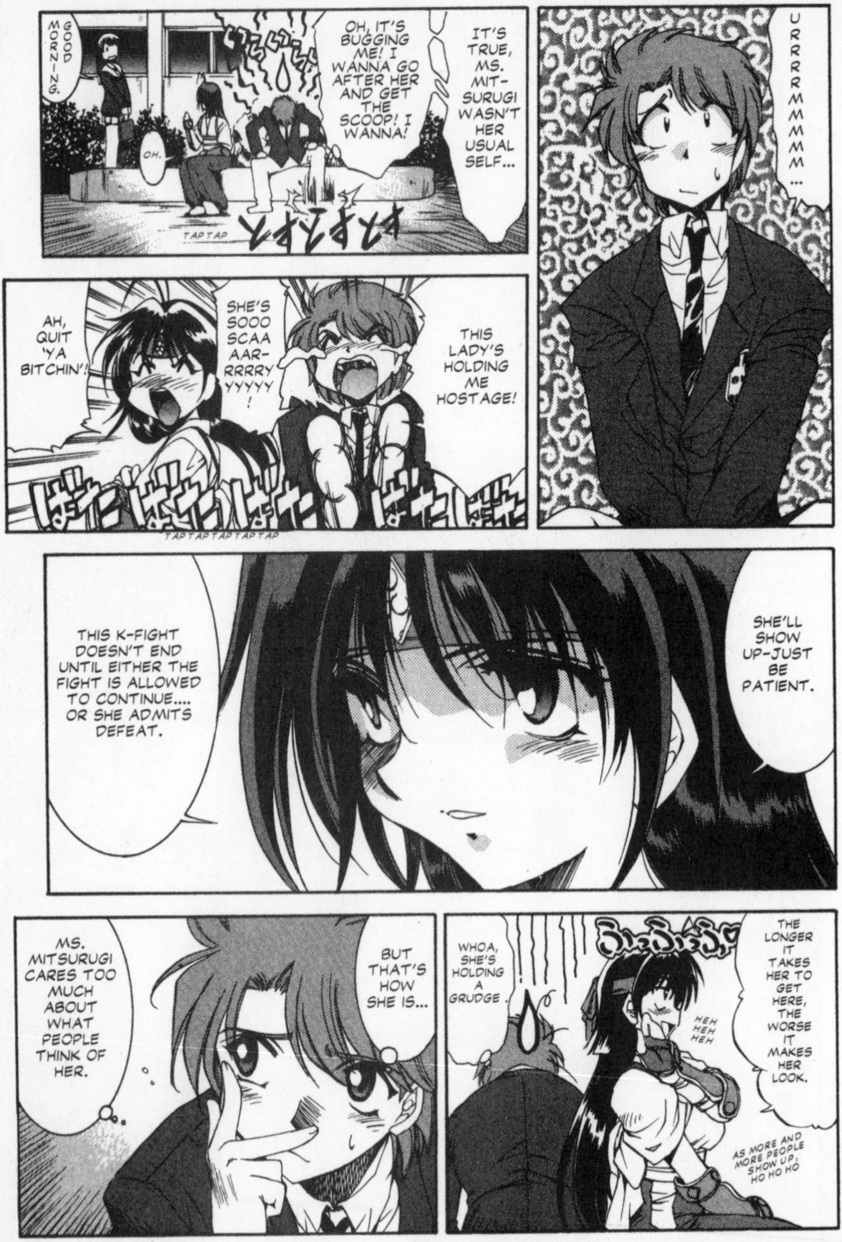
URRRRMMMMMM...
IT'S TRUE, MS. MIT-SURUGI WASN'T HER USUAL SELF...
OH, IT'S BUGGING ME! I WANNA GO AFTER HER AND GET THE SCOOP! I WANNA!
GOOD MORNING.
OH.
TAPTAP
THIS LADY'S HOLDING ME HOSTAGE!
SHE'S SOOO SCAAAAR-RRRRYYYYYY!
AH, QUIT 'YA BITCHIN'!
TAPTAPTAPTAPTAP
SHE'LL SHOW UP-JUST BE PATIENT.
THIS K-FIGHT DOESN'T END UNTIL EITHER THE FIGHT IS ALLOWED TO CONTINUE.... OR SHE ADMITS DEFEAT.
THE LONGER IT TAKES HER TO GET HERE, THE WORSE IT MAKES HER LOOK.
HEH HEH HEH
WHOA, SHE'S HOLDING A GRUDGE.
AS MORE AND MORE PEOPLE SHOW UP, HO HO HO
BUT THAT'S HOW SHE IS...
MS. MITSURUGI CARES TOO MUCH ABOUT WHAT PEOPLE THINK OF HER.

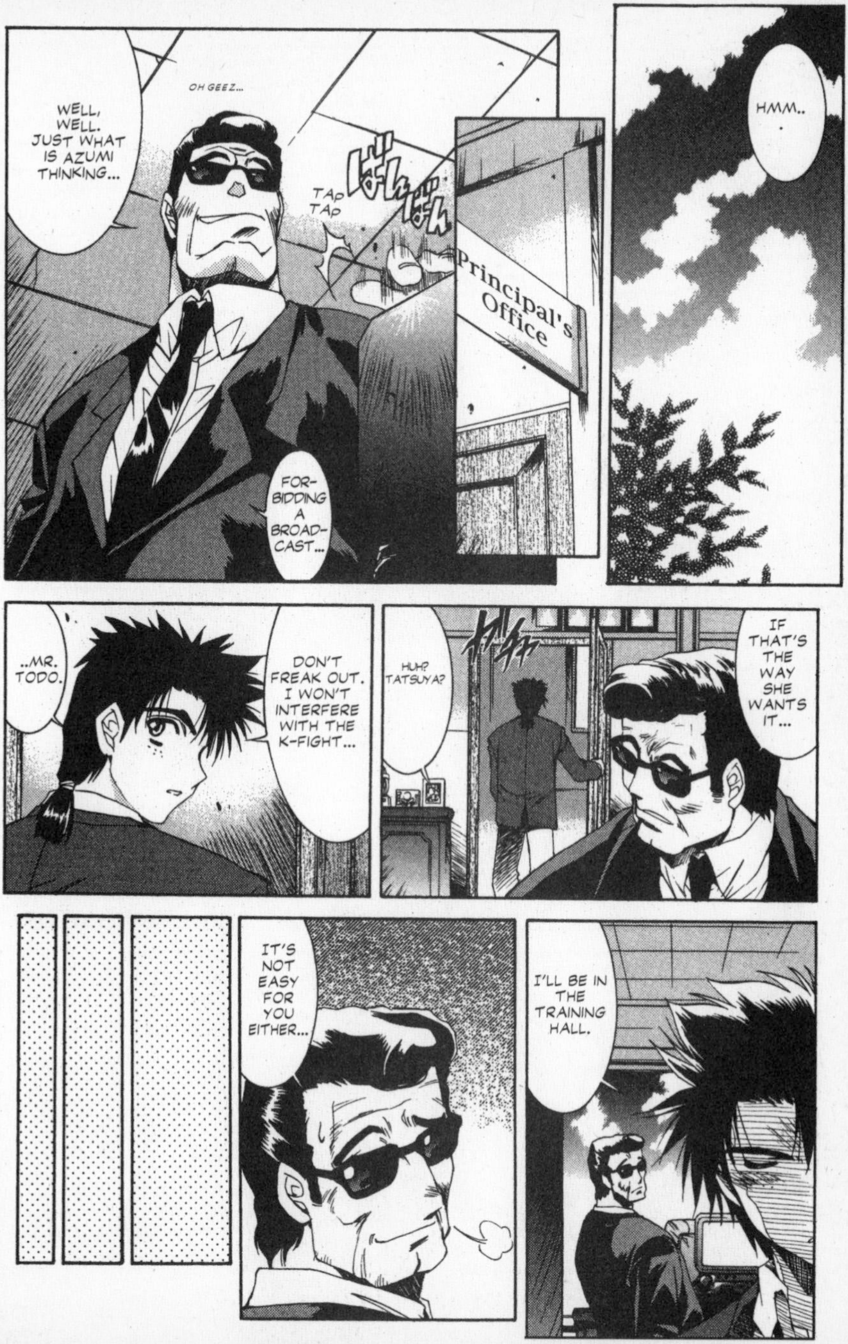
HMM..
ばんばん
TAp TAp
OH GEEZ...
WELL, WELL. JUST WHAT IS AZUMI THINKING...
FOR-BIDDING A BROAD-CAST...
IF THAT'S THE WAY SHE WANTS IT...
HUH? TATSUYA?
DON'T FREAK OUT. I WON'T INTERFERE WITH THE K-FIGHT...
..MR. TODO.
I'LL BE IN THE TRAINING HALL.
IT'S NOT EASY FOR YOU EITHER...

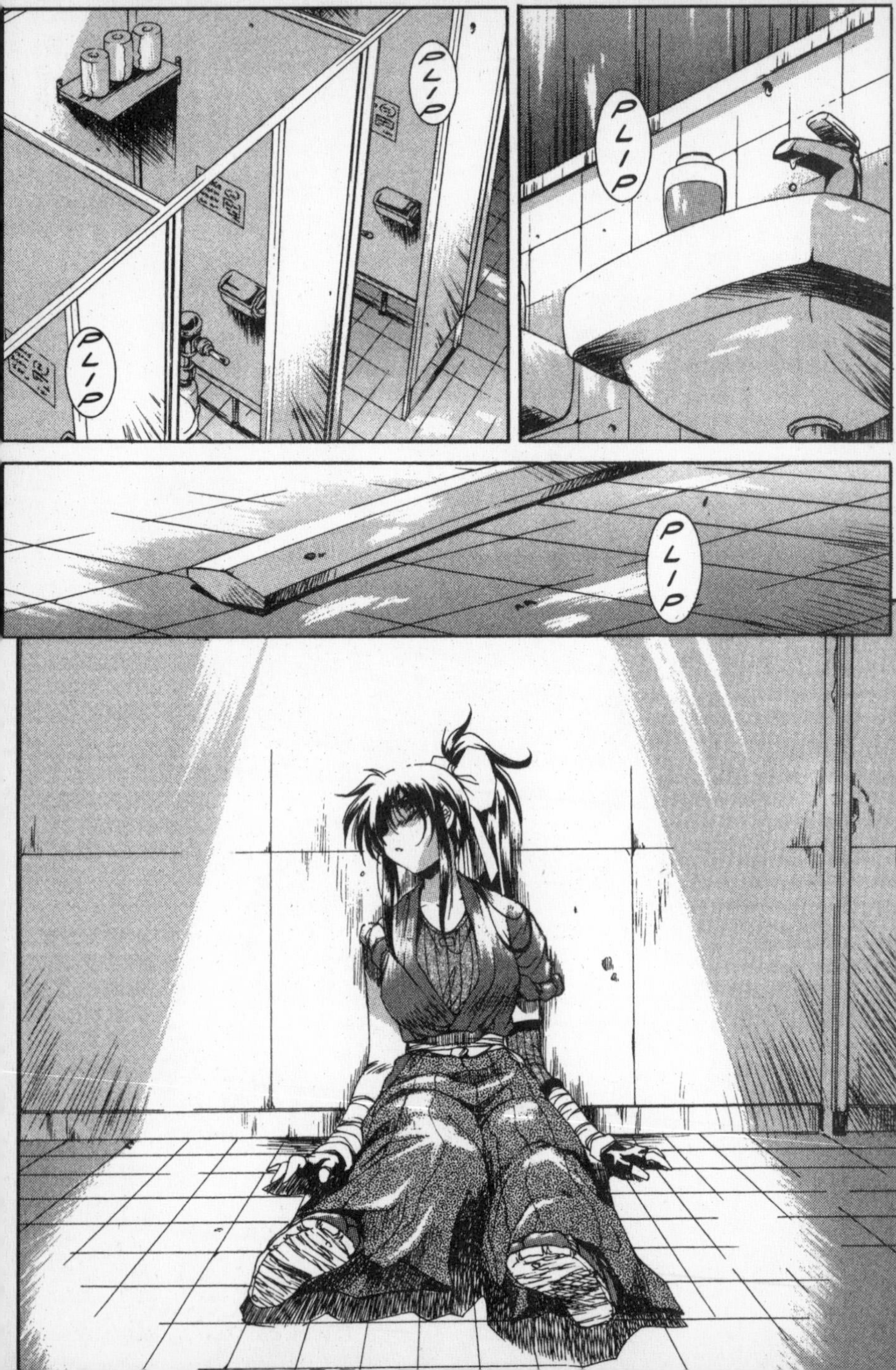
PLIP
PLIP
PLIP
PLIP

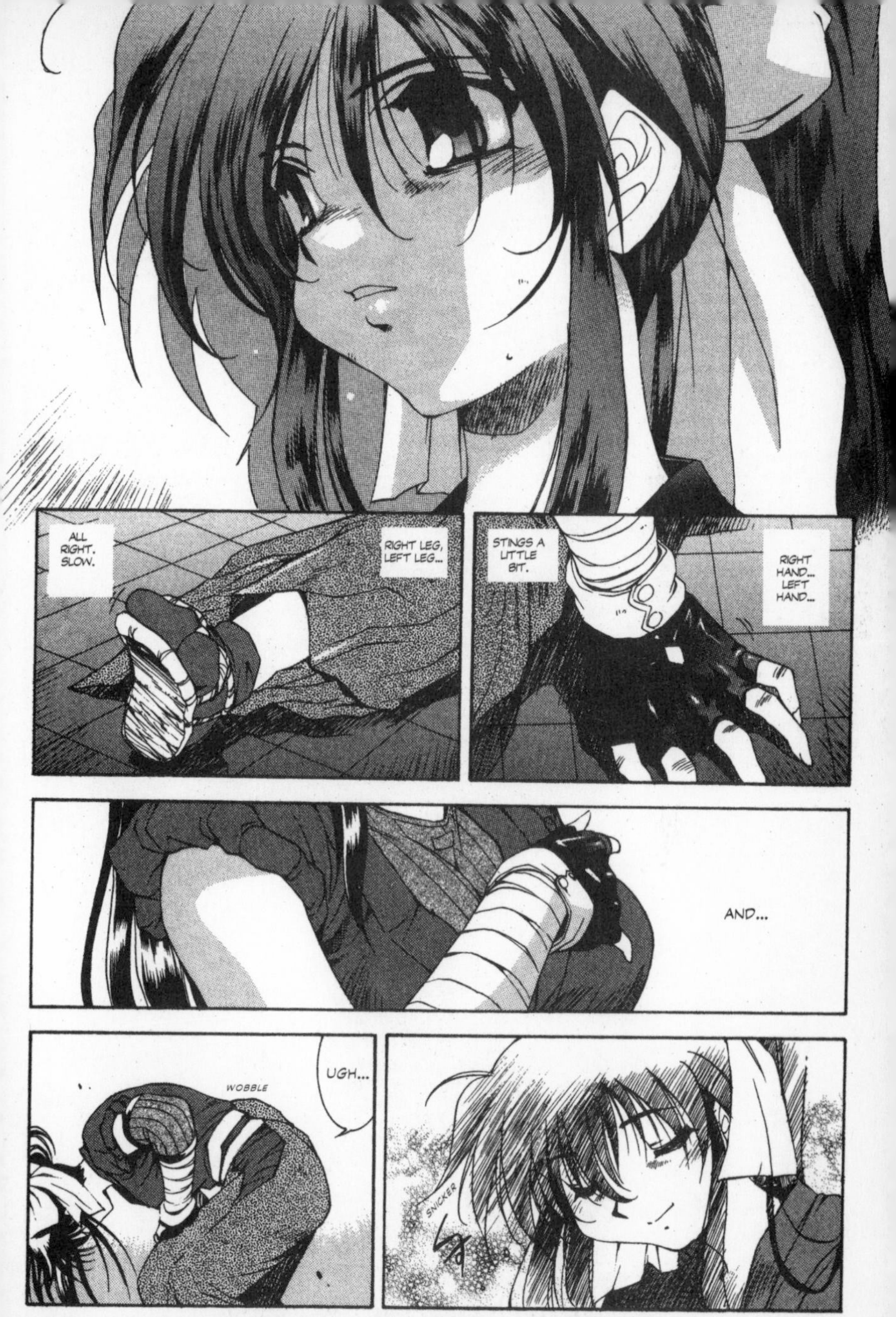
RIGHT HAND... LEFT HAND...
STINGS A LITTLE BIT.
RIGHT LEG, LEFT LEG...
ALL RIGHT. SLOW.
AND...
SNICKER
UGH...
WOBBLE

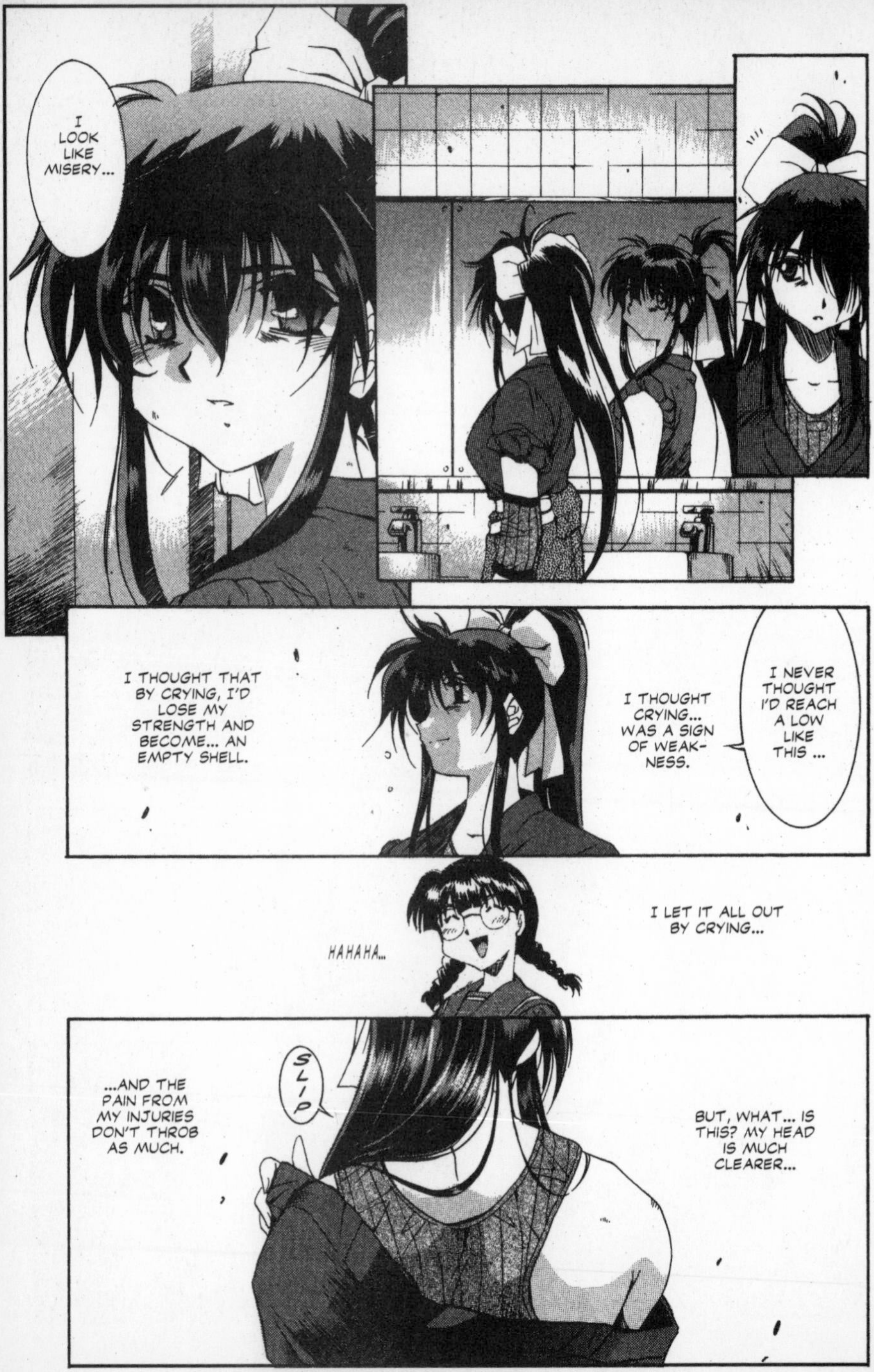
I LOOK LIKE MISERY...
I NEVER THOUGHT I'D REACH A LOW LIKE THIS ...
I THOUGHT CRYING... WAS A SIGN OF WEAK-NESS.
I THOUGHT THAT BY CRYING, I'D LOSE MY STRENGTH AND BECOME... AN EMPTY SHELL.
I LET IT ALL OUT BY CRYING...
HAHAHA...
BUT, WHAT... IS THIS? MY HEAD IS MUCH CLEARER...
SLIP
...AND THE PAIN FROM MY INJURIES DON'T THROB AS MUCH.

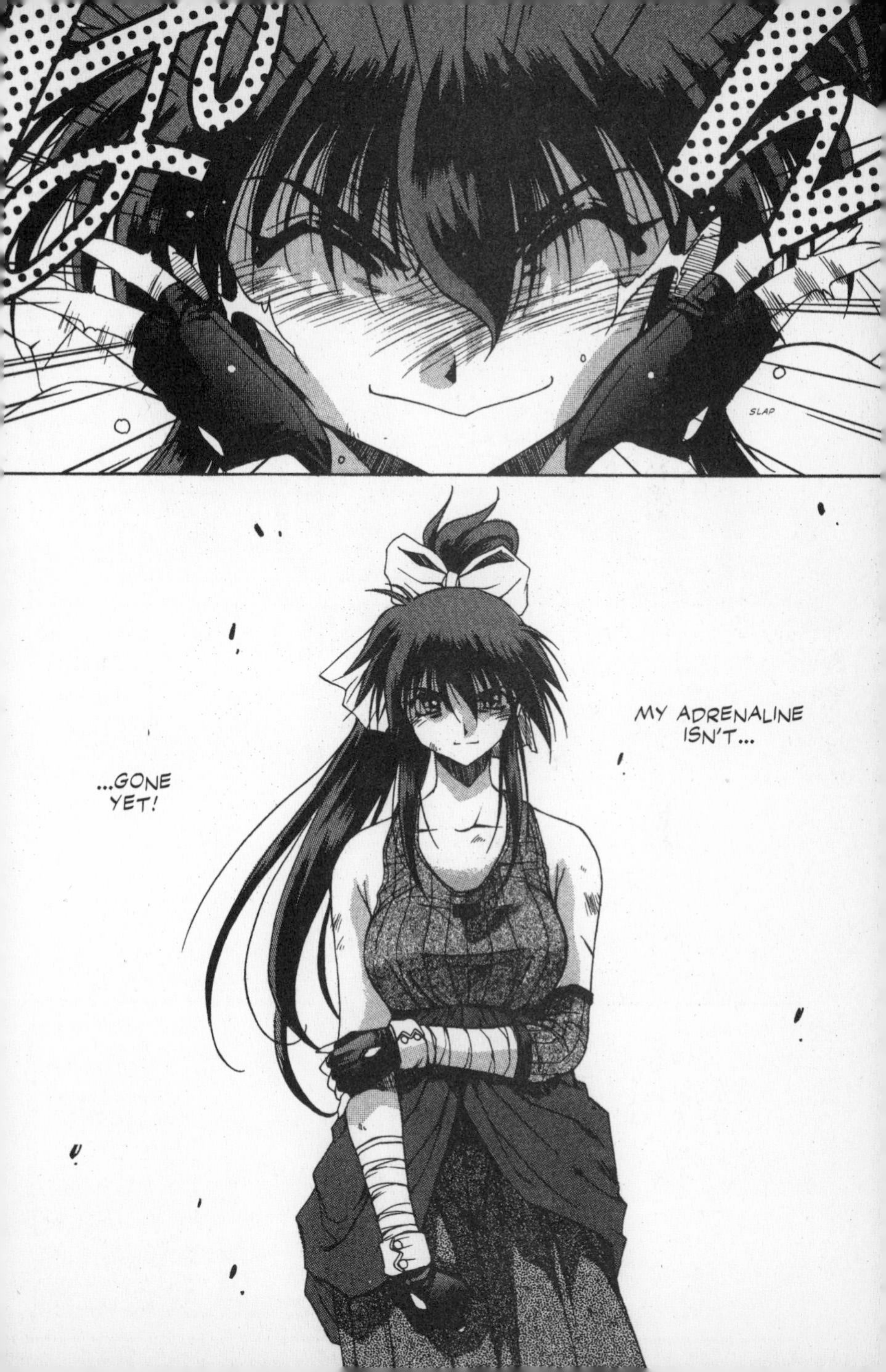
SLAP
MY ADRENALINE ISN'T...
...GONE YET!

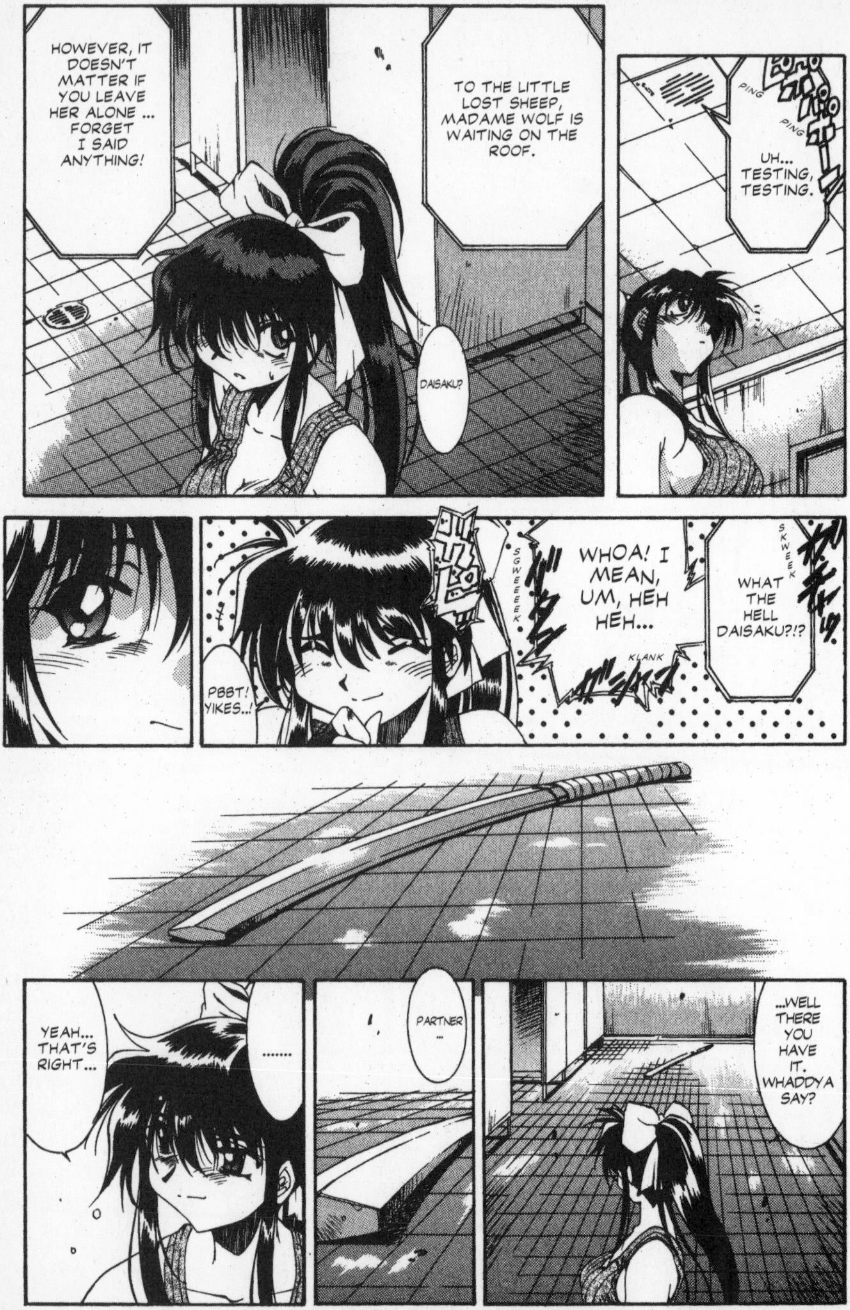
PING
PING
UH... TESTING, TESTING.
TO THE LITTLE LOST SHEEP, MADAME WOLF IS WAITING ON THE ROOF.
HOWEVER, IT DOESN'T MATTER IF YOU LEAVE HER ALONE ... FORGET I SAID ANYTHING!
DAISAKU?
SKWEEK
WHAT THE HELL DAISAKU?!?
SGWEEEEK
WHOA! I MEAN, UM, HEH HEH...
KLANK
PBBT! YIKES..!
...WELL THERE YOU HAVE IT. WHADDYA SAY?
PARTNER ...
....
YEAH... THAT'S RIGHT...

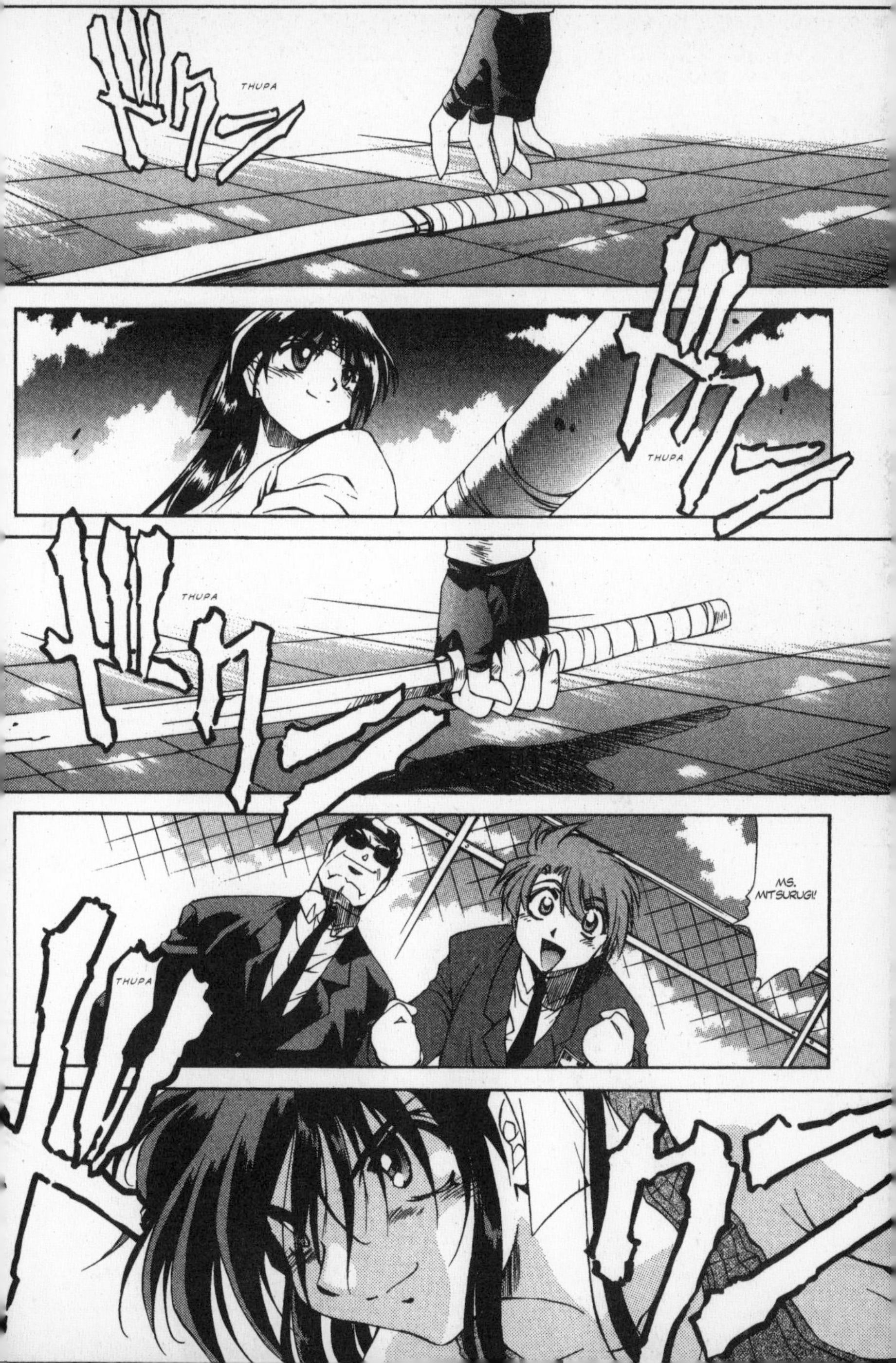
THUPA
THUPA
THUPA
MS. MITSURUGI!
THUPA

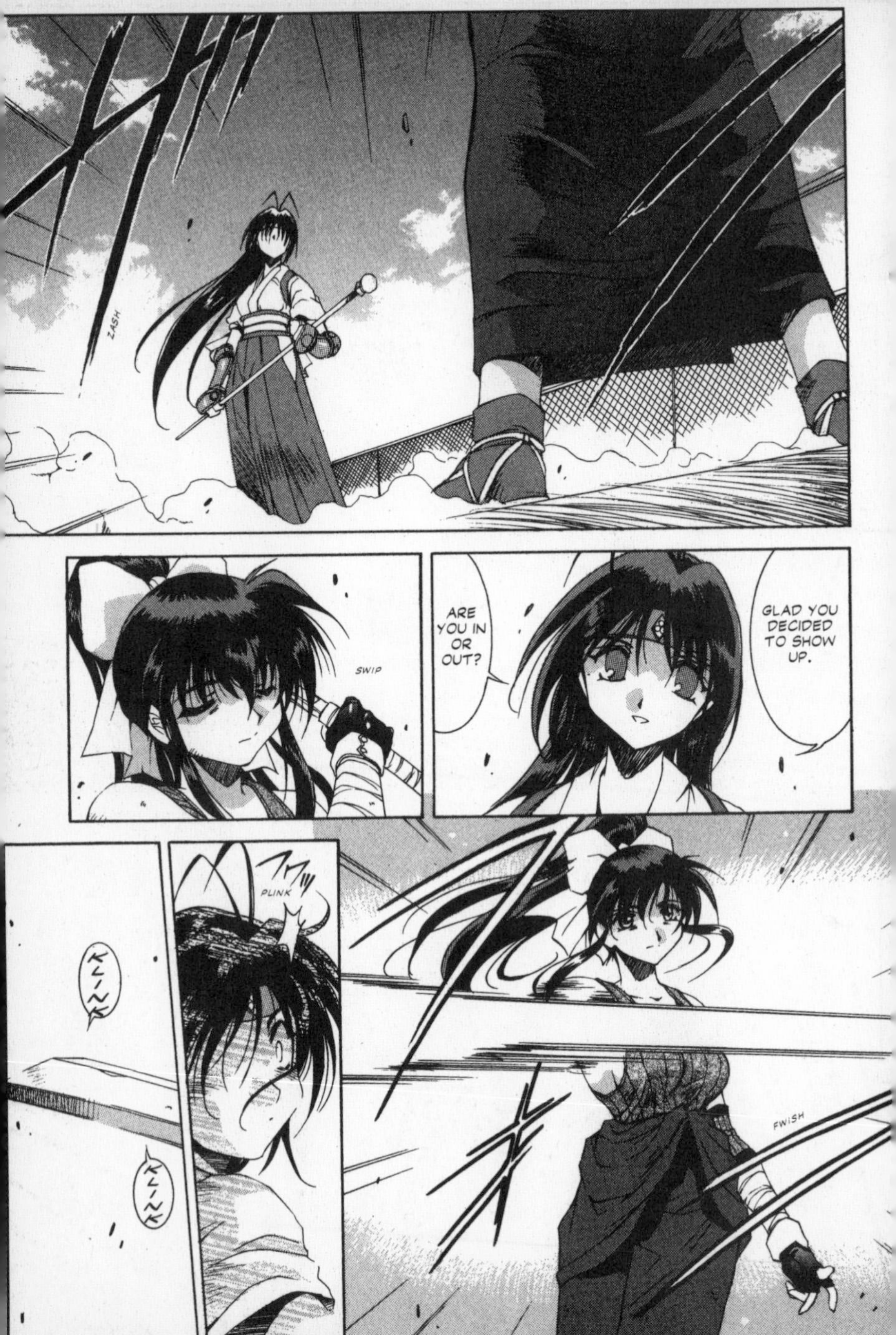
ZASH
GLAD YOU DECIDED TO SHOW UP.
ARE YOU IN OR OUT?
SWIP
FWISH
PLINK
KLINK
KLINK

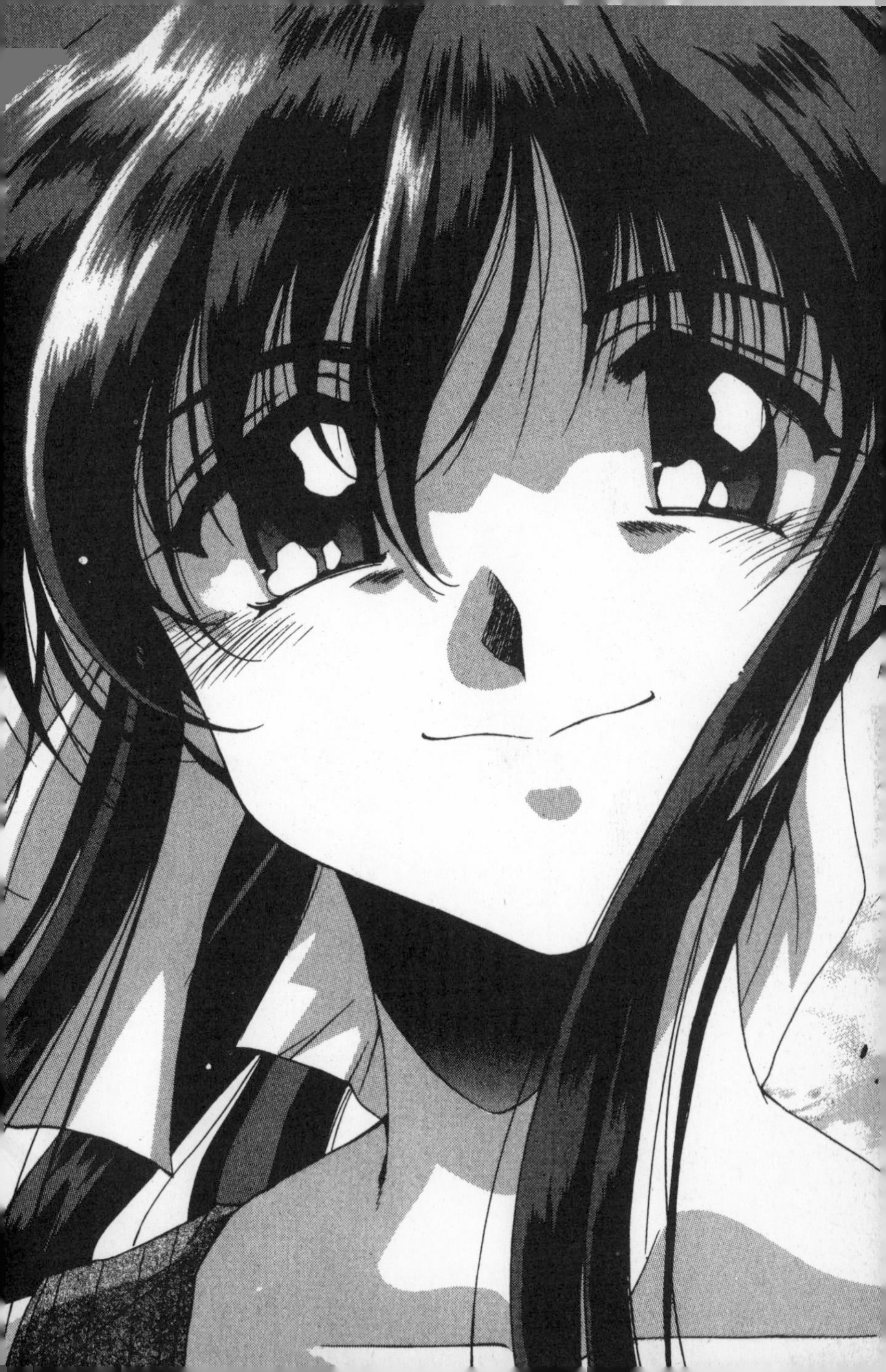

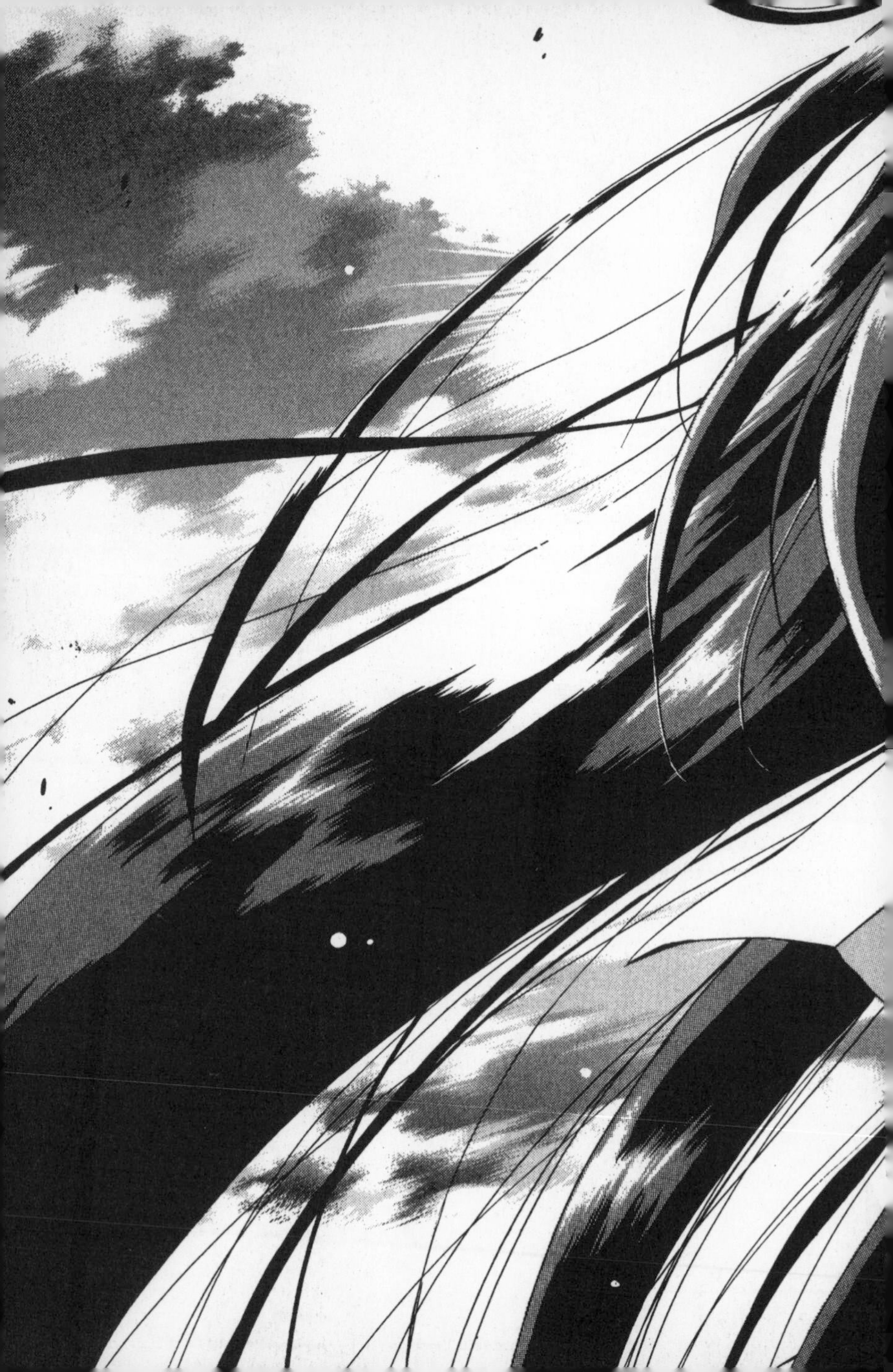

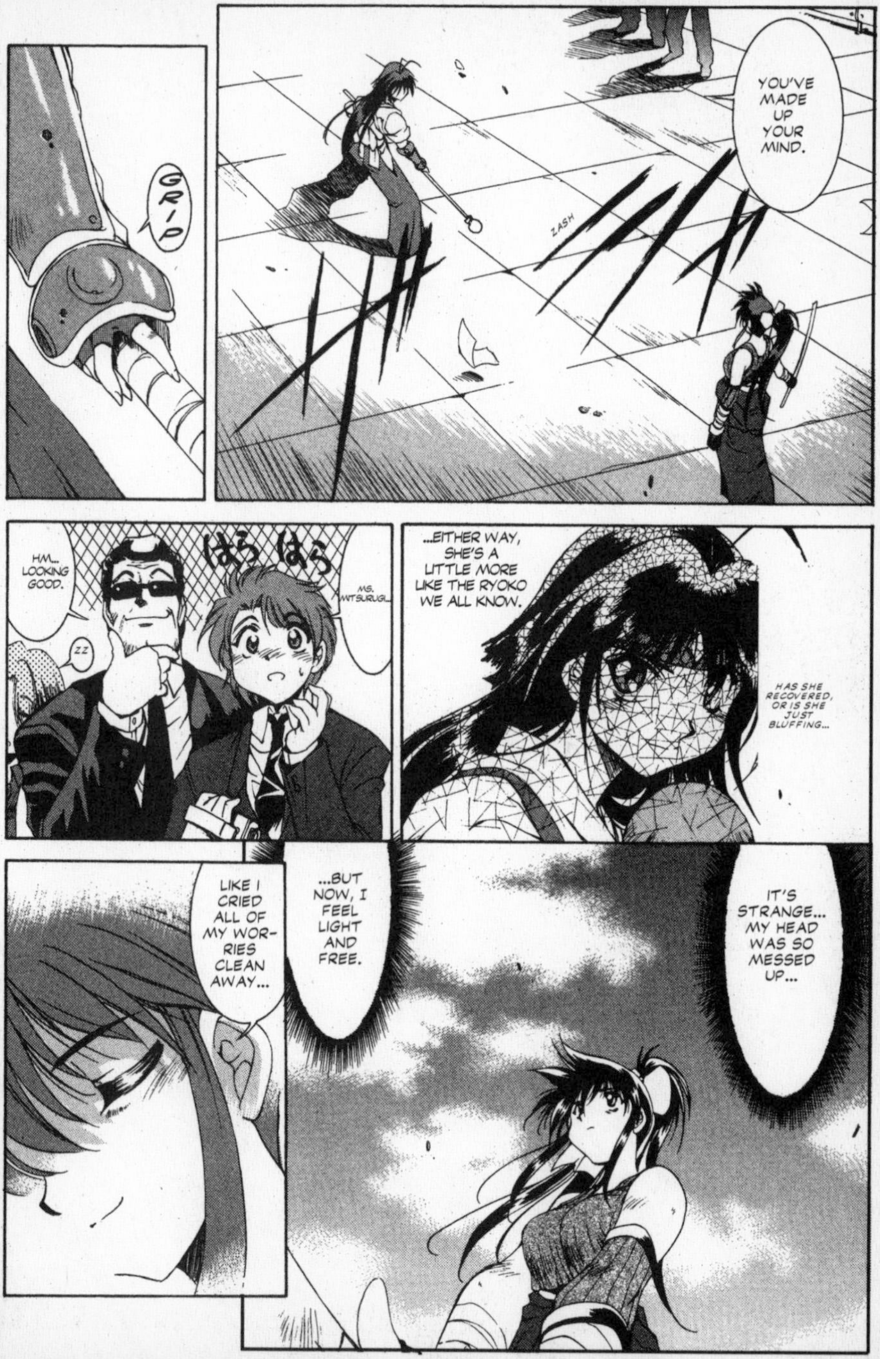
YOU'VE MADE UP YOUR MIND.
ZASH
GRIP
...EITHER WAY, SHE'S A LITTLE MORE LIKE THE RYOKO WE ALL KNOW.
HAS SHE RECOVERED, OR IS SHE JUST BLUFFING...
はら はら
MS. MITSURUGI...
HM... LOOKING GOOD.
ZZ
IT'S STRANGE... MY HEAD WAS SO MESSED UP...
...BUT NOW, I FEEL LIGHT AND FREE.
LIKE I CRIED ALL OF MY WOR-RIES CLEAN AWAY...

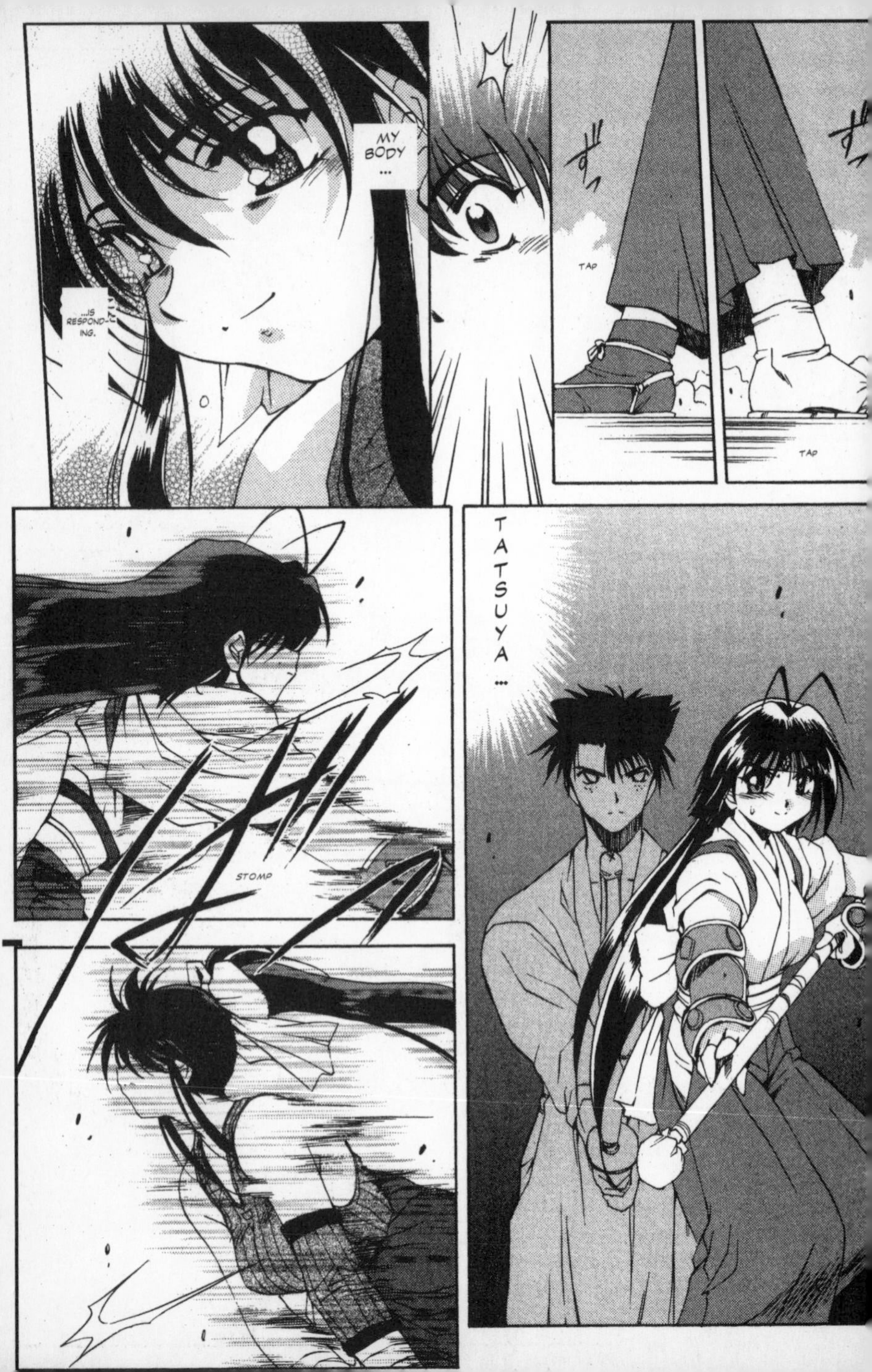

ずっ
TAP
ずっ
TAP
MY BODY ...
...IS RESPOND-ING.
TATSUYA ...
STOMP

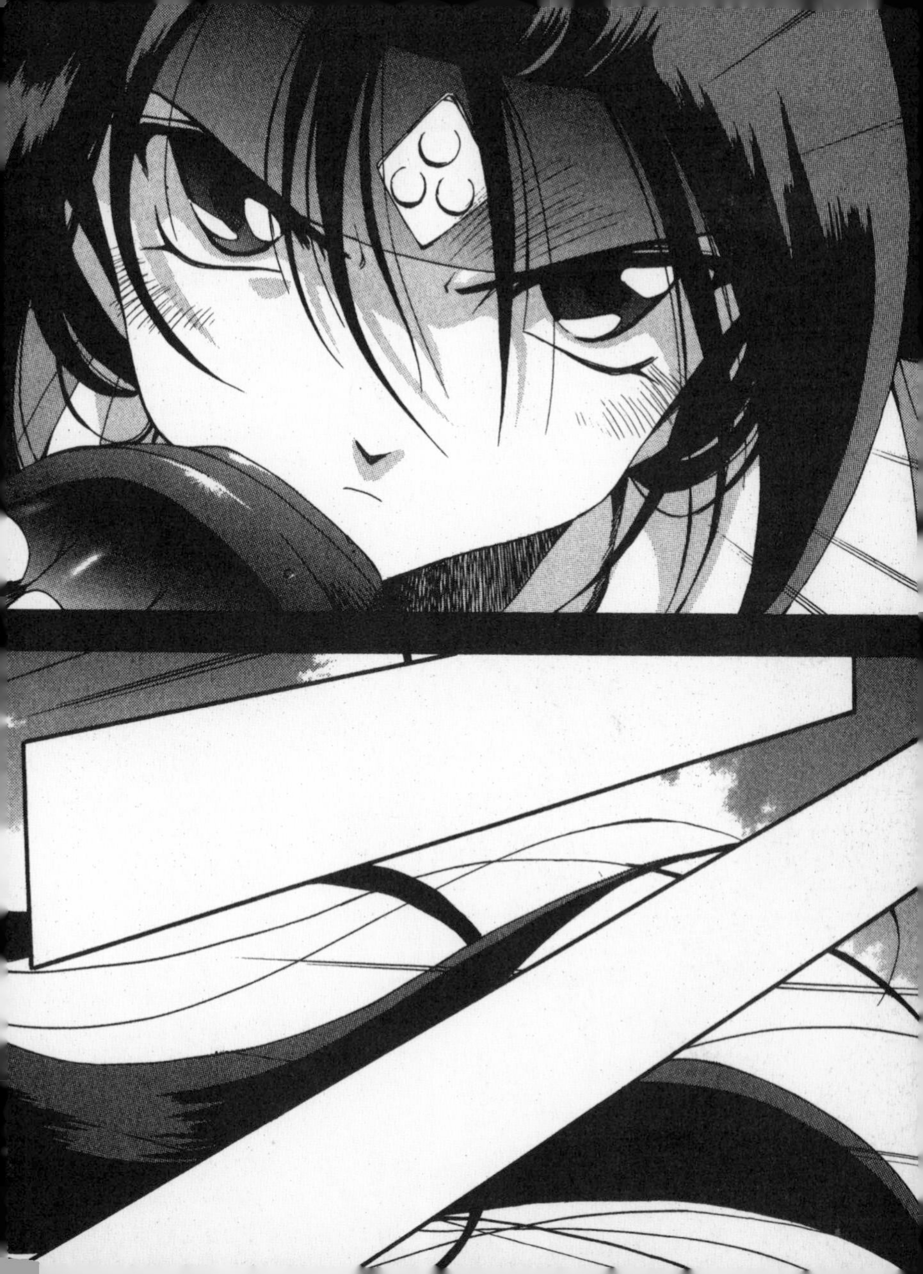

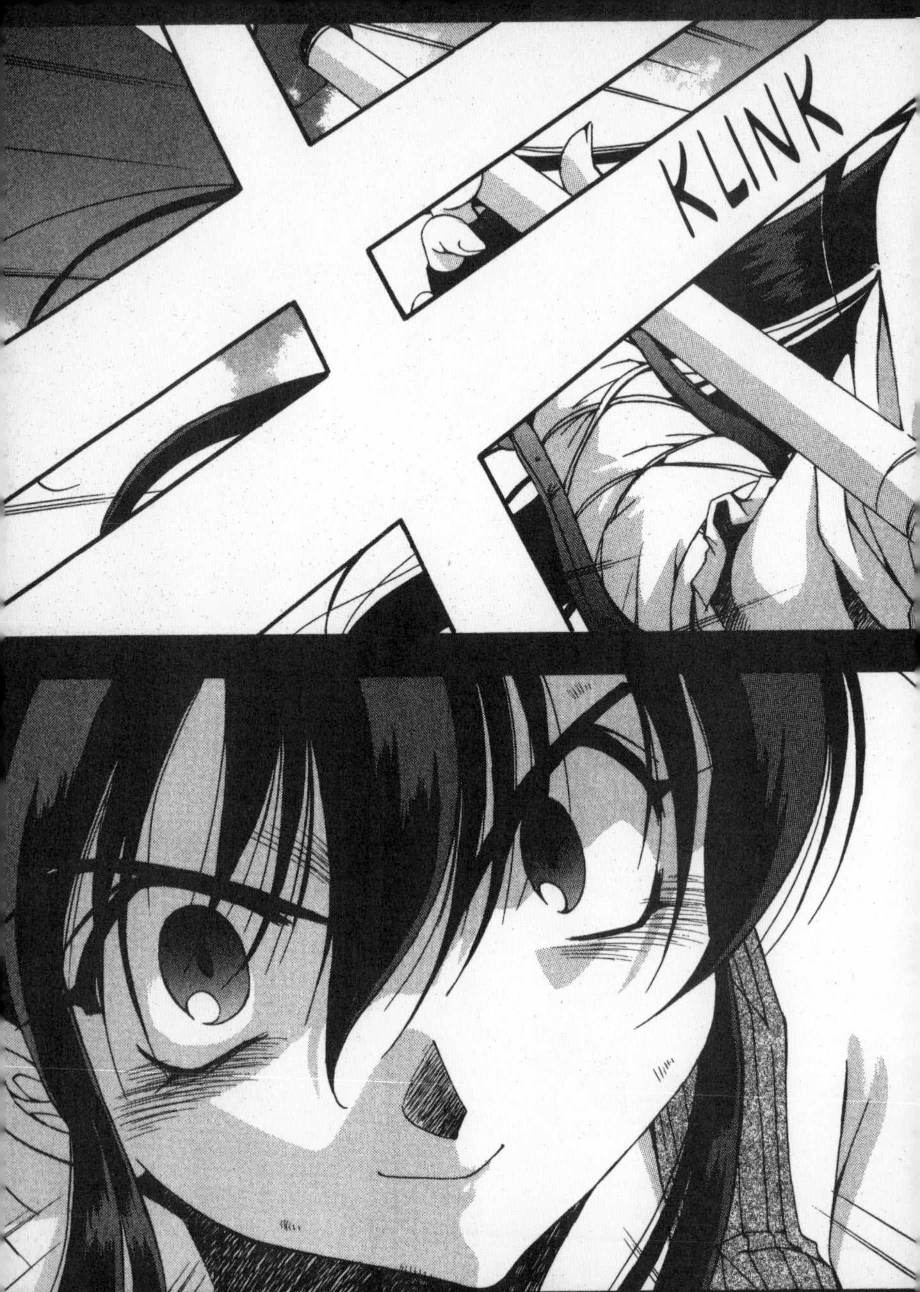
KLINK

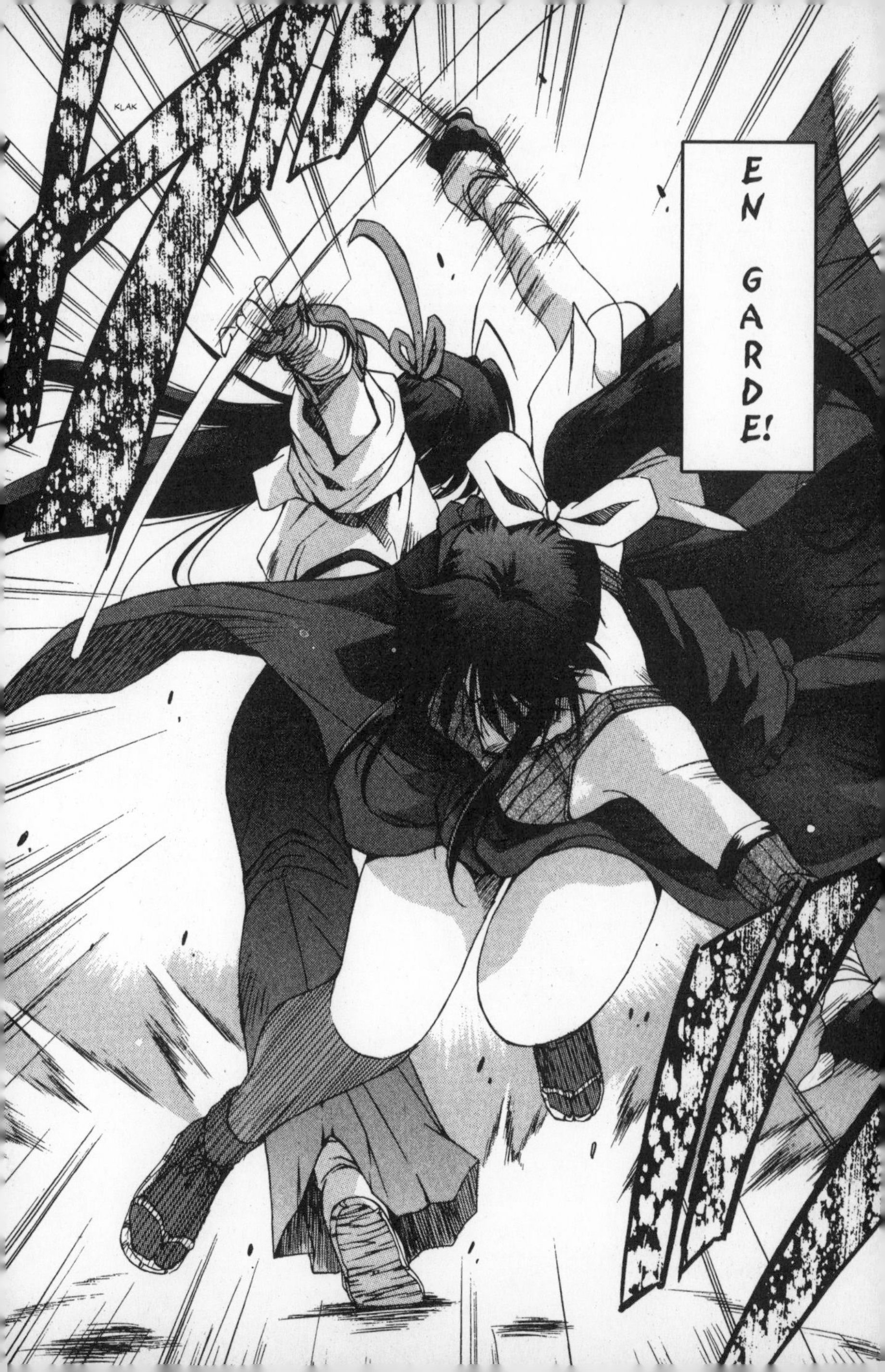
EN GARDE!
KLAK

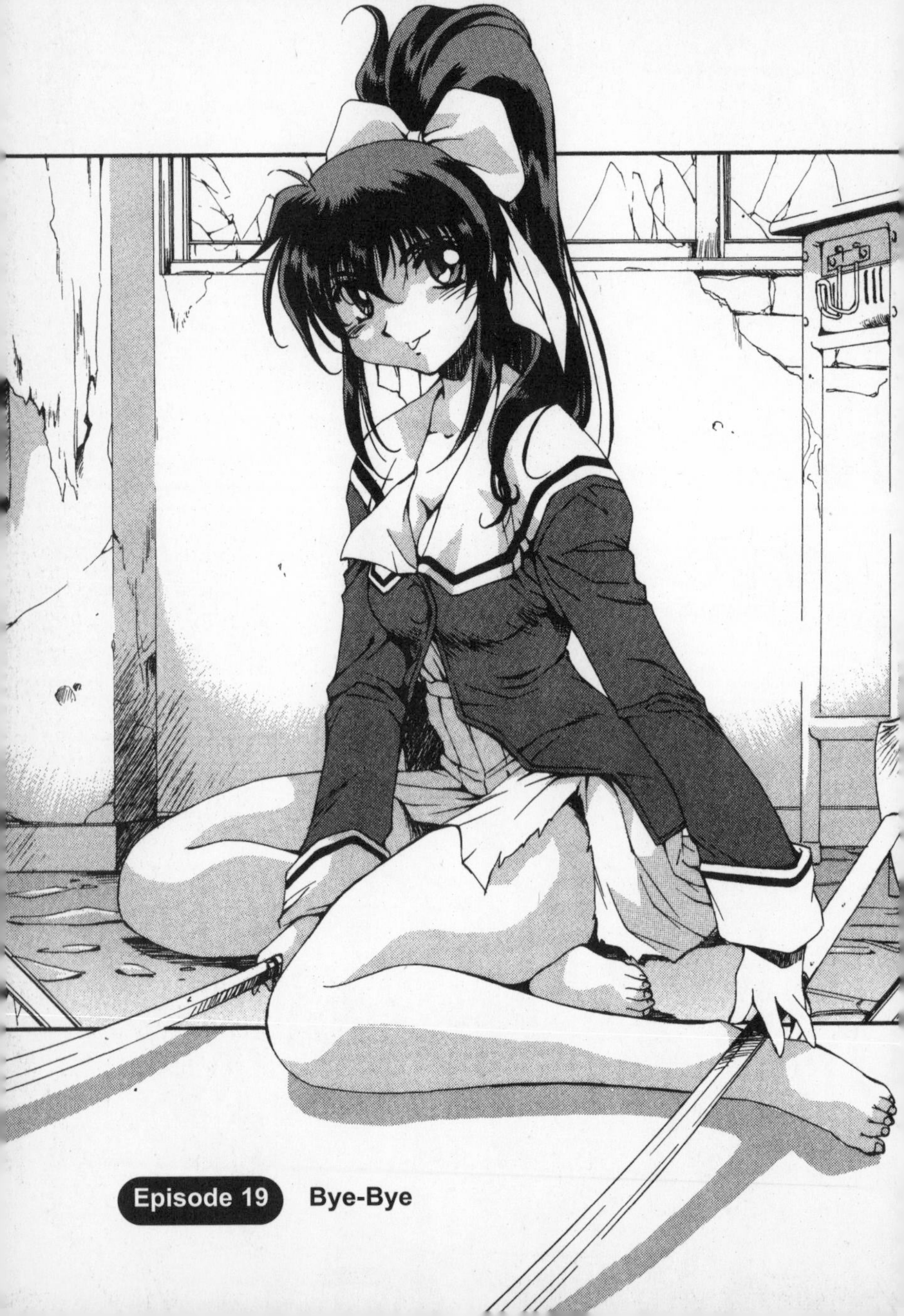

Episode 19 Bye-Bye

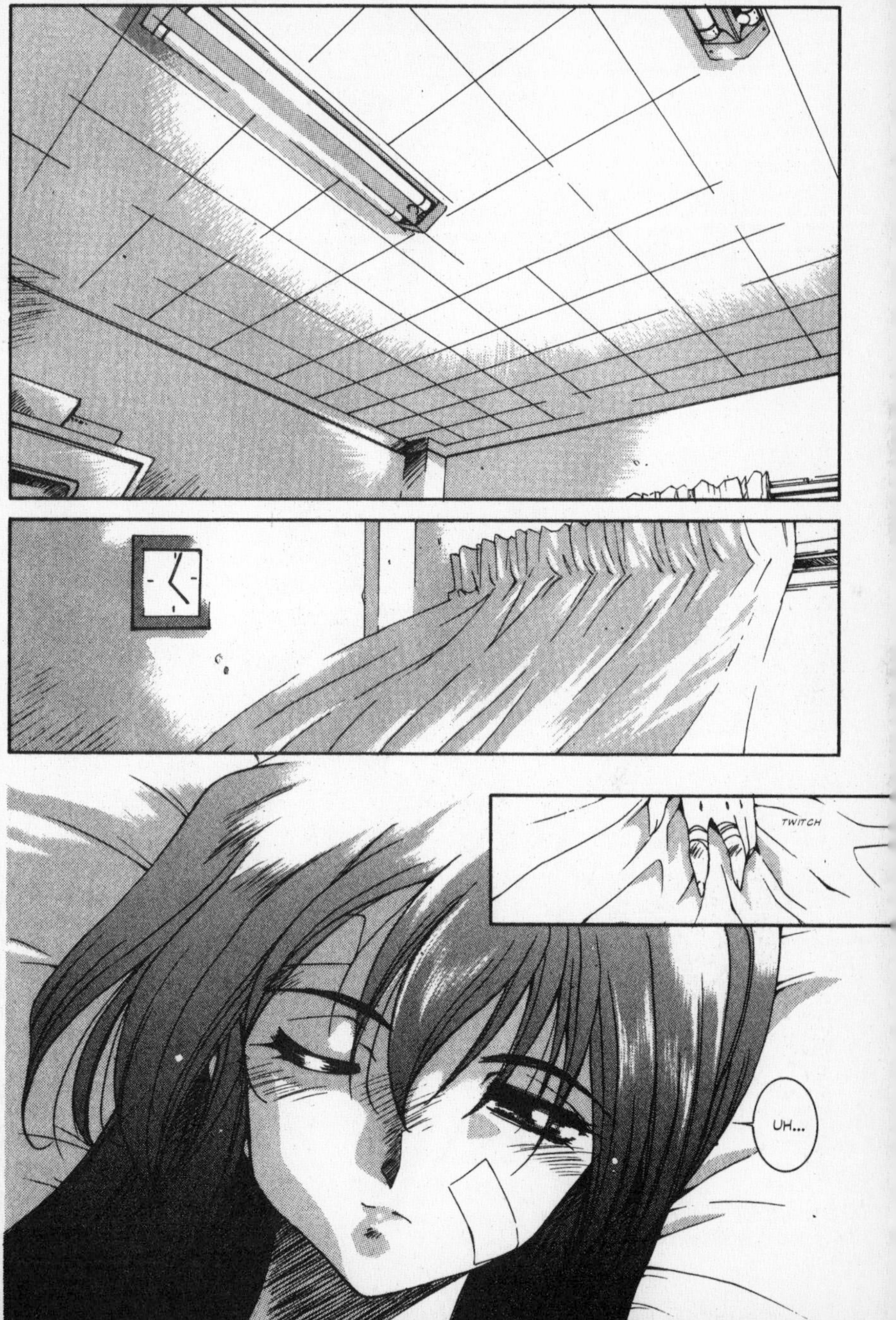
TWITCH
UH...

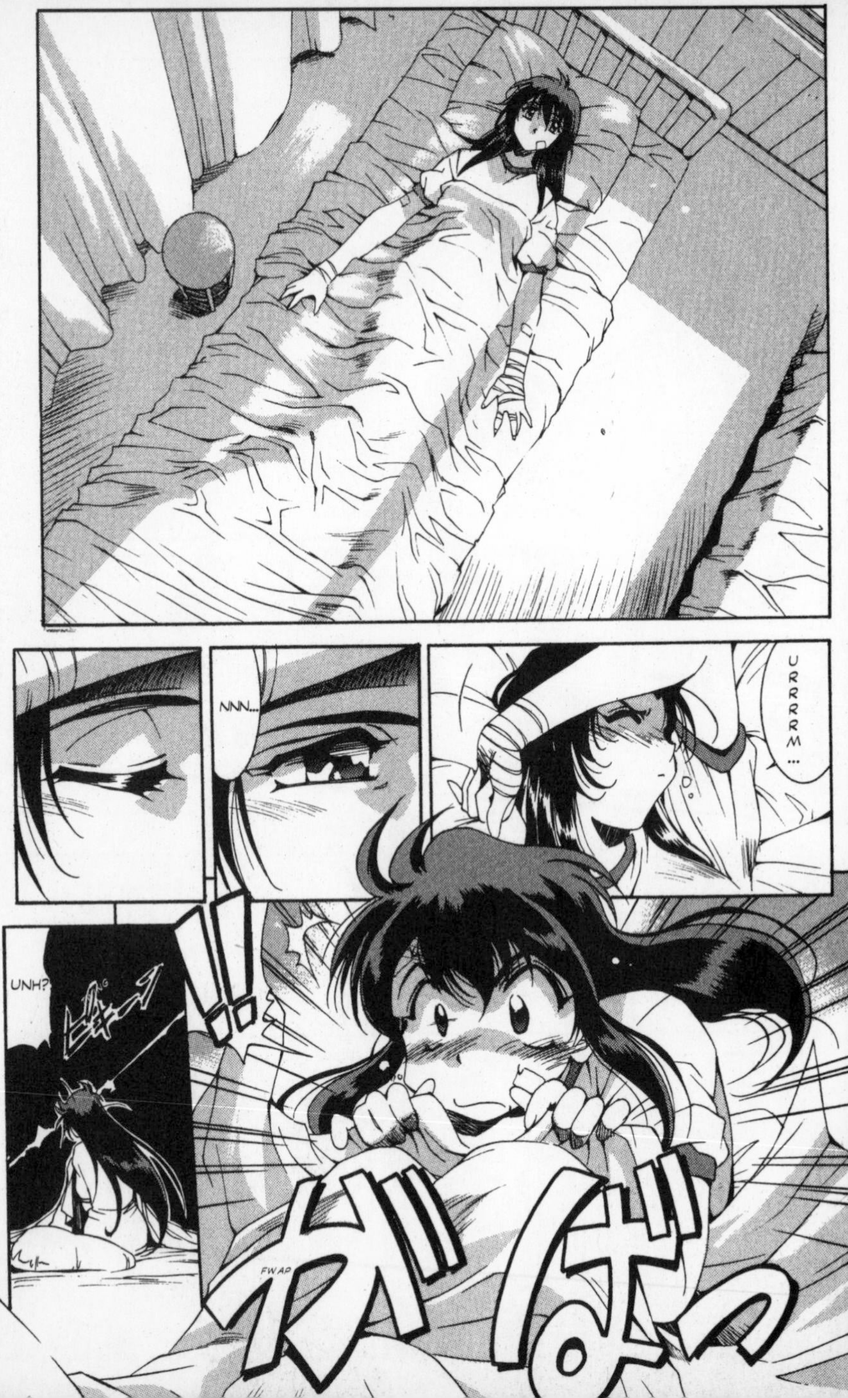
URRRRM...
NNN...
!!
FWAP
がばっ
UNH?

I WONDER IF RYOKO'S AWAKE YET...

NURSE'S OFFICE

YEUU''
EEE OUU''
OO,''

EEK

WOW!

YEOW! IT HUUURRRRRTS!!!

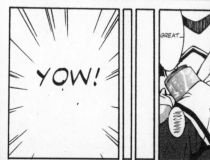

YOW!

GREAT...

HA...
HA...
HA...
RYOKO...

PHEW!

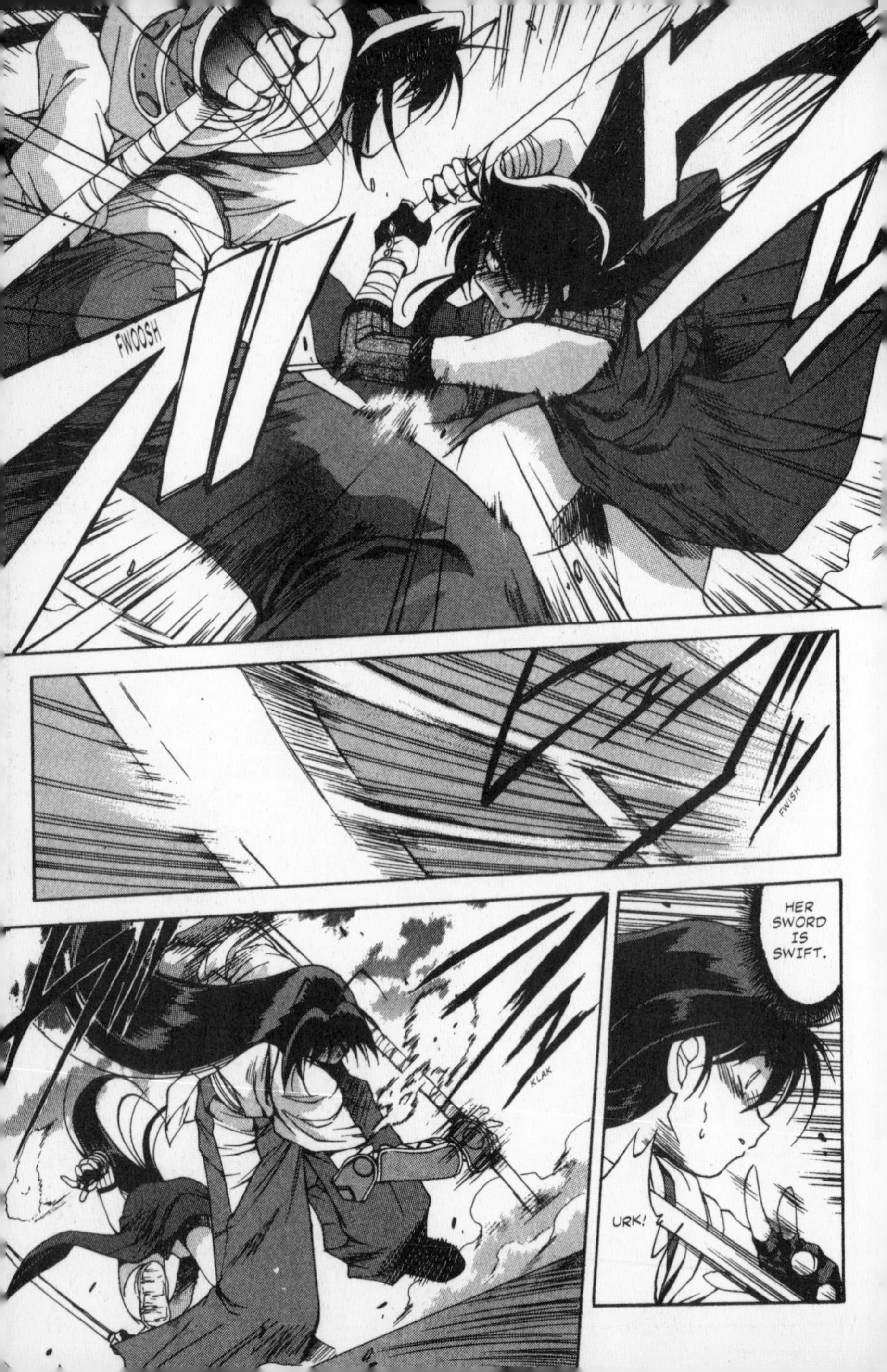
FWOOSH
FWISH
HER SWORD IS SWIFT.
URK!
KLAK

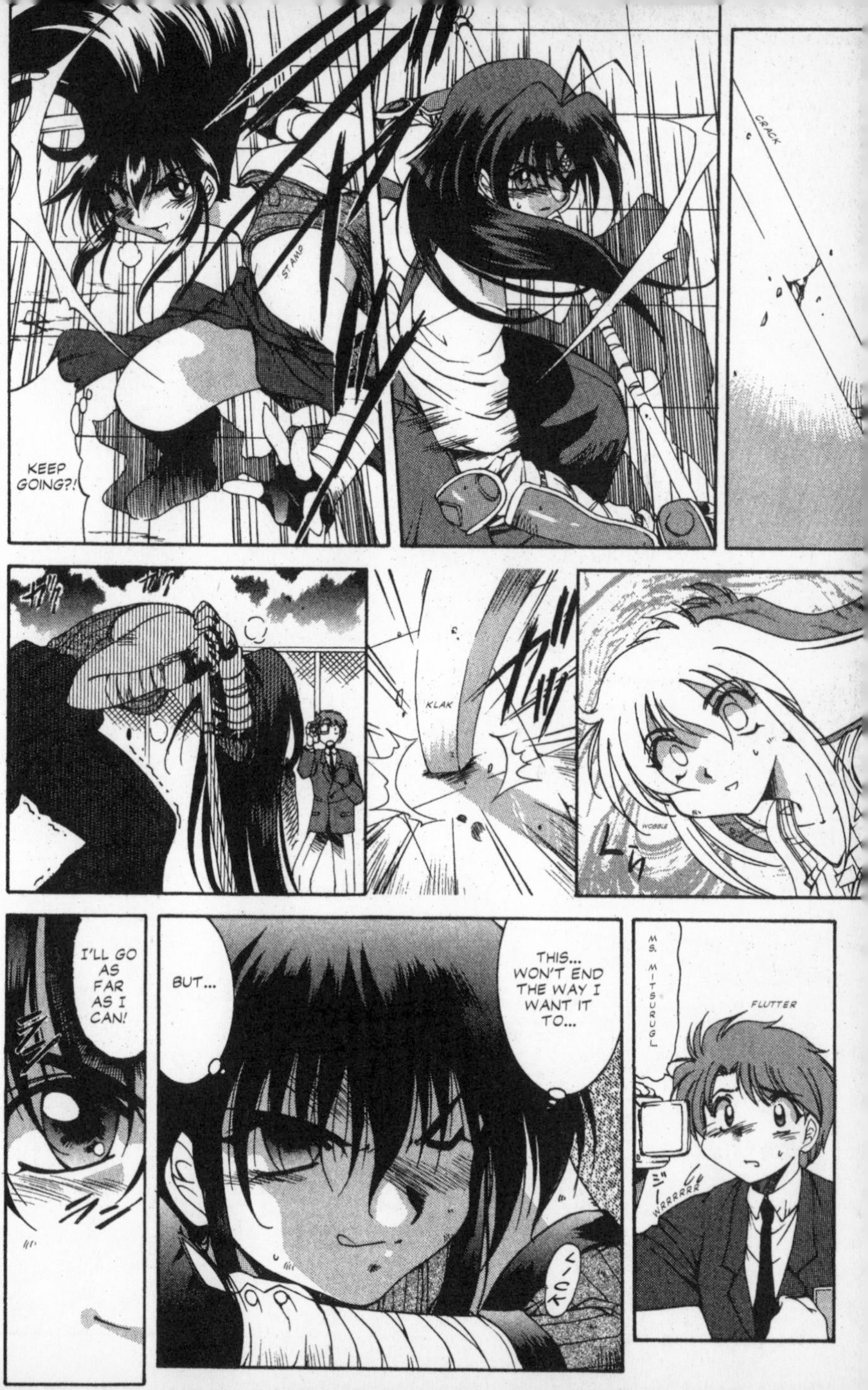
CRACK
STAMP
KEEP GOING?!
WOBBLE
KLAK
MS. MITSURUGI.
FLUTTER
WRRRRRR
THIS... WON'T END THE WAY I WANT IT TO...
BUT...
LICK
I'LL GO AS FAR AS I CAN!

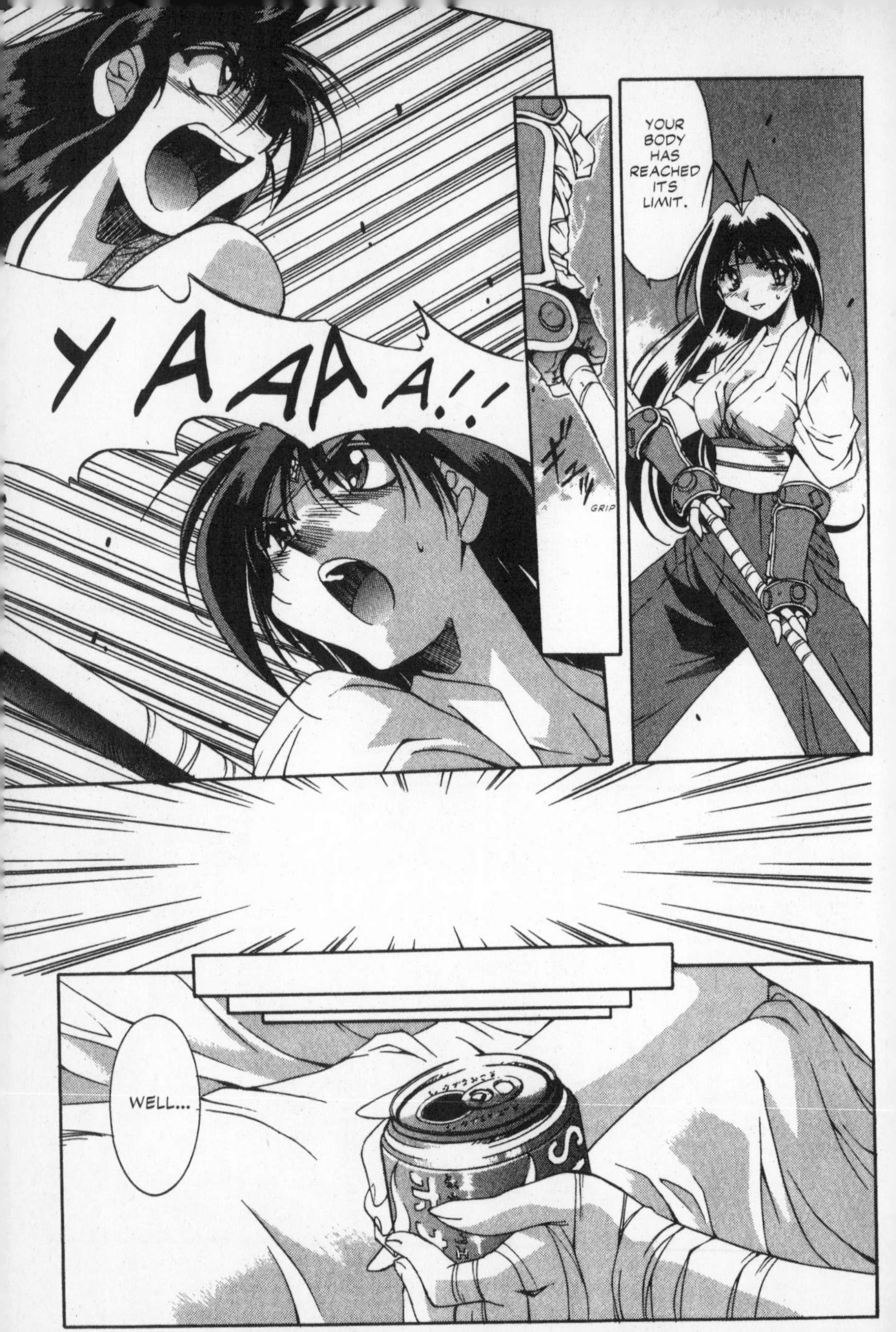
YOUR BODY HAS REACHED ITS LIMIT.
GRIP
YAAAA!!!
WELL...

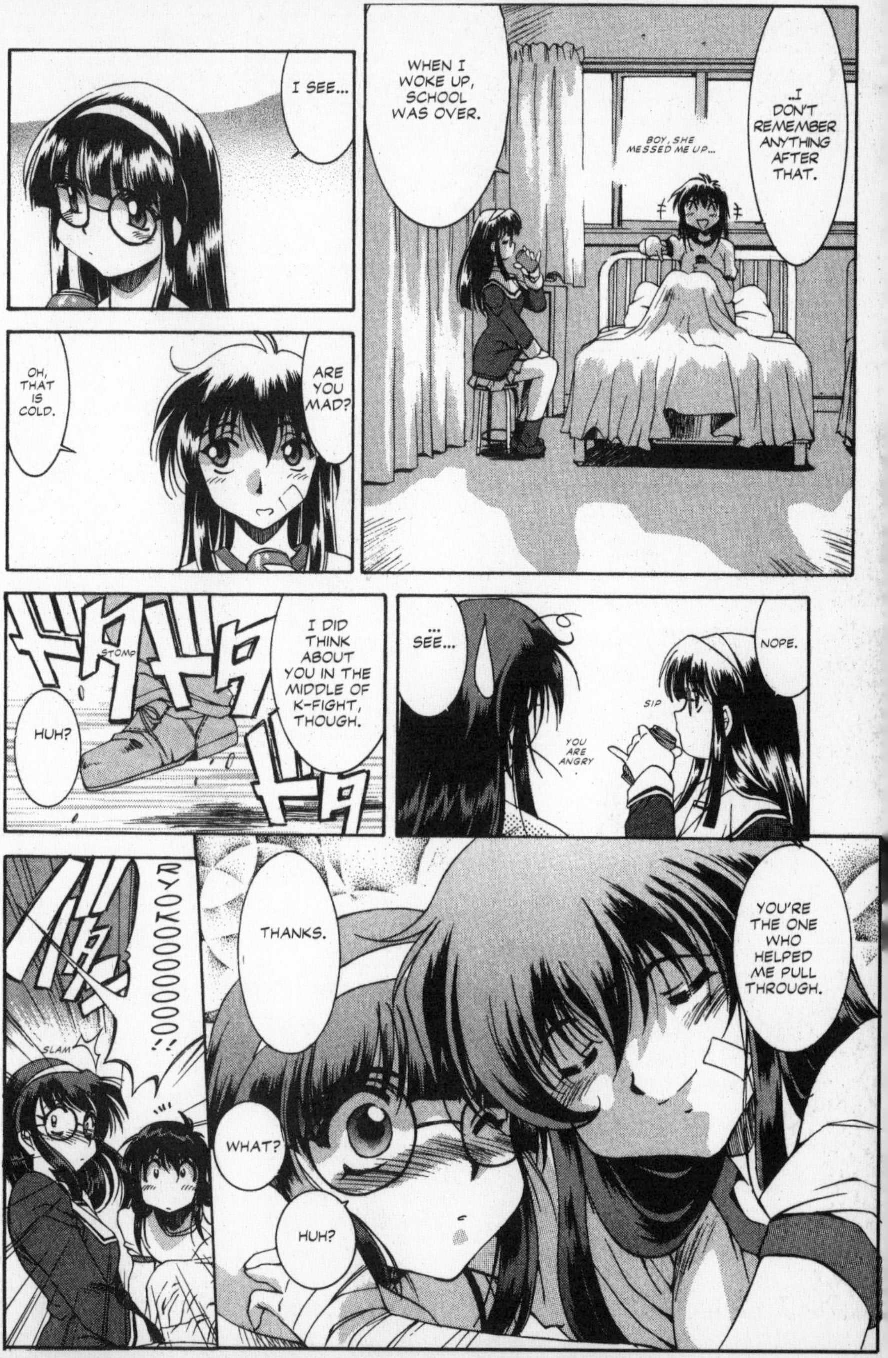

..I DON'T REMEMBER ANYTHING AFTER THAT.
BOY, SHE MESSED ME UP...
WHEN I WOKE UP, SCHOOL WAS OVER.
I SEE...
ARE YOU MAD?
OH, THAT IS COLD.
NOPE.
SIP
YOU ARE ANGRY
... SEE...
I DID THINK ABOUT YOU IN THE MIDDLE OF K-FIGHT, THOUGH.
STOMP
HUH?
YOU'RE THE ONE WHO HELPED ME PULL THROUGH.
THANKS.
WHAT?
HUH?
RYOKOOOOOOO!!
SLAM

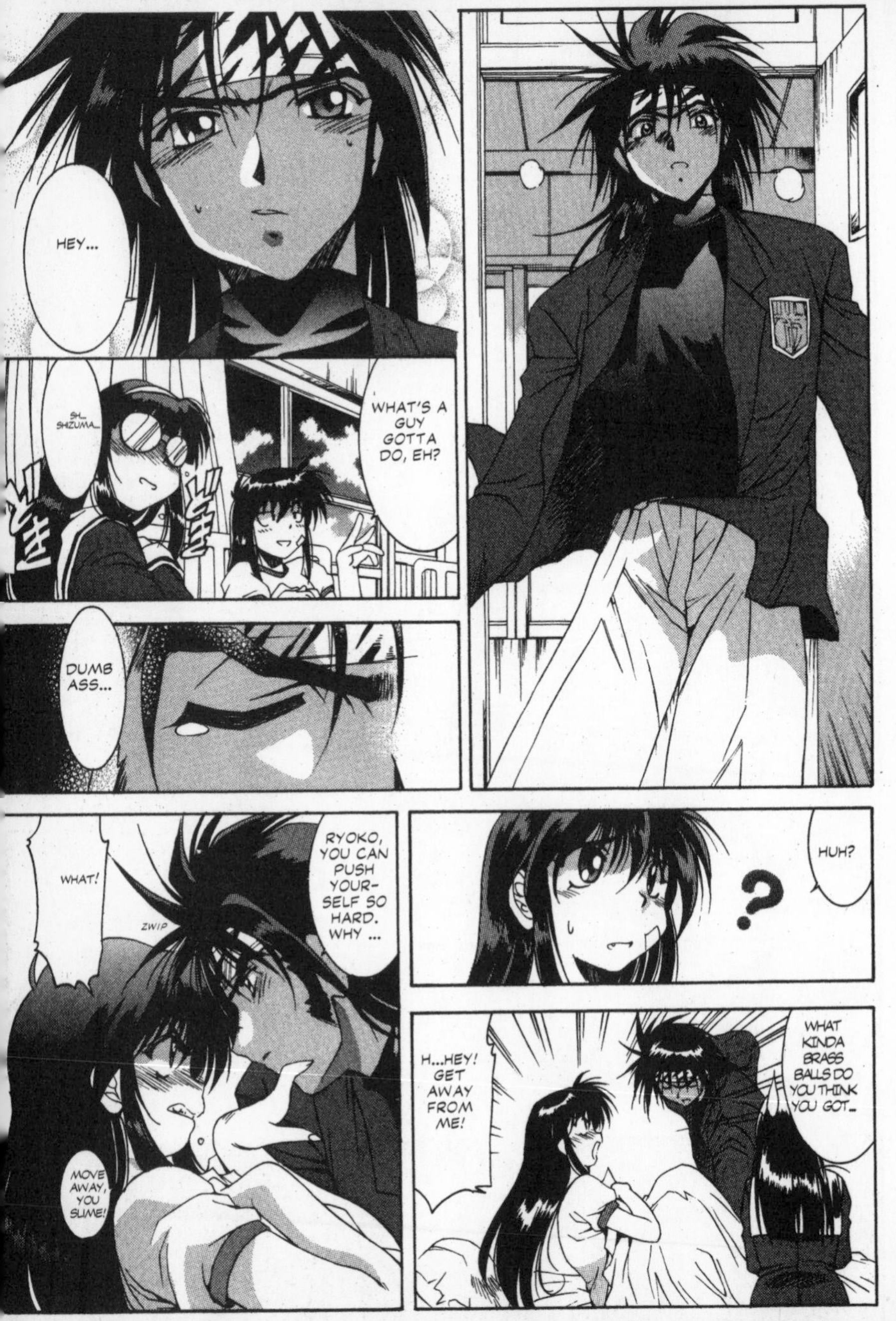
HEY...
WHAT'S A GUY GOTTA DO, EH?
SH.. SHIZUMA...
DUMB ASS...
HUH?
WHAT KINDA BRASS BALLS DO YOU THINK YOU GOT...
H...HEY! GET AWAY FROM ME!
RYOKO, YOU CAN PUSH YOUR-SELF SO HARD. WHY ...
WHAT!
ZWIP
MOVE AWAY, YOU SLIME!

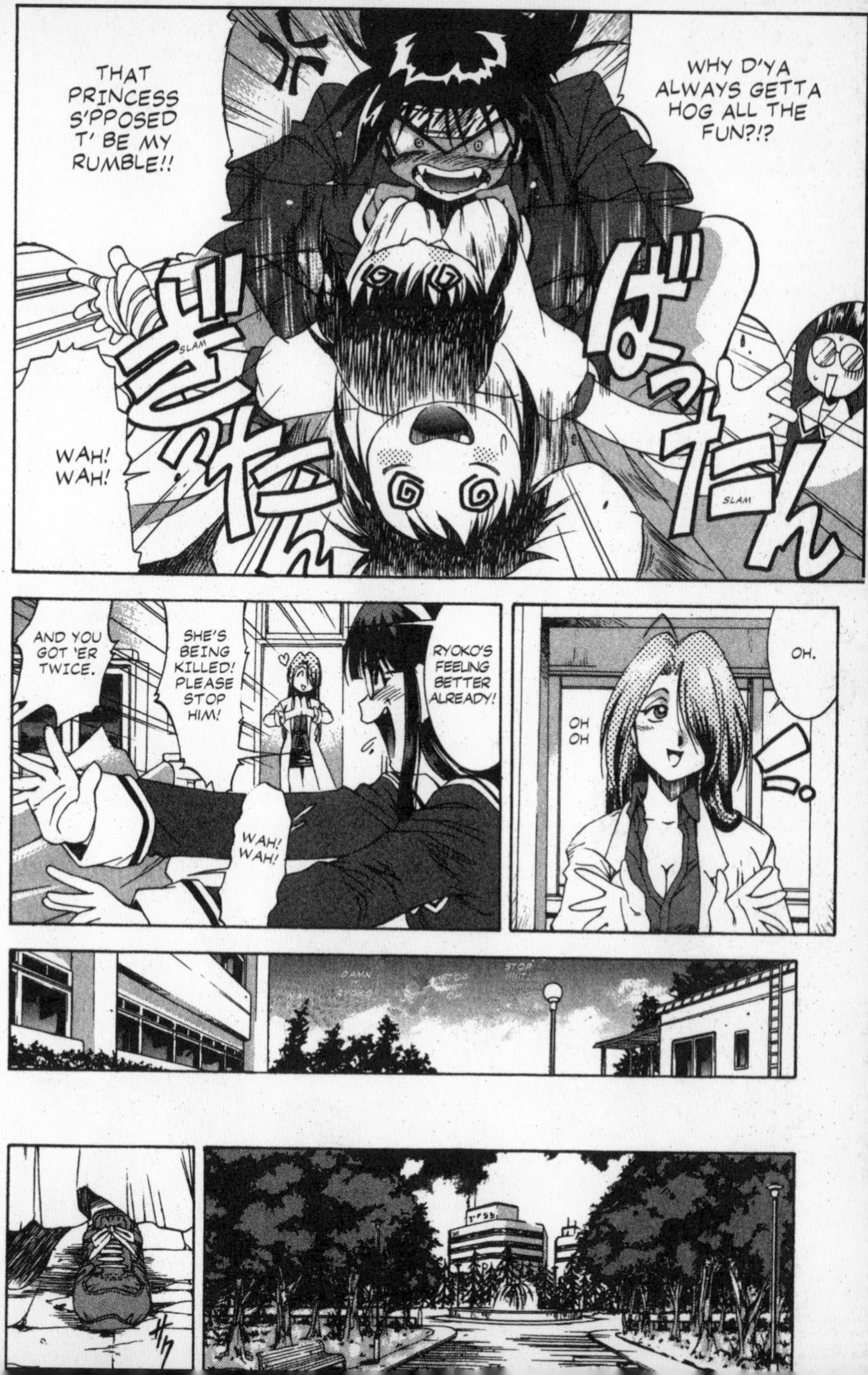
WHY D'YA ALWAYS GETTA HOG ALL THE FUN?!?
THAT PRINCESS S'PPOSED T' BE MY RUMBLE!!
SLAM
SLAM
WAH! WAH!
OH.
OH OH
RYOKO'S FEELING BETTER ALREADY!
SHE'S BEING KILLED! PLEASE STOP HIM!
AND YOU GOT 'ER TWICE.
WAH! WAH!
STOP
DAMN

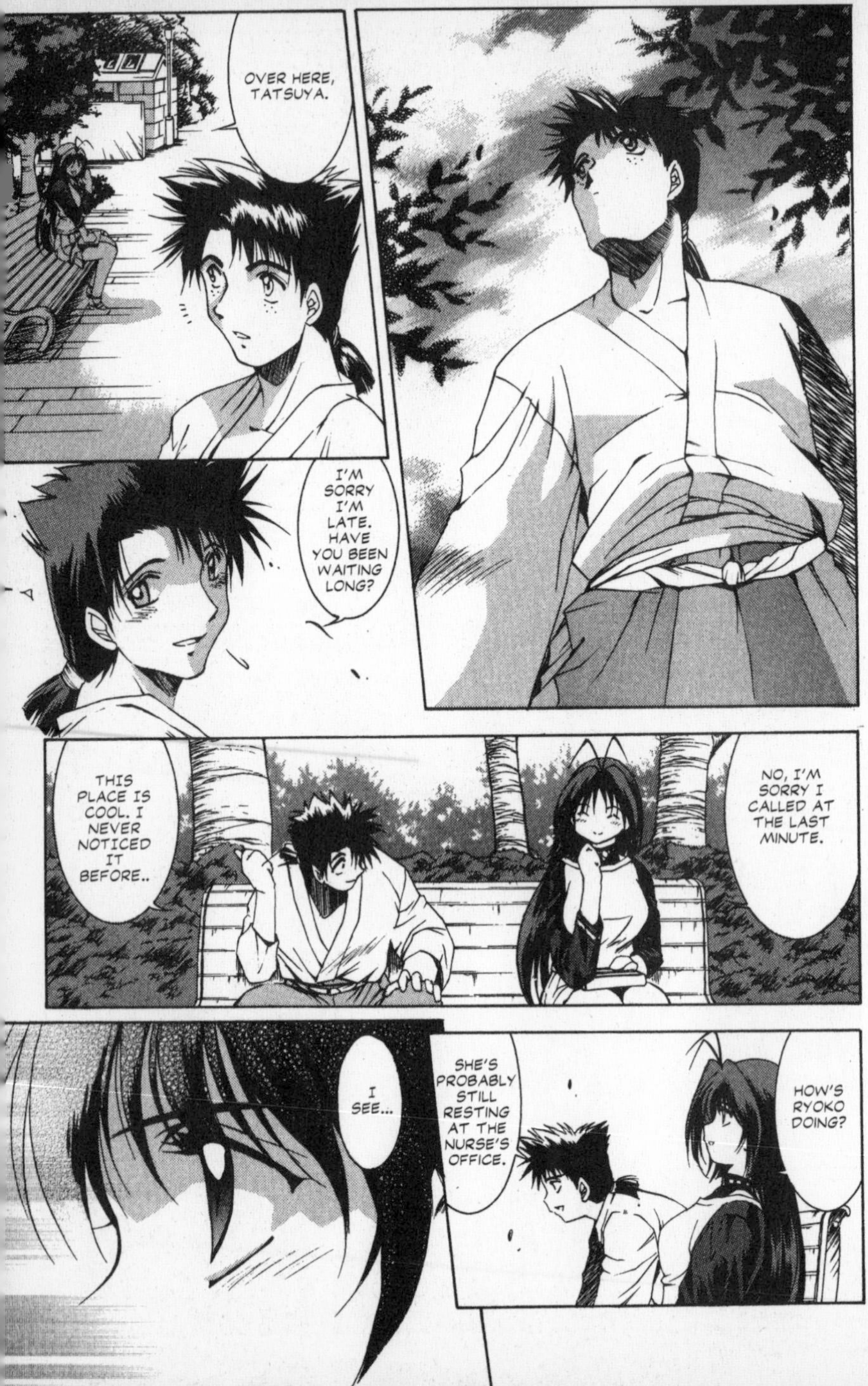
OVER HERE, TATSUYA.
I'M SORRY I'M LATE. HAVE YOU BEEN WAITING LONG?
NO, I'M SORRY I CALLED AT THE LAST MINUTE.
THIS PLACE IS COOL. I NEVER NOTICED IT BEFORE..
HOW'S RYOKO DOING?
SHE'S PROBABLY STILL RESTING AT THE NURSE'S OFFICE.
I SEE...

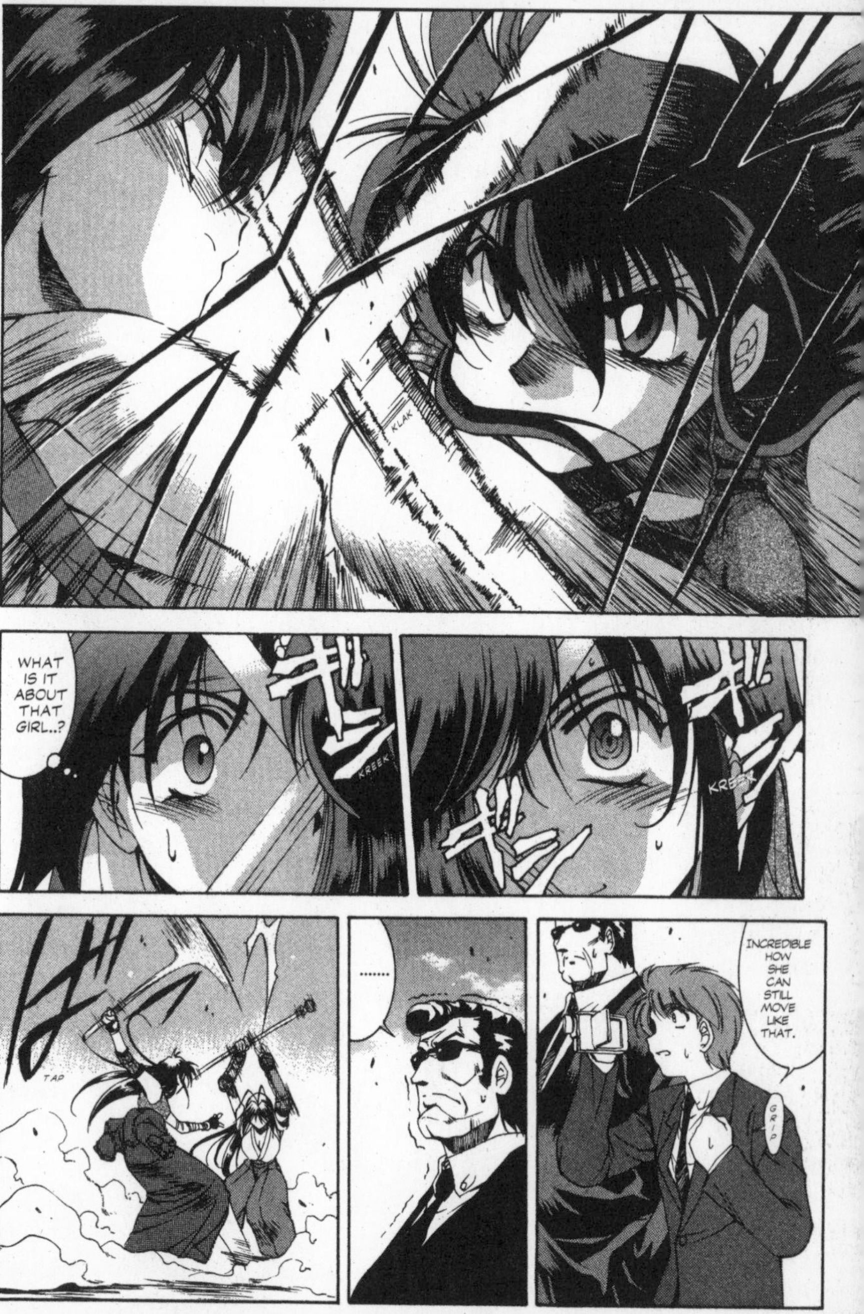
KLAK
KREEK
WHAT IS IT ABOUT THAT GIRL..?
KREEK
INCREDIBLE HOW SHE CAN STILL MOVE LIKE THAT.
GRIP
....
TAP

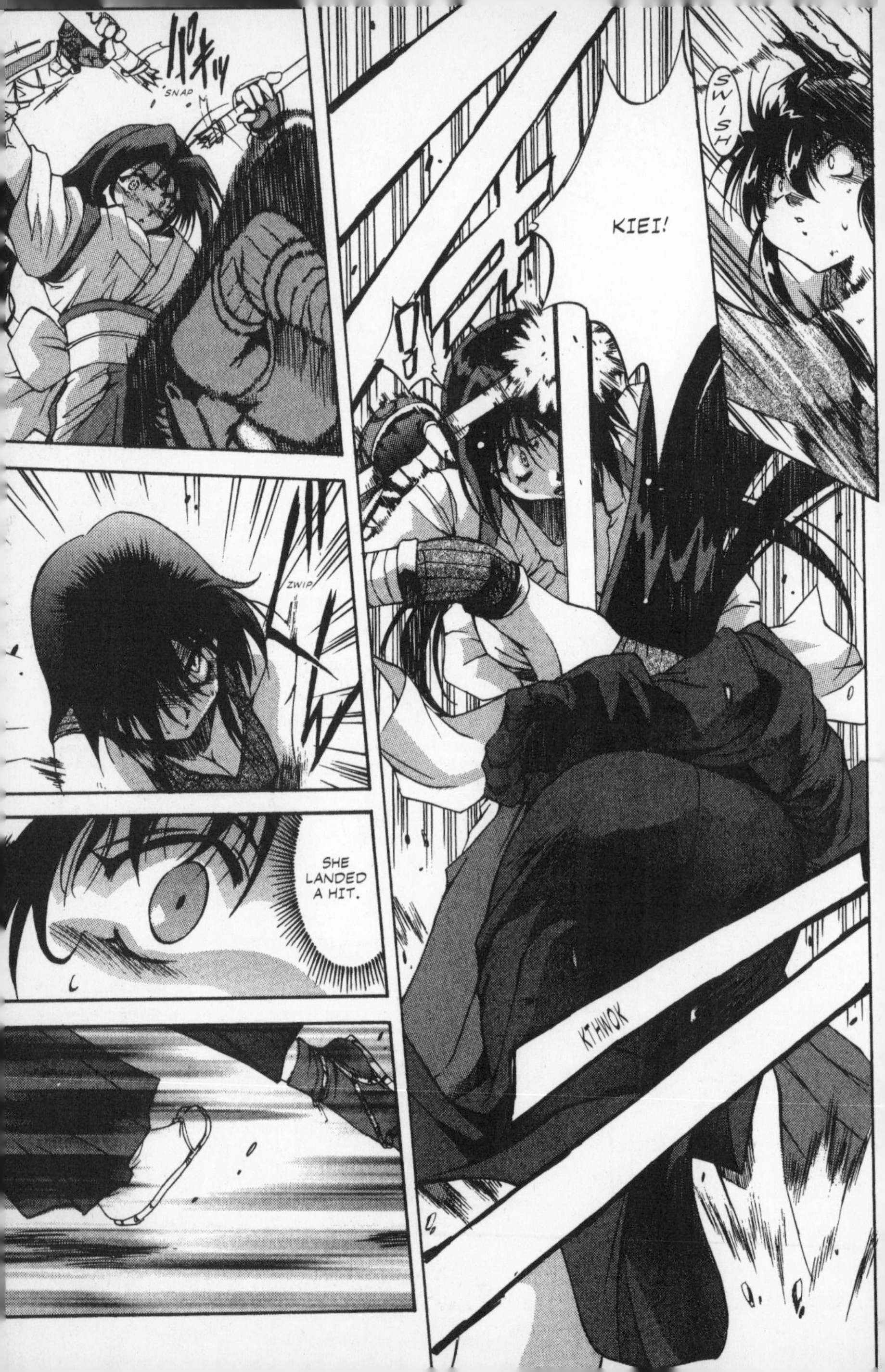
SWISH
KIEI!
KTHWOK
SNAP
ZWIP
SHE LANDED A HIT.

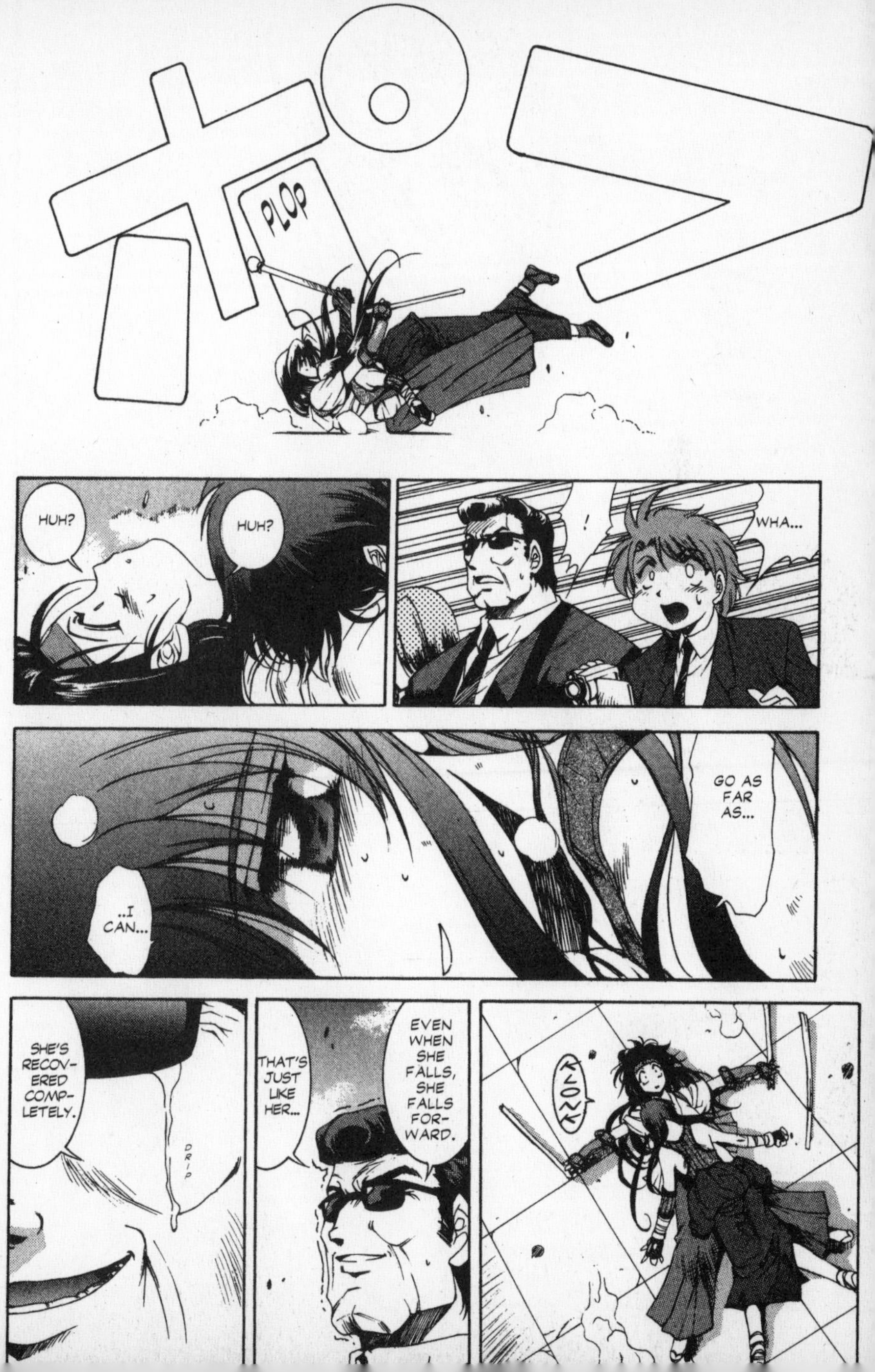
PLOP
!
WHA...
HUH?
HUH?
GO AS FAR AS...
..I CAN...
KLONK
EVEN WHEN SHE FALLS, SHE FALLS FOR-WARD.
THAT'S JUST LIKE HER...
SHE'S RECOV-ERED COMP-LETELY.
DRIP

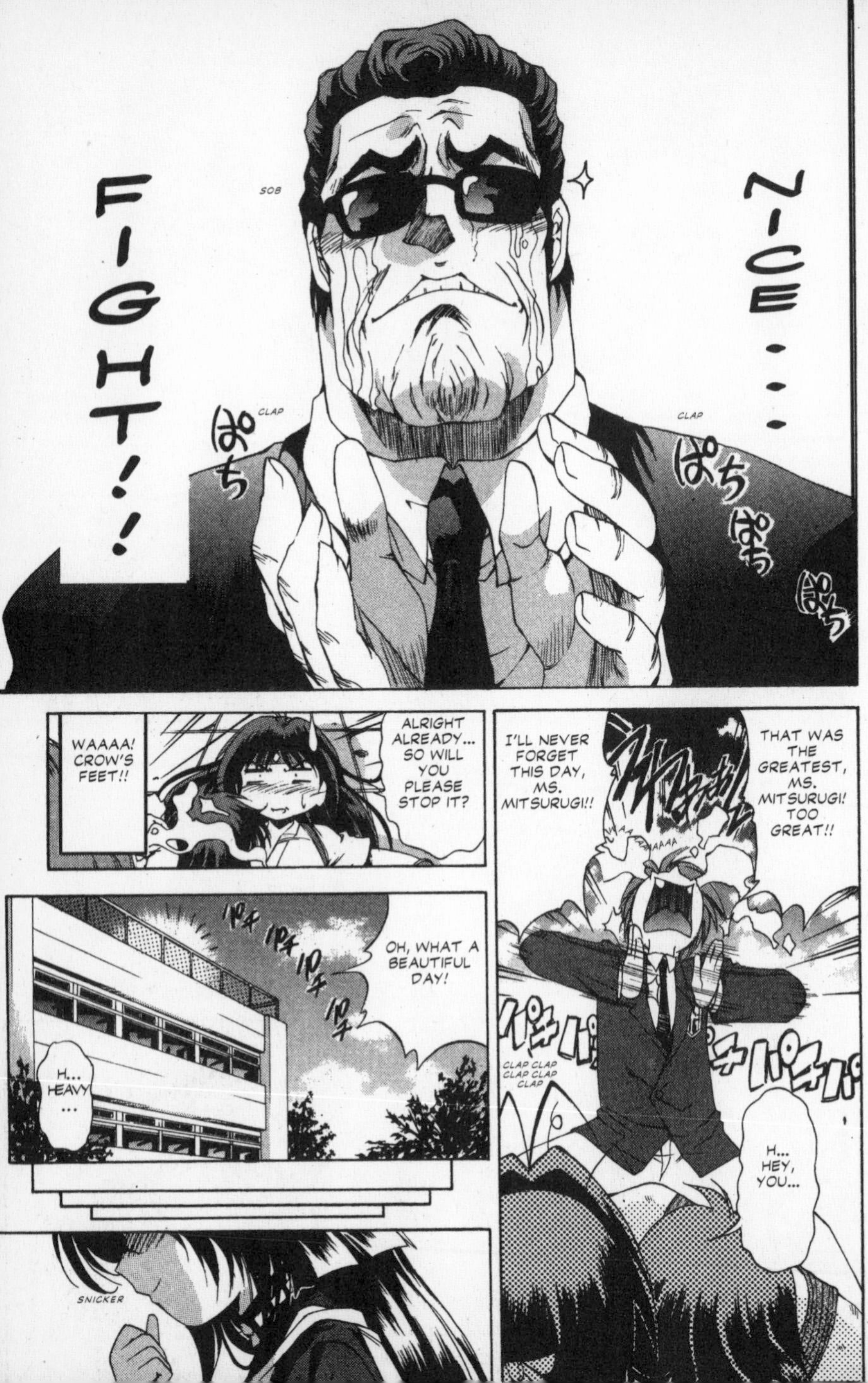
NICE...
CLAP
ぱちぱちぱち
SOB
FIGHT!!
CLAP
ぱち
THAT WAS THE GREATEST, MS. MITSURUGI! TOO GREAT!!
I'LL NEVER FORGET THIS DAY, MS. MITSURUGI!!
AAAA
パチパチパチパ
CLAP CLAP CLAP CLAP CLAP
ALRIGHT ALREADY... SO WILL YOU PLEASE STOP IT?
WAAAA! CROW'S FEET!!
パチパチパチパチ
OH, WHAT A BEAUTIFUL DAY!
H... HEAVY ...
H... HEY, YOU...
SNICKER

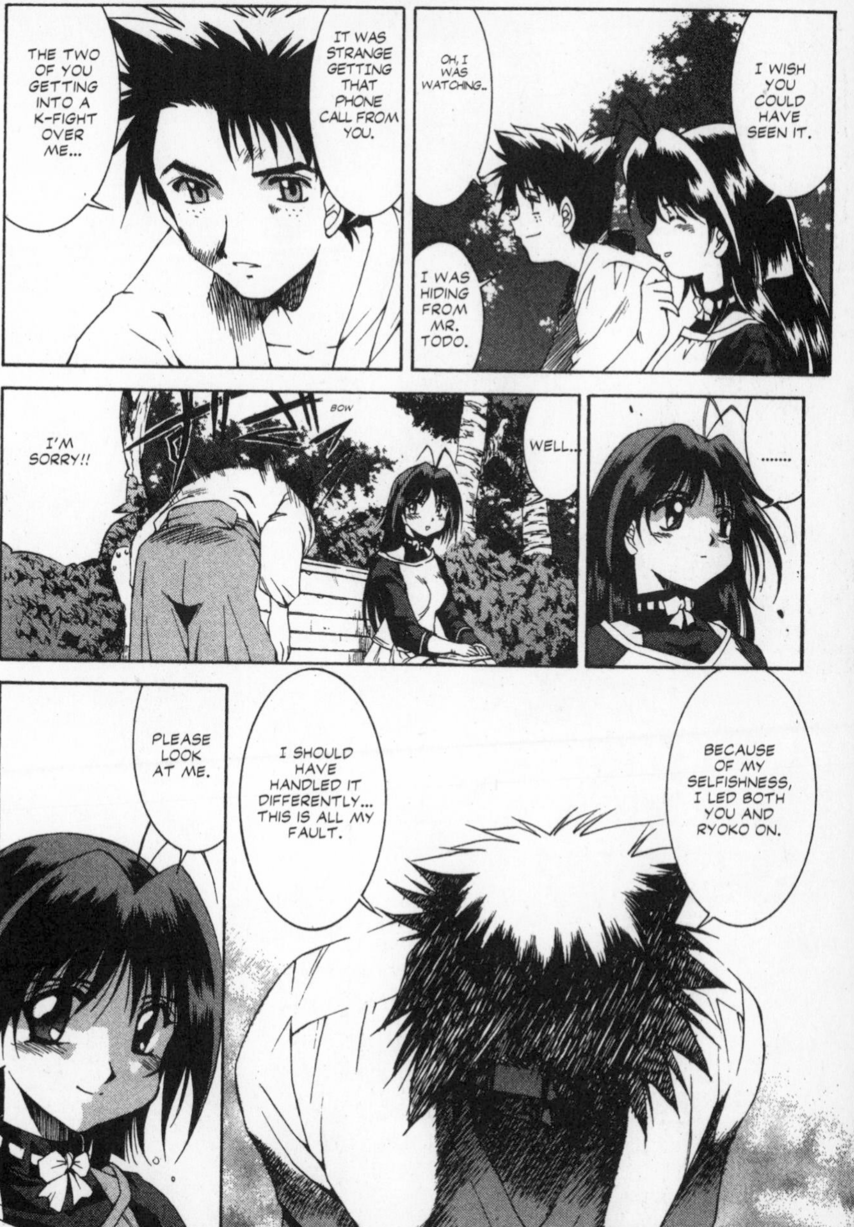
I WISH YOU COULD HAVE SEEN IT.
OH, I WAS WATCHING..
I WAS HIDING FROM MR. TODO.
IT WAS STRANGE GETTING THAT PHONE CALL FROM YOU.
THE TWO OF YOU GETTING INTO A K-FIGHT OVER ME...
....
WELL...
BOW
I'M SORRY!!
BECAUSE OF MY SELFISHNESS, I LED BOTH YOU AND RYOKO ON.
I SHOULD HAVE HANDLED IT DIFFERENTLY... THIS IS ALL MY FAULT.
PLEASE LOOK AT ME.

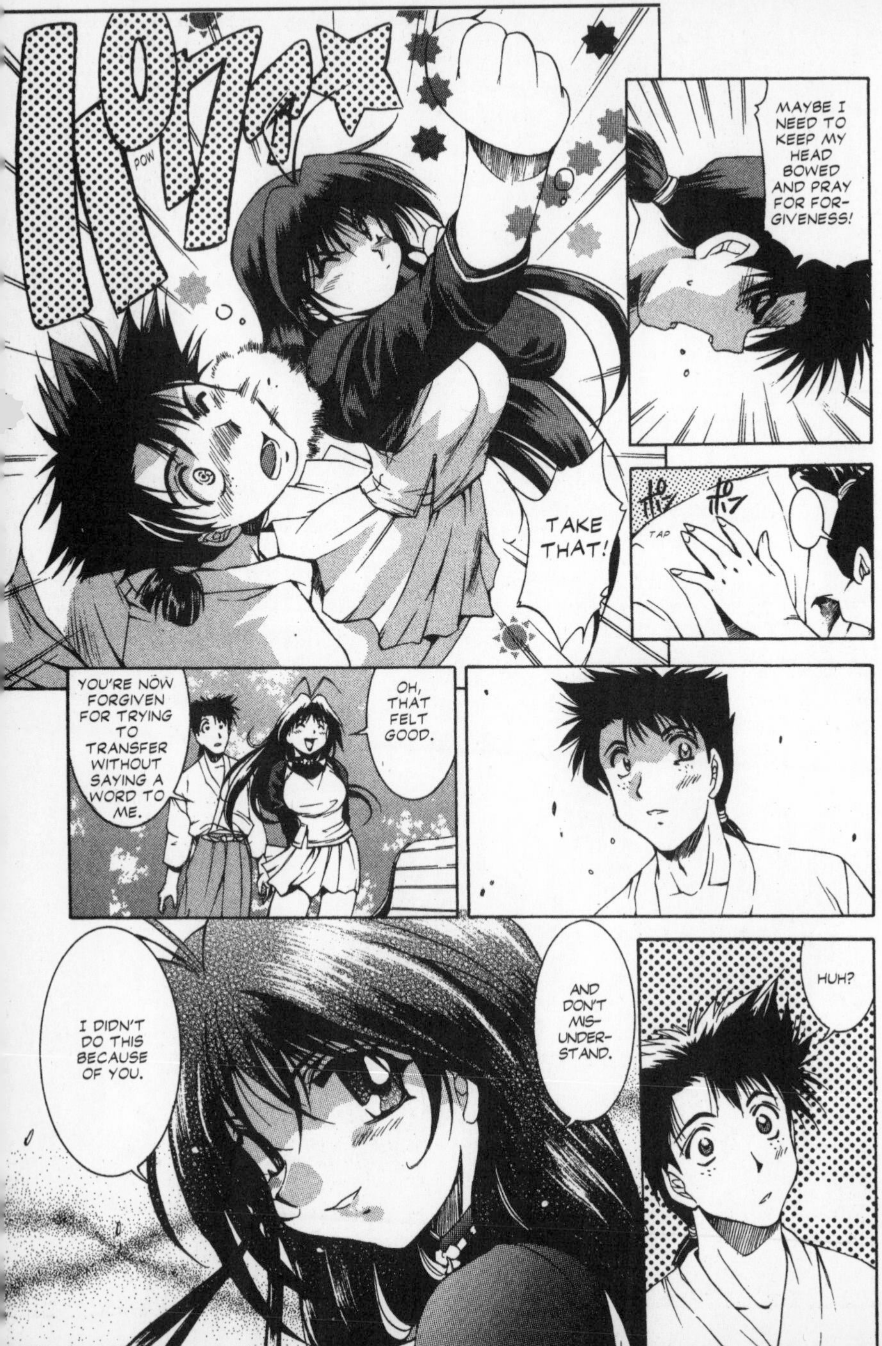
MAYBE I NEED TO KEEP MY HEAD BOWED AND PRAY FOR FOR-GIVENESS!
TAP
POW
TAKE THAT!
OH, THAT FELT GOOD.
YOU'RE NOW FORGIVEN FOR TRYING TO TRANSFER WITHOUT SAYING A WORD TO ME.
HUH?
AND DON'T MIS-UNDER-STAND.
I DIDN'T DO THIS BECAUSE OF YOU.

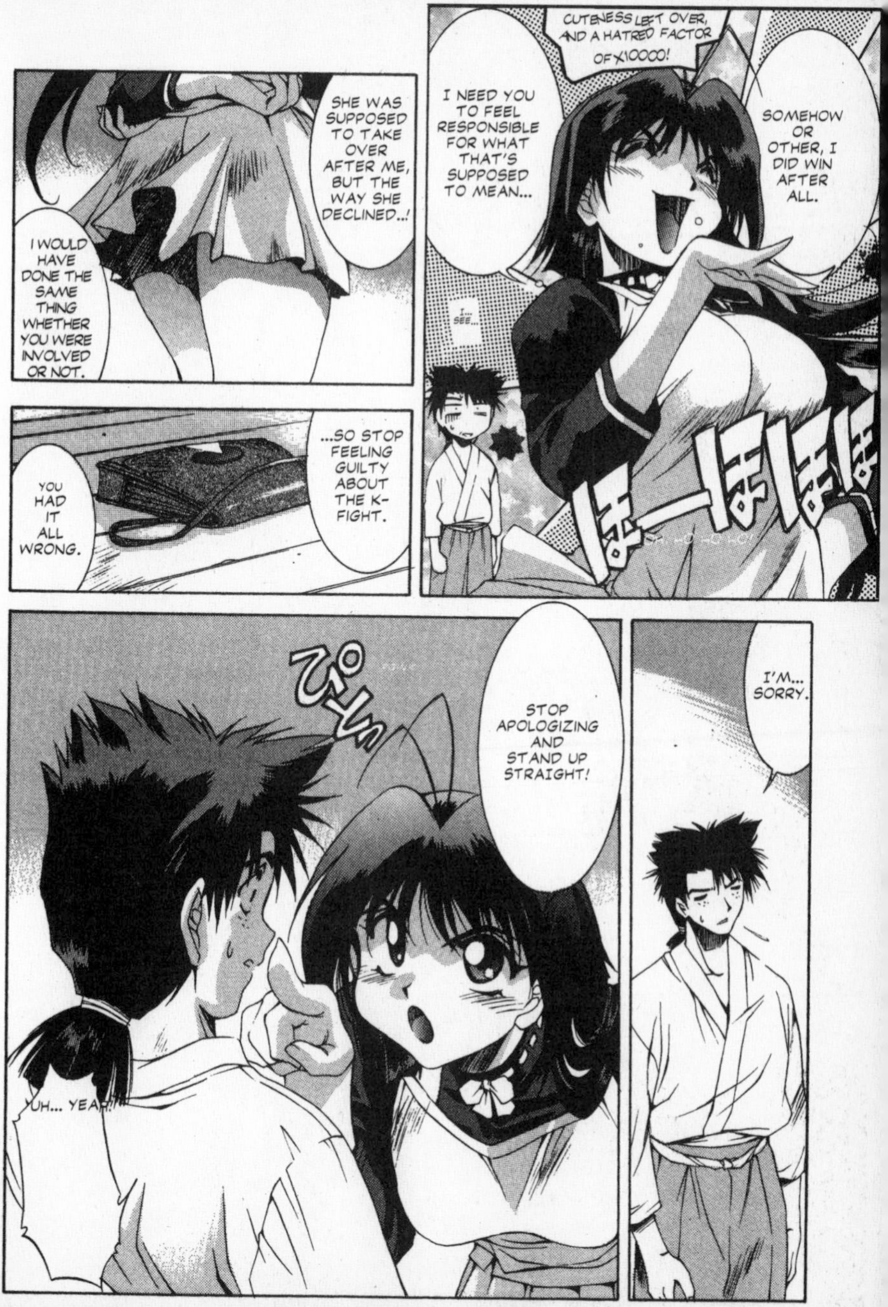
SOMEHOW OR OTHER, I DID WIN AFTER ALL.
CUTENESS LEFT OVER, AND A HATRED FACTOR OF X10000!
I NEED YOU TO FEEL RESPONSIBLE FOR WHAT THAT'S SUPPOSED TO MEAN...
I... SEE...
ほーほほほ
OH HO HO HO!
SHE WAS SUPPOSED TO TAKE OVER AFTER ME, BUT THE WAY SHE DECLINED..!
I WOULD HAVE DONE THE SAME THING WHETHER YOU WERE INVOLVED OR NOT.
...SO STOP FEELING GUILTY ABOUT THE K-FIGHT.
YOU HAD IT ALL WRONG.
I'M... SORRY.
STOP APOLOGIZING AND STAND UP STRAIGHT!
ぴょん
UH... YEAH.

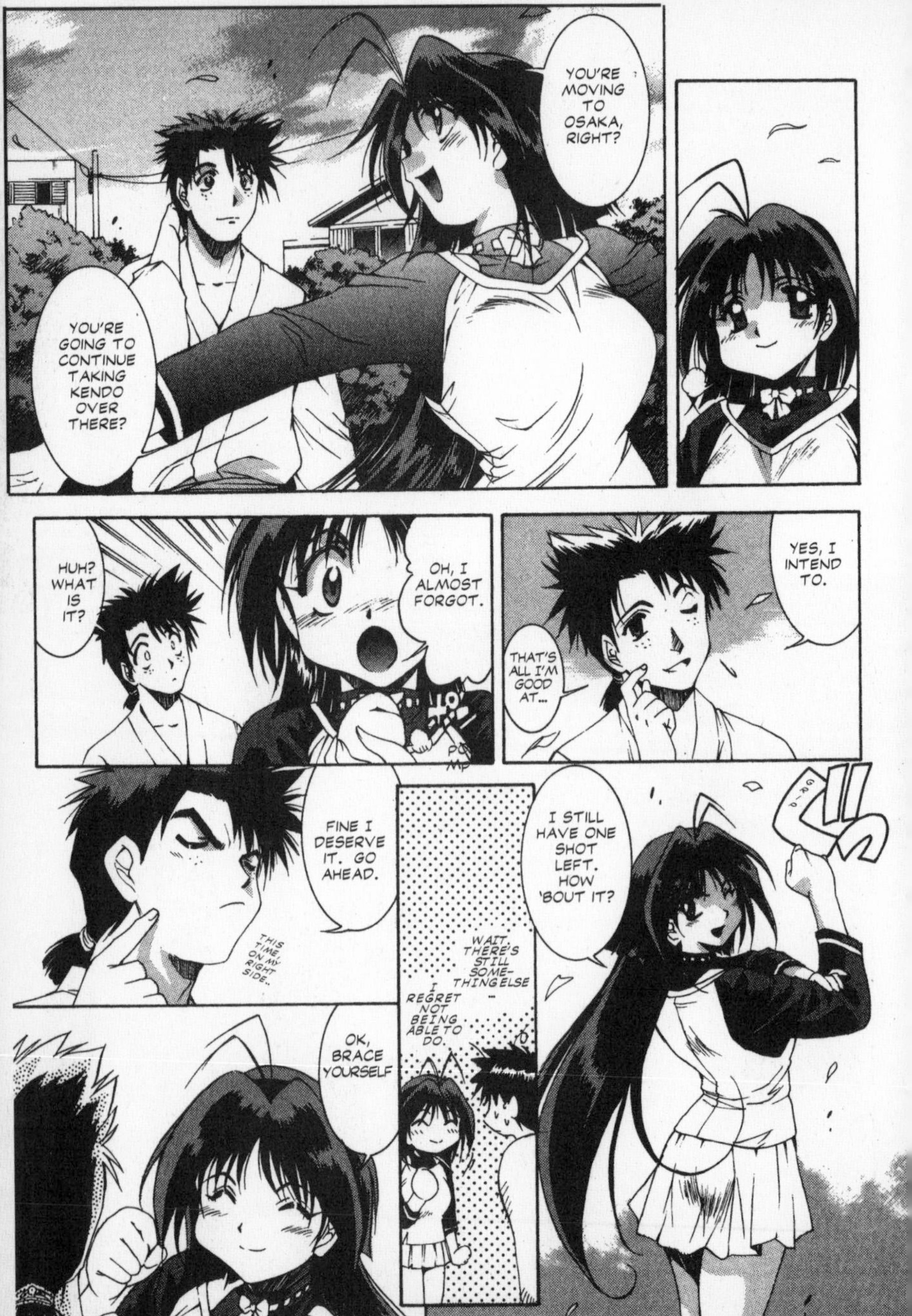
YOU'RE MOVING TO OSAKA, RIGHT?
YOU'RE GOING TO CONTINUE TAKING KENDO OVER THERE?
YES, I INTEND TO.
THAT'S ALL I'M GOOD AT...
OH, I ALMOST FORGOT.
HUH? WHAT IS IT?
POMP
GRIP
I STILL HAVE ONE SHOT LEFT. HOW 'BOUT IT?
WAIT. THERE'S STILL SOMETHING ELSE ...
I REGRET NOT BEING ABLE TO DO.
FINE I DESERVE IT. GO AHEAD.
THIS TIME, ON MY RIGHT SIDE..
OK, BRACE YOURSELF

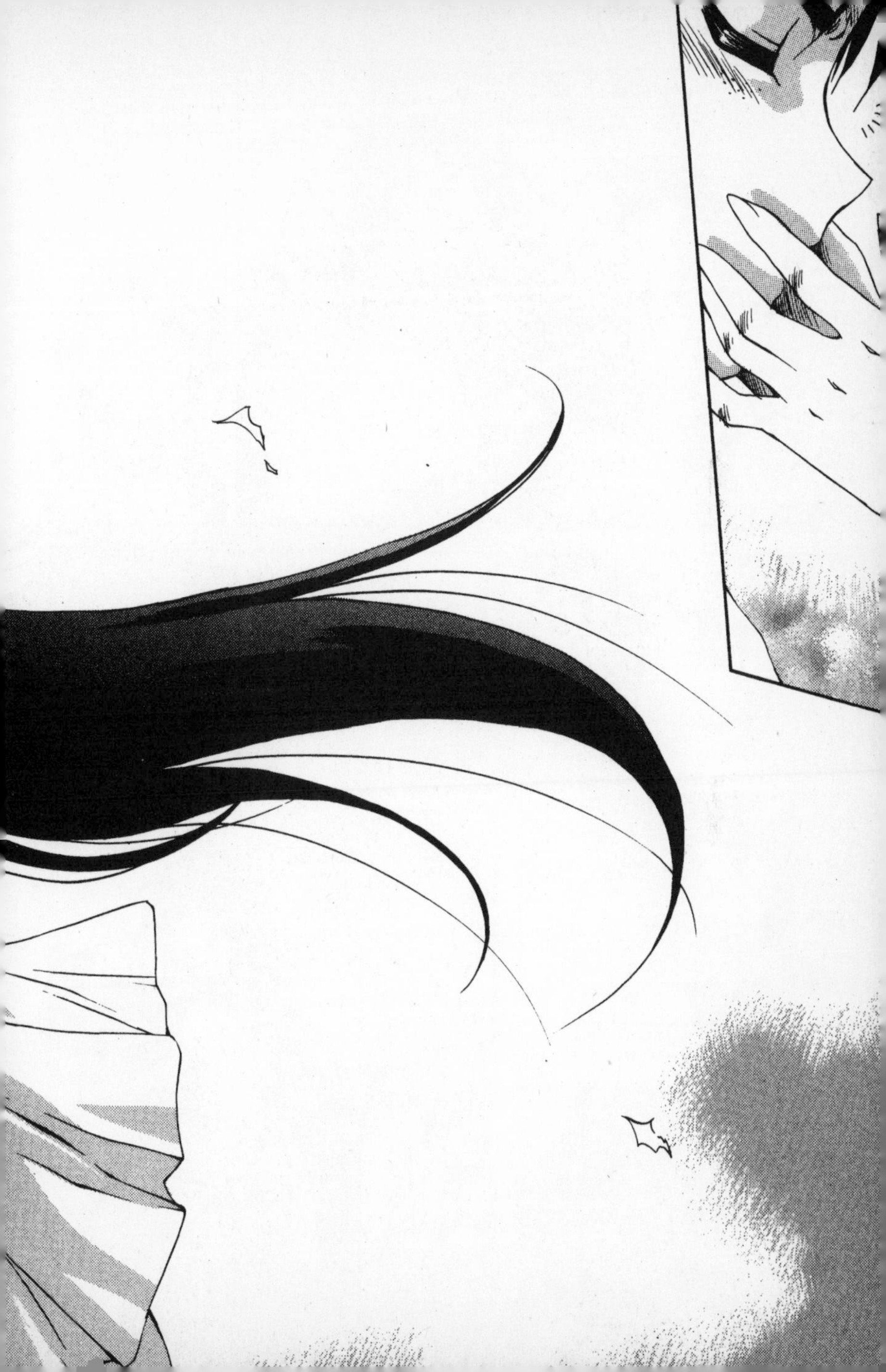

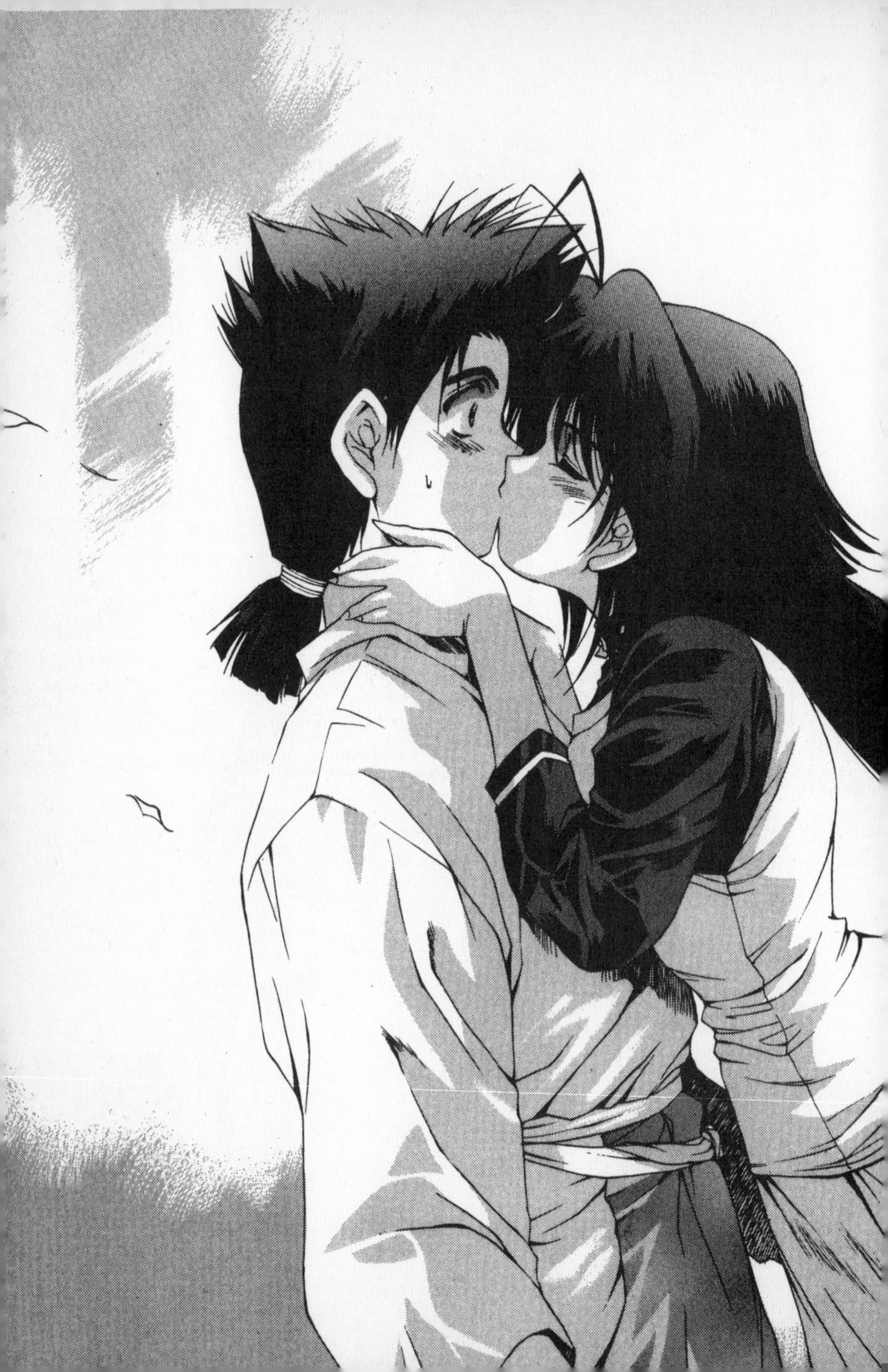

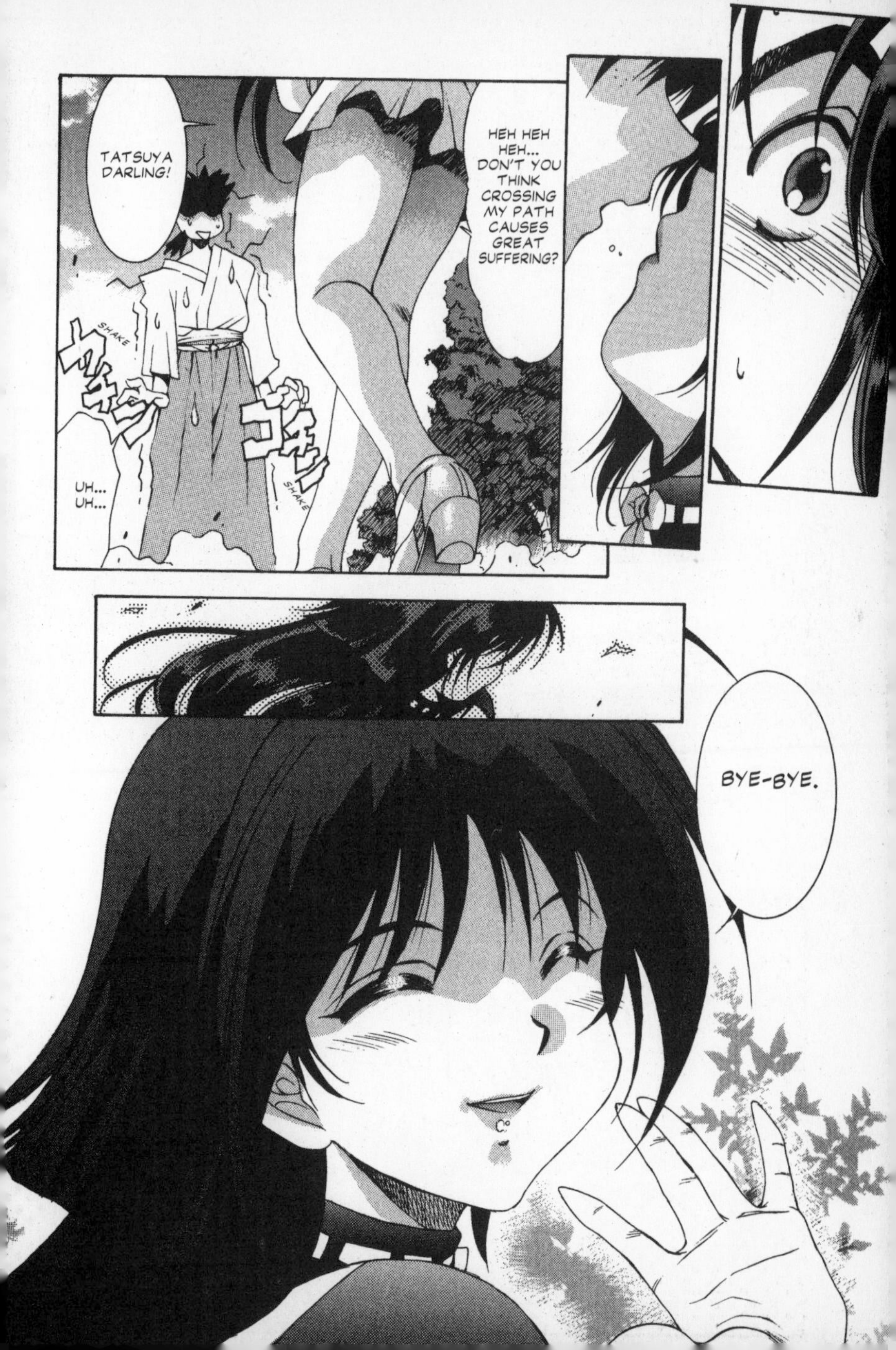
HEH HEH HEH... DON'T YOU THINK CROSSING MY PATH CAUSES GREAT SUFFERING?
TATSUYA DARLING!
SHAKE
SHAKE
UH... UH...
BYE-BYE.

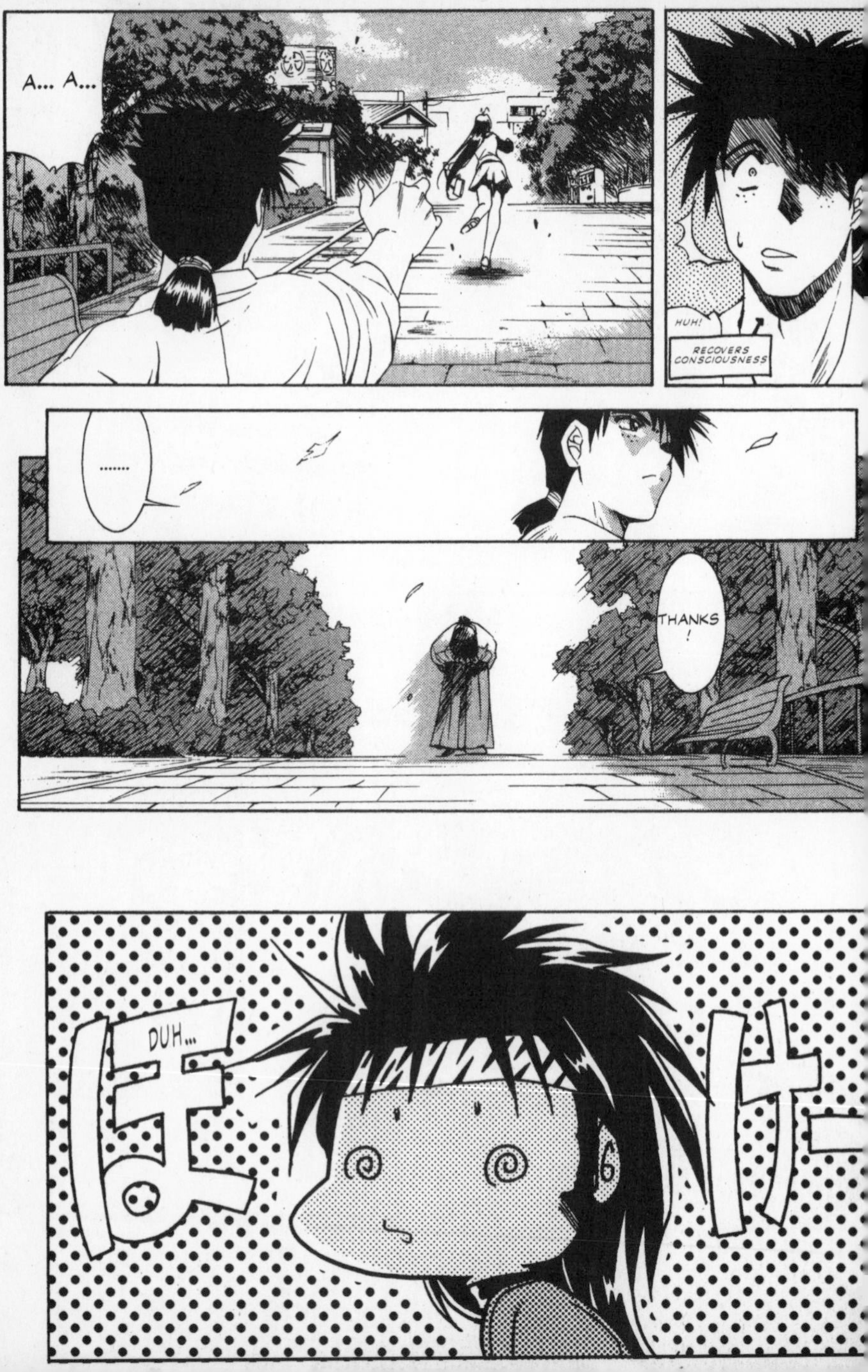
HUH!
RECOVERS CONSCIOUSNESS
A... A...
......
THANKS!
DUH...

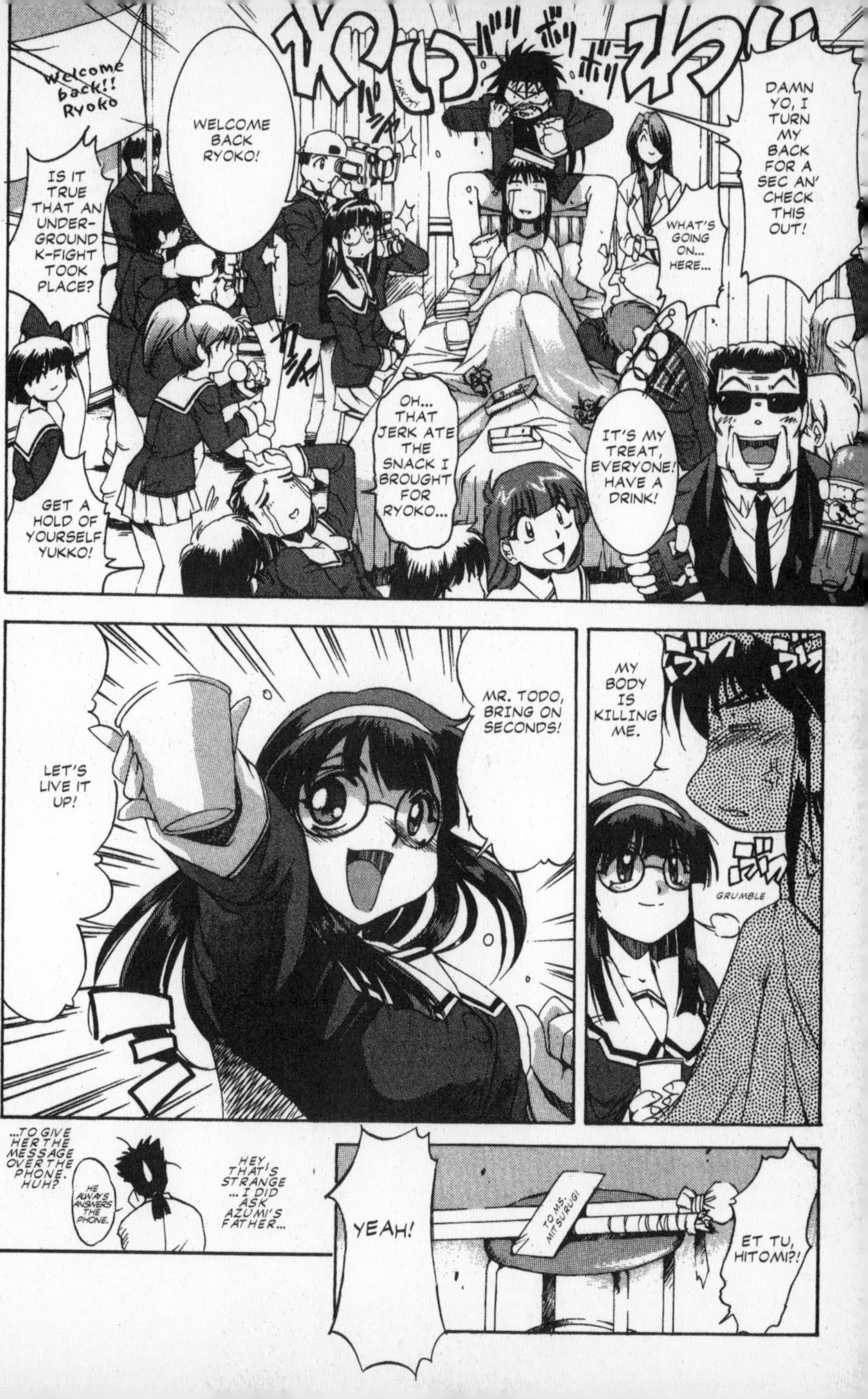
DAMN YO, I TURN MY BACK FOR A SEC AN' CHECK THIS OUT!
WHAT'S GOING ON... HERE...
YAKITY
WELCOME BACK RYOKO!
Welcome back!! Ryoko
IS IT TRUE THAT AN UNDERGROUND K-FIGHT TOOK PLACE?
IT'S MY TREAT, EVERYONE! HAVE A DRINK!
OH... THAT JERK ATE THE SNACK I BROUGHT FOR RYOKO...
GET A HOLD OF YOURSELF YUKKO!
MY BODY IS KILLING ME.
GRUMBLE
MR. TODO, BRING ON SECONDS!
LET'S LIVE IT UP!
ET TU, HITOMI?!
TO MS. MITSURUGI
YEAH!
HEY THAT'S STRANGE ...I DID ASK AZUMI'S FATHER...
HE ALWAYS ANSWERS THE PHONE.
...TO GIVE HER THE MESSAGE OVER THE PHONE. HUH?

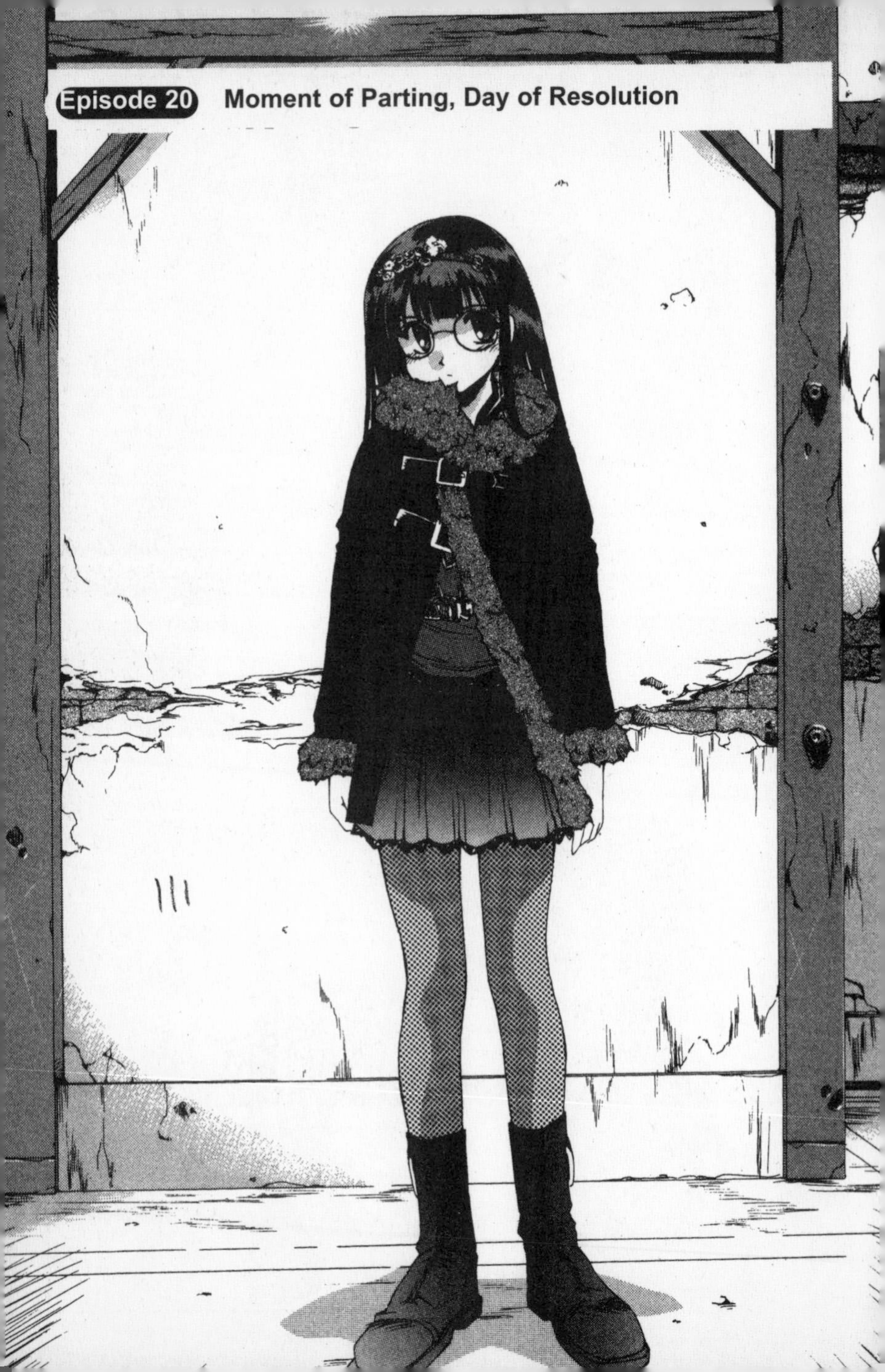
Episode 20 Moment of Parting, Day of Resolution

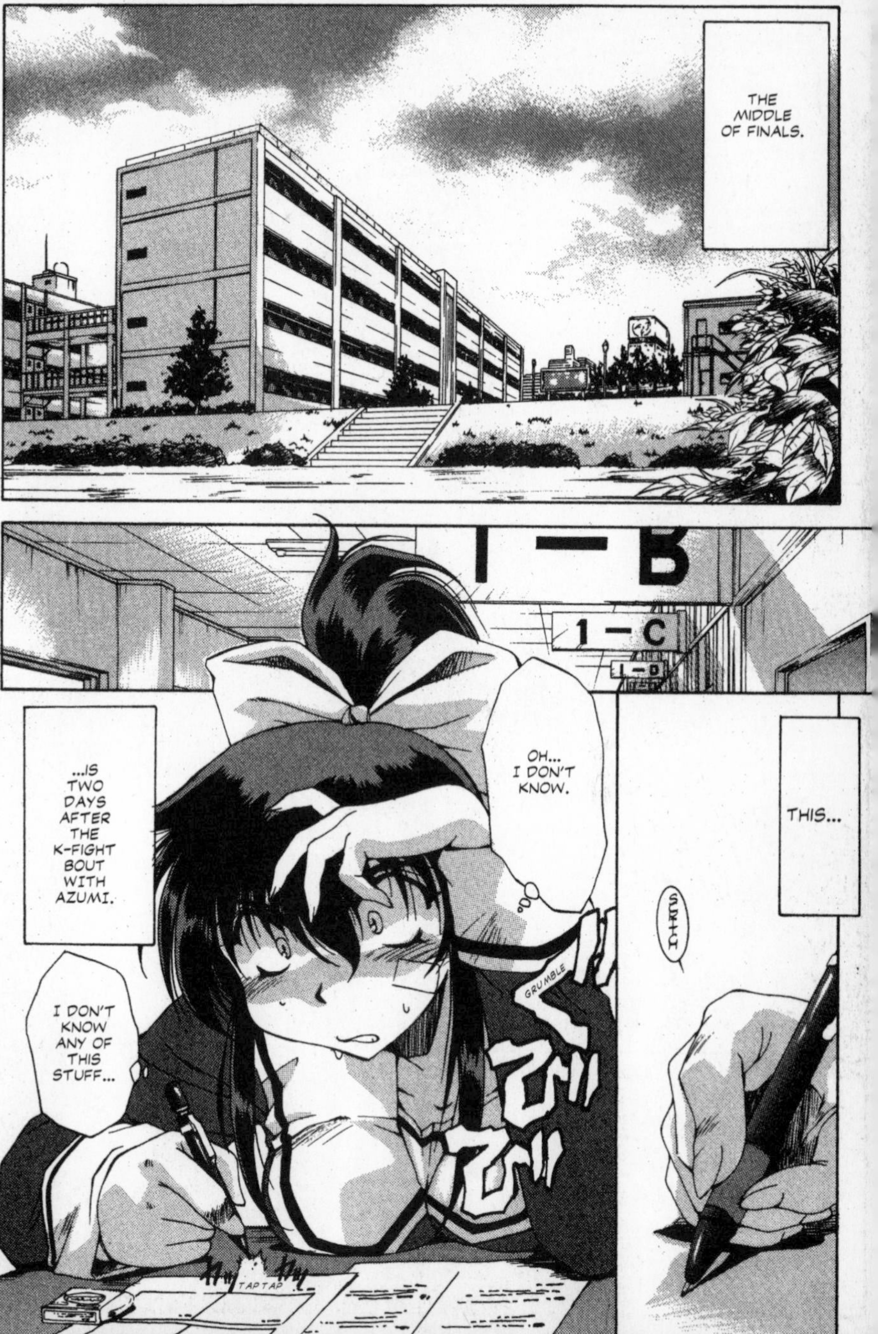
THE MIDDLE OF FINALS.
1-B
1-C
1-D
THIS...
OH... I DON'T KNOW.
...IS TWO DAYS AFTER THE K-FIGHT BOUT WITH AZUMI.
GRUMBLE
I DON'T KNOW ANY OF THIS STUFF...
TAPTAP

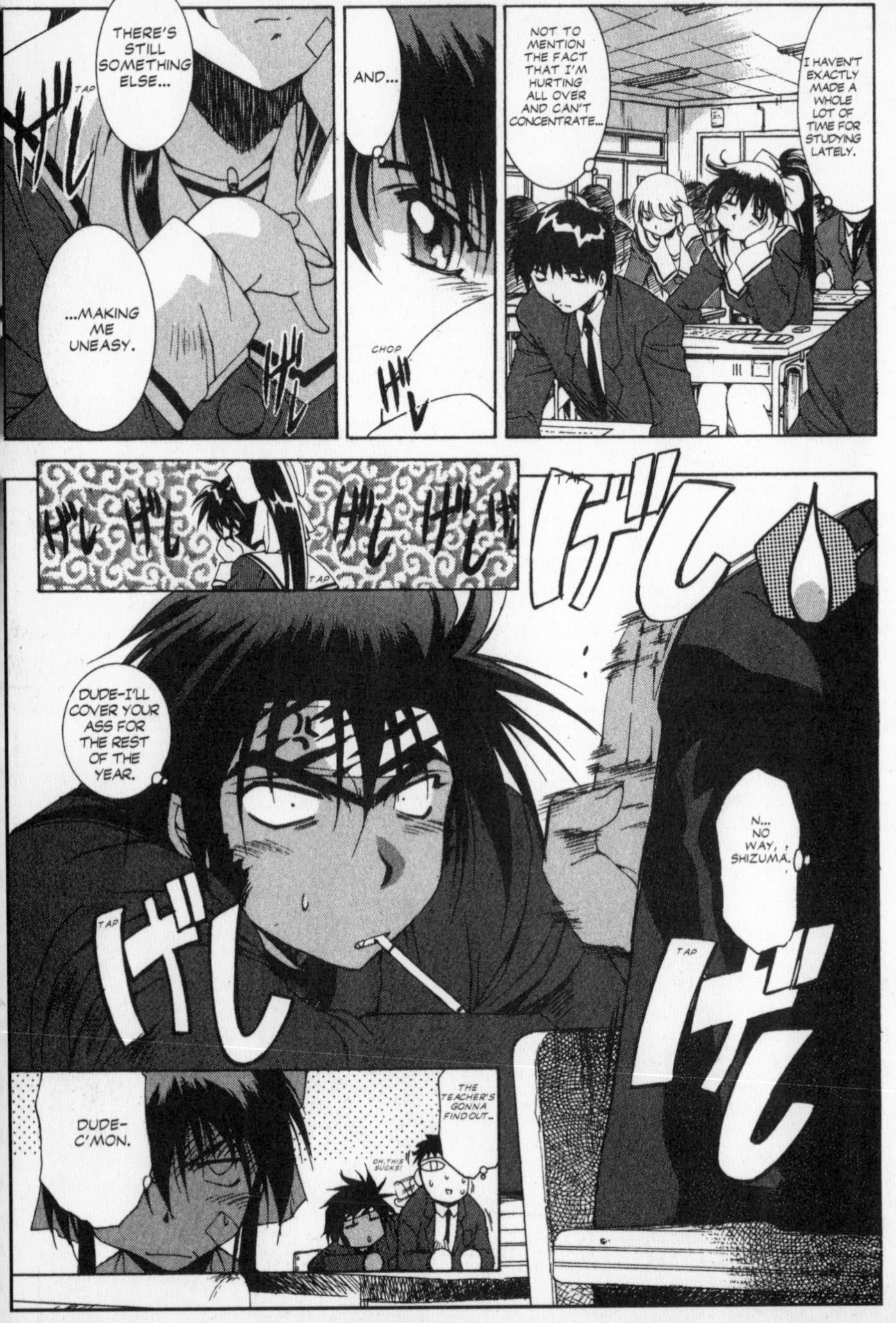
I HAVEN'T EXACTLY MADE A WHOLE LOT OF TIME FOR STUDYING LATELY.
NOT TO MENTION THE FACT THAT I'M HURTING ALL OVER AND CAN'T CONCENTRATE...
AND...
CHOP
THERE'S STILL SOMETHING ELSE...
TAP
...MAKING ME UNEASY.
TAP
N... NO WAY, SHIZUMA.
DUDE-I'LL COVER YOUR ASS FOR THE REST OF THE YEAR.
TAP
TAP
TAP
THE TEACHER'S GONNA FIND OUT...
OH, THIS SUCKS!
DUDE- C'MON.

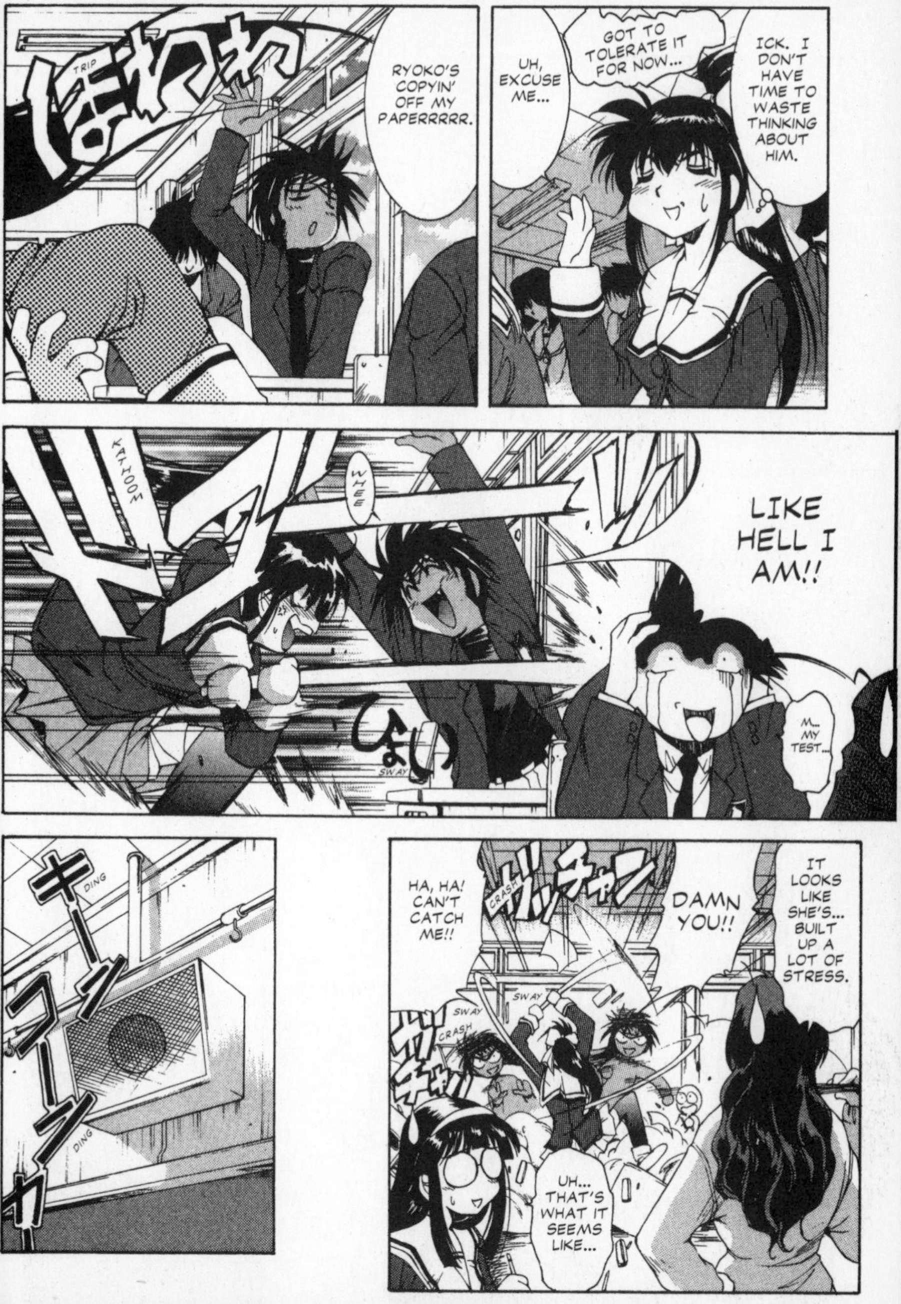
ICK. I DON'T HAVE TIME TO WASTE THINKING ABOUT HIM.
GOT TO TOLERATE IT FOR NOW...
UH, EXCUSE ME...
RYOKO'S COPYIN' OFF MY PAPERRRRR.
TRIP
LIKE HELL I AM!!
WHEE
KATHOOM
M... MY TEST...
SWAY
IT LOOKS LIKE SHE'S... BUILT UP A LOT OF STRESS.
DAMN YOU!!
CRASH
HA, HA! CAN'T CATCH ME!!
SWAY
SWAY
CRASH
UH... THAT'S WHAT IT SEEMS LIKE...
DING
DING

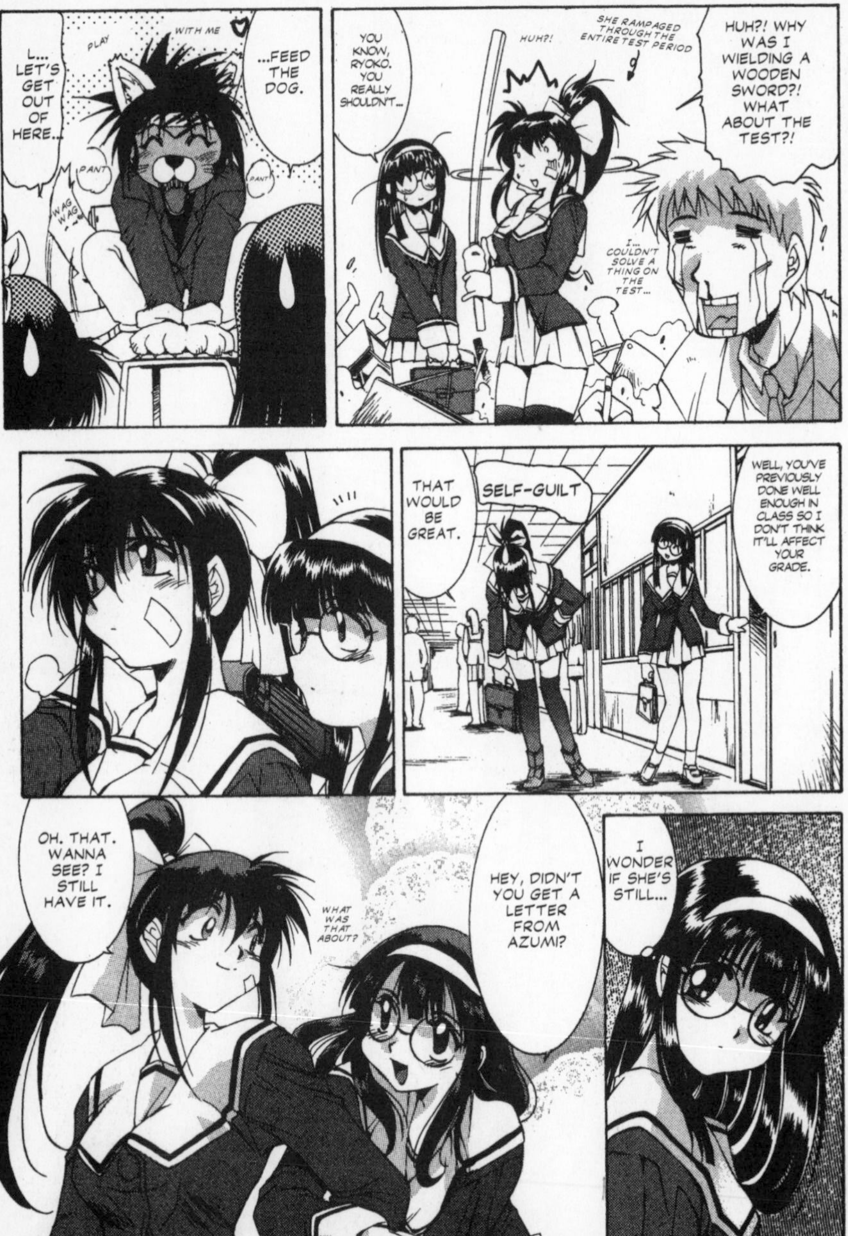
HUH?! WHY WAS I WIELDING A WOODEN SWORD?! WHAT ABOUT THE TEST?!
SHE RAMPAGED THROUGH THE ENTIRE TEST PERIOD
HUH?!
YOU KNOW, RYOKO. YOU REALLY SHOULDN'T...
I... COULDN'T SOLVE A THING ON THE TEST...
...FEED THE DOG.
WITH ME
PLAY
L... LET'S GET OUT OF HERE...
PANT
PANT
WAG WAG
WELL, YOU'VE PREVIOUSLY DONE WELL ENOUGH IN CLASS SO I DON'T THINK IT'LL AFFECT YOUR GRADE.
SELF-GUILT
THAT WOULD BE GREAT.
I WONDER IF SHE'S STILL...
HEY, DIDN'T YOU GET A LETTER FROM AZUMI?
WHAT WAS THAT ABOUT?
OH. THAT. WANNA SEE? I STILL HAVE IT.

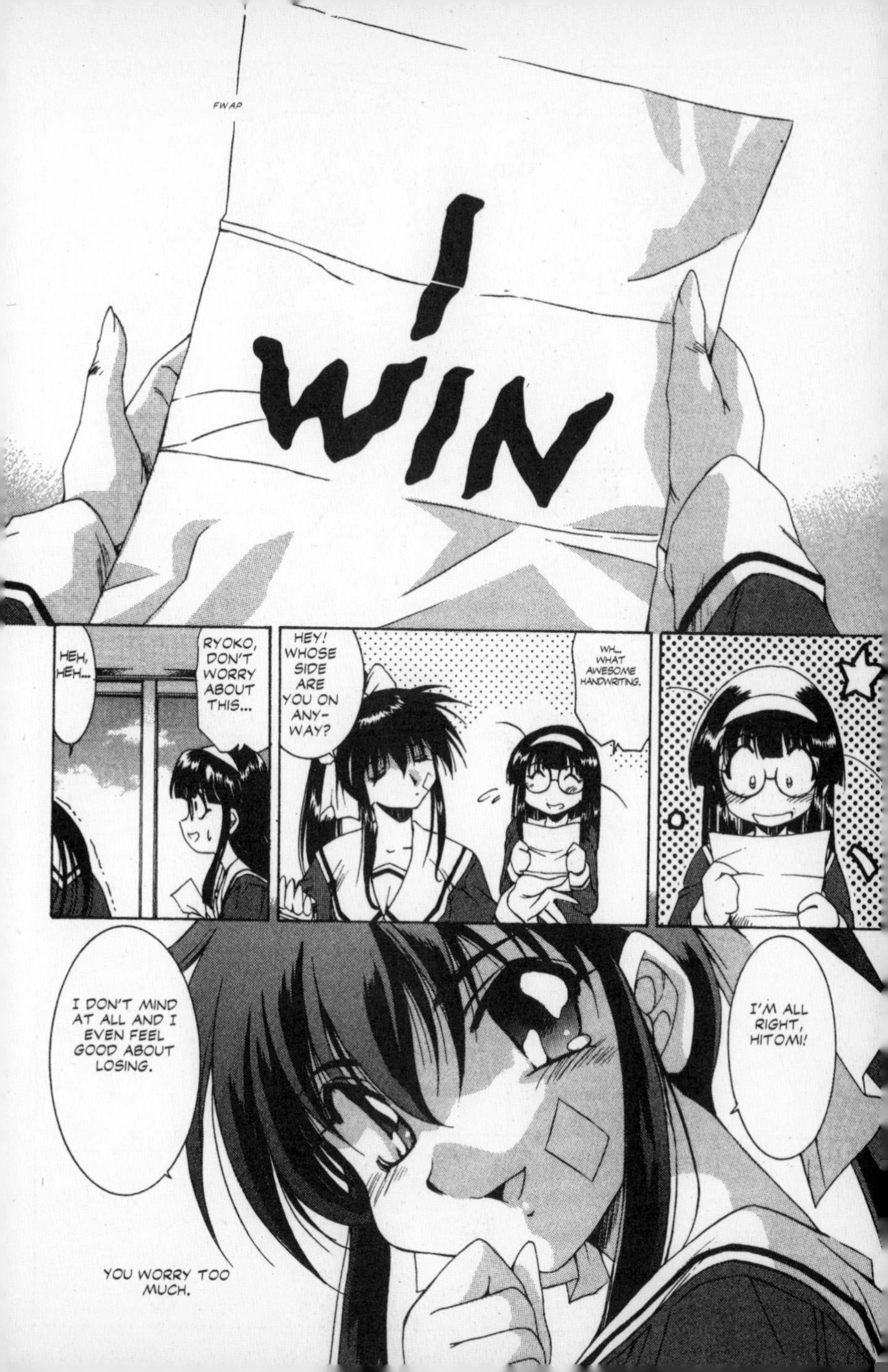
FWAP
I WIN
WH... WHAT AWESOME HANDWRITING.
HEY! WHOSE SIDE ARE YOU ON ANY-WAY?
RYOKO, DON'T WORRY ABOUT THIS...
HEH, HEH...
I'M ALL RIGHT, HITOMI!
I DON'T MIND AT ALL AND I EVEN FEEL GOOD ABOUT LOSING.
YOU WORRY TOO MUCH.

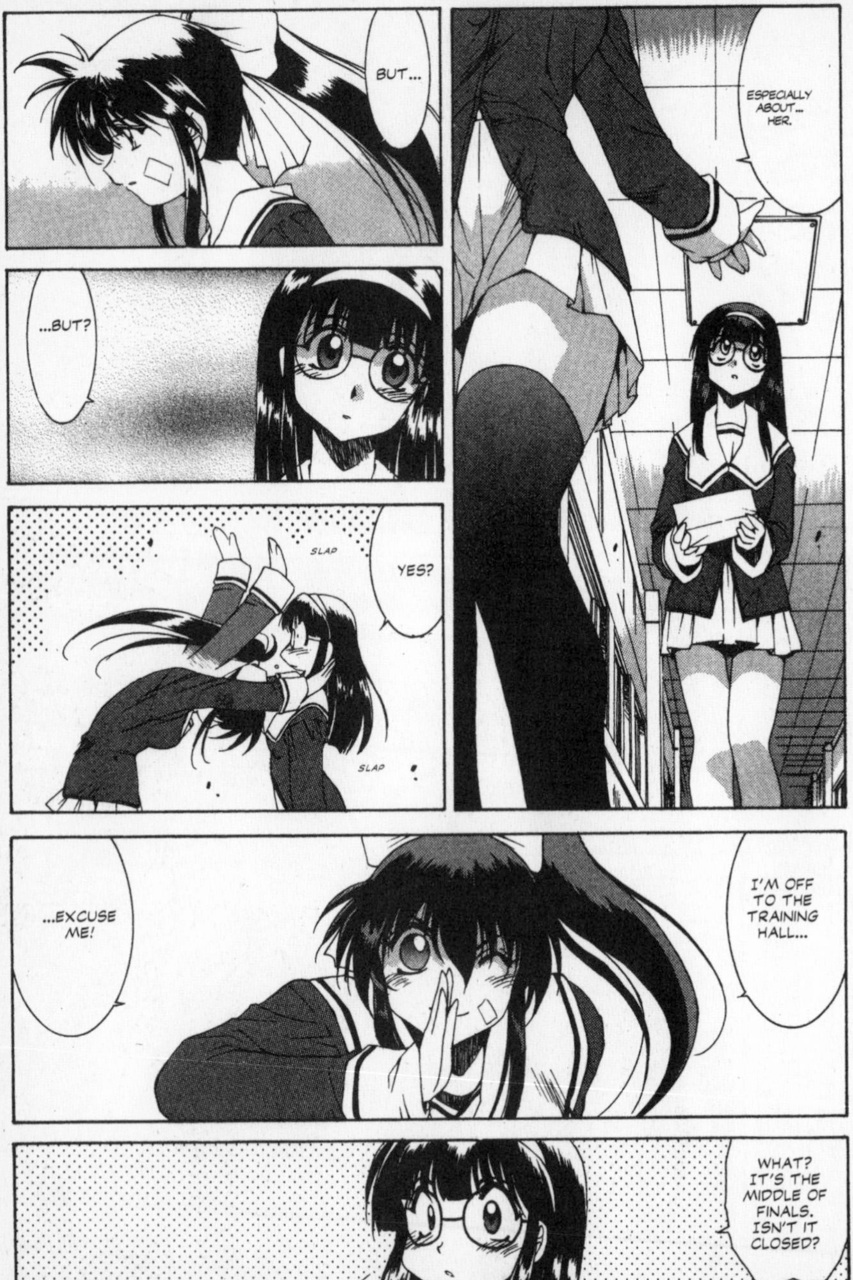
ESPECIALLY ABOUT... HER.
BUT...
...BUT?
YES?
SLAP
SLAP
I'M OFF TO THE TRAINING HALL...
...EXCUSE ME!
WHAT? IT'S THE MIDDLE OF FINALS. ISN'T IT CLOSED?

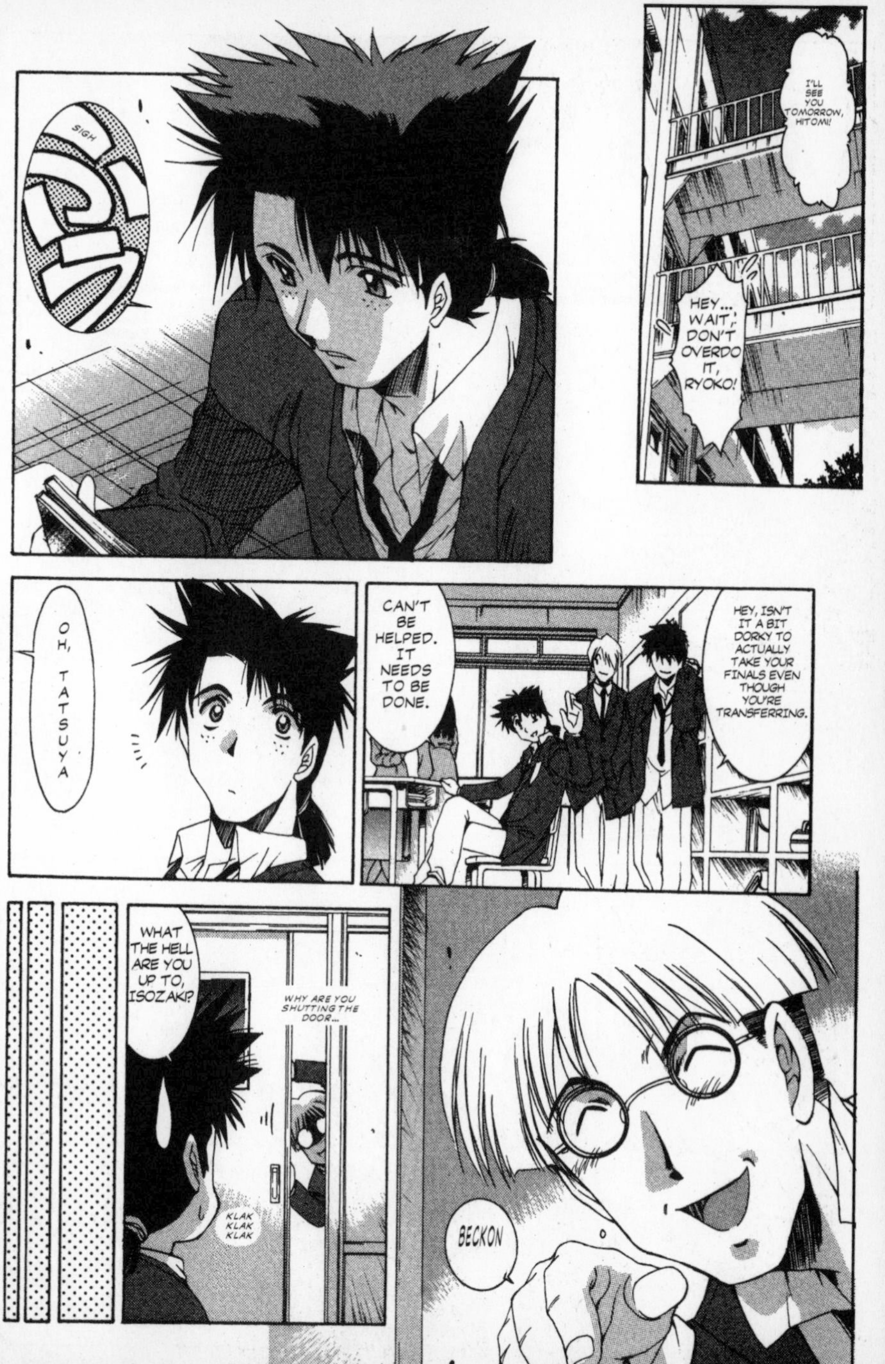
I'LL SEE YOU TOMORROW, HITOMI!
HEY... WAIT, DON'T OVERDO IT, RYOKO!
SIGH
HEY, ISN'T IT A BIT DORKY TO ACTUALLY TAKE YOUR FINALS EVEN THOUGH YOU'RE TRANSFERRING.
CAN'T BE HELPED. IT NEEDS TO BE DONE.
OH, TATSUYA
BECKON
WHY ARE YOU SHUTTING THE DOOR...
WHAT THE HELL ARE YOU UP TO, ISOZAKI?
KLAK KLAK KLAK

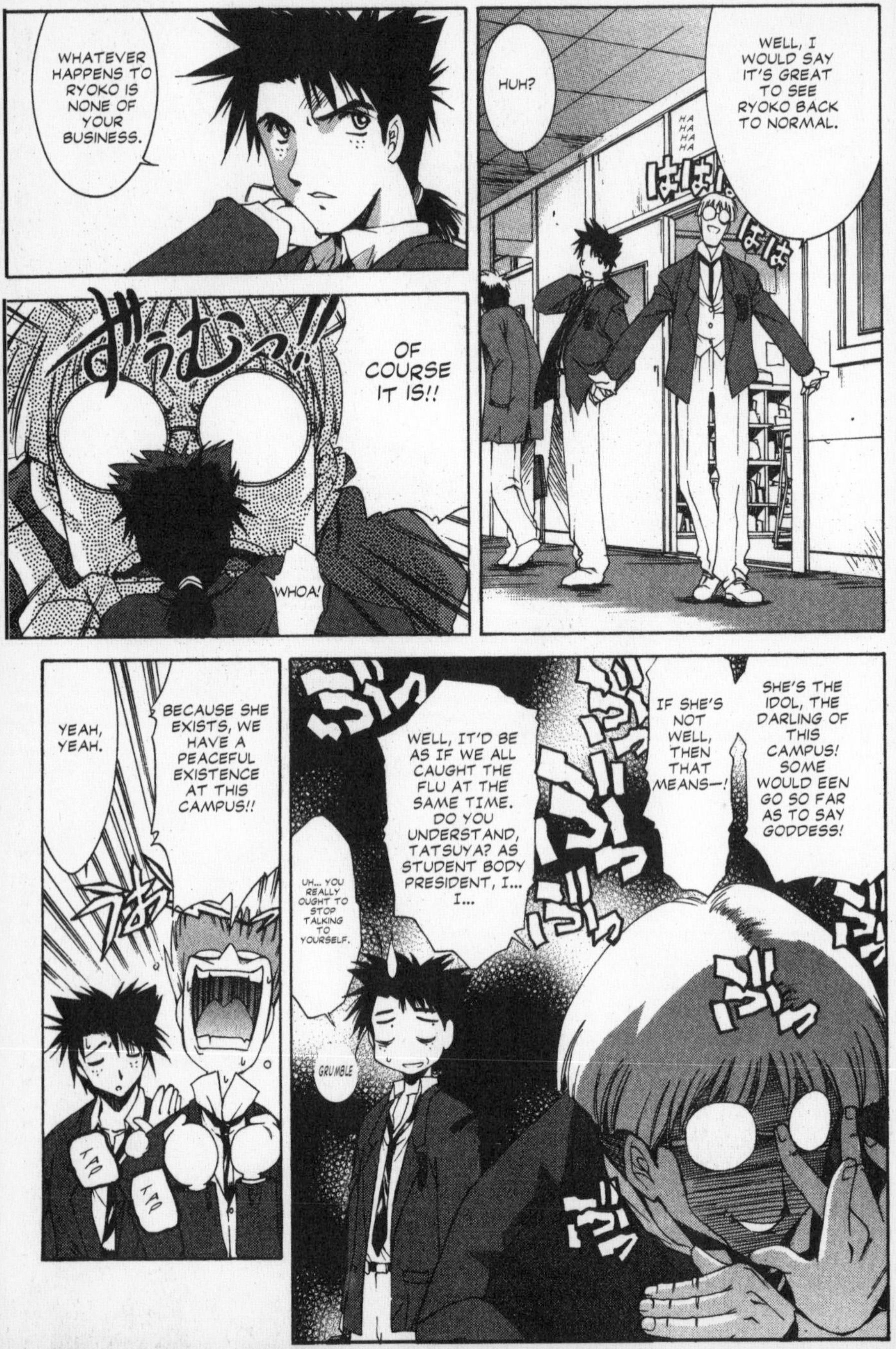
WELL, I WOULD SAY IT'S GREAT TO SEE RYOKO BACK TO NORMAL.
HUH?
HA HA HA HA
WHATEVER HAPPENS TO RYOKO IS NONE OF YOUR BUSINESS.
OF COURSE IT IS!!
WHOA!
SHE'S THE IDOL, THE DARLING OF THIS CAMPUS! SOME WOULD EEN GO SO FAR AS TO SAY GODDESS!
IF SHE'S NOT WELL, THEN THAT MEANS—!
WELL, IT'D BE AS IF WE ALL CAUGHT THE FLU AT THE SAME TIME. DO YOU UNDERSTAND, TATSUYA? AS STUDENT BODY PRESIDENT, I... I...
UH... YOU REALLY OUGHT TO STOP TALKING TO YOURSELF.
GRUMBLE
BECAUSE SHE EXISTS, WE HAVE A PEACEFUL EXISTENCE AT THIS CAMPUS!!
YEAH, YEAH.

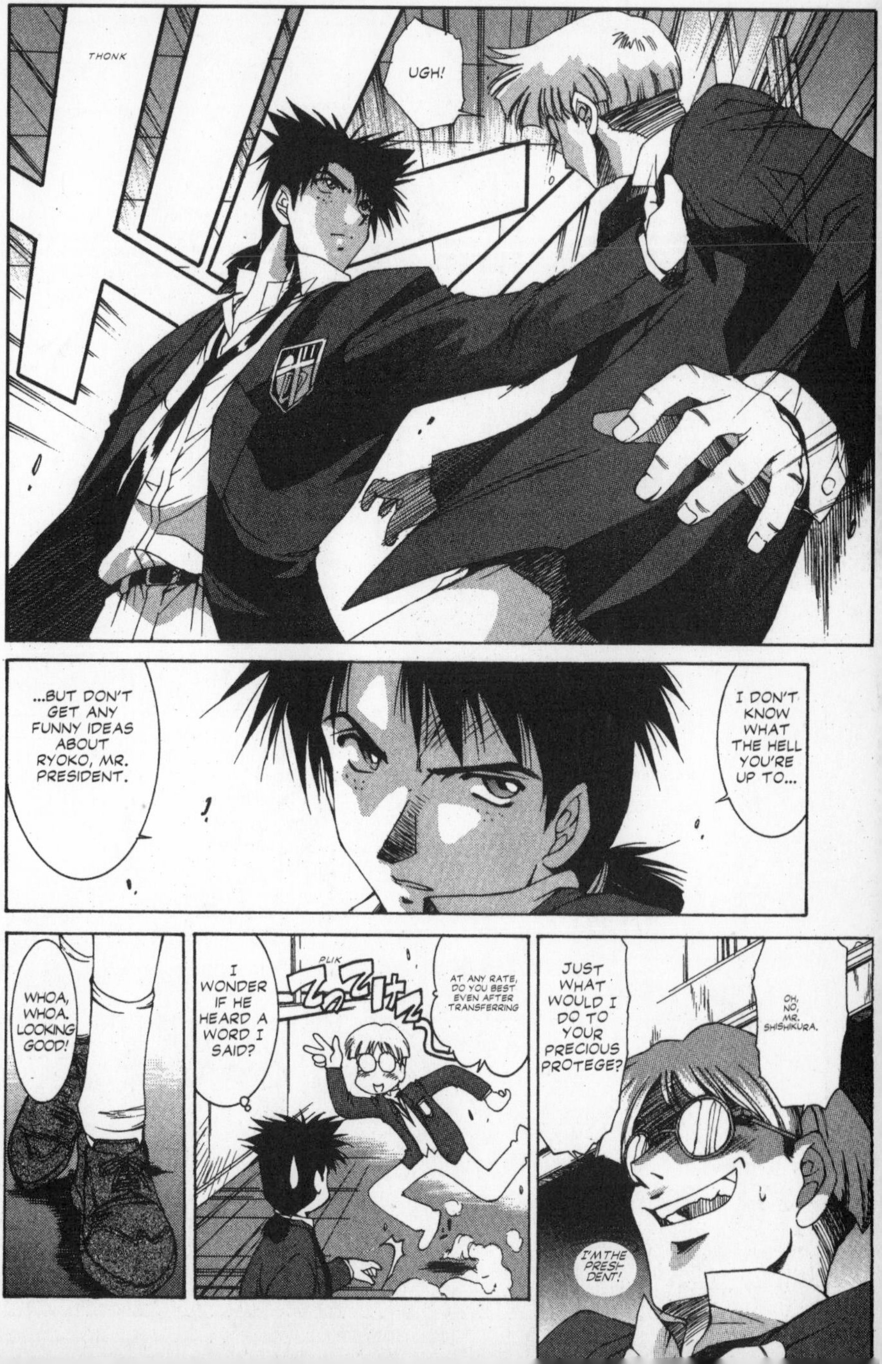
THONK
UGH!
I DON'T KNOW WHAT THE HELL YOU'RE UP TO...
...BUT DON'T GET ANY FUNNY IDEAS ABOUT RYOKO, MR. PRESIDENT.
JUST WHAT WOULD I DO TO YOUR PRECIOUS PROTEGE?
OH, NO, MR. SHISHIKURA.
I'M THE PRESI-DENT!
AT ANY RATE, DO YOU BEST EVEN AFTER TRANSFERRING
PLIK
I WONDER IF HE HEARD A WORD I SAID?
WHOA, WHOA. LOOKING GOOD!

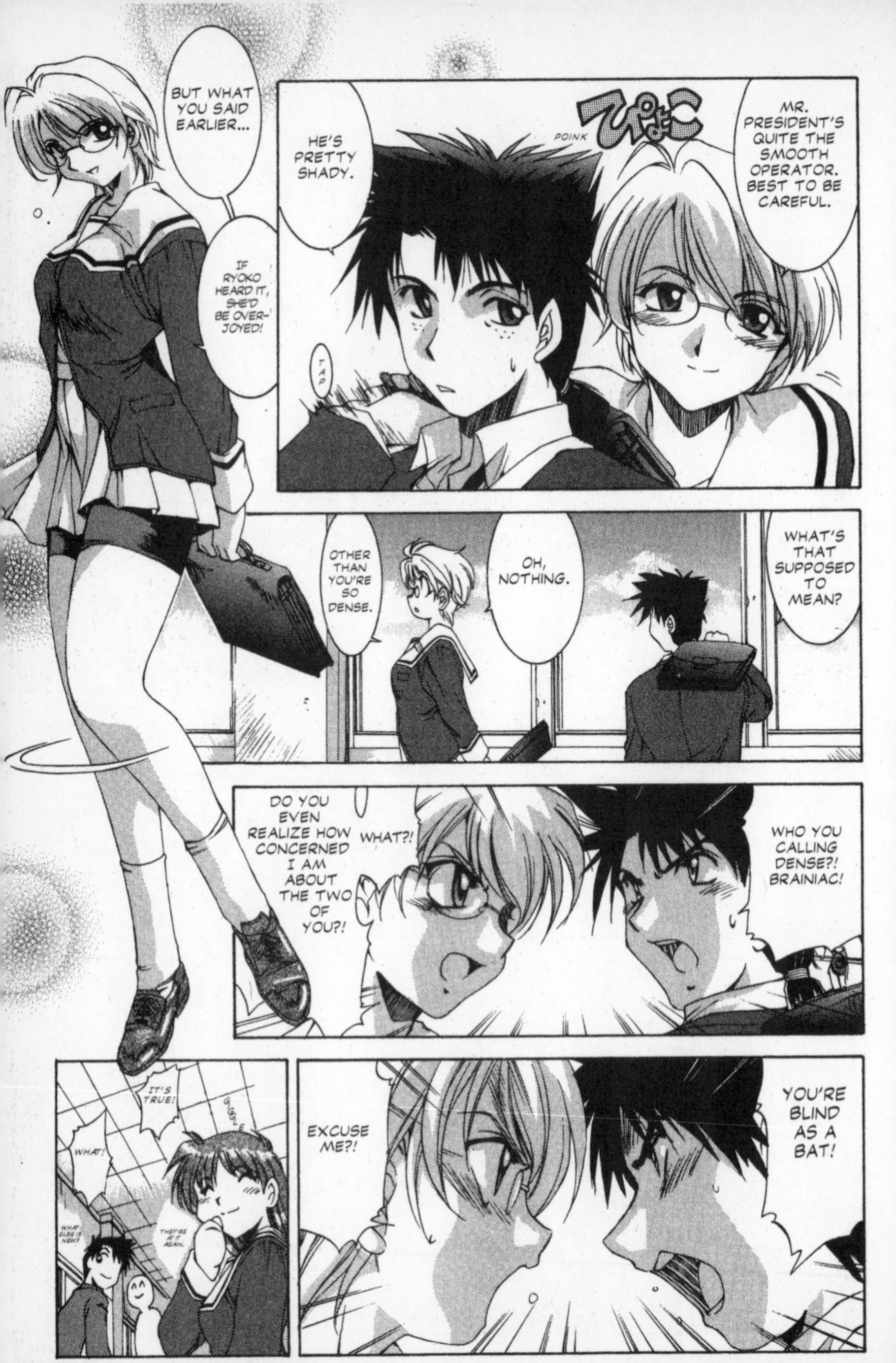
MR. PRESIDENT'S QUITE THE SMOOTH OPERATOR. BEST TO BE CAREFUL.
ぴょこ
POINK
HE'S PRETTY SHADY.
TAP
WHAT'S THAT SUPPOSED TO MEAN?
OH, NOTHING.
OTHER THAN YOU'RE SO DENSE.
WHO YOU CALLING DENSE?! BRAINIAC!
WHAT?!
DO YOU EVEN REALIZE HOW CONCERNED I AM ABOUT THE TWO OF YOU?!
BUT WHAT YOU SAID EARLIER...
IF RYOKO HEARD IT, SHE'D BE OVER-JOYED!
YOU'RE BLIND AS A BAT!
EXCUSE ME?!
IT'S TRUE!
GIGGLE
WHAT!
THEY'RE AT IT AGAIN.
WHAT ELSE IS NEW?

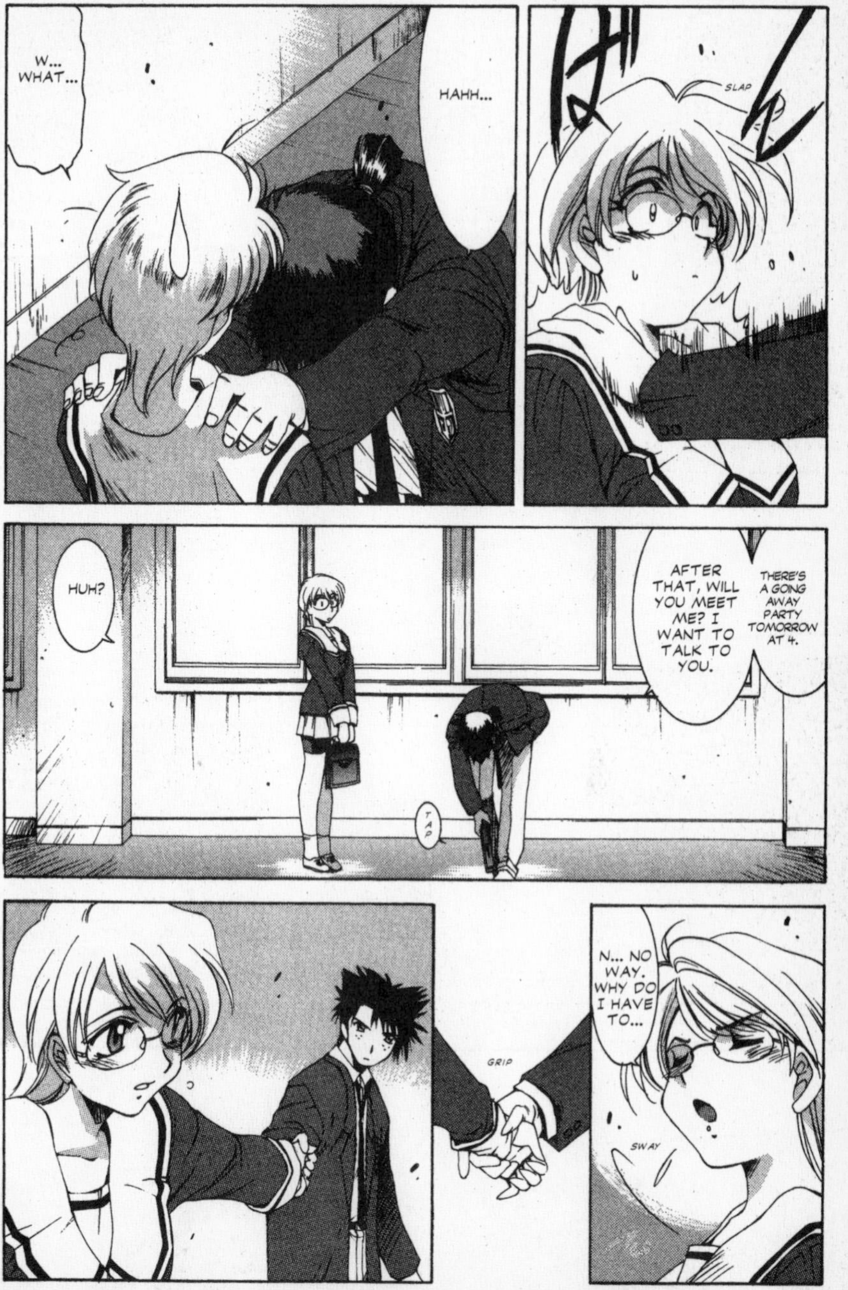
ばん
SLAP
HAHH...
W... WHAT...
THERE'S A GOING AWAY PARTY TOMORROW AT 4.
AFTER THAT, WILL YOU MEET ME? I WANT TO TALK TO YOU.
HUH?
TAP
N... NO WAY. WHY DO I HAVE TO...
SWAY
GRIP

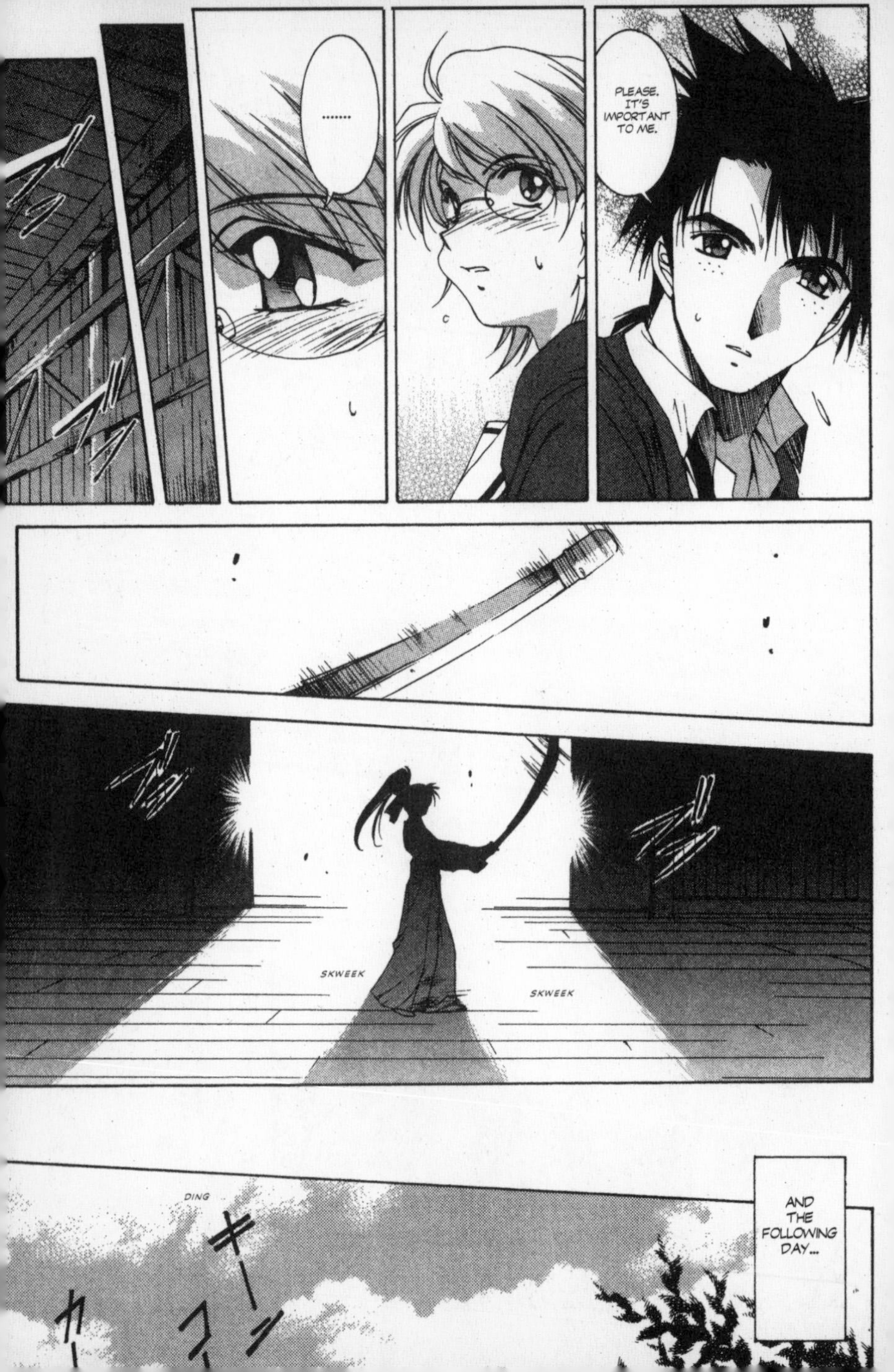
PLEASE. IT'S IMPORTANT TO ME.
....
SKWEEK
SKWEEK
AND THE FOLLOWING DAY...
DING ...

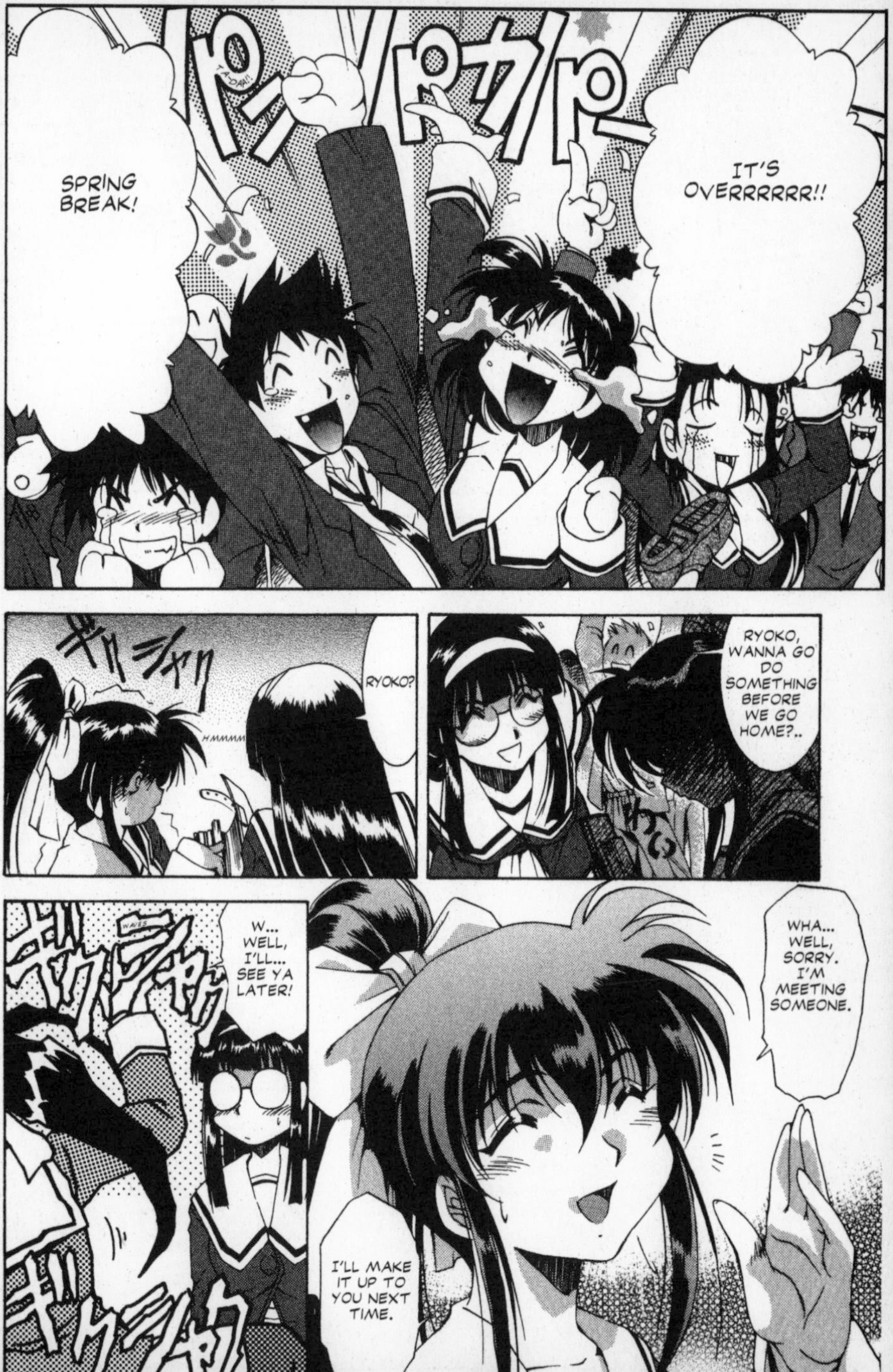
TA-DAA!!
IT'S OVERRRRRR!!
SPRING BREAK!
RYOKO, WANNA GO DO SOMETHING BEFORE WE GO HOME?..
RYOKO?
HMMMM
WHA... WELL, SORRY. I'M MEETING SOMEONE.
I'LL MAKE IT UP TO YOU NEXT TIME.
W... WELL, I'LL... SEE YA LATER!
WAVES

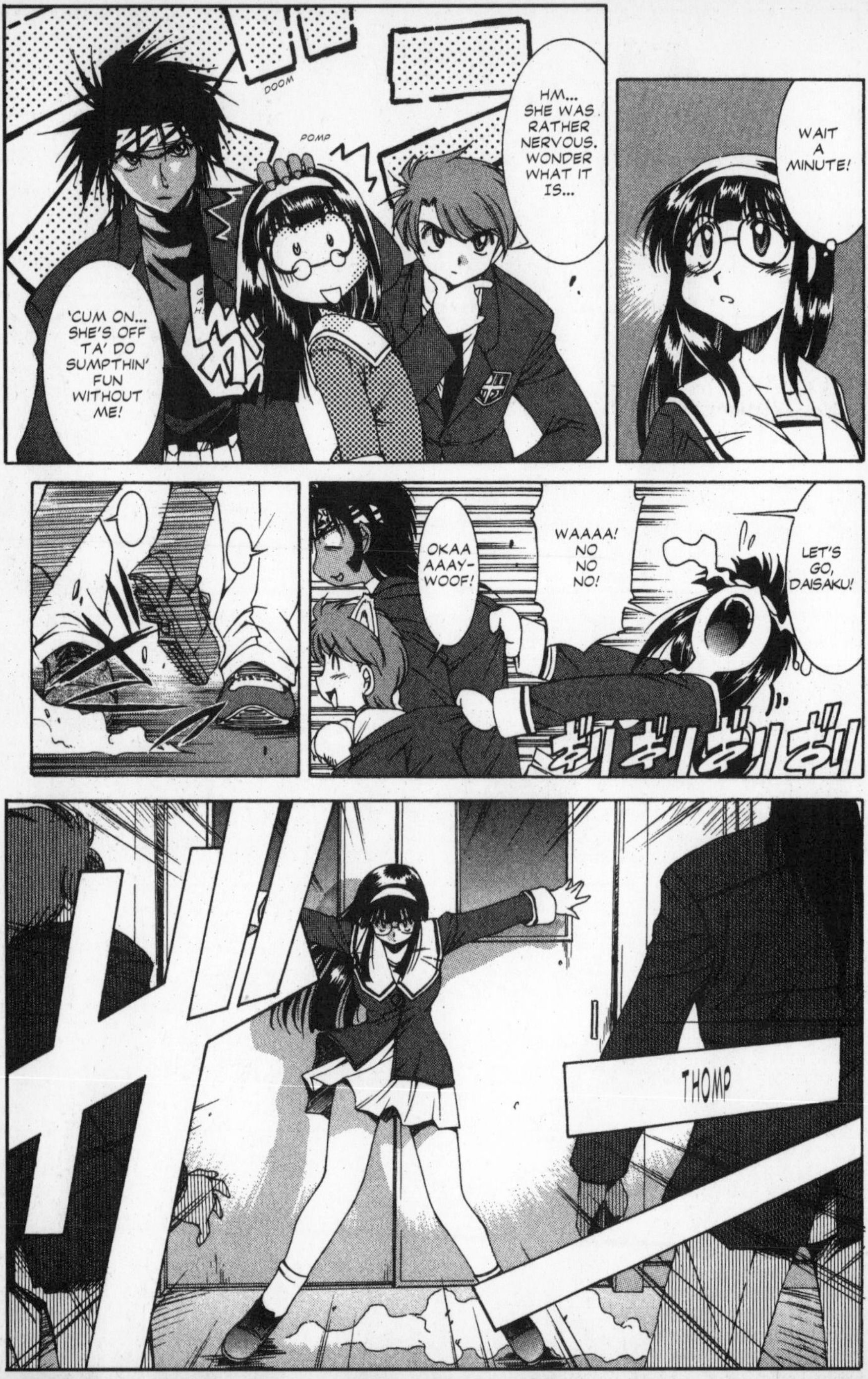
WAIT A MINUTE!
HM... SHE WAS RATHER NERVOUS. WONDER WHAT IT IS...
POMP
DOOM
'CUM ON... SHE'S OFF TA' DO SUMPTHIN' FUN WITHOUT ME!
LET'S GO, DAISAKU!
WAAAA! NO NO NO!
OKAA AAAY-WOOF!
THOMP

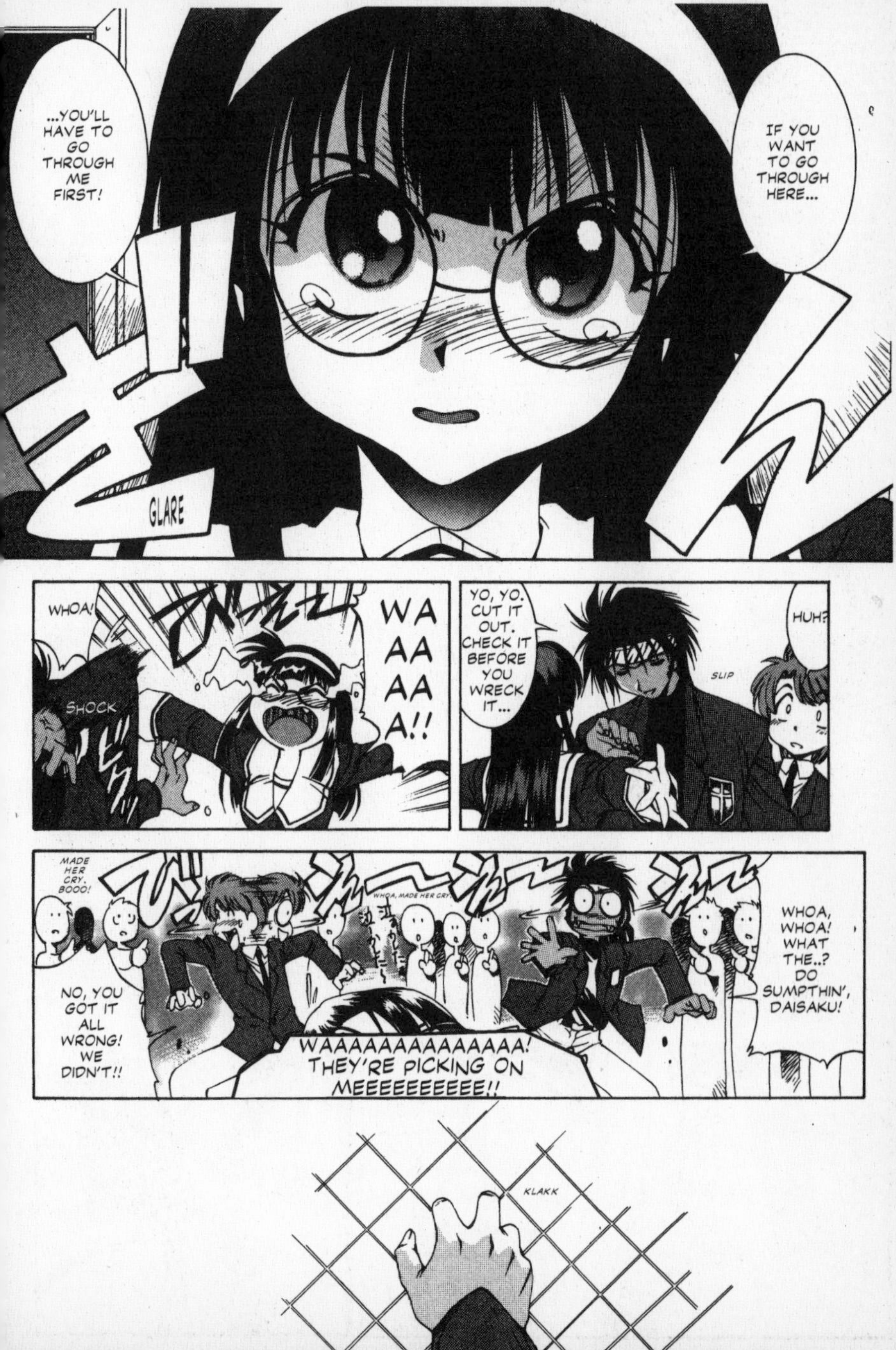
IF YOU WANT TO GO THROUGH HERE...
...YOU'LL HAVE TO GO THROUGH ME FIRST!
GLARE
HUH?
SLIP
YO, YO. CUT IT OUT. CHECK IT BEFORE YOU WRECK IT...
WA AA AA AA A!!
WHOA!
SHOCK
WHOA, WHOA! WHAT THE..? DO SUMPTHIN', DAISAKU!
WAAAAAAAAAAAAAA! THEY'RE PICKING ON MEEEEEEEEEEE!!
WHOA, MADE HER CRY
MADE HER CRY. BOOO!
NO, YOU GOT IT ALL WRONG! WE DIDN'T!!
KLAKK

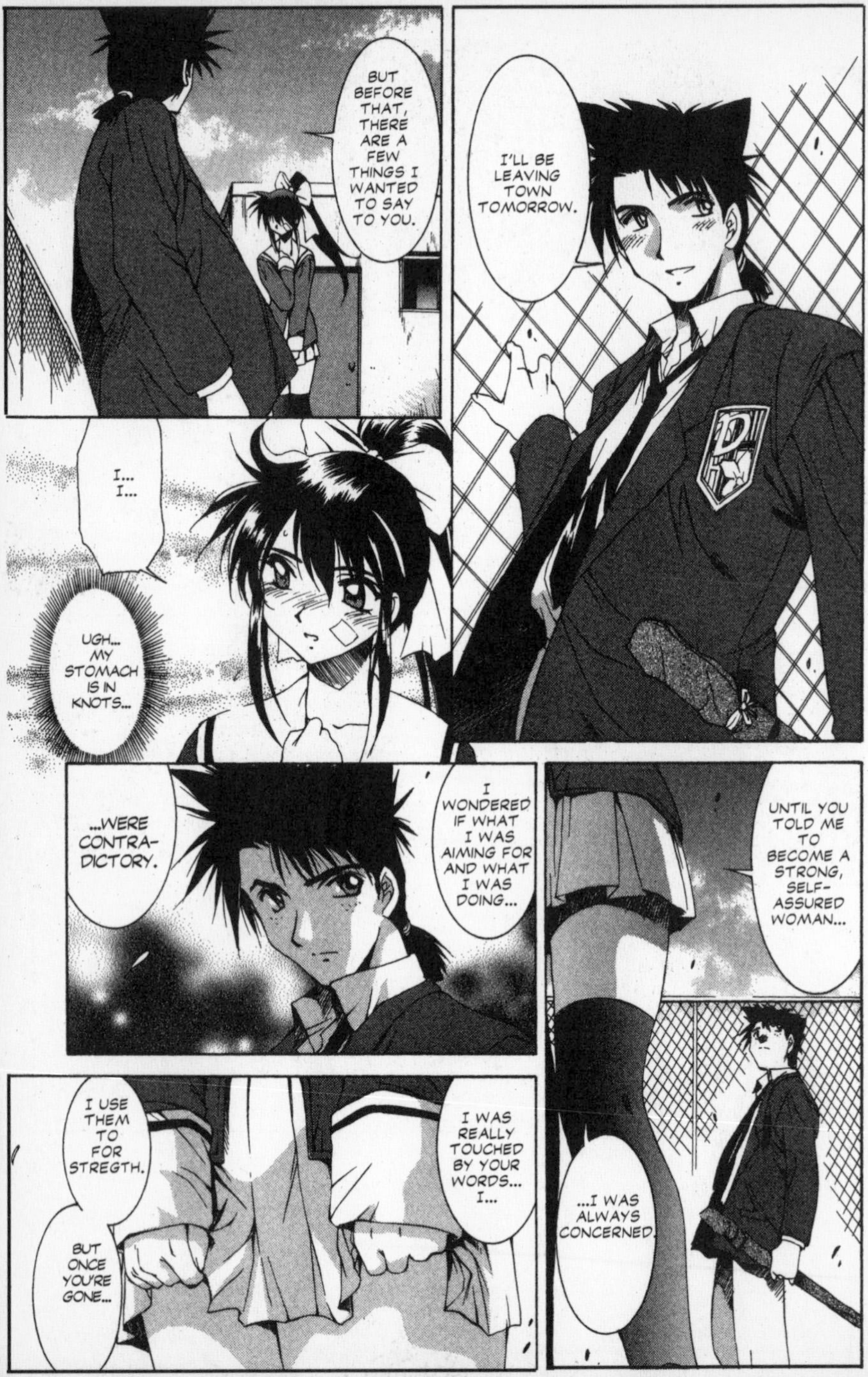
I'LL BE LEAVING TOWN TOMORROW.
BUT BEFORE THAT, THERE ARE A FEW THINGS I WANTED TO SAY TO YOU.
I... I...
UGH... MY STOMACH IS IN KNOTS...
UNTIL YOU TOLD ME TO BECOME A STRONG, SELF-ASSURED WOMAN...
...I WAS ALWAYS CONCERNED.
I WONDERED IF WHAT I WAS AIMING FOR AND WHAT I WAS DOING...
...WERE CONTRA-DICTORY.
I WAS REALLY TOUCHED BY YOUR WORDS... I...
I USE THEM TO FOR STREGTH.
BUT ONCE YOU'RE GONE...

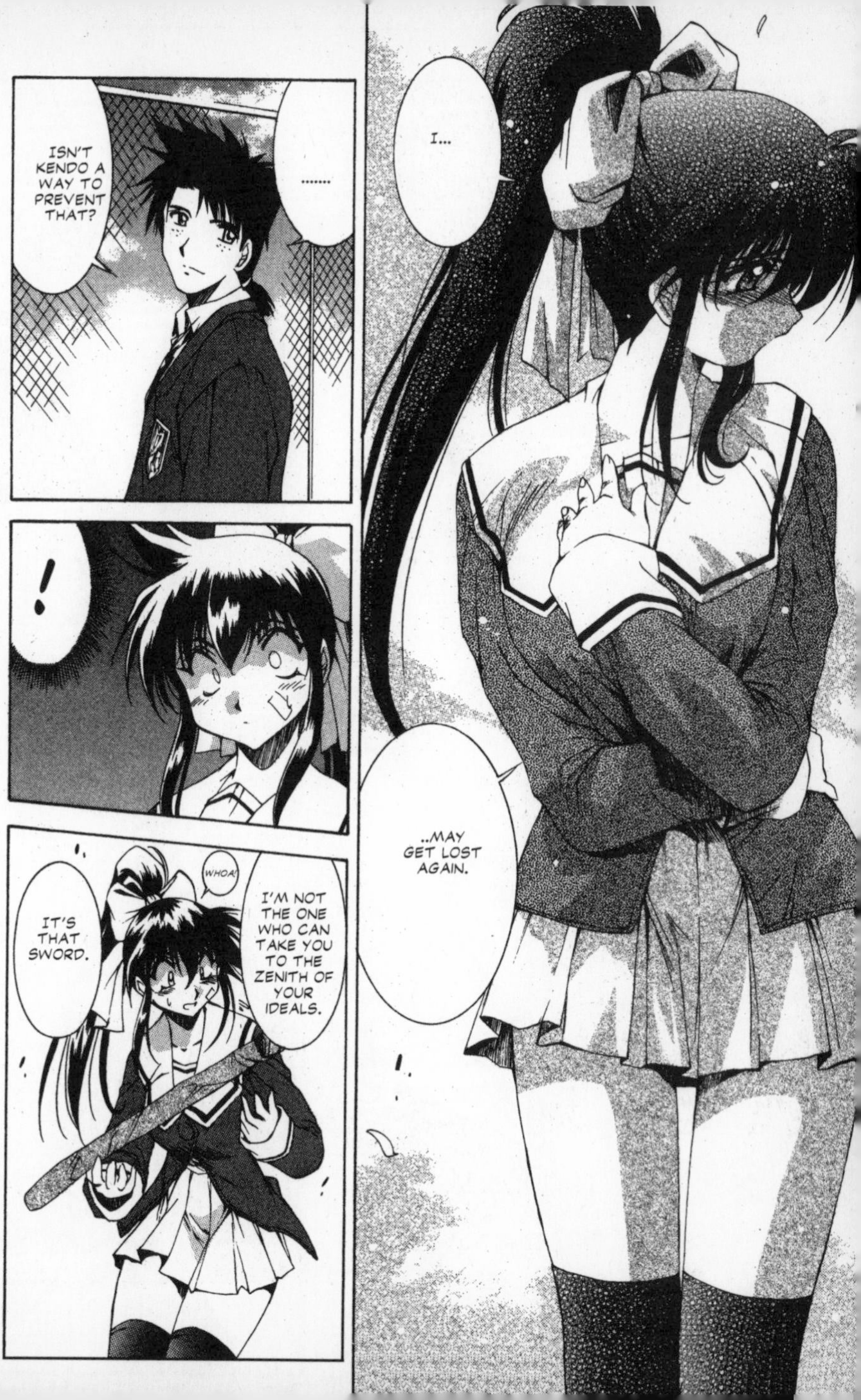
I...
..MAY GET LOST AGAIN.
....
ISN'T KENDO A WAY TO PREVENT THAT?
!
I'M NOT THE ONE WHO CAN TAKE YOU TO THE ZENITH OF YOUR IDEALS.
WHOA!
IT'S THAT SWORD.

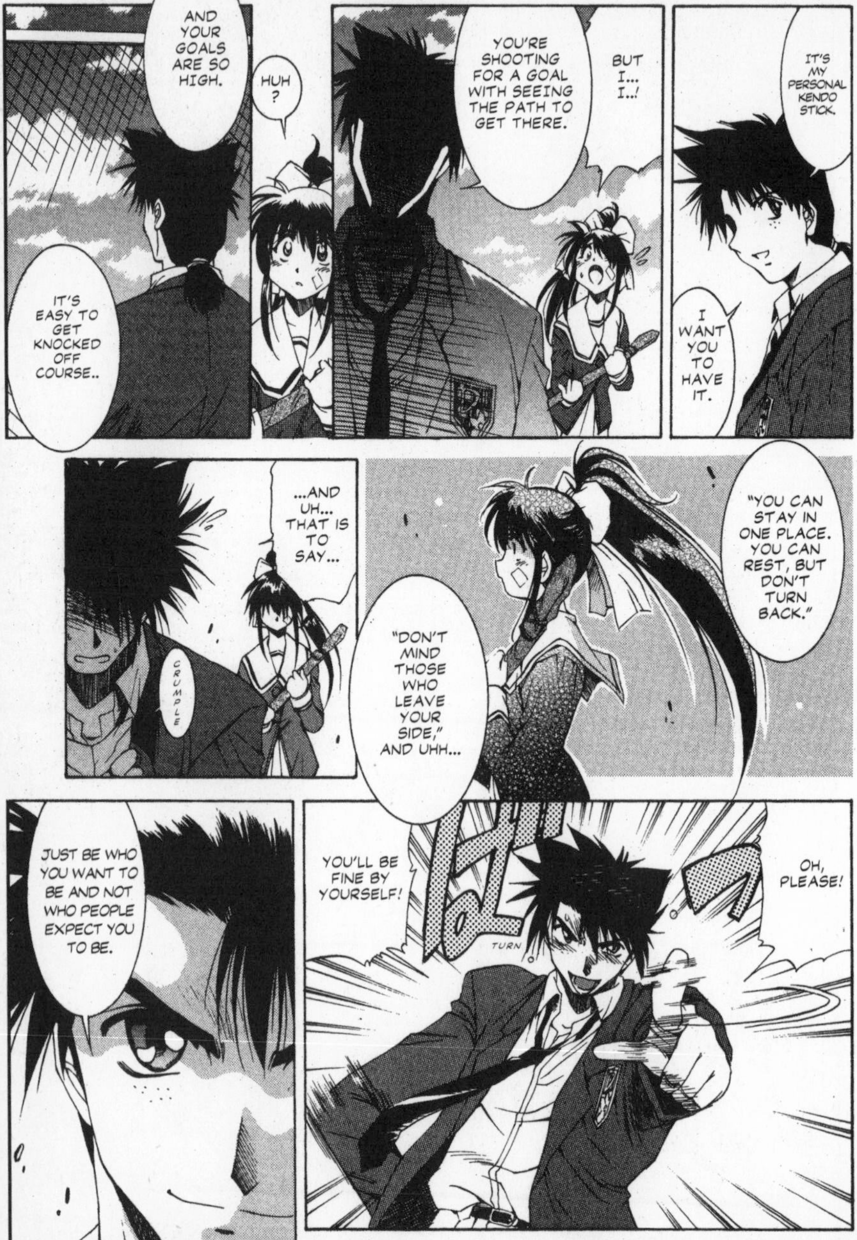
IT'S MY PERSONAL KENDO STICK.
I WANT YOU TO HAVE IT.
BUT I... I...!
YOU'RE SHOOTING FOR A GOAL WITH SEEING THE PATH TO GET THERE.
HUH?
AND YOUR GOALS ARE SO HIGH.
IT'S EASY TO GET KNOCKED OFF COURSE..
"YOU CAN STAY IN ONE PLACE. YOU CAN REST, BUT DON'T TURN BACK."
"DON'T MIND THOSE WHO LEAVE YOUR SIDE," AND UHH...
...AND UH... THAT IS TO SAY...
CRUMPLE
OH, PLEASE!
YOU'LL BE FINE BY YOURSELF!
TURN
JUST BE WHO YOU WANT TO BE AND NOT WHO PEOPLE EXPECT YOU TO BE.

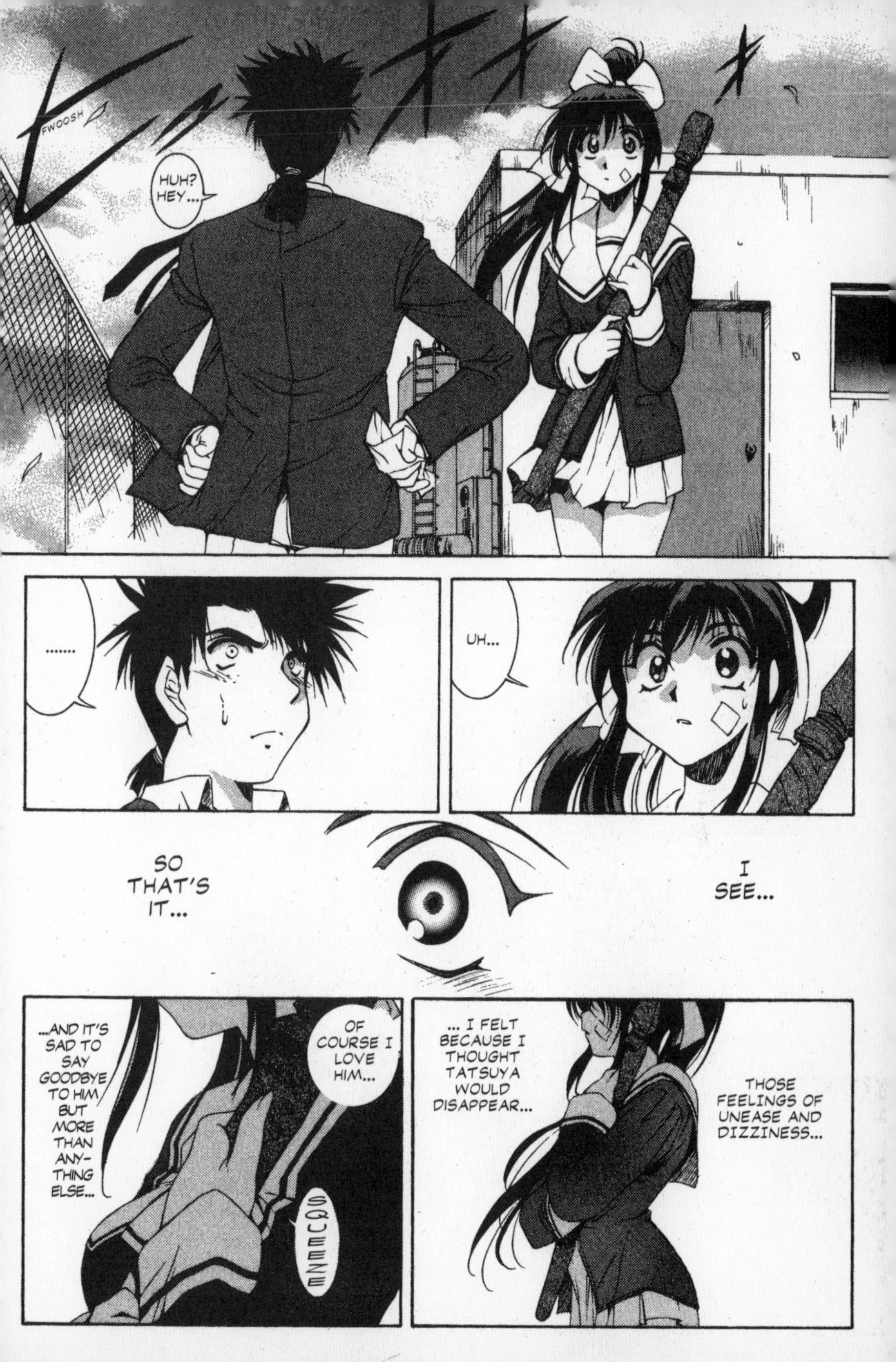
FWOOSH
HUH? HEY...
UH...
....
I SEE...
SO THAT'S IT...
THOSE FEELINGS OF UNEASE AND DIZZINESS...
... I FELT BECAUSE I THOUGHT TATSUYA WOULD DISAPPEAR...
OF COURSE I LOVE HIM...
...AND IT'S SAD TO SAY GOODBYE TO HIM BUT MORE THAN ANY-THING ELSE...
SQUEEZE

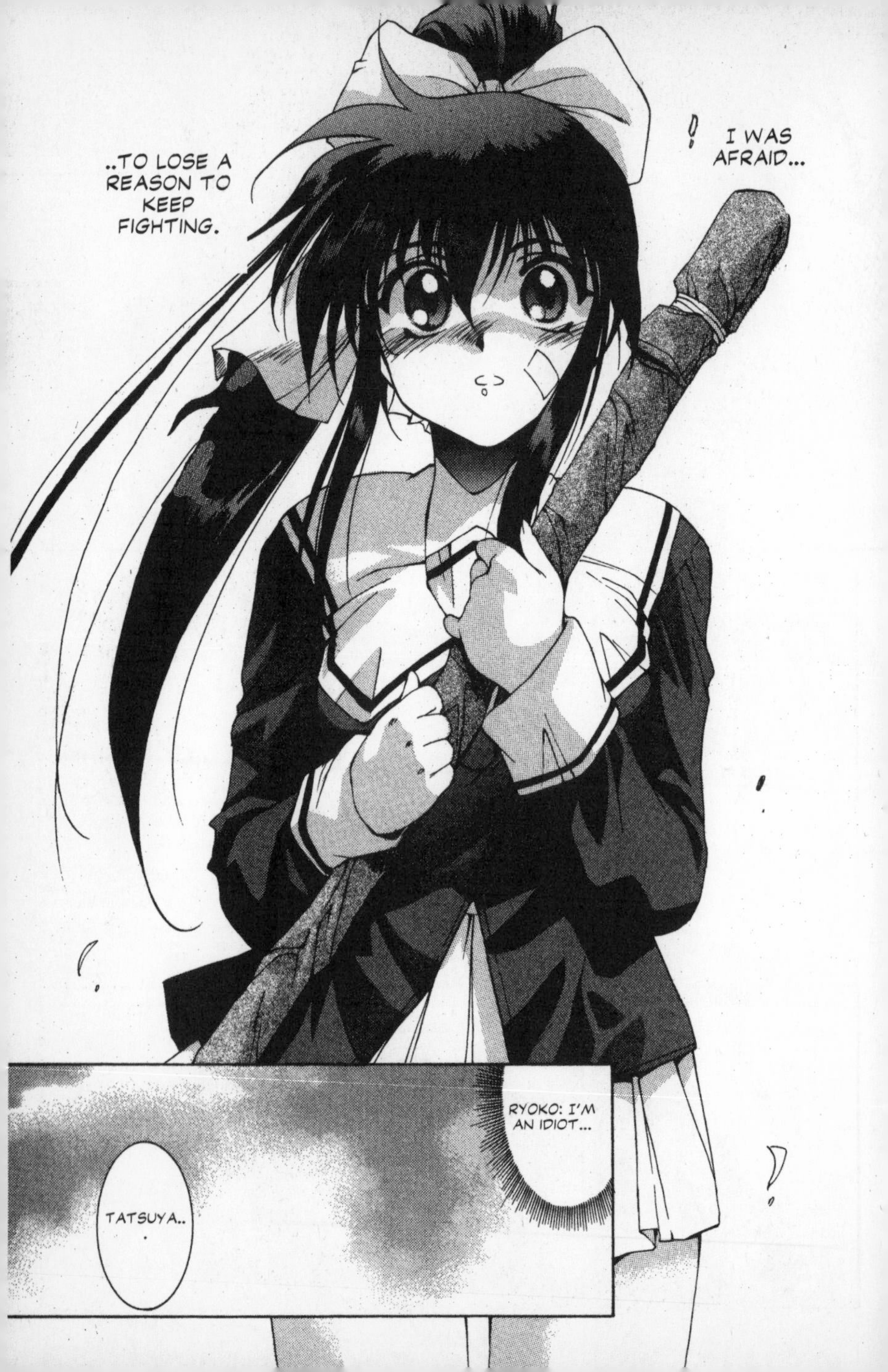
I WAS AFRAID...
..TO LOSE A REASON TO KEEP FIGHTING.
RYOKO: I'M AN IDIOT...
TATSUYA...

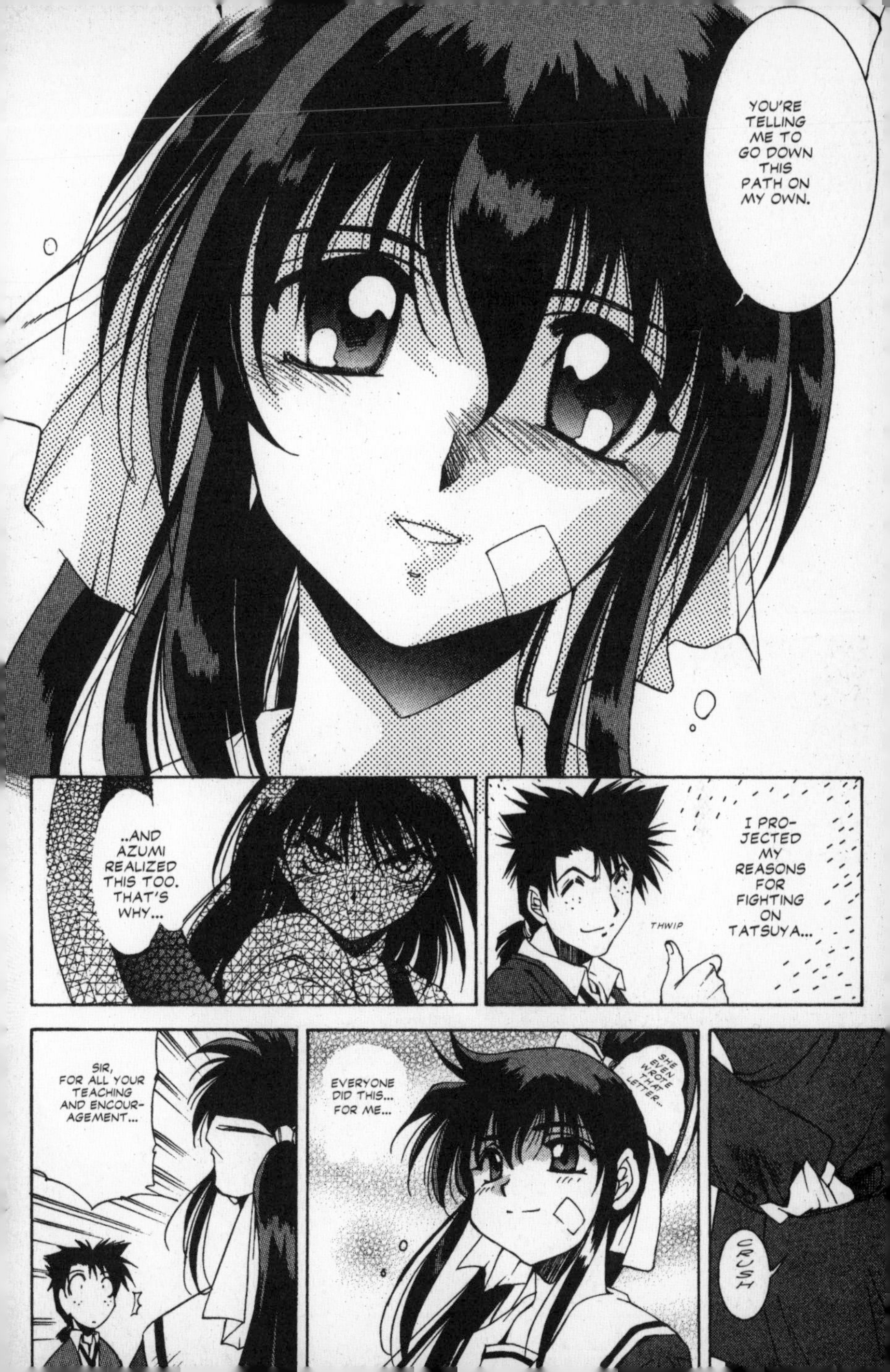
YOU'RE TELLING ME TO GO DOWN THIS PATH ON MY OWN.
I PRO-JECTED MY REASONS FOR FIGHTING ON TATSUYA...
THWIP
..AND AZUMI REALIZED THIS TOO. THAT'S WHY...
CRUSH
SHE EVEN WROTE THAT LETTER...
EVERYONE DID THIS... FOR ME...
SIR, FOR ALL YOUR TEACHING AND ENCOUR-AGEMENT...

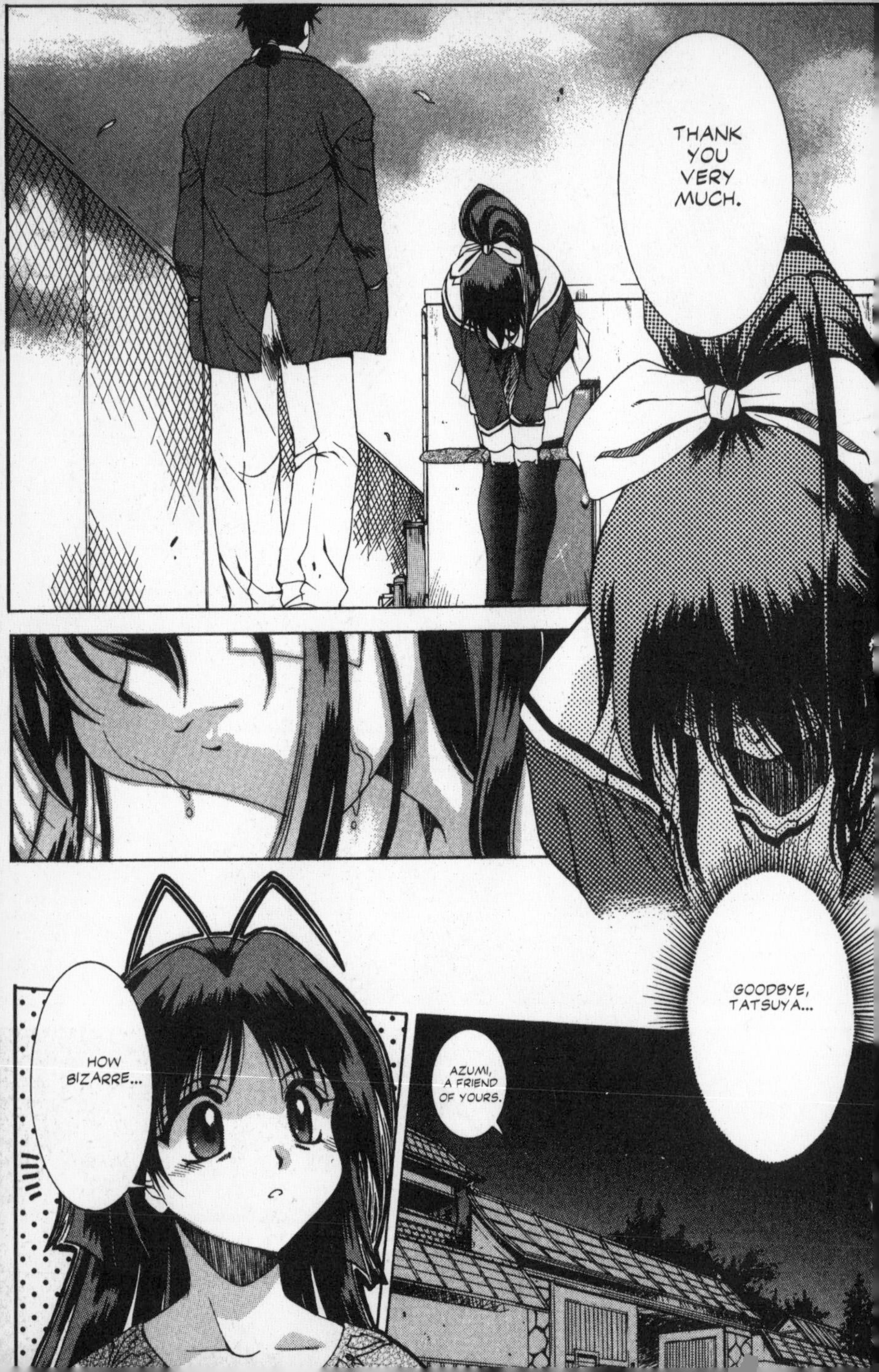
THANK YOU VERY MUCH.
GOODBYE, TATSUYA...
AZUMI, A FRIEND OF YOURS.
HOW BIZARRE...

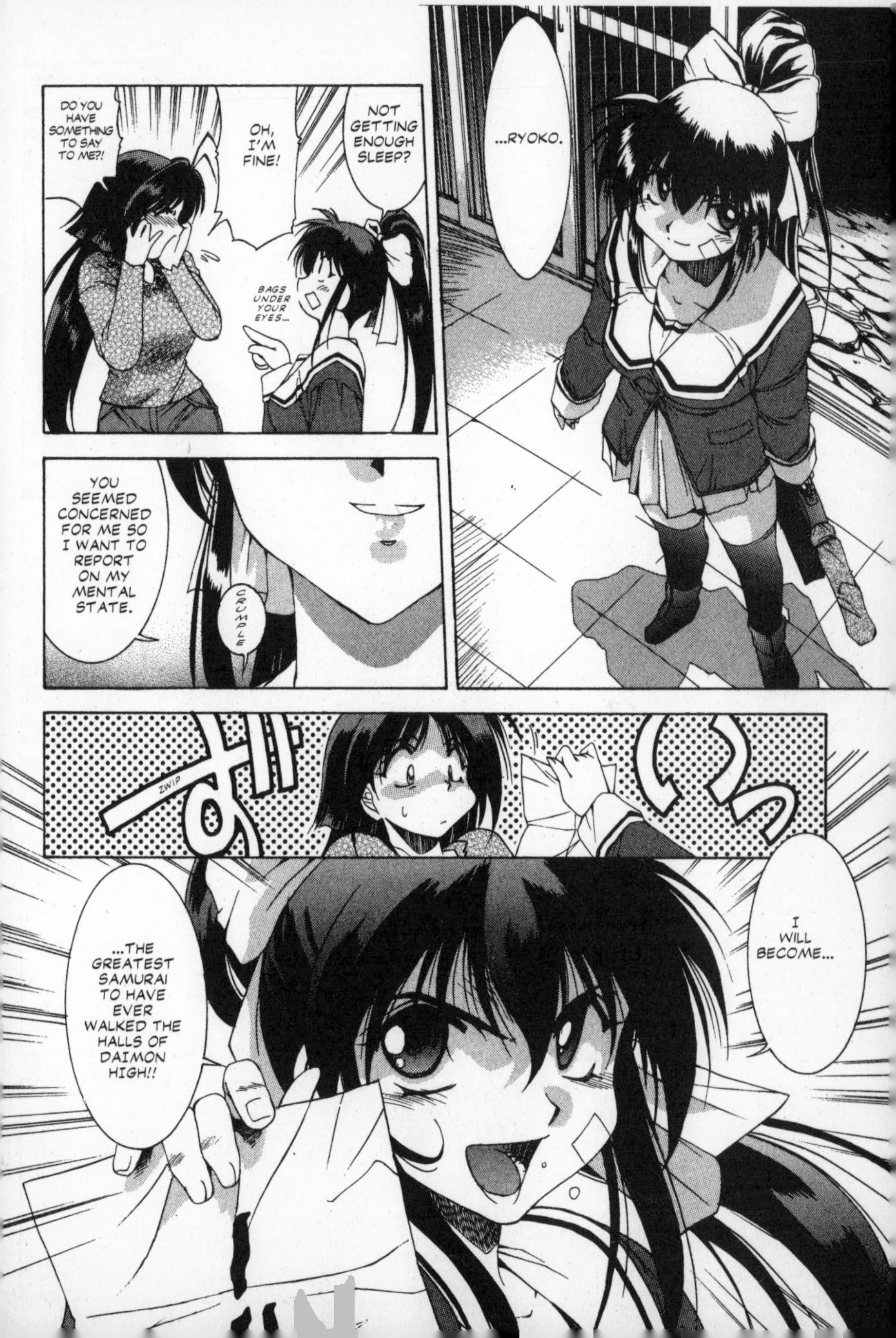
...RYOKO.
NOT GETTING ENOUGH SLEEP?
OH, I'M FINE!
DO YOU HAVE SOMETHING TO SAY TO ME?!
BAGS UNDER YOUR EYES...
YOU SEEMED CONCERNED FOR ME SO I WANT TO REPORT ON MY MENTAL STATE.
CRUMPLE
ZWIP
I WILL BECOME...
...THE GREATEST SAMURAI TO HAVE EVER WALKED THE HALLS OF DAIMON HIGH!!

Episode 21 Wartime in Spring, Ryoko and Shizuma and...

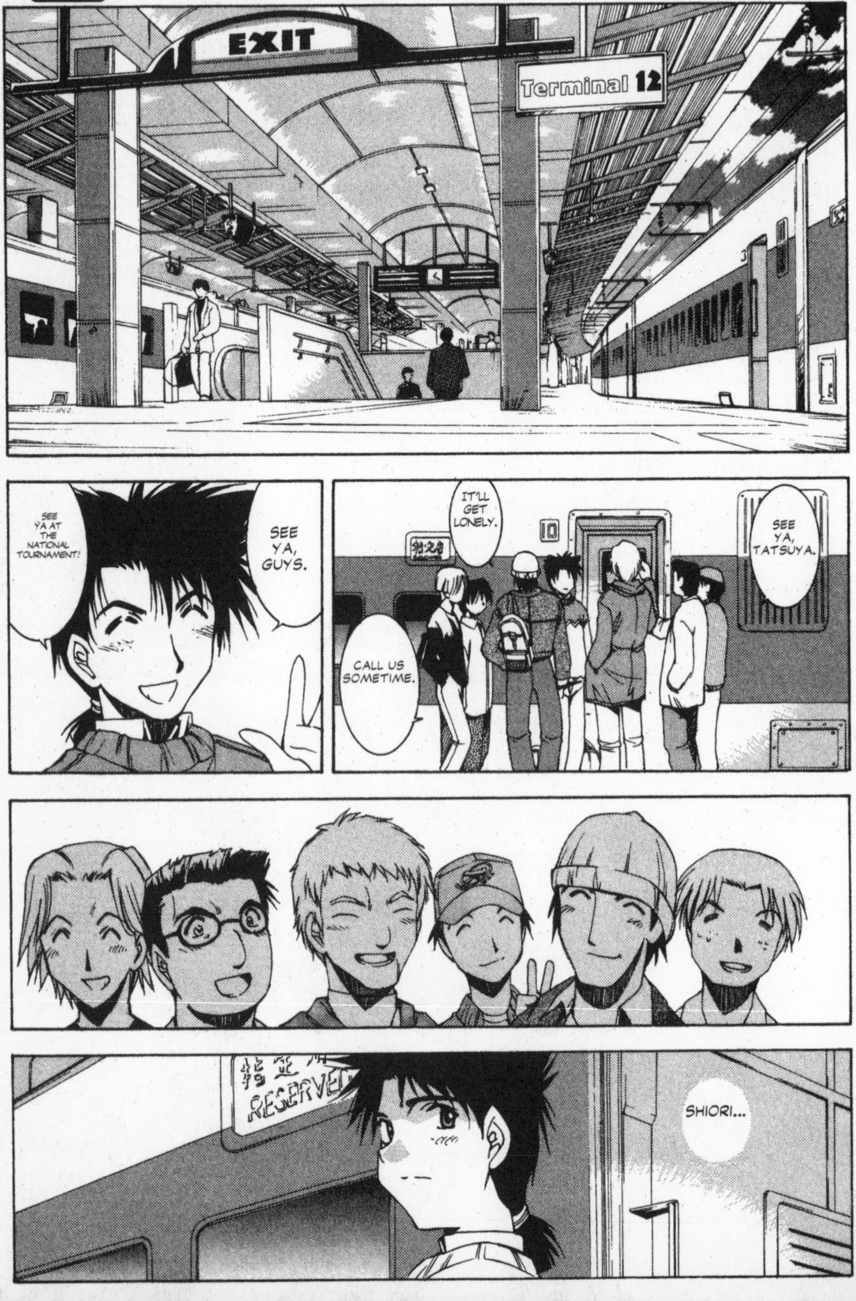
EXIT
Terminal 12
SEE YA, TATSUYA.
IT'LL GET LONELY.
10
CALL US SOMETIME.
SEE YA, GUYS.
SEE YA AT THE NATIONAL TOURNAMENT!
RESERVED
SHIORI...

Episode 21 Wartime in Spring, Ryoko and Shizuma and...

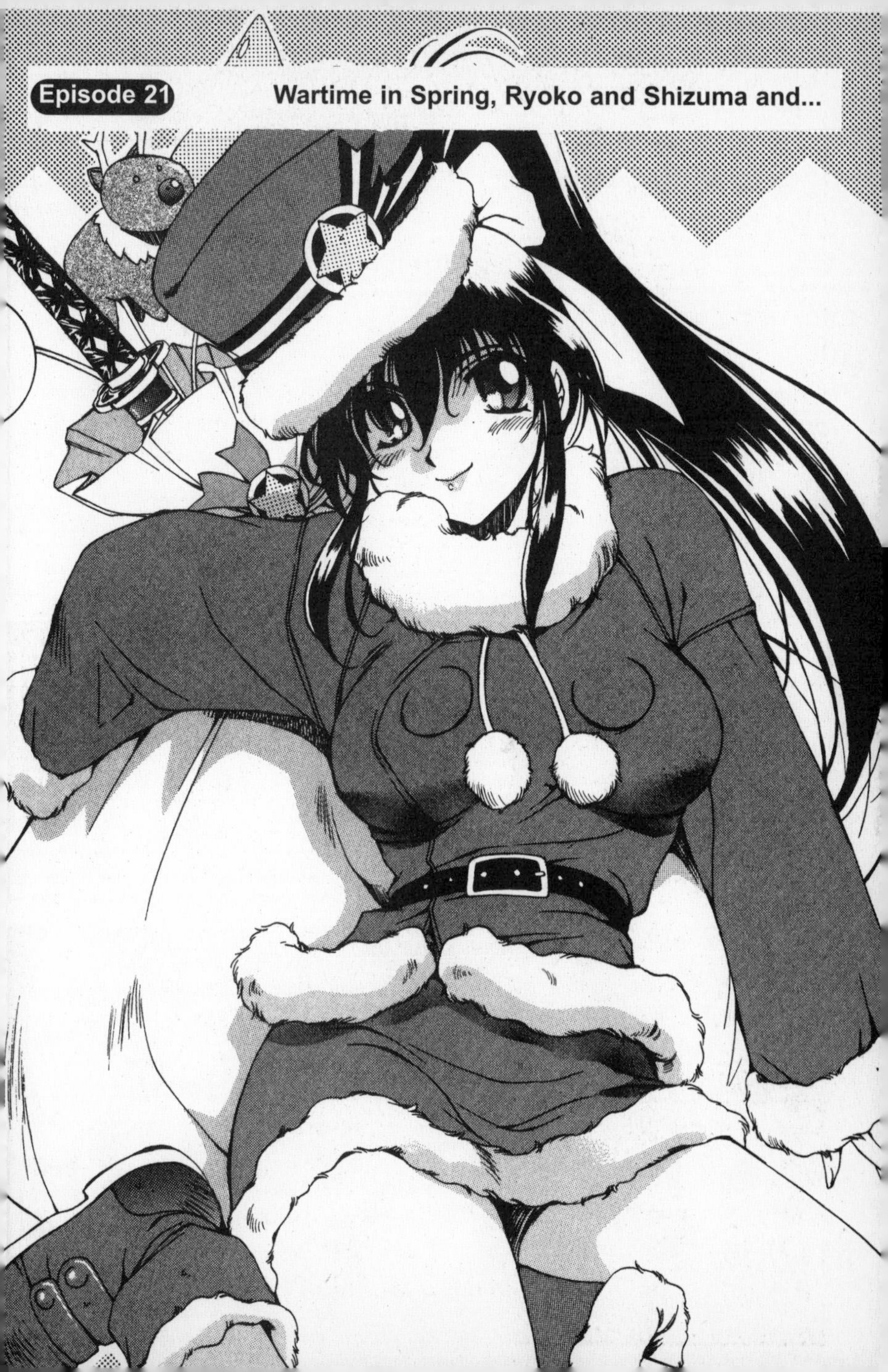

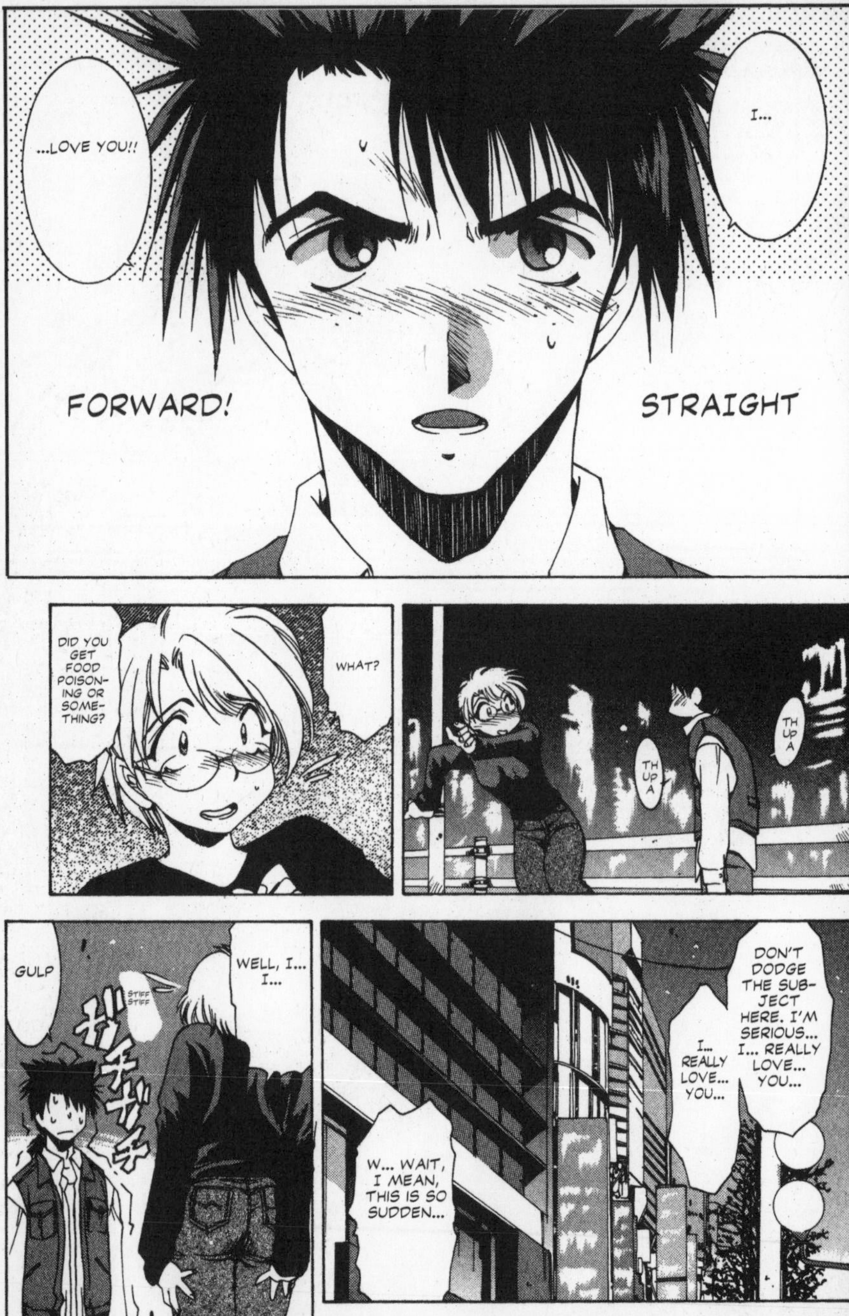
I...
...LOVE YOU!!
STRAIGHT
FORWARD!
THUPA
THUPA
WHAT?
DID YOU GET FOOD POISONING OR SOMETHING?
DON'T DODGE THE SUBJECT HERE. I'M SERIOUS... I... REALLY LOVE... YOU...
I... REALLY LOVE... YOU...
W... WAIT, I MEAN, THIS IS SO SUDDEN...
WELL, I... I...
STIFF STIFF
GULP

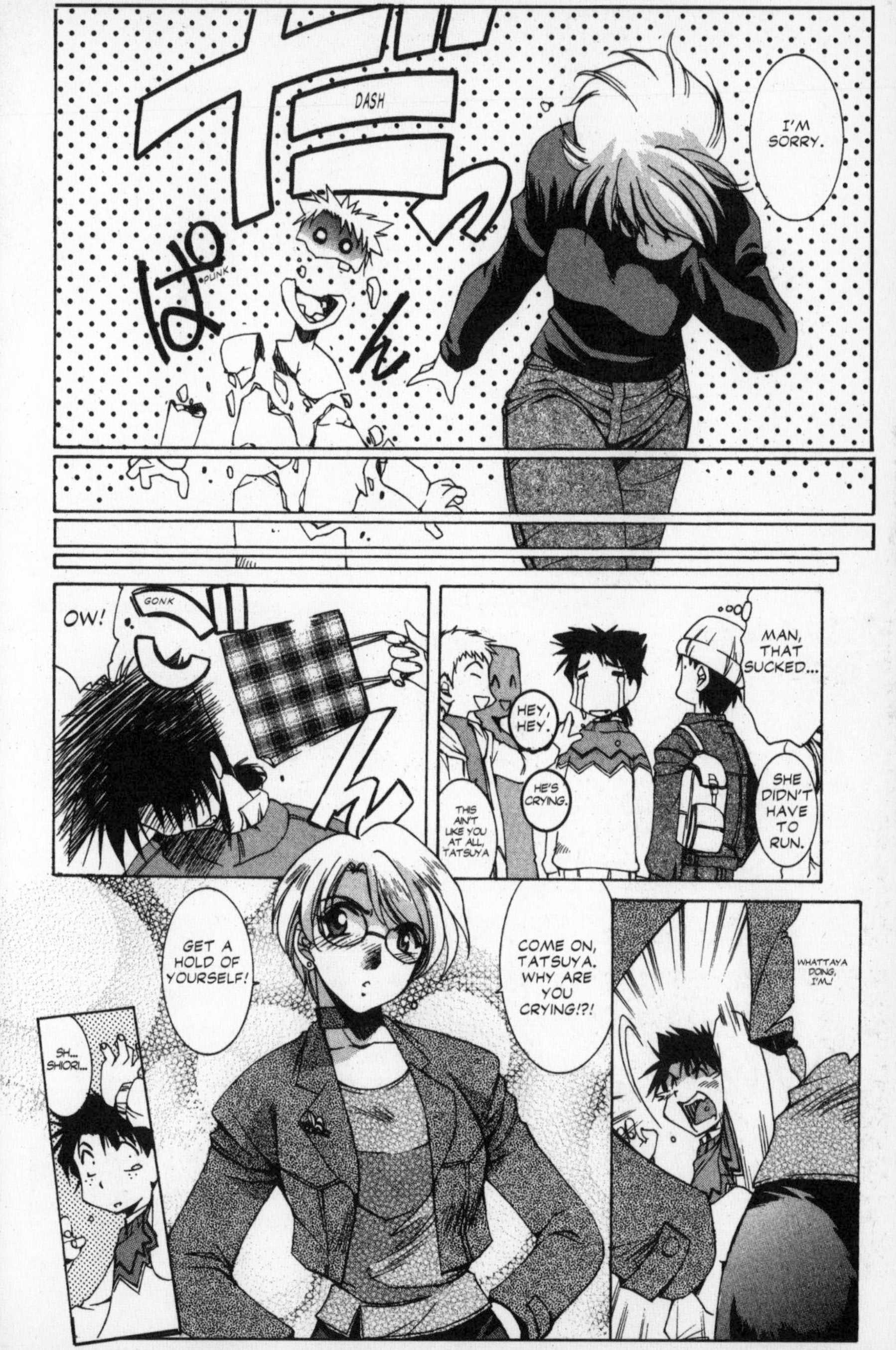
I'M SORRY.
DASH
PUNK
MAN, THAT SUCKED...
HEY, HEY.
SHE DIDN'T HAVE TO RUN.
HE'S CRYING.
THIS AIN'T LIKE YOU AT ALL, TATSUYA
OW!
GONK
WHATTAYA DOING, I'M..!
COME ON, TATSUYA. WHY ARE YOU CRYING!?!
GET A HOLD OF YOURSELF!
SH... SHIORI...

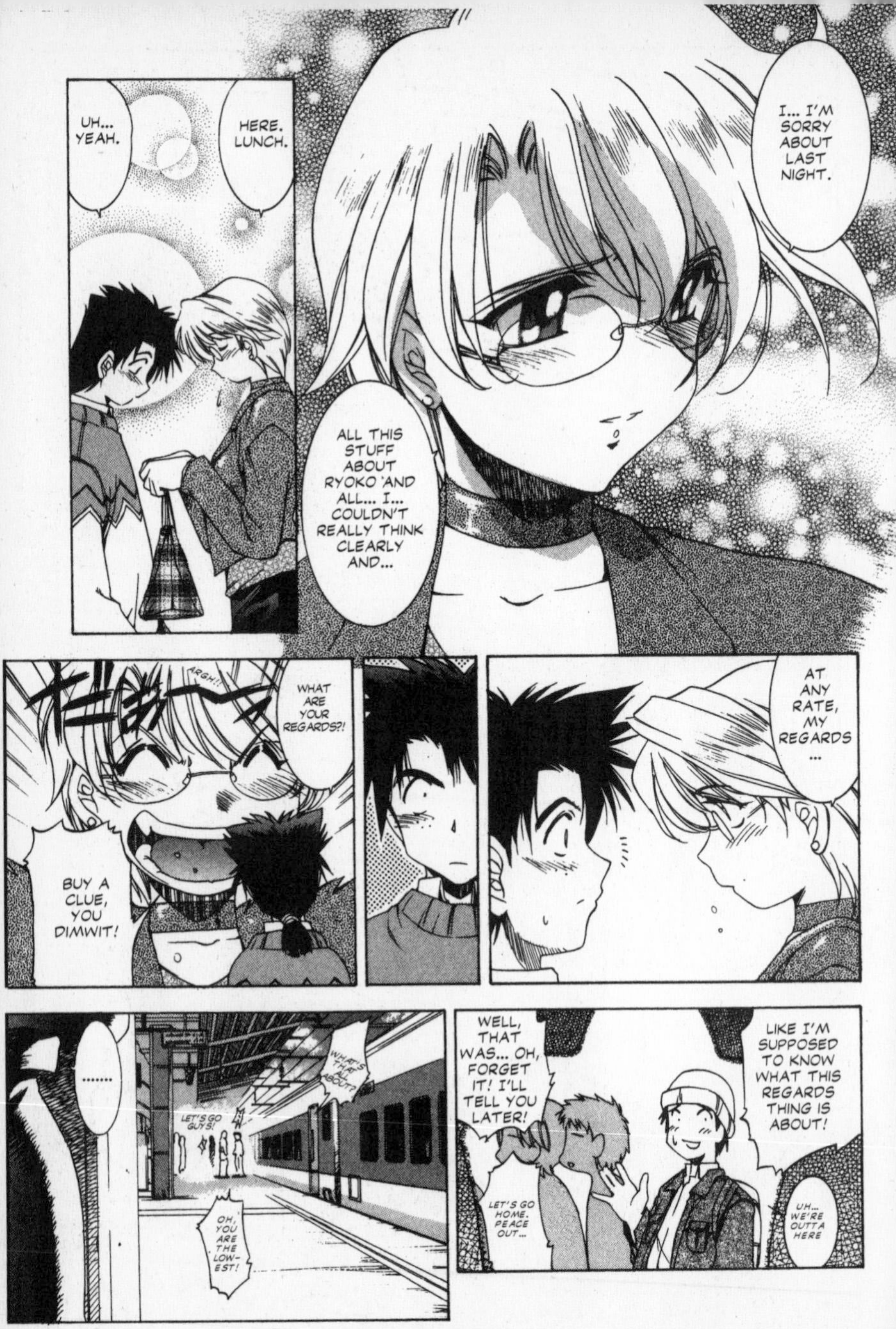
I... I'M SORRY ABOUT LAST NIGHT.
ALL THIS STUFF ABOUT RYOKO 'AND ALL... I... COULDN'T REALLY THINK CLEARLY AND...
HERE. LUNCH.
UH... YEAH.
AT ANY RATE, MY REGARDS ...
WHAT ARE YOUR REGARDS?!
ARGH!!
BUY A CLUE, YOU DIMWIT!
LIKE I'M SUPPOSED TO KNOW WHAT THIS REGARDS THING IS ABOUT!
UH... WE'RE OUTTA HERE
WELL, THAT WAS... OH, FORGET IT! I'LL TELL YOU LATER!
LET'S GO HOME. PEACE OUT...
WHAT'S THAT ALL ABOUT?
....
LET'S GO GUYS!
OH, YOU ARE THE LOW-EST!

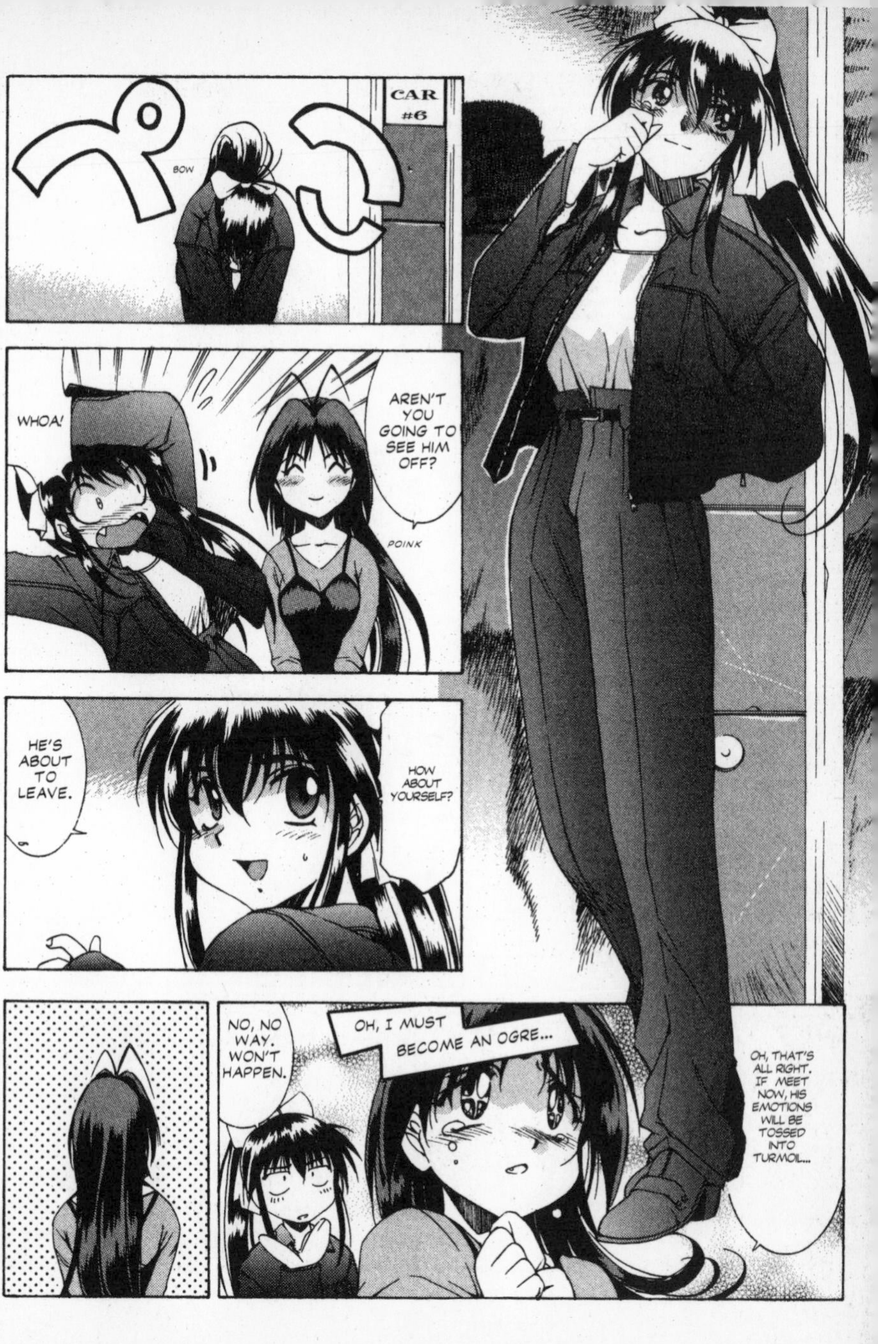

CAR #6
ペこ
BOW
AREN'T YOU GOING TO SEE HIM OFF?
POINK
WHOA!
HOW ABOUT YOURSELF?
HE'S ABOUT TO LEAVE.
OH, THAT'S ALL RIGHT. IF MEET NOW, HIS EMOTIONS WILL BE TOSSED INTO TURMOIL...
OH, I MUST BECOME AN OGRE...
NO, NO WAY. WON'T HAPPEN.

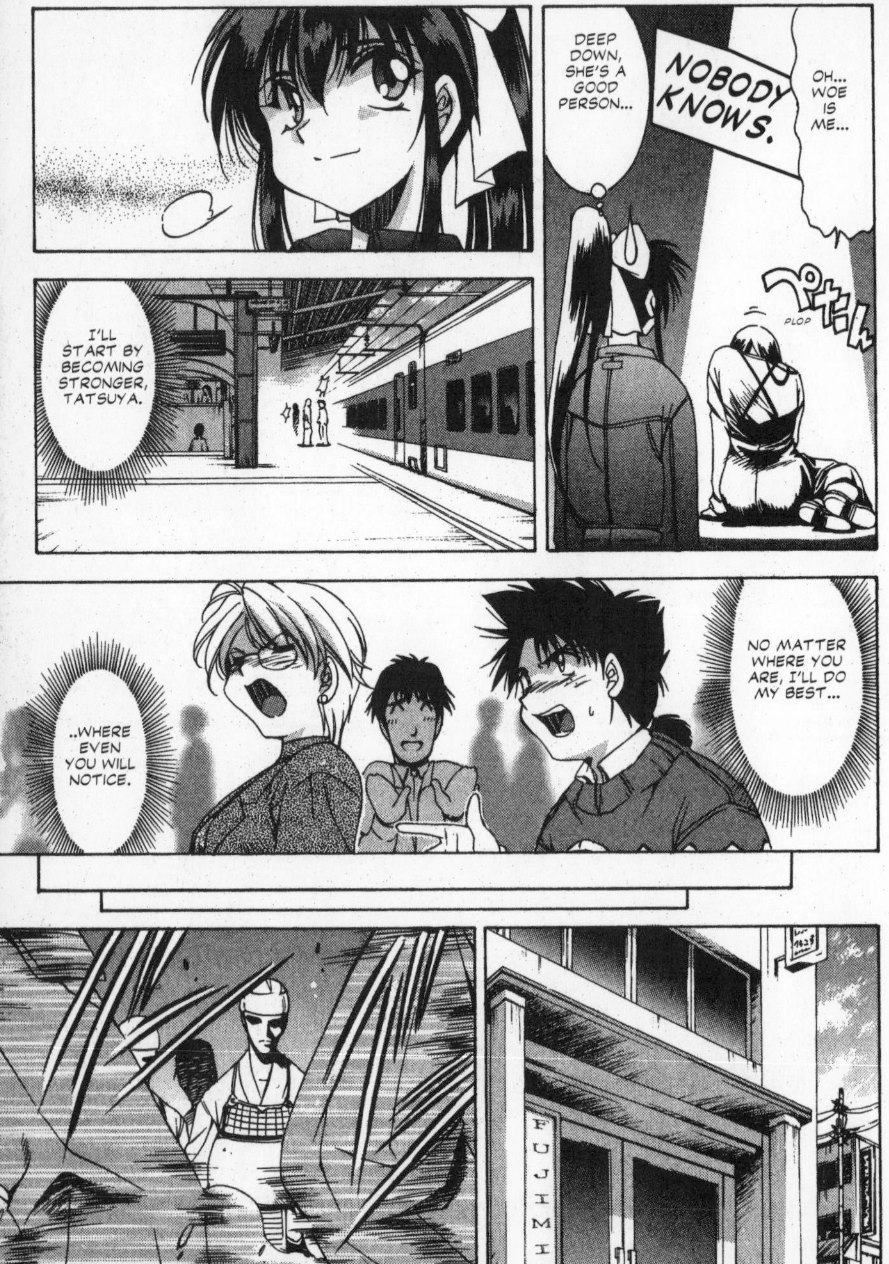
OH... WOE IS ME...
NOBODY KNOWS.
DEEP DOWN, SHE'S A GOOD PERSON...
PLOP
I'LL START BY BECOMING STRONGER, TATSUYA.
NO MATTER WHERE YOU ARE, I'LL DO MY BEST...
..WHERE EVEN YOU WILL NOTICE.
FUJIMIK

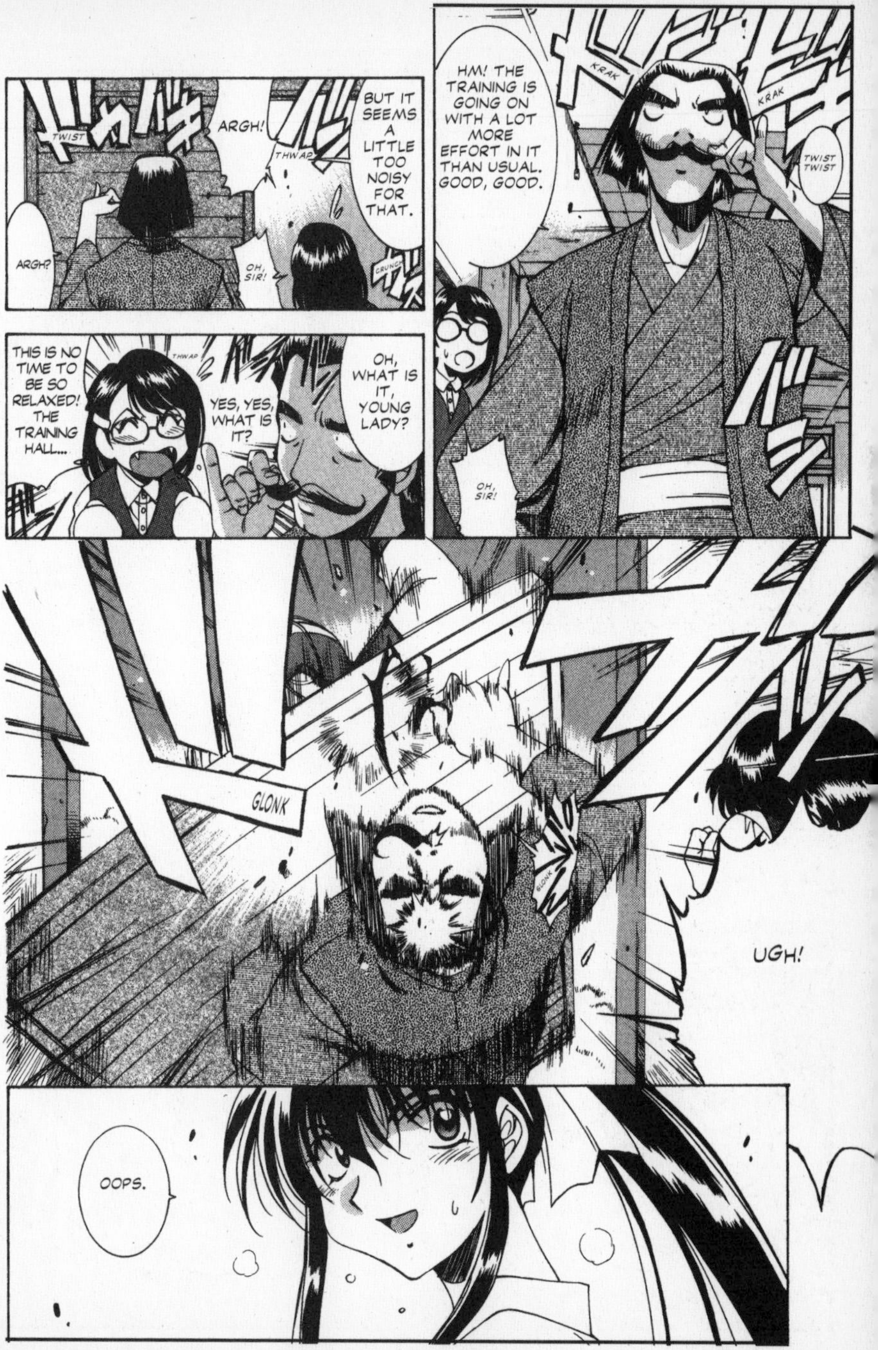
KRAK
KRAK
HM! THE TRAINING IS GOING ON WITH A LOT MORE EFFORT IN IT THAN USUAL. GOOD, GOOD.
TWIST TWIST
OH, SIR!
BUT IT SEEMS A LITTLE TOO NOISY FOR THAT.
ARGH!
THWAP
TWIST
GRUNCH
OH, SIR!
ARGH?
OH, WHAT IS IT, YOUNG LADY?
YES, YES, WHAT IS IT?
THWAP
THIS IS NO TIME TO BE SO RELAXED! THE TRAINING HALL...
UGH!
GLONK
GLONK
OOPS.

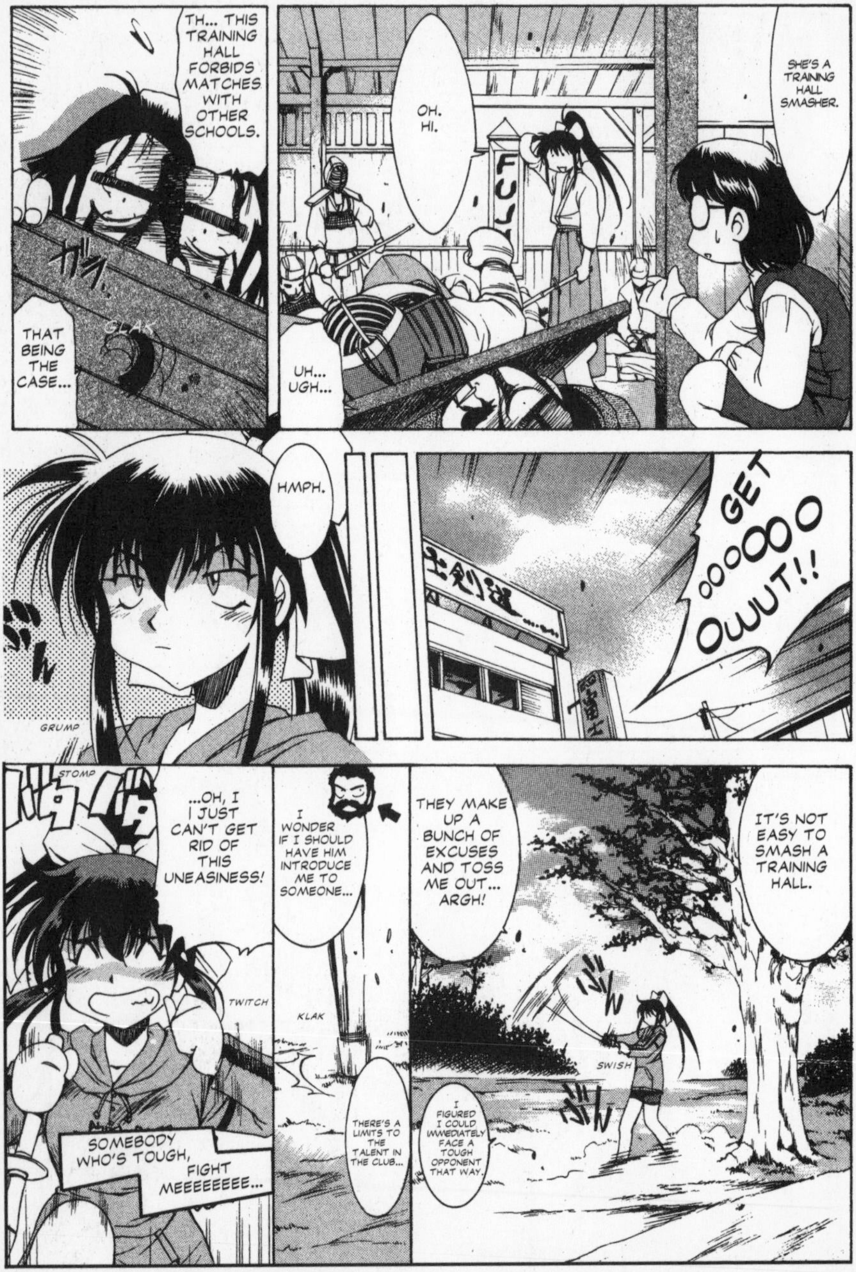
SHE'S A TRAINING HALL SMASHER.
OH. HI.
UH... UGH...
TH... THIS TRAINING HALL FORBIDS MATCHES WITH OTHER SCHOOLS.
GLAK
THAT BEING THE CASE...
GET OOOOOOO OWUT!!
HMPH.
GRUMP
IT'S NOT EASY TO SMASH A TRAINING HALL.
THEY MAKE UP A BUNCH OF EXCUSES AND TOSS ME OUT... ARGH!
SWISH
I FIGURED I COULD IMMEDIATELY FACE A TOUGH OPPONENT THAT WAY.
I WONDER IF I SHOULD HAVE HIM INTRODUCE ME TO SOMEONE...
KLAK
THERE'S A LIMITS TO THE TALENT IN THE CLUB...
STOMP
...OH, I I JUST CAN'T GET RID OF THIS UNEASINESS!
TWITCH
SOMEBODY WHO'S TOUGH, FIGHT MEEEEEEEE...

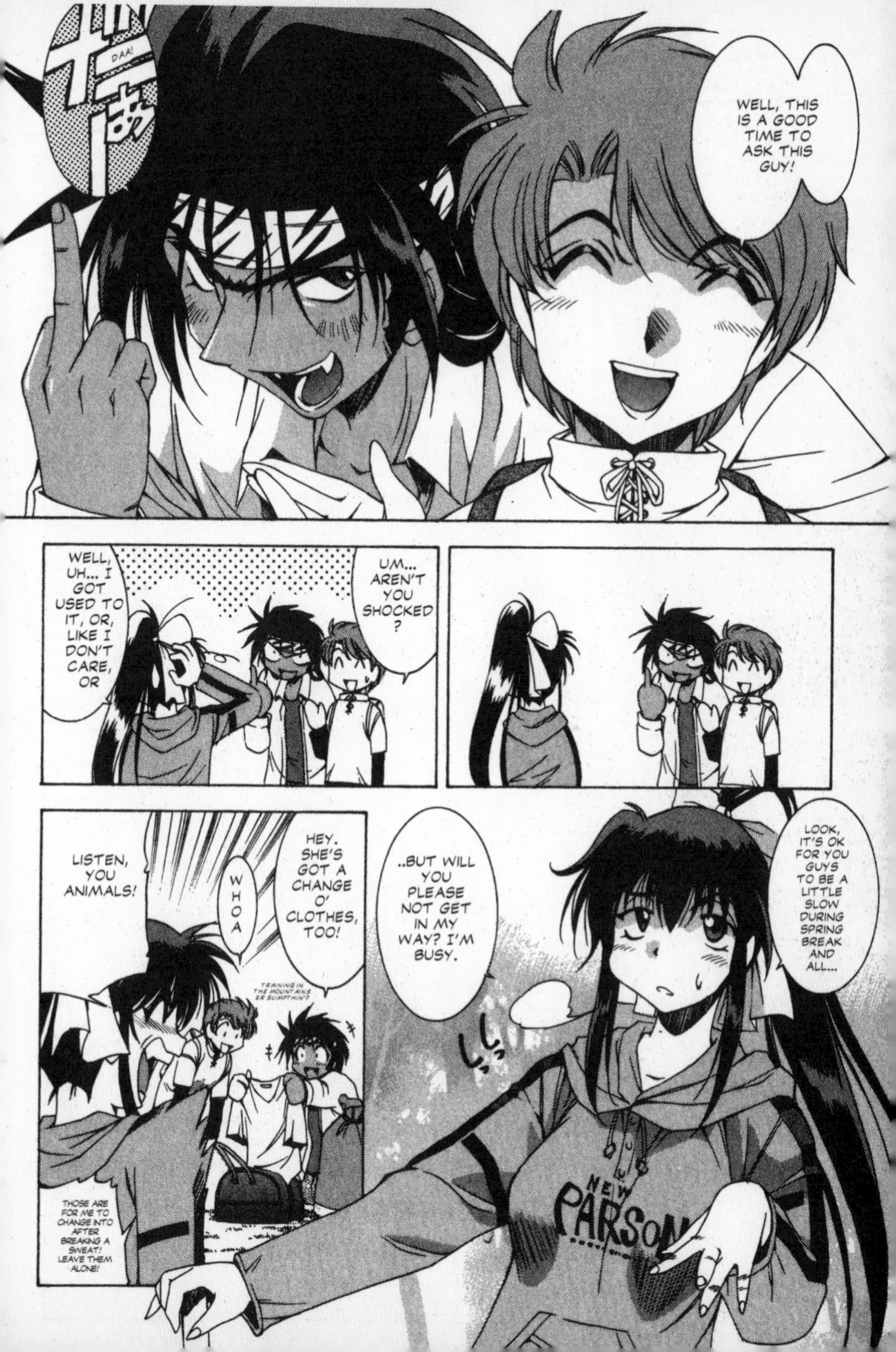
WELL, THIS IS A GOOD TIME TO ASK THIS GUY!
DAA!
UM... AREN'T YOU SHOCKED?
WELL, UH... I GOT USED TO IT, OR, LIKE I DON'T CARE, OR
LOOK, IT'S OK FOR YOU GUYS TO BE A LITTLE SLOW DURING SPRING BREAK AND ALL...
..BUT WILL YOU PLEASE NOT GET IN MY WAY? I'M BUSY.
HEY. SHE'S GOT A CHANGE O' CLOTHES, TOO!
TRAINING IN THE MOUNTAINS ER SUMPTHIN'?
WHOA
LISTEN, YOU ANIMALS!
THOSE ARE FOR ME TO CHANGE INTO AFTER BREAKING A SWEAT! LEAVE THEM ALONE!

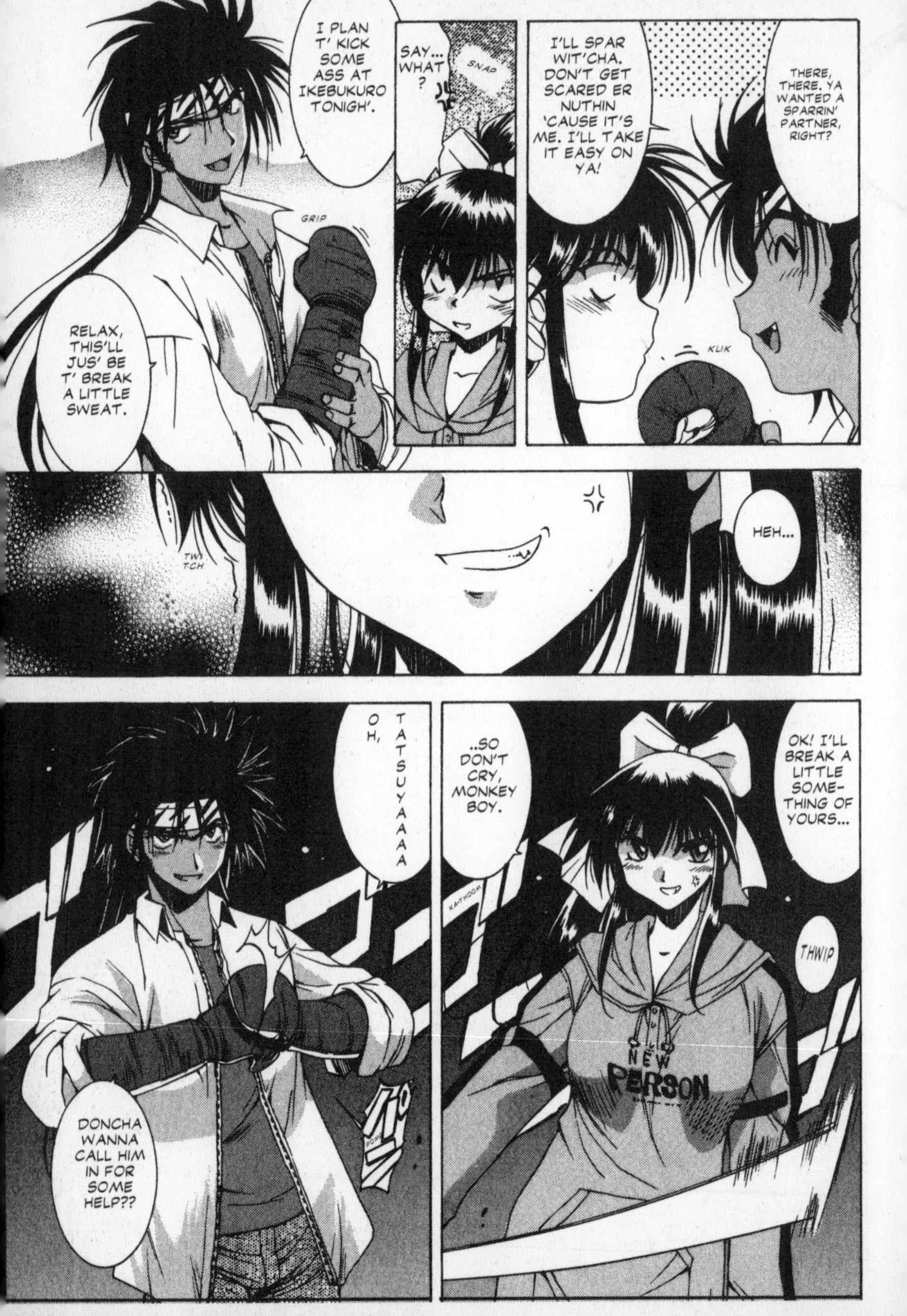
THERE, THERE. YA WANTED A SPARRIN' PARTNER, RIGHT?
I'LL SPAR WIT'CHA. DON'T GET SCARED ER NUTHIN 'CAUSE IT'S ME. I'LL TAKE IT EASY ON YA!
KLIK
SAY... WHAT?
SNAP
I PLAN T' KICK SOME ASS AT IKEBUKURO TONIGH'.
GRIP
RELAX, THIS'LL JUS' BE T' BREAK A LITTLE SWEAT.
HEH...
TWITCH
OK! I'LL BREAK A LITTLE SOME-THING OF YOURS...
THWIP
..SO DON'T CRY, MONKEY BOY.
NEW PERSON
KA-THOOM
OH, TATSUYAAAAA
DONCHA WANNA CALL HIM IN FOR SOME HELP??
POM

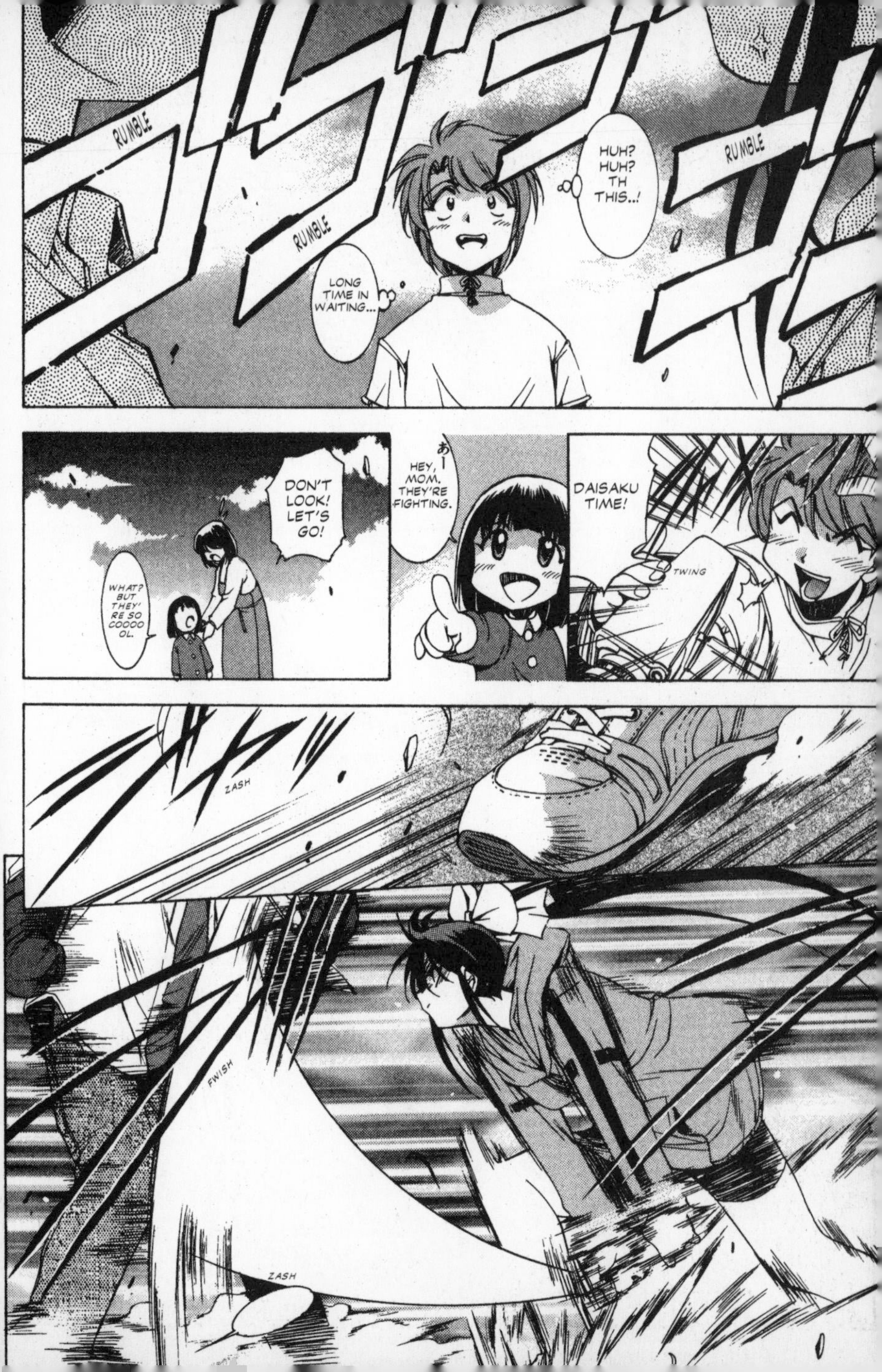
RUMBLE
HUH? HUH? TH THIS...!
RUMBLE
LONG TIME IN WAITING...
RUMBLE
DAISAKU TIME!
TWING
あー
HEY, MOM. THEY'RE FIGHTING.
DON'T LOOK! LET'S GO!
WHAT? BUT THEY'RE SO COOOOOL.
ZASH
FWISH
ZASH

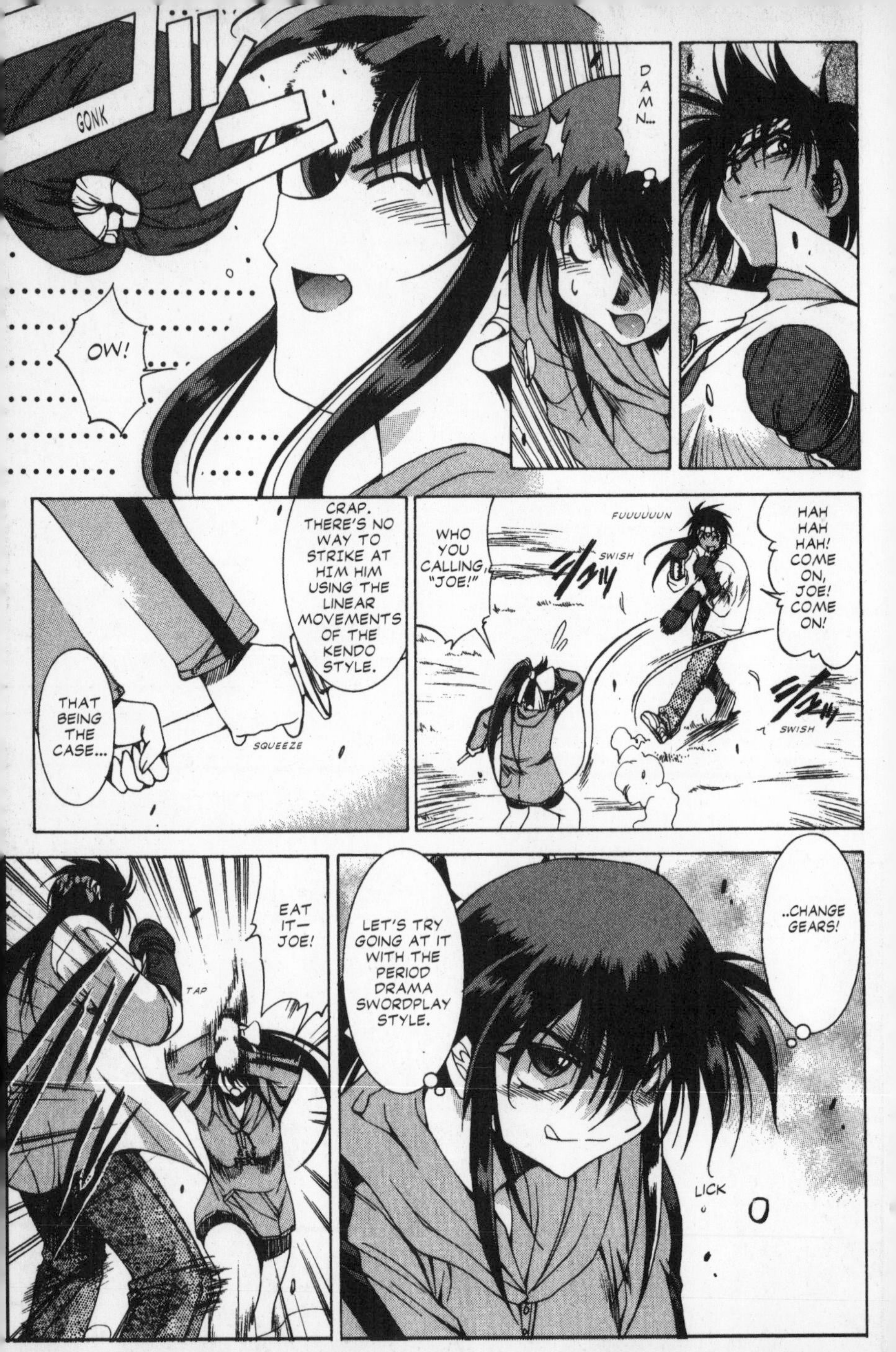
DAMN...
GONK
OW!
HAH HAH HAH! COME ON, JOE! COME ON!
FUUUUUUN
SWISH
WHO YOU CALLING, "JOE!"
SWISH
CRAP. THERE'S NO WAY TO STRIKE AT HIM HIM USING THE LINEAR MOVEMENTS OF THE KENDO STYLE.
THAT BEING THE CASE...
SQUEEZE
..CHANGE GEARS!
LET'S TRY GOING AT IT WITH THE PERIOD DRAMA SWORDPLAY STYLE.
LICK
EAT IT—JOE!
TAP

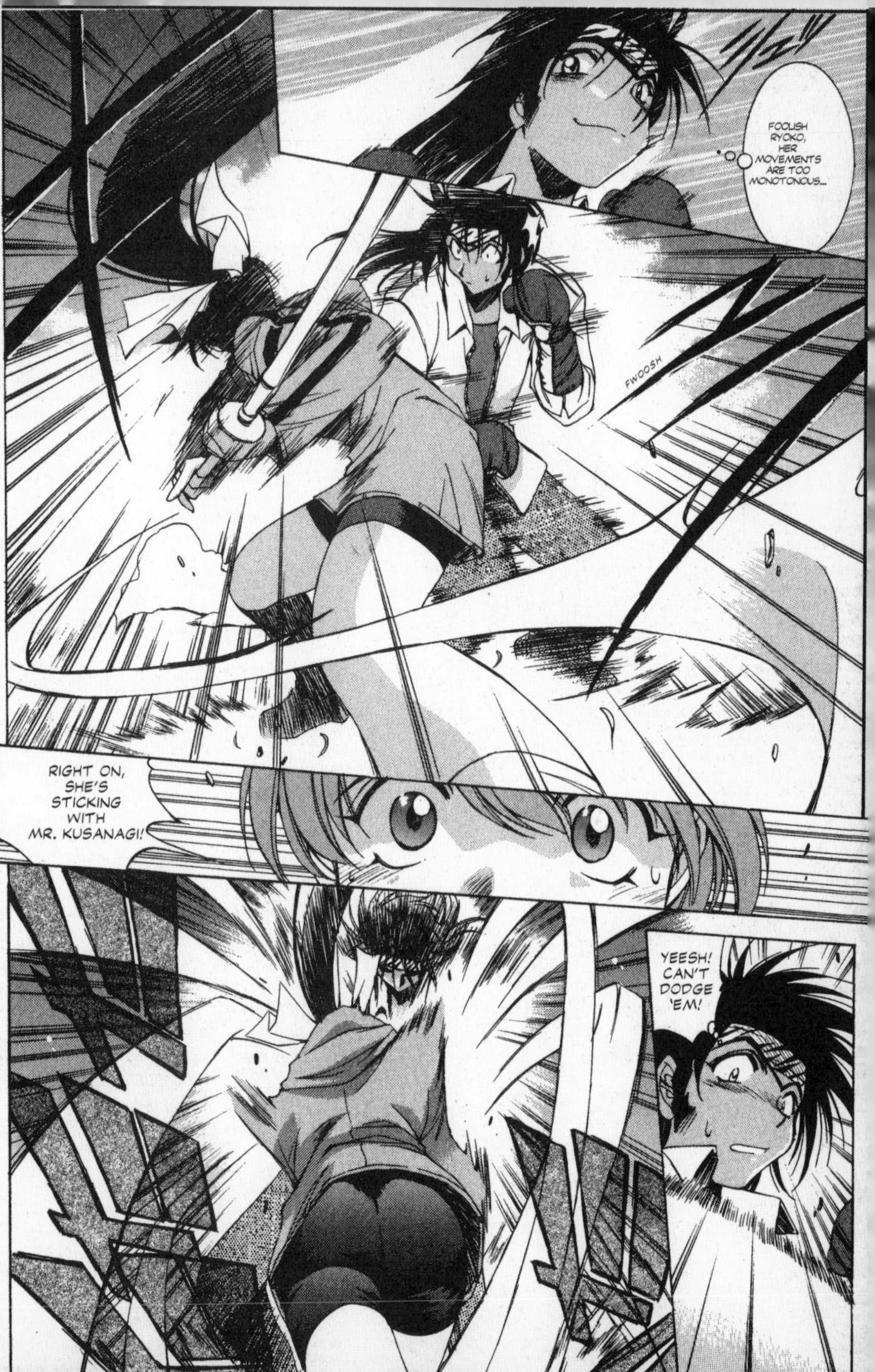
FOOLISH RYOKO, HER MOVEMENTS ARE TOO MONOTONOUS...
FWOOSH
RIGHT ON, SHE'S STICKING WITH MR. KUSANAGI!
YEESH! CAN'T DODGE 'EM!

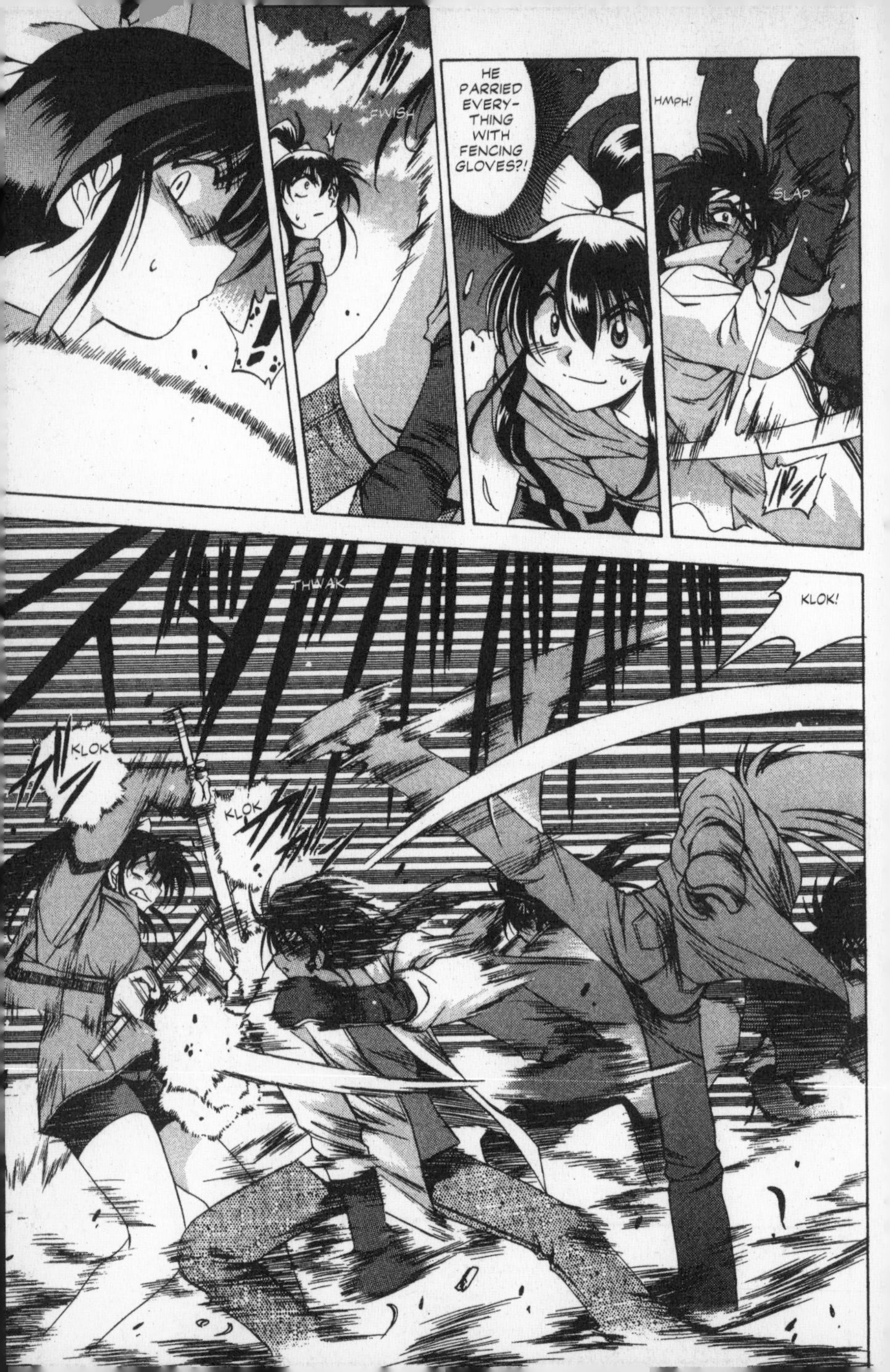
HMPH!
SLAP
HE PARRIED EVERY-THING WITH FENCING GLOVES?!
FWISH
KLOK!
THWAK
KLOK
KLOK

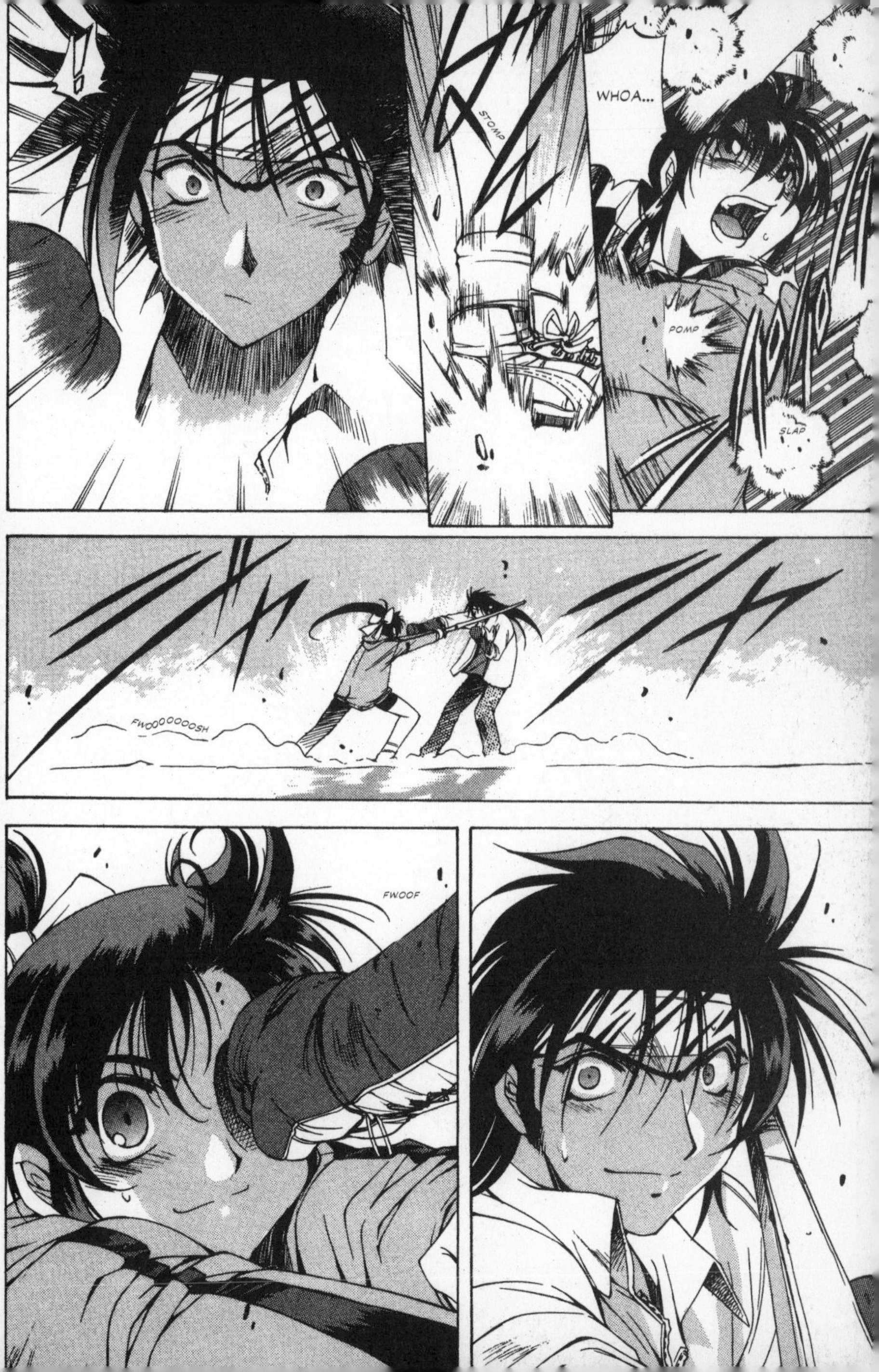
WHOA...
POMP
SLAP
STOMP
FWOOOOOOOSH
FWOOF

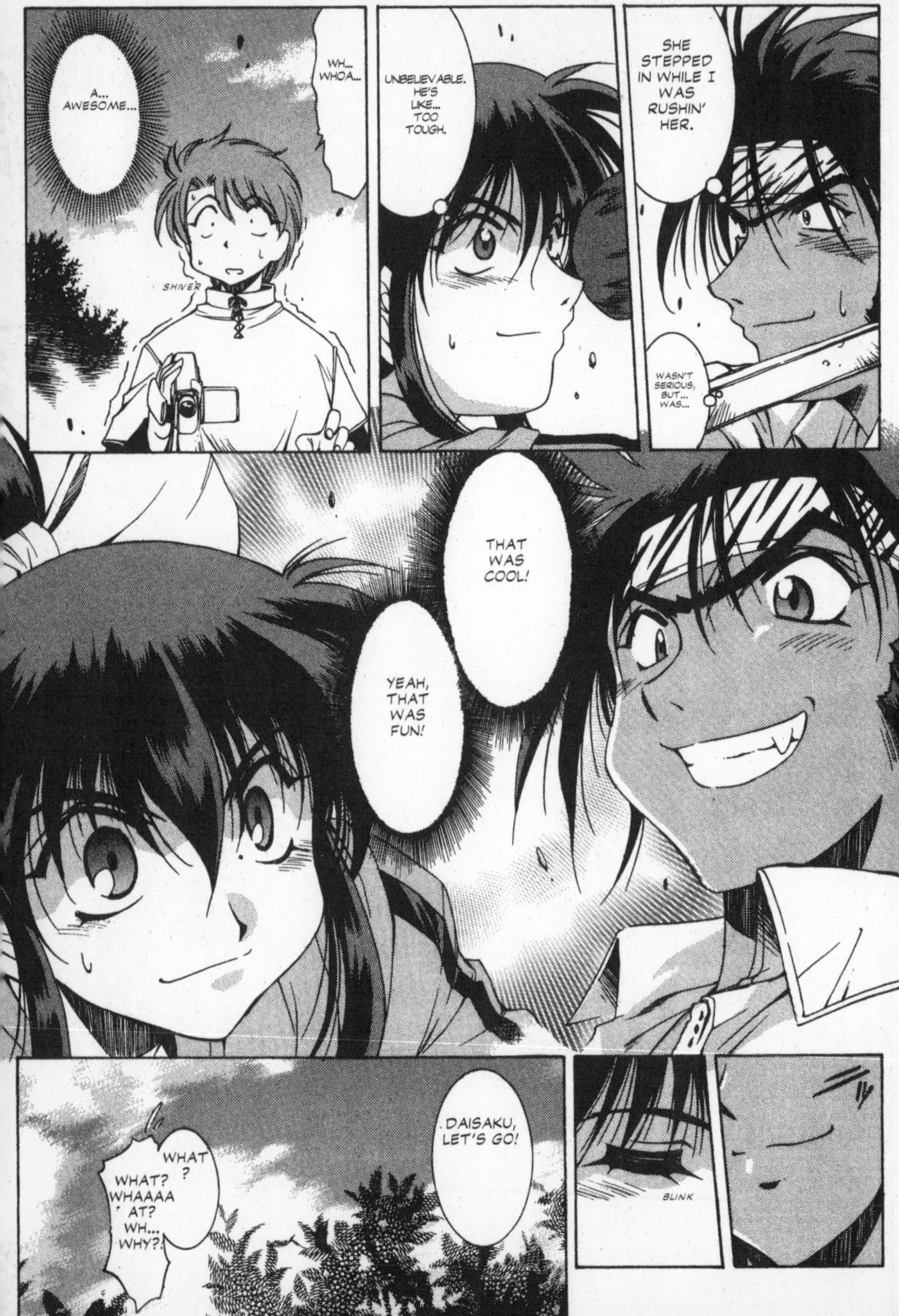
SHE STEPPED IN WHILE I WAS RUSHIN' HER.
WASN'T SERIOUS, BUT... WAS...
UNBELIEVABLE. HE'S LIKE... TOO TOUGH.
WH... WHOA...
A... AWESOME...
SHIVER
THAT WAS COOL!
YEAH, THAT WAS FUN!
BLINK
DAISAKU, LET'S GO!
WHAT ?
WHAT? WHAAAA AT? WH... WHY?

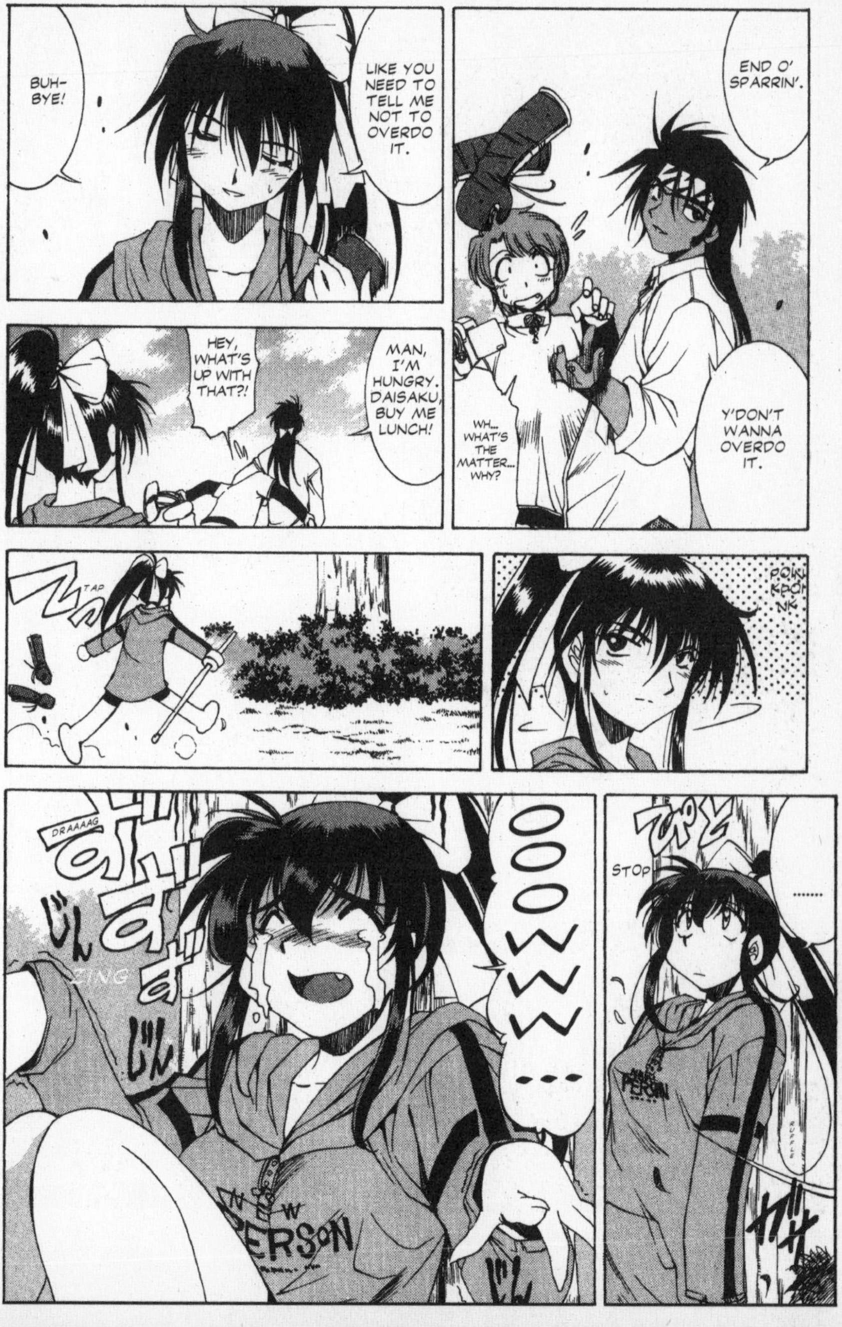
END O' SPARRIN'.
Y'DON'T WANNA OVERDO IT.
WH... WHAT'S THE MATTER... WHY?
LIKE YOU NEED TO TELL ME NOT TO OVERDO IT.
BUH-BYE!
MAN, I'M HUNGRY. DAISAKU, BUY ME LUNCH!
HEY, WHAT'S UP WITH THAT?!
POINK KPOINK
TAP
STOP
....
RUFFLE
DRAAAAG
ZING
OOOWWW...

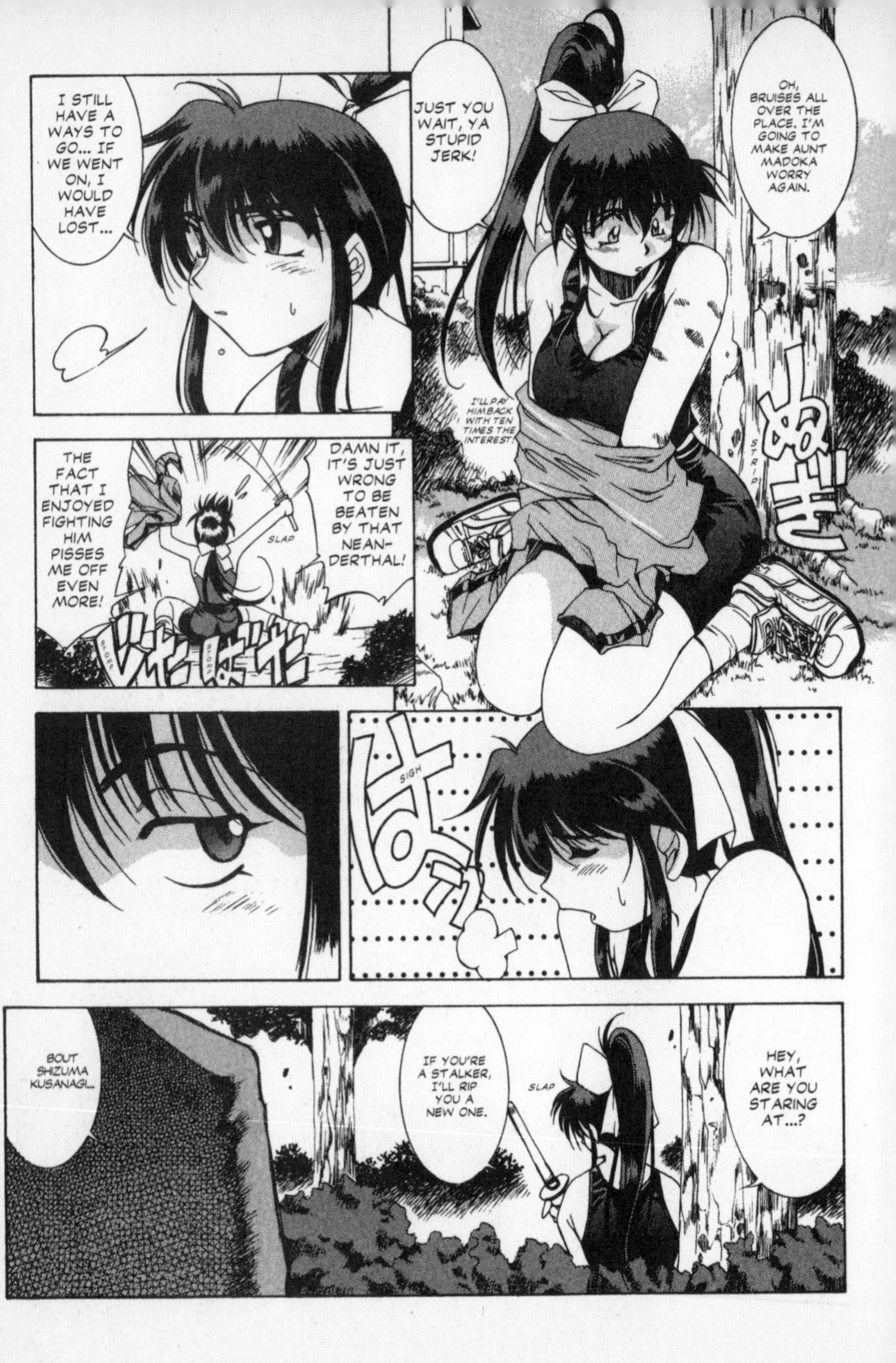
OH, BRUISES ALL OVER THE PLACE. I'M GOING TO MAKE AUNT MADOKA WORRY AGAIN.
JUST YOU WAIT, YA STUPID JERK!
I'LL PAY HIMBACK WITH TEN TIMES THE INTEREST!
STRIP
I STILL HAVE A WAYS TO GO... IF WE WENT ON, I WOULD HAVE LOST...
DAMN IT, IT'S JUST WRONG TO BE BEATEN BY THAT NEAN-DERTHAL!
THE FACT THAT I ENJOYED FIGHTING HIM PISSES ME OFF EVEN MORE!
SLAP
SIGH
HEY, WHAT ARE YOU STARING AT...?
SLAP
IF YOU'RE A STALKER, I'LL RIP YOU A NEW ONE.
BOUT SHIZUMA KUSANAGI...

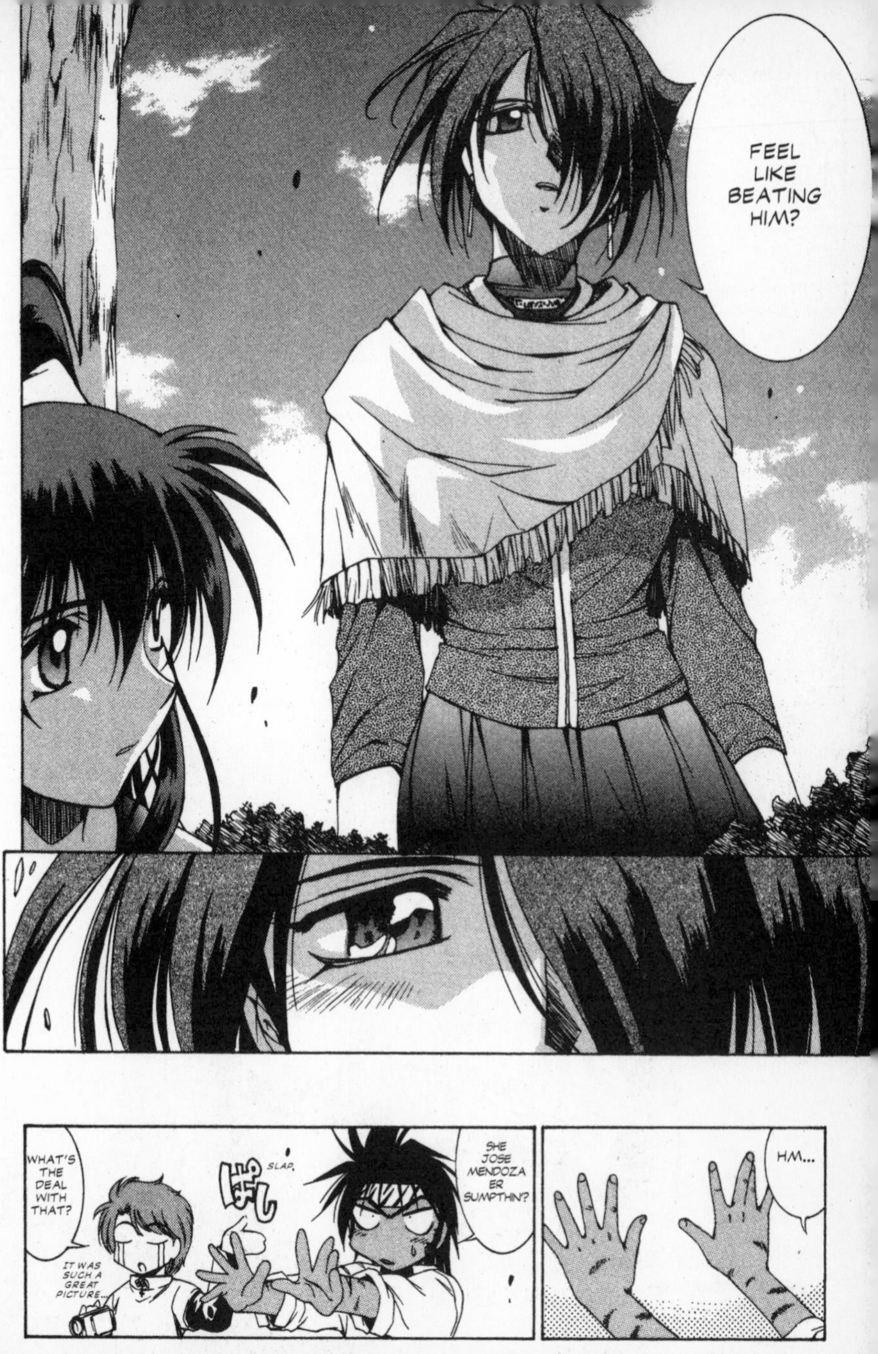
FEEL LIKE BEATING HIM?
HM...
SHE JOSE MENDOZA ER SUMPTHIN?
SLAP
ぱし
WHAT'S THE DEAL WITH THAT?
IT WAS SUCH A GREAT PICTURE...

Side Stories Real Bout High School Short Shorts

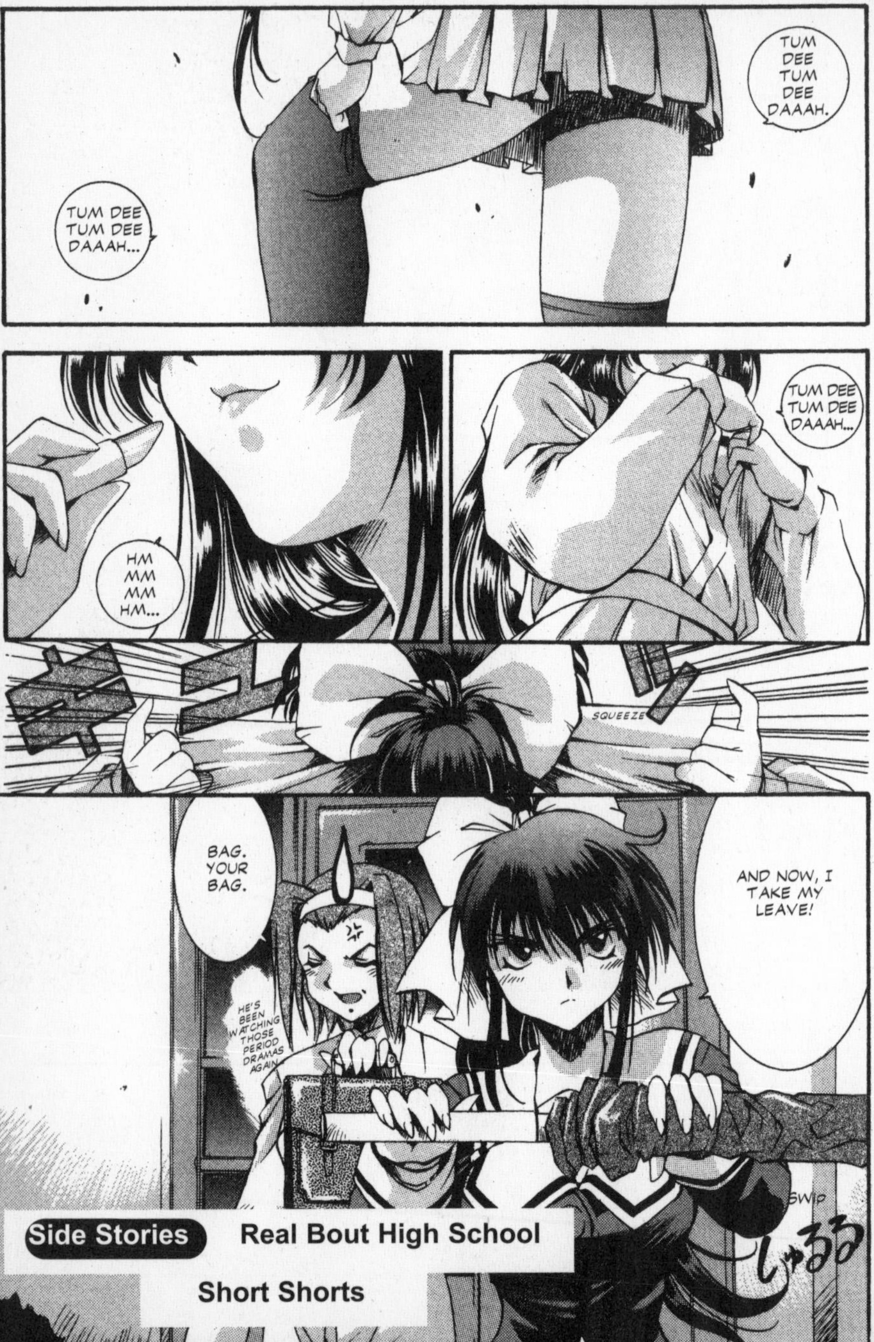

TUM DEE TUM DEE DAAAH.
TUM DEE TUM DEE DAAAH...
TUM DEE TUM DEE DAAAH...
HM MM MM HM...
SQUEEZE
AND NOW, I TAKE MY LEAVE!
BAG. YOUR BAG.
HE'S BEEN WATCHING THOSE PERIOD DRAMAS AGAIN.
SWIP
しゅるる

A Tranquil Day

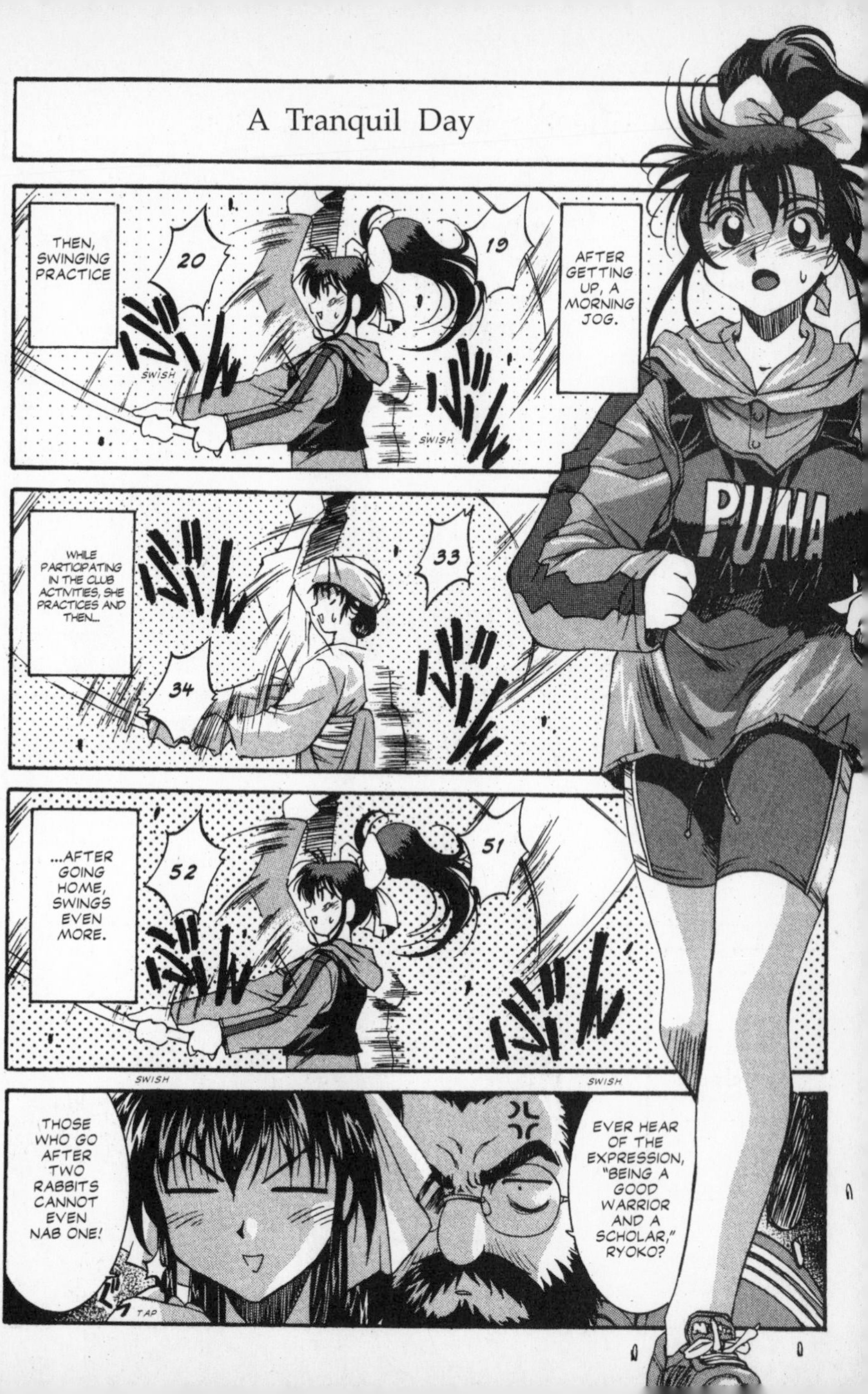
AFTER GETTING UP, A MORNING JOG.
THEN, SWINGING PRACTICE
19
20
SWISH
SWISH
WHILE PARTICIPATING IN THE CLUB ACTIVITIES, SHE PRACTICES AND THEN...
33
34
...AFTER GOING HOME, SWINGS EVEN MORE.
51
52
SWISH
SWISH
EVER HEAR OF THE EXPRESSION, "BEING A GOOD WARRIOR AND A SCHOLAR," RYOKO?
THOSE WHO GO AFTER TWO RABBITS CANNOT EVEN NAB ONE!
TAP

The Sleeping Prince at the Desk

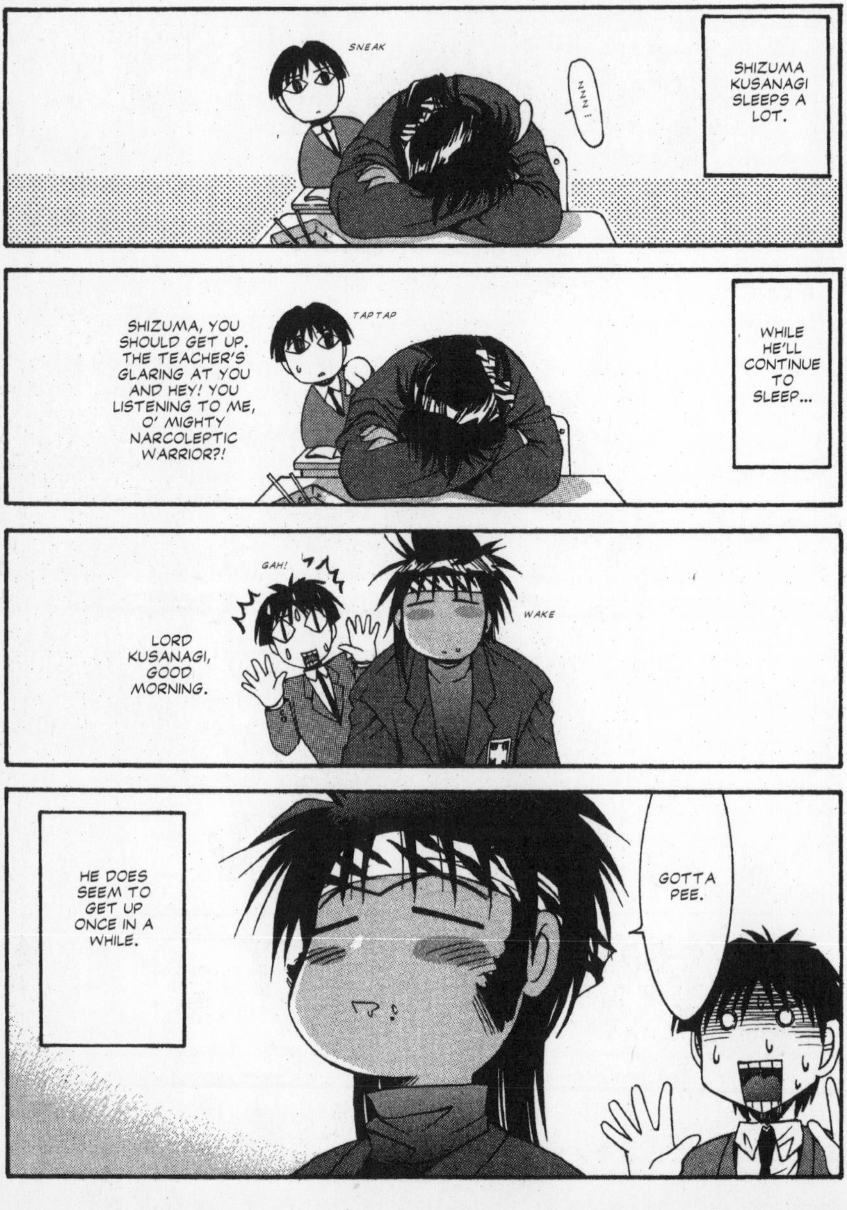
SHIZUMA KUSANAGI SLEEPS A LOT.
ZZZ!!
SNEAK
WHILE HE'LL CONTINUE TO SLEEP...
TAPTAP
SHIZUMA, YOU SHOULD GET UP. THE TEACHER'S GLARING AT YOU AND HEY! YOU LISTENING TO ME, O' MIGHTY NARCOLEPTIC WARRIOR?!
WAKE
GAH!
LORD KUSANAGI, GOOD MORNING.
GOTTA PEE.
HE DOES SEEM TO GET UP ONCE IN A WHILE.

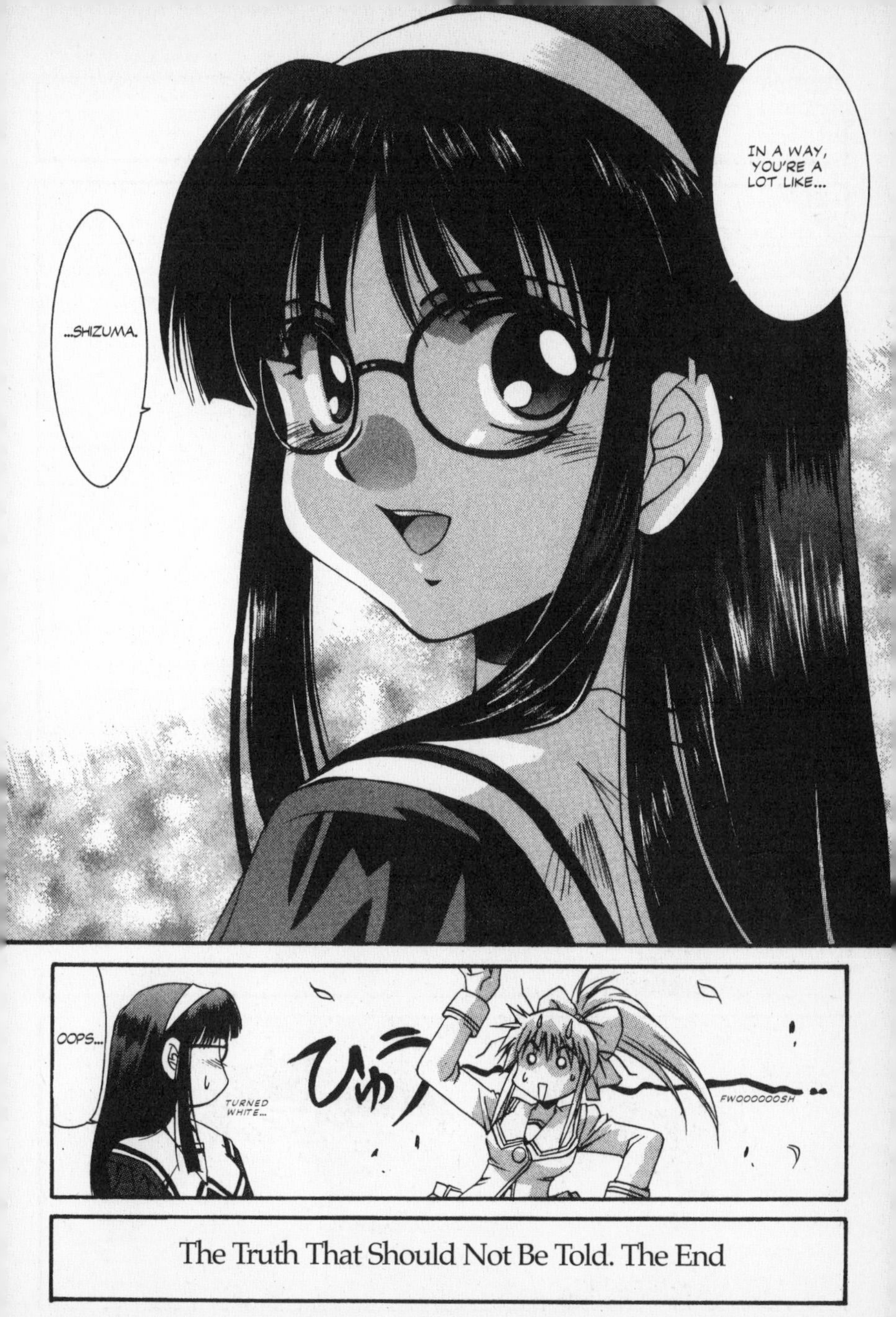
IN A WAY, YOU'RE A LOT LIKE...
...SHIZUMA.
FWOOOOOOSH
TURNED WHITE...
OOPS...

The Truth That Should Not Be Told. The End

Ambition

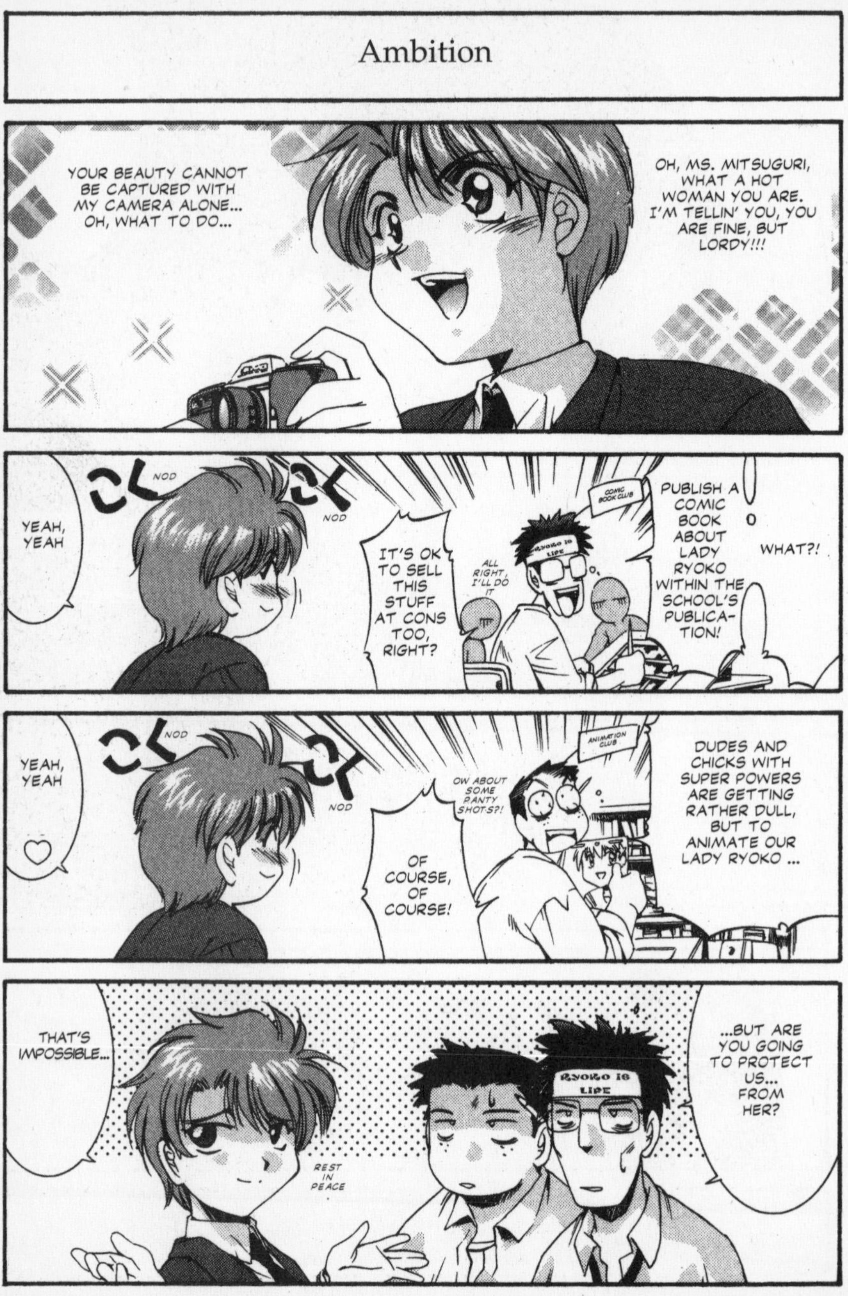
OH, MS. MITSUGURI, WHAT A HOT WOMAN YOU ARE. I'M TELLIN' YOU, YOU ARE FINE, BUT LORDY!!!
YOUR BEAUTY CANNOT BE CAPTURED WITH MY CAMERA ALONE... OH, WHAT TO DO...
WHAT?!
PUBLISH A COMIC BOOK ABOUT LADY RYOKO WITHIN THE SCHOOL'S PUBLICATION!
COMIC BOOK CLUB
RYOKO IS LIFE
ALL RIGHT, I'LL DO IT
IT'S OK TO SELL THIS STUFF AT CONS TOO, RIGHT?
こく
NOD
こく
NOD
YEAH, YEAH
DUDES AND CHICKS WITH SUPER POWERS ARE GETTING RATHER DULL, BUT TO ANIMATE OUR LADY RYOKO ...
ANIMATION CLUB
OW ABOUT SOME PANTY SHOTS?!
OF COURSE, OF COURSE!
こく
NOD
こく
NOD
YEAH, YEAH ♡
...BUT ARE YOU GOING TO PROTECT US... FROM HER?
RYOKO IS LIFE
REST IN PEACE
THAT'S IMPOSSIBLE...

A Man's Ideal

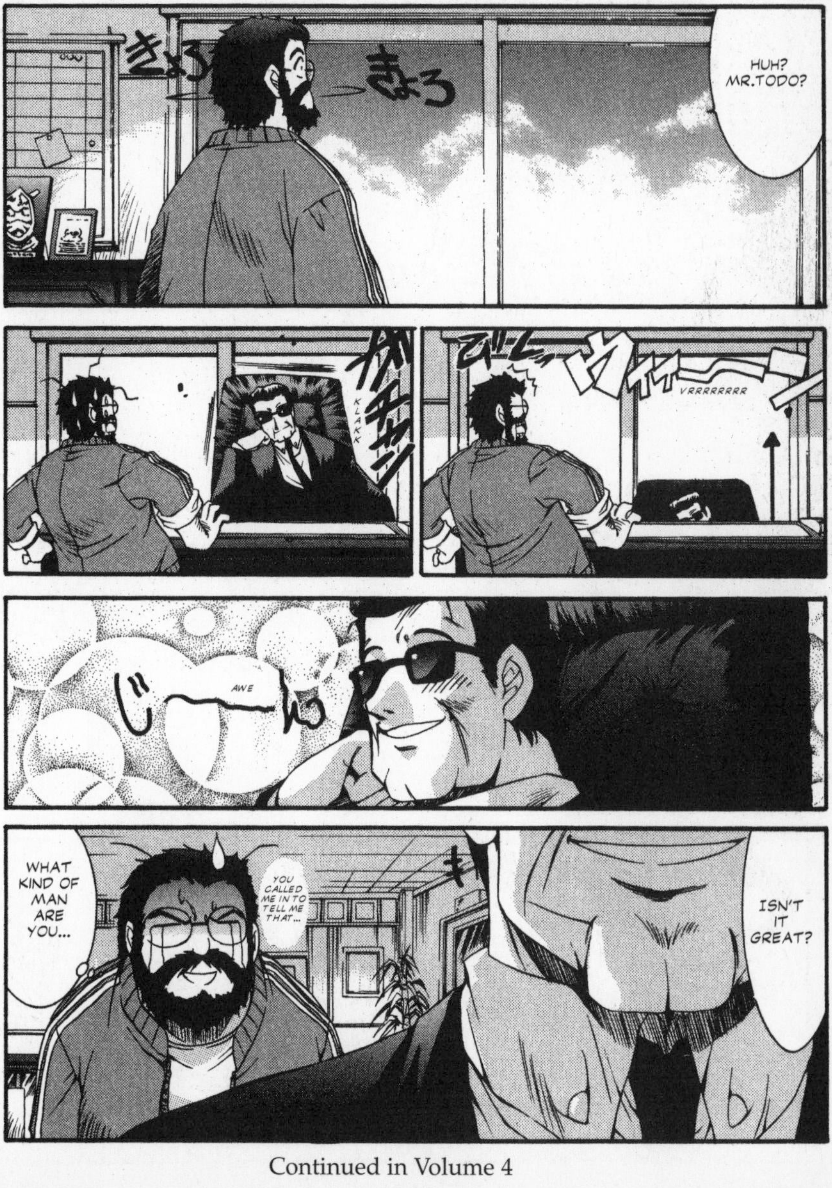
HUH? MR.TODO?
きょろ
きょろ
VRRRRRRRR
KLAKK
AWE
ISN'T IT GREAT?
YOU CALLED ME IN TO TELL ME THAT...
WHAT KIND OF MAN ARE YOU...

Continued in Volume 4

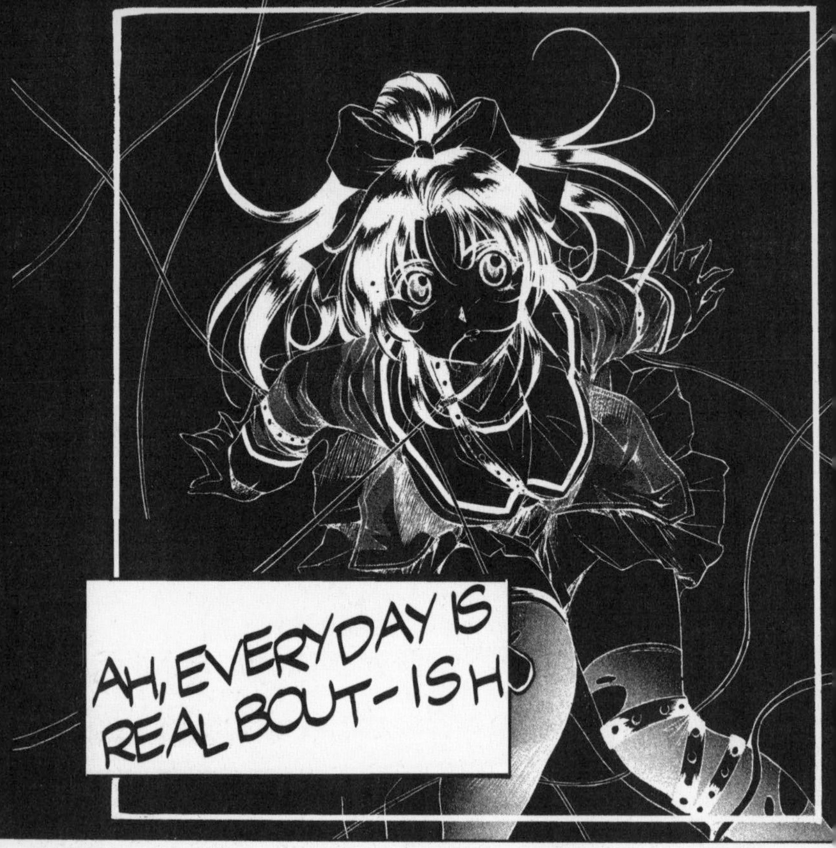
AH, EVERYDAY IS REAL BOUT-ISH

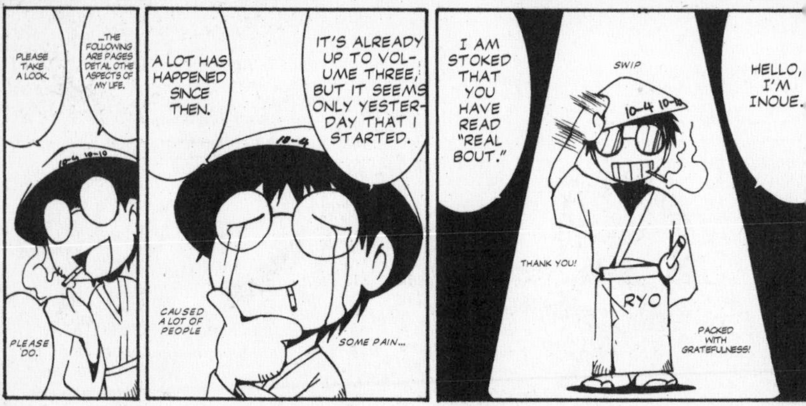
HELLO, I'M INOUE.
I AM STOKED THAT YOU HAVE READ "REAL BOUT."
SWIP
THANK YOU!
RYO
PACKED WITH GRATEFULNESS!
IT'S ALREADY UP TO VOL-UME THREE, BUT IT SEEMS ONLY YESTER-DAY THAT I STARTED.
A LOT HAS HAPPENED SINCE THEN.
CAUSED A LOT OF PEOPLE
SOME PAIN...
...THE FOLLOWING ARE PAGES DETAIL OTHE ASPECTS OF MY LIFE.
PLEASE TAKE A LOOK.
PLEASE DO.

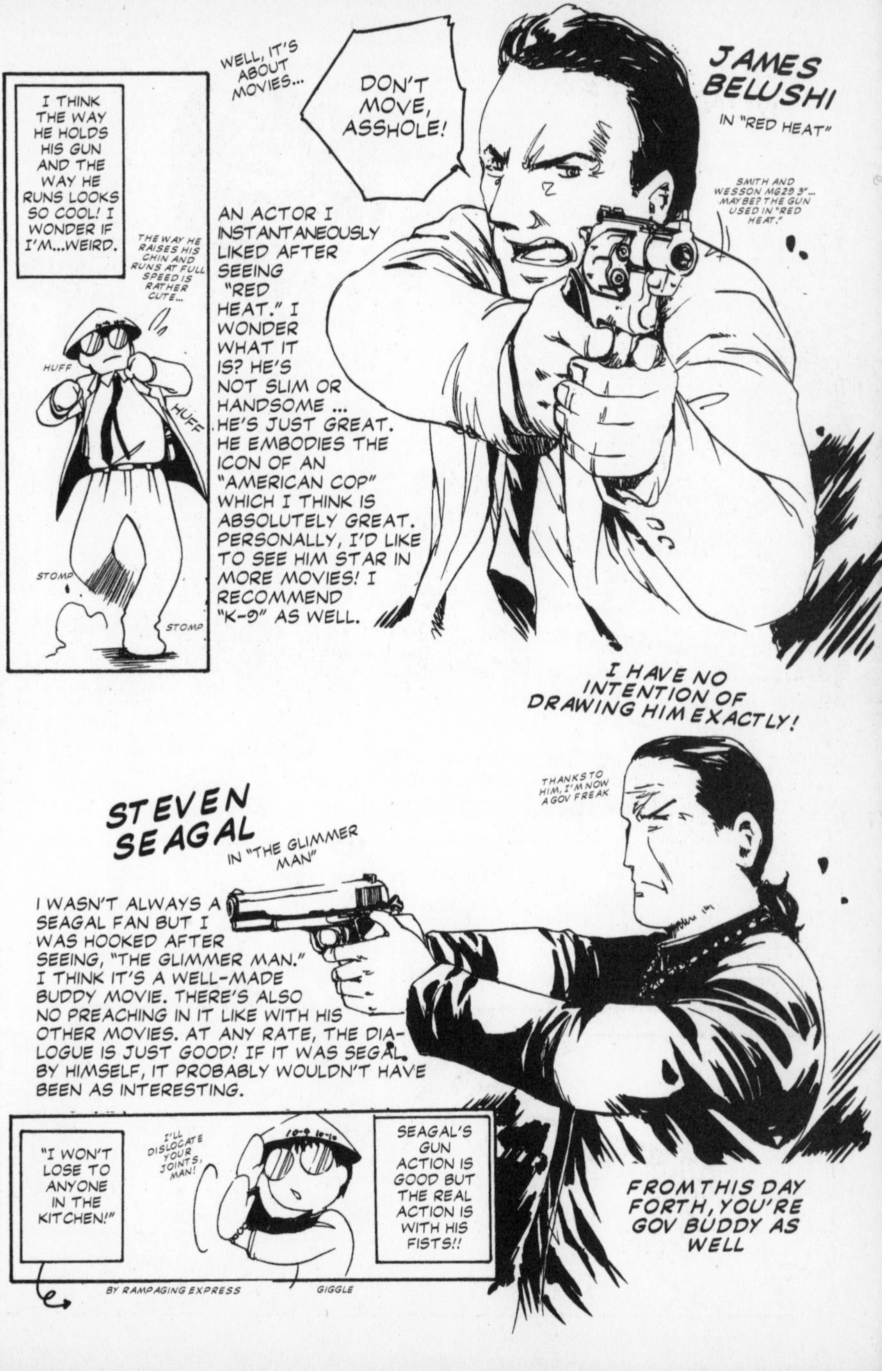

JAMES BELUSHI
IN "RED HEAT"
SMITH AND WESSON MG29 3"... MAYBE? THE GUN USED IN "RED HEAT."
DON'T MOVE, ASSHOLE!
WELL, IT'S ABOUT MOVIES...
AN ACTOR I INSTANTANEOUSLY LIKED AFTER SEEING "RED HEAT." I WONDER WHAT IT IS? HE'S NOT SLIM OR HANDSOME ... HE'S JUST GREAT. HE EMBODIES THE ICON OF AN "AMERICAN COP" WHICH I THINK IS ABSOLUTELY GREAT. PERSONALLY, I'D LIKE TO SEE HIM STAR IN MORE MOVIES! I RECOMMEND "K-9" AS WELL.
I THINK THE WAY HE HOLDS HIS GUN AND THE WAY HE RUNS LOOKS SO COOL! I WONDER IF I'M...WEIRD.
THE WAY HE RAISES HIS CHIN AND RUNS AT FULL SPEED IS RATHER CUTE...
HUFF
HUFF
STOMP
STOMP
I HAVE NO INTENTION OF DRAWING HIM EXACTLY!
THANKS TO HIM, I'M NOW A GOV FREAK
STEVEN SEAGAL
IN "THE GLIMMER MAN"
I WASN'T ALWAYS A SEAGAL FAN BUT I WAS HOOKED AFTER SEEING, "THE GLIMMER MAN." I THINK IT'S A WELL-MADE BUDDY MOVIE. THERE'S ALSO NO PREACHING IN IT LIKE WITH HIS OTHER MOVIES. AT ANY RATE, THE DIALOGUE IS JUST GOOD! IF IT WAS SEGAL BY HIMSELF, IT PROBABLY WOULDN'T HAVE BEEN AS INTERESTING.
FROM THIS DAY FORTH, YOU'RE GOV BUDDY AS WELL
SEAGAL'S GUN ACTION IS GOOD BUT THE REAL ACTION IS WITH HIS FISTS!!
I'LL DISLOCATE YOUR JOINTS, MAN!
"I WON'T LOSE TO ANYONE IN THE KITCHEN!"
GIGGLE
BY RAMPAGING EXPRESS

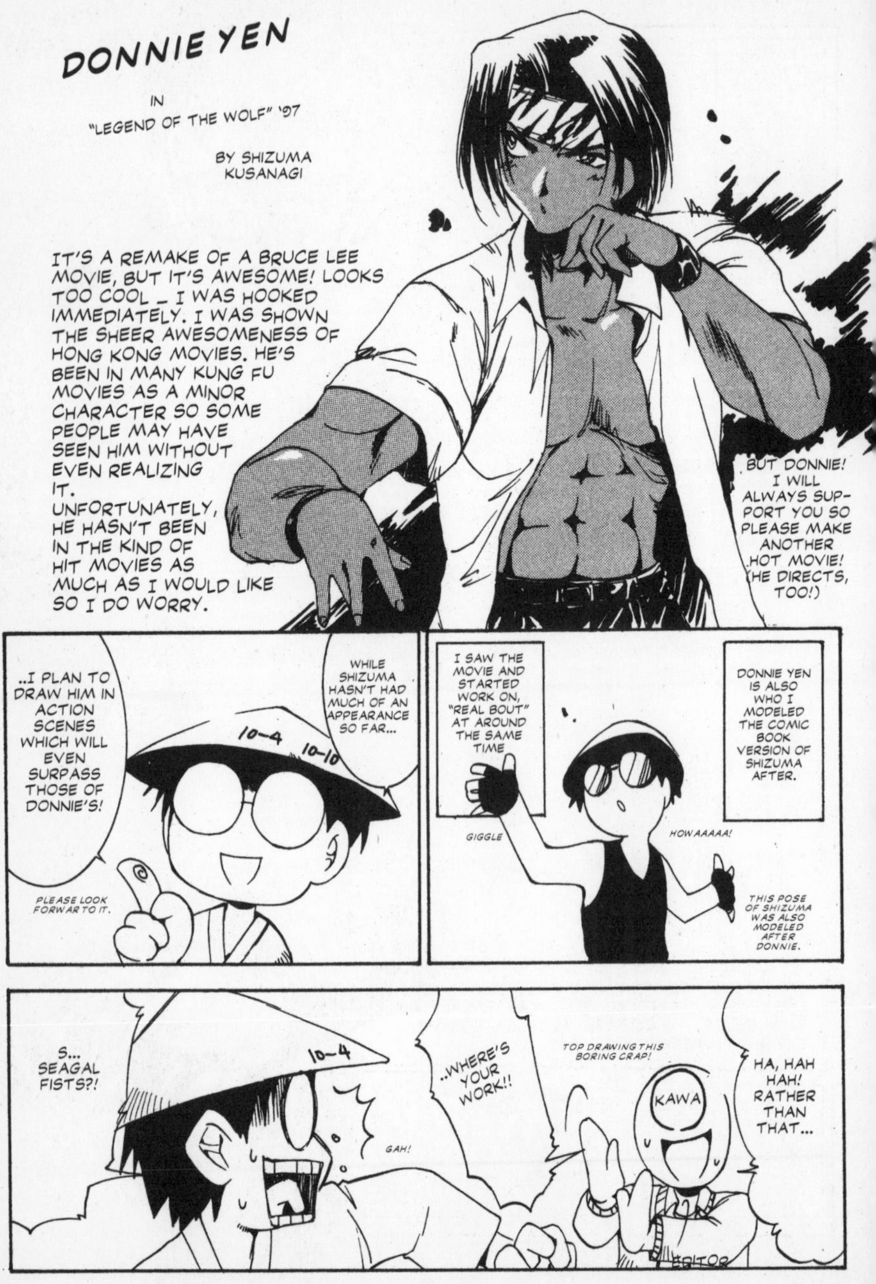
DONNIE YEN
IN
"LEGEND OF THE WOLF" '97
BY SHIZUMA KUSANAGI
IT'S A REMAKE OF A BRUCE LEE MOVIE, BUT IT'S AWESOME! LOOKS TOO COOL _ I WAS HOOKED IMMEDIATELY. I WAS SHOWN THE SHEER AWESOMENESS OF HONG KONG MOVIES. HE'S BEEN IN MANY KUNG FU MOVIES AS A MINOR CHARACTER SO SOME PEOPLE MAY HAVE SEEN HIM WITHOUT EVEN REALIZING IT.
UNFORTUNATELY, HE HASN'T BEEN IN THE KIND OF HIT MOVIES AS MUCH AS I WOULD LIKE SO I DO WORRY.
BUT DONNIE! I WILL ALWAYS SUPPORT YOU SO PLEASE MAKE ANOTHER HOT MOVIE! (HE DIRECTS, TOO!)
DONNIE YEN IS ALSO WHO I MODELED THE COMIC BOOK VERSION OF SHIZUMA AFTER.
I SAW THE MOVIE AND STARTED WORK ON, "REAL BOUT" AT AROUND THE SAME TIME
HOWAAAAA!
GIGGLE
THIS POSE OF SHIZUMA WAS ALSO MODELED AFTER DONNIE.
WHILE SHIZUMA HASN'T HAD MUCH OF AN APPEARANCE SO FAR...
..I PLAN TO DRAW HIM IN ACTION SCENES WHICH WILL EVEN SURPASS THOSE OF DONNIE'S!
10-10
10-4
PLEASE LOOK FORWAR TO IT.
HA, HAH HAH! RATHER THAN THAT...
TOP DRAWING THIS BORING CRAP!
KAWA
EDITOR
..WHERE'S YOUR WORK!!
GAH!
10-4
S... SEAGAL FISTS?!

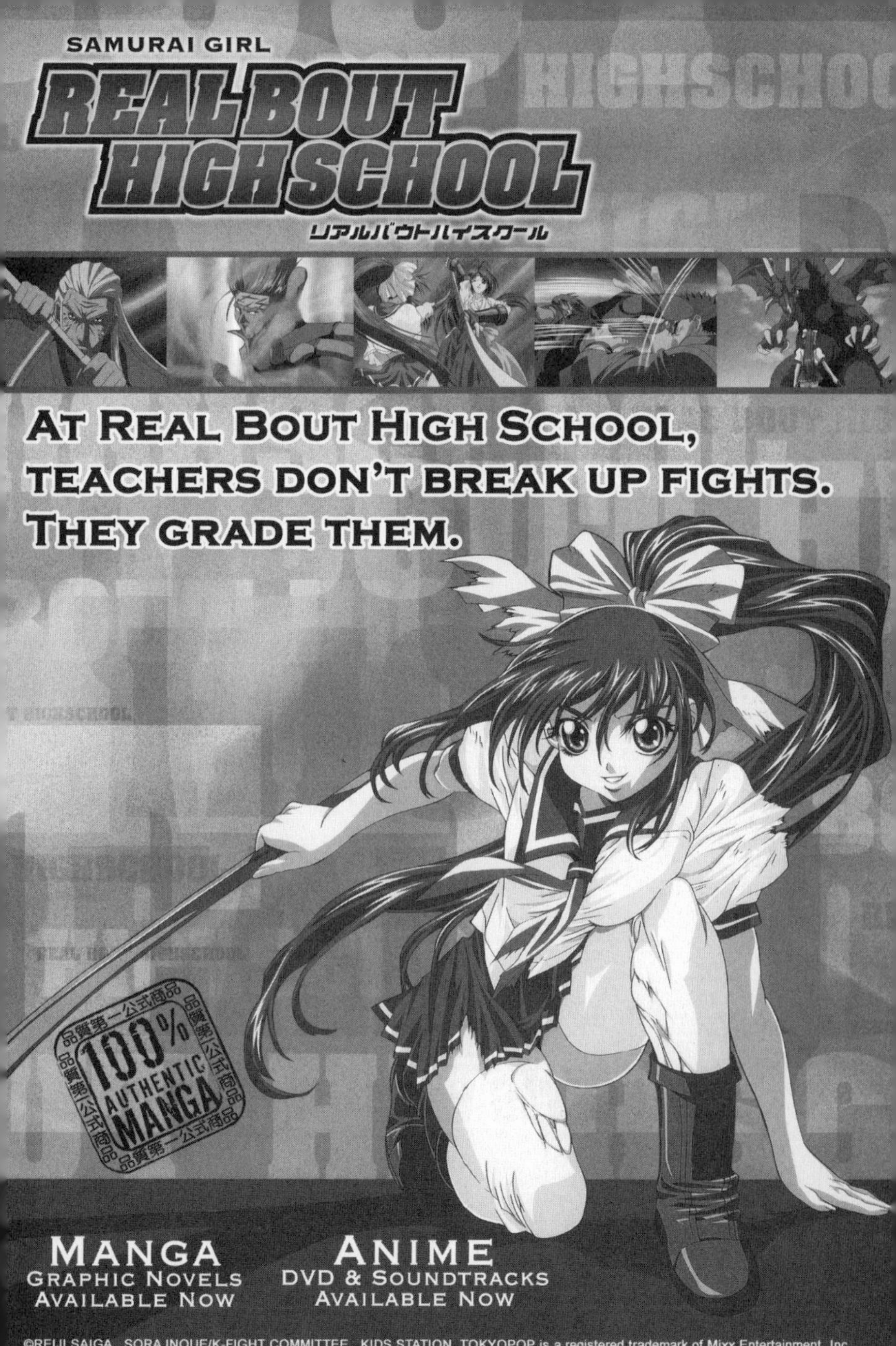
SAMURAI GIRL
REAL BOUT HIGH SCHOOL
リアルバウトハイスクール
AT REAL BOUT HIGH SCHOOL, TEACHERS DON'T BREAK UP FIGHTS. THEY GRADE THEM.
品質第一公式商品
100% AUTHENTIC MANGA
MANGA
GRAPHIC NOVELS
AVAILABLE NOW
ANIME
DVD & SOUNDTRACKS
AVAILABLE NOW

The latest best-seller from CLAMP!!

In the Future, Boys will be Boys and Girls will be Robots.

Graphic Novels Available Now

See TOKYOPOP.com for other CLAMP titles.

100% AUTHENTIC MANGA

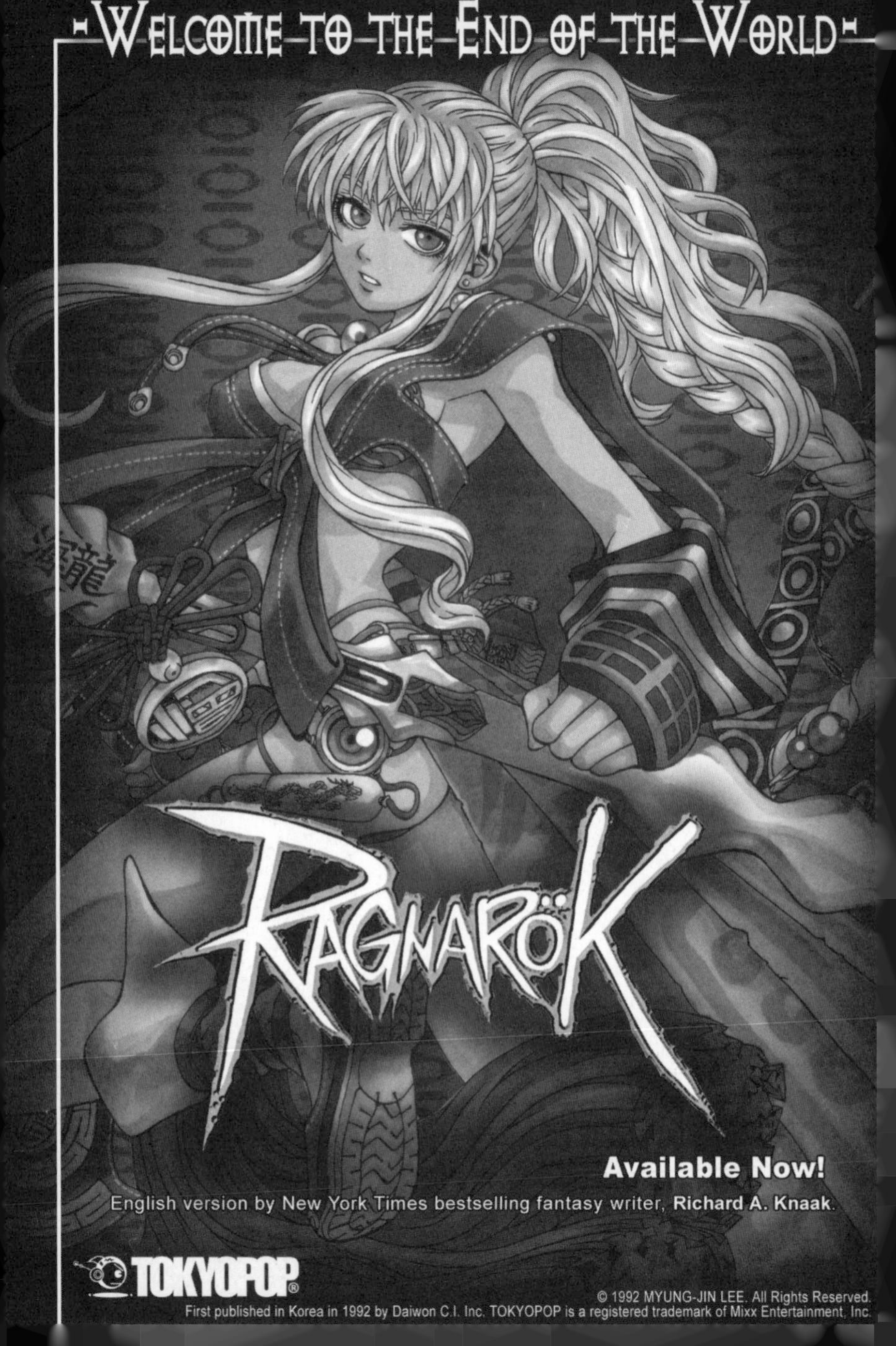
Welcome to the End of the World
Ragnarök
Available Now!
English version by New York Times bestselling fantasy writer, Richard A. Knaak.
TOKYOPOP
© 1992 MYUNG-JIN LEE. All Rights Reserved.
First published in Korea in 1992 by Daiwon C.I. Inc. TOKYOPOP is a registered trademark of Mixx Entertainment, Inc.

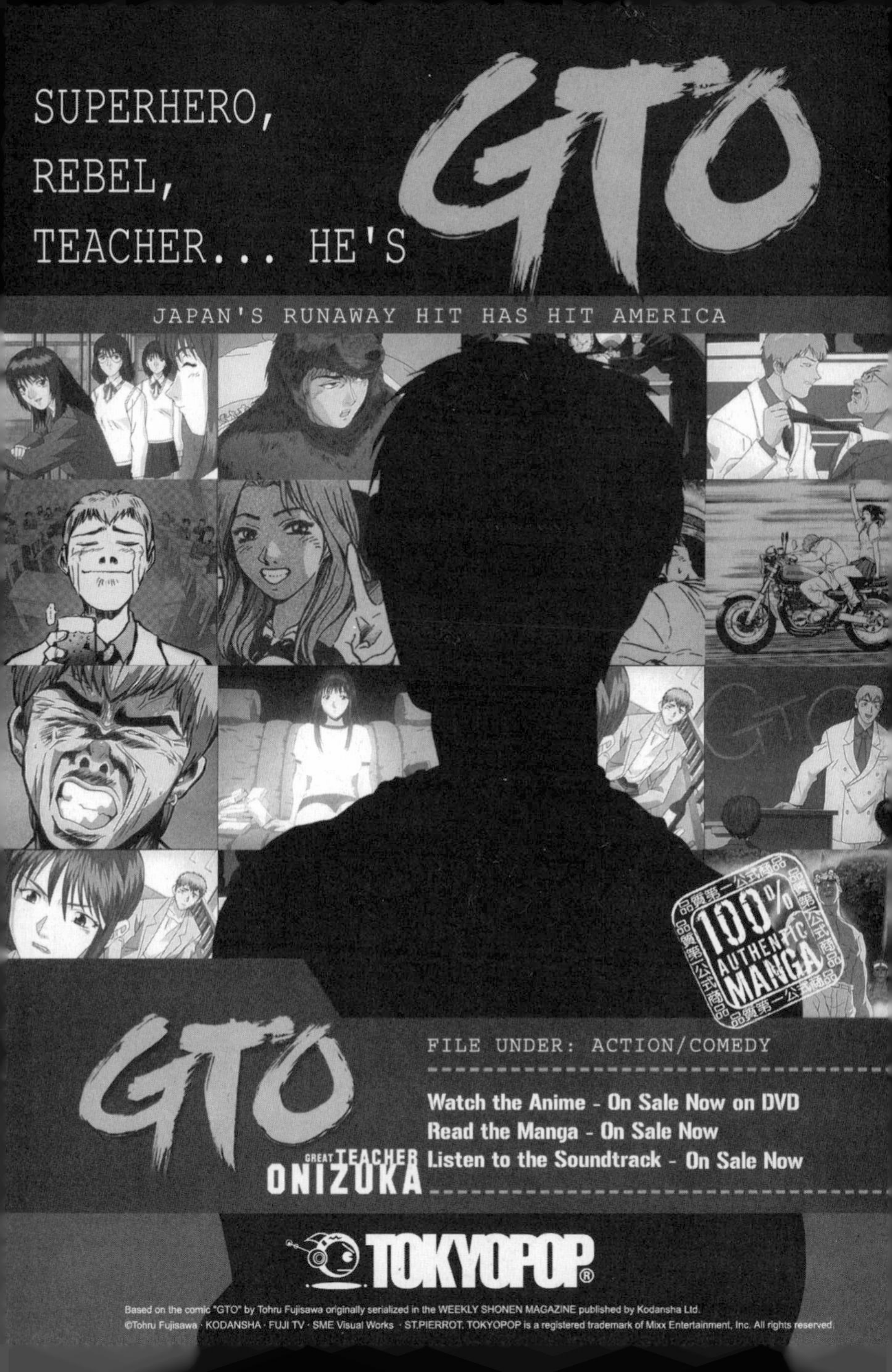

SUPERHERO,
REBEL,
TEACHER... HE'S
GTO
JAPAN'S RUNAWAY HIT HAS HIT AMERICA
GTO
100% AUTHENTIC MANGA
品質第一公式商品
GTO
GREAT TEACHER ONIZUKA
FILE UNDER: ACTION/COMEDY
Watch the Anime - On Sale Now on DVD
Read the Manga - On Sale Now
Listen to the Soundtrack - On Sale Now
TOKYOPOP®
Based on the comic "GTO" by Tohru Fujisawa originally serialized in the WEEKLY SHONEN MAGAZINE published by Kodansha Ltd.
©Tohru Fujisawa · KODANSHA · FUJI TV · SME Visual Works · ST.PIERROT. TOKYOPOP is a registered trademark of Mixx Entertainment, Inc. All rights reserved.

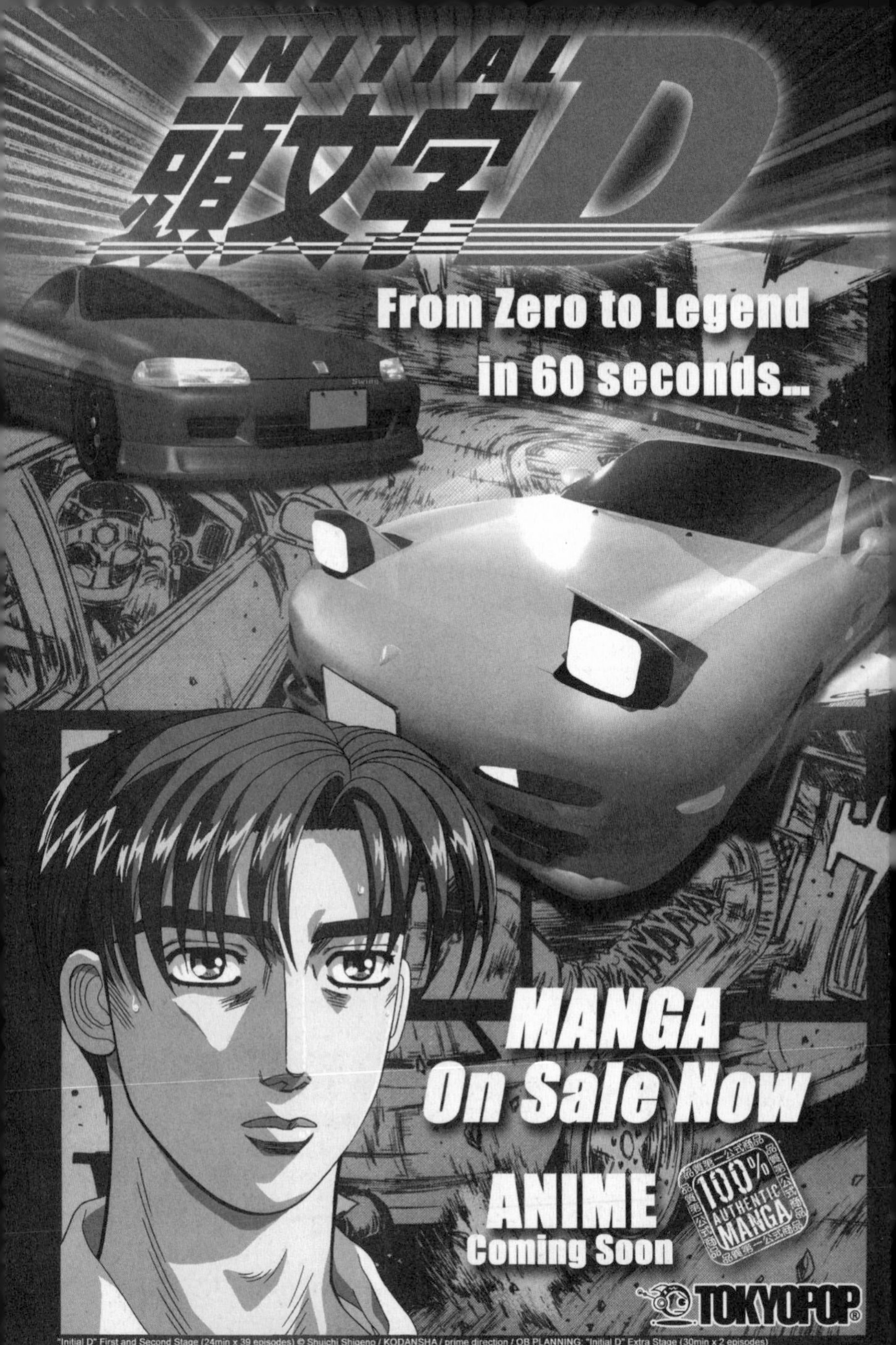
INITIAL
頭文字D
From Zero to Legend
in 60 seconds...
MANGA
On Sale Now
ANIME
Coming Soon
100% AUTHENTIC MANGA
TOKYOPOP

FEB 22 2016

STOP!

This is the back of the book.
You wouldn't want to spoil a great ending!

This book is printed "manga-style," in the authentic Japanese right-to-left format. Since none of the artwork has been flipped or altered, readers get to experience the story just as the creator intended. You've been asking for it, so TOKYOPOP® delivered: authentic, hot-off-the-press, and far more fun!

DIRECTIONS

If this is your first time reading manga-style, here's a quick guide to help you understand how it works.

It's easy... just start in the top right panel and follow the numbers. Have fun, and look for more 100% authentic manga from TOKYOPOP®!

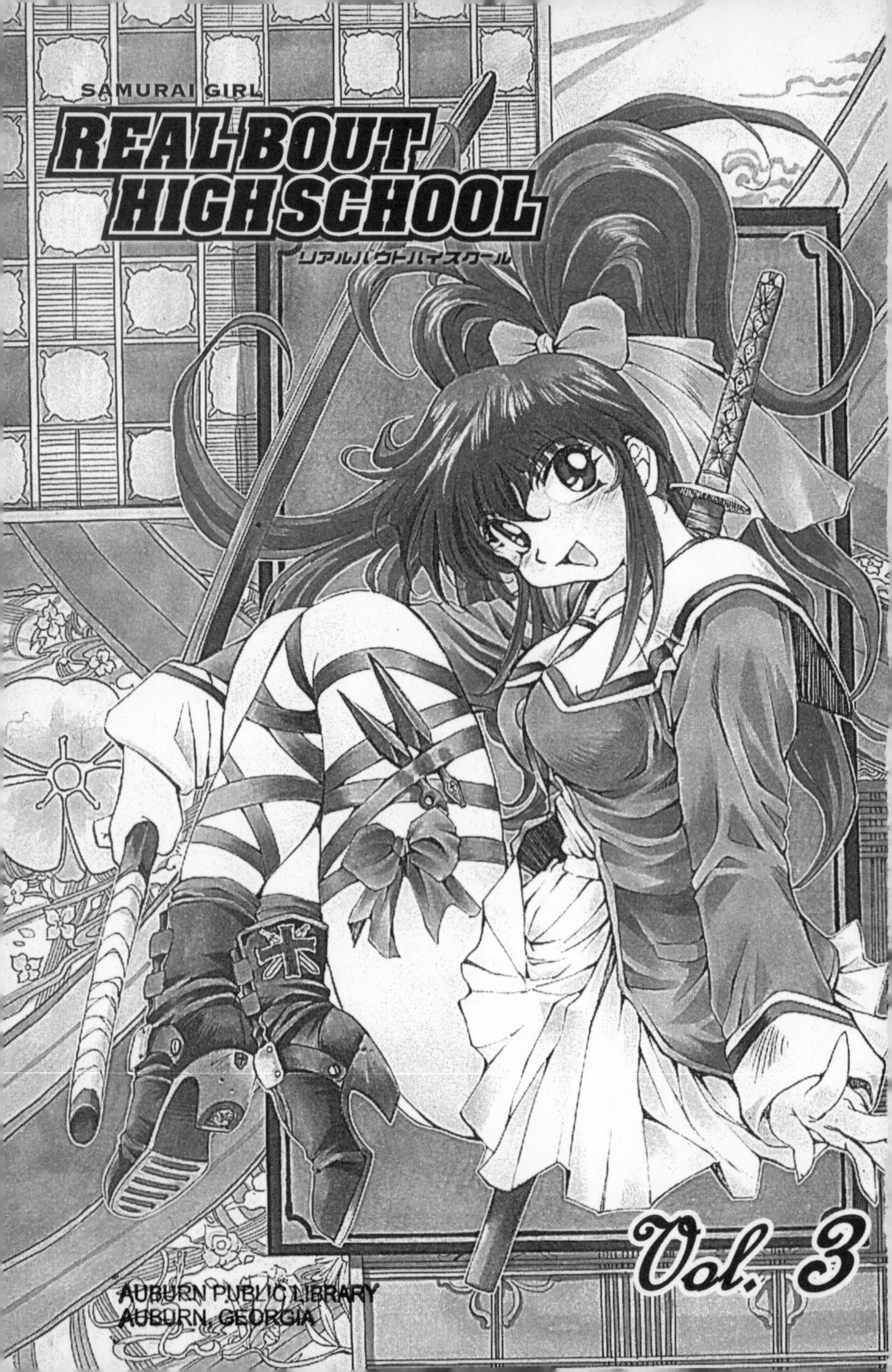
SAMURAI GIRL
REAL BOUT HIGH SCHOOL
リアルバウトハイスクール
Vol. 3

Other 100% Authentic Manga Available from TOKYOPOP®:

COWBOY BEBOP 1-3 (of 3)
All-new adventures of interstellar bounty hunting, based on the hit anime seen on Cartoon Network.

MARMALADE BOY 1-2 (of 8)
A tangled teen romance for the new millennium.

MARS 1-3 (of 15)
Biker Rei and artist Kira are as different as night and day, but fate binds them in this angst-filled romance.

GTO 1-4 (of 23+)
Biker gang member Onizuka is going back to school…as a teacher!

CHOBITS 1-2 (of 5+)
In the future, boys will be boys and girls will be…robots? The newest hit series from CLAMP!

SKULL MAN 1-3 (of 7+)
They took his family. They took his face. They took his soul. Now, he's going to take his revenge.

DRAGON KNIGHTS 1-3 (of 17)
Part dragon, part knight, ALL glam. The most inept knights on the block are out to kick some demon butt.

INITIAL D 1-2 (of 23+)
Delivery boy Tak has a gift for driving, but can he compete in the high-stakes world of street racing?

PARADISE KISS 1-2 (of 3+)
High fashion and deep passion collide in this hot new shojo series!

KODOCHA: Sana's Stage 1-2 (of 10)
There's a rumble in the jungle gym when child star Sana Kurata and bully Akito Hayama collide.

ANGELIC LAYER 1 (of 5)
In the future, the most popular game is Angelic Layer, where hand-raised robots battle for supremacy.

LOVE HINA 1-4 (of 14)
Can Keitaro handle living in a dorm with five cute girls…and still make it through school?

Coming Soon from TOKYOPOP®:

SHAOLIN SISTERS 1 (of 5)
The epic martial-arts/fantasy sequel to Juline, by the creator of Vampire Princess Miyu.

KARE KANO: He Says, She Says 1 (of 12+)
What happens when the smartest girl in school gets competition from the cutest guy?

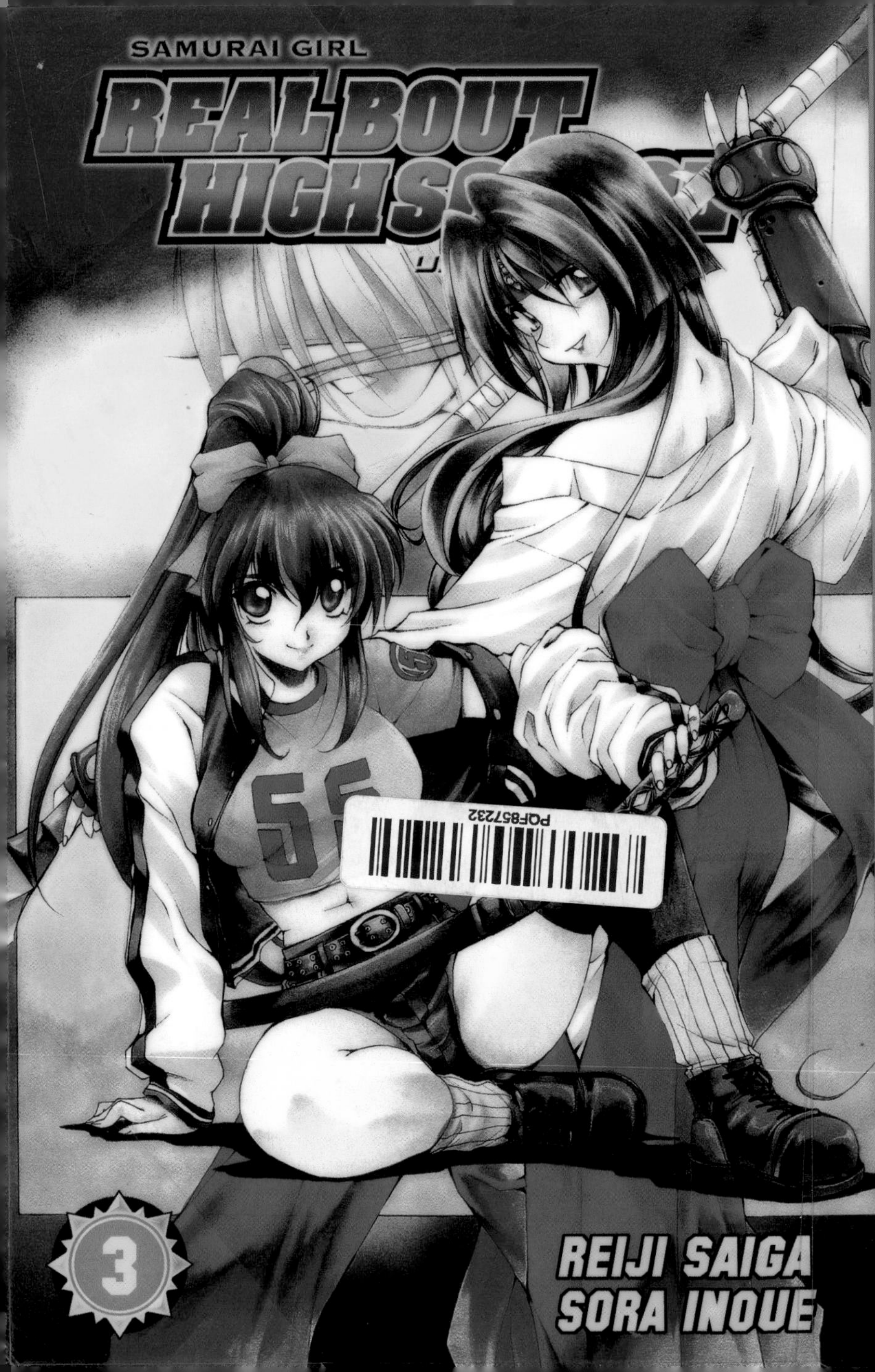
SAMURAI GIRL
REAL BOUT
HIGH S
3
REIJI SAIGA
SORA INOUE

ISBN 1591820200